European social democracy during the global economic crisis

Manchester University Press

European social democracy during the global economic crisis: renovation or resignation?

Edited by
DAVID J. BAILEY, JEAN-MICHEL DE WAELE,
FABIEN ESCALONA AND MATHIEU VIEIRA

Manchester University Press

Published by Manchester University Press
c/o the Renold Building, Oxford Road, Manchester M13 9PL, UK
and Room 400, 175 Fifth Avenue, New York, NY 10010, USA
www.manchesteruniversitypress.co.uk

Distributed in the United States exclusively by
Palgrave Macmillan, 175 Fifth Avenue, New York,
NY 10010, USA

Distributed in Canada exclusively by
UBC Press, University of British Columbia, 2029 West Mall,
Vancouver, BC, Canada V6T 1Z2

British Library Cataloguing-in-Publication Data
A catalogue record for this book is available from the British Library

Library of Congress Cataloging-in-Publication Data applied for

ISBN 978 07190 9195 7 hardback

First published 2014

The publisher has no responsibility for the persistence or accuracy of URLs for any external or third-party internet websites referred to in this book, and does not guarantee that any content on such websites is, or will remain, accurate or appropriate.

Typeset by Servis Filmsetting Ltd, Stockport, Cheshire
Printed in Great Britain by
CPI Group (UK) Ltd, Croydon, CR0 4YY

Contents

Tables

Contributors

JENNY ANDERSSON is CNRS Fellow and Researcher, Centre d'Etudes Européennes, Sciences Po Paris.

DAVID J. BAILEY is Lecturer in Politics, University of Birmingham.

CHRISTOPHE BOUILLAUD is Professor of Political Science, Sciences Po Grenoble.

JOHN CALLAGHAN is Professor of Politics and Contemporary History, University of Salford.

JEAN-MICHEL DE WAELE is Professor of Political Science, Université Libre de Bruxelles.

FABIEN ESCALONA is Ph.D. candidate in Political Science and ATER at Sciences Po Grenoble.

MICHAEL HOLMES is Lecturer in Politics, University of Liverpool.

PAUL KENNEDY is Lecturer in Spanish and European Studies, University of Bath.

ASHLEY LAVELLE is Lecturer in Politics, Macquarie University.

SIMON LIGHTFOOT is Senior Lecturer in European Politics, University of Leeds.

PHILIPPE MARLIÈRE is Professor of French and European Politics, University College of London.

GERASSIMOS MOSCHONAS is Professor of Comparative Politics, Panteion University of Athens.

GEORGE ROSS is Professor Emeritus of Labor and Social Thought, Brandeis University; Chaire Jean Monnet *ad personam*, University of Montréal.

MAGNUS RYNER is Reader in International Political Economy, King's College of London.

INGO SCHMIDT is Academic Coordinator of Labour Studies, Athabasca University.

DIMITRI A. SOTIROPOULOS is Associate Professor of Political Science and Public Administration, University of Athens.

MATHIEU VIEIRA is ATER at Sciences Po Lille, Ph.D. candidate in political science, Sciences Po Grenoble and Université Libre de Bruxelles.

Acknowledgements

We thank all the authors for their excellent contributions, and their responsiveness to our requests. Most of all we acknowledge the help and financial support of the Faculty of Social and Political Sciences, Université Libre de Bruxelles; the research centre Pacte and the Institut d'Etudes Politiques of Grenoble; the Foundation for European Progressive Studies; and the Fondation Jean Jaurès.

Finally we want to thank our families, our friends and especially Alix and Fanny for their everyday support, and to Emma Bailey, for always providing a source of optimism.

David J. Bailey
Jean-Michel De Waele
Fabien Escalona
Mathieu Vieira

July 2013

Abbreviations

AES	Alternative Economic Strategy
ANI	Interprofessional National Agreement
ATTAC	Association for the Taxation of Financial Transactions and for Citizens' Action
BDI	German Employers' Federation
BPI	Public Bank for Investment
CBI	Confederation of British Industry
CDU	Christian Democratic Union
CFDT	French Democratic Confederation of Labor
CFE–CGC	French Management Confederation – General Confederation of Managers
CFTC	French Confederation of Christian Workers
CGPME	General Confederation of Medium and Small Businesses.
DEA	Department of Economic Affairs
ECB	European Central Bank
ECT	European Constitutional Treaty
EKAP	PASOK Committee on the party's statutes and accreditation
EL	Red–Green Alliance [Denmark]
EMU	Economic and Monetary Union
EP	European Parliament
EU	European Union
FPÖ	Freedom Party of Austria
FSA	Financial Services Authority
GATT	General Agreement on Tariffs and Trade
GDP	gross domestic product
GEC	global economic crisis
HCFP	Higher Council on Public Finance
IMF	International Monetary Fund

KOES	PASOK Central Organizing Committee of the Congress
MAP	Modernization of Public Action
MEDEF	Movement of French Businesses
MPC	Monetary Policy Committee
NEC	National Executive Committee
NGO	non-governmental organisation
NIB	National Investment Board
OECD	Organisation for Economic Co-operation and Development
PASOK	Panhellenic Socialist Movement
PCE	Communist Party of Spain
PCF	French Communist Party
PCP	Portuguese Communist Party
PdCI	Party of Italian Communists
PES	Party of European Socialists
PES–ECOFIN	Party of European Socialists Economic and Finance Ministers
PIIGS	Portugal, Ireland, Italy, Greece and Spain
PR	proportional representation
PRC	Communist Refoundation Party [Italy]
PS	French socialist party [after 1969]
PSOE	Spanish Socialist Workers' Party
PVV	Party for Freedom [Netherlands]
RGPP	General Review of Public Policies
SD	Sweden Democrats
SDF	Social Democratic Federation
SF	Socialist People's Party [Denmark]
SFIO	French socialist party [1905–69]
SIB	Securities and Investment Board
SMIC	Growth-oriented Interprofessionnal Minimum Wage
SP	Socialist Party [Netherlands]
SPD	Social Democratic Party of Germany
SPÖ	Social Democratic Party of Austria
TINA	'there is no alternative'
TSCG	Treaty on Stability, Coordination and Governance in the Economic and Monetary Union
TUC	Trades Union Congress
UMP	Union for a People's Movement
UN	United Nations
V	Left Party [Sweden]
VAS	Left Alliance [Finland]
WTO	World Trade Organization

1

Introduction

David J. Bailey, Jean-Michel De Waele, Fabien Escalona and Mathieu Vieira

The global economic crisis (GEC) began as a housing market crisis in 2007, and rapidly developed into the subprime crisis before subsequently transforming (with the collapse of Lehman Brothers in 2008) into a global financial crisis. From that point, it morphed into a prolonged Great Recession that has seen growth stagnate across the developed world since 2009, and has simultaneously been accompanied by the Euro-zone crisis and severe fiscal and monetary instability for both the PIIGS member states and the Euro as a whole. In terms of centre-left social democratic party politics, however, what has perhaps been most notable throughout this period is the coexistence of two contrasting trends. On the one hand, prominent social democrats and social democratic parties have been repeatedly looked to as the political vehicle through which a coherent crisis resolution could and should be coordinated (see, for instance, the contributions to Callaghan *et al.*, 2009). Financial regulation, housing market regulation, fiscal reflation and redistribution, quantitative easing, a tempering of austerity measures and the defence of the welfare state have been consistently identified as part of a centre-left, social democratic response to the crisis that could and/ or should be adopted as a means of tackling the clear examples of market failure witnessed over the past decade. This, so the argument goes, represents a viable alternative to the current range of policy responses – which essentially (especially in the European context) amounts to a neo-liberal remedy to cure a crisis caused by neo-liberalism. On the other hand, and despite widespread anticipation for a social democratic remedy, we have also witnessed repeated frustration that empirically such a response has consistently failed to materialise (on this mismatch between social democratic expectations and outcomes, see also Bailey and Bates, 2012: 195–6). This frustration was perhaps most clearly visible in the surprise that met the decline in social democratic votes in the 2009 European Parliament. But it also met the ejection from office of the British Labour Party, the Spanish Socialist Workers' Party (PSOE), and the massive decline in electoral support for PASOK in Greece. In the view of many observers, social democratic parties have responded (or, rather, failed to respond) to the global economic crisis (GEC) with a continuation of the capitulation to neo-liberalism that also characterised the social democratic party family during the pre-2007 period. This coexists with a corresponding inability by social democratic parties to appeal to an electorate that desires a coherent and progressive alternative.

This therefore represents something of a paradox. Despite a crisis of neo-liberalism, no clear and viable social democratic alternative appears to have (thus far) been forthcoming. Of course, some might respond that this non-social democratic response is to be expected, particularly given the widespread jettisoning of traditional social democratic values during the move to 'third way' social democracy, which most social democratic parties actively embraced. Nevertheless, the pro-market position adopted by social democratic parties during the 'third way' period was more often than not legitimated through a 'logic of no alternative' discourse (Watson and Hay, 2003), according to which social democratic parties presented the jettisoning of some of their core aims as part of a wider attempt to ensure their continued relevance (and that of their remaining social democratic values) to contemporary politics (Klitgaard, 2007). From this perspective, the global economic and financial crisis creates a potential opportunity to question the 'logic of no alternative'. The paradox, therefore, is that so few social democratic parties have seemingly taken up this opportunity. While it would be simplistic to expect an 'automatic' resurgence of support for, or the renewed promotion of, a revived centre-left programme, it is nevertheless the case that the historic episode of the Great Depression of the 1930s has taught us that social democrats have in the past proved able to welcome and conceive of new ideas, and in some cases to implement them in the context of prolonged economic crisis (in Scandinavia in particular) (Blyth, 2002; Ryner, 2002). In addition, we have seen some centre-left parties returning to power after 2008, in some cases on an agenda that proclaimed a forthcoming leftward shift. The election of François Hollande is perhaps the most obvious example. Although in this case it is not clear that the record in office matches the ambitions held while out of office.

The present book therefore seeks to address an apparent dilemma facing social democracy and social democratic parties. The opportunities seem ripe for social democratic alternatives, but no such viable alternative appears to be forthcoming. This raises a number of questions. Is social democracy even capable of producing a response to the GEC that will see its renovation and rejuvenation as a political movement able to mobilise support for a coherent and progressive alternative to neo-liberalism's crisis? Or are we witnessing (and likely to continue to witness) a sustained incapacity by social democratic parties and a continued resignation in the face of an apparently hegemonic neo-liberal global economic (dis)order?

In opting to focus on social democratic parties in the *European* context we seek to explore the point at which this dilemma is perhaps most pronounced: social democratic parties have been historically strong within Europe; the European Union has often been noted as a means by which social democracy could overcome some of the problems associated with 'globalisation'; and the European integration project itself is currently in crisis (thereby potentially creating a new set of opportunities for change). The book therefore hopes to consider ways in which *European* social democratic parties – at both the national and European level – have responded to the GEC, and the extent to which we might envisage alternatives to the neo-liberal consensus being successfully promoted by those parties within the European Union. We have also chosen to select our cases from 'western Europe' – i.e. we include no country cases from the 2004–07 EU accession. This reflects our desire to consider those social democratic parties with the strongest historical tradition of social democracy, considered particularly in terms of their commitment to reformism, Keynesianism and parliamentarism – with social democratic parties absent from eastern Europe prior to 1989, we have chosen not to focus there. The book is therefore focused in large part upon western Europe, due in part to its being in many ways the ideological and historical centre of social democracy. Of the West European countries, perhaps most notable by its absence is the Italian case. Indeed, we decided not to include a chapter on Italy due largely to problems in terms of categorising a social democratic party within that country. Thus, the dominant historic left party in Italy was, throughout most of the post-war period, the Italian Communist Party (PCI). This has subsequently morphed into the Democratic Party, itself not a straightforward social democratic party.

Social democracy and economic crisis: a historical relationship?

The question of social democracy's response to the GEC can also be situated historically. Commentators have commonly identified the Great Depression as the period during which 'traditional' social democracy was first formulated. Thus, the failure of democratic capitalism to produce either stable democracy or stable capitalism during the inter-war period has been shown by scholars such as Mark Blyth (2002) and Sheri Berman (2006) to have been a prompt for social democratic actors to experiment with new policy responses that would both (in a mutually dependent way) stabilise capitalism through the Keynesian solution of reflationary measures that simultaneously redistribute resources to social democracy's core industrial working-class constituents.

It is perhaps this experience – of social democratic parties constructing a coherent 'Keynesian' macroeconomic programme, as a response to, and in the light of, the Great Depression – that continues to most inform the current commonly held anticipation that the GEC will witness a similarly coherent social democratic response emerge in an attempt to counter the recurrent bouts of economic crisis, stagnation and austerity measures that characterise the present. If Polanyi's 'double movement' could emerge out of the Great Depression and crystallise in the form of the traditional, Keynesian, social democratic party programme, so this reasoning goes, so we should expect and anticipate another 'double movement', again led by social democratic parties, in response to the current GEC. Others, meanwhile, have been less optimistic. As Nancy Fraser has argued, the lack of political leadership on the left, the disorganised state of the working class, and the absence of a territorialised (nation state) authority through which to focus demands for renewed social protection, have each been cited as reasons for the absence of a so-called 'double movement' during the present crisis. Further still, Fraser highlights how the political terrain has changed since the 1930s, in that political movements and social struggles are now far more attuned to the limitations of a strategy focused solely on social protection without an equally keen awareness of the risks of introducing other forms of inequalities and hierarchies apart from those arising solely from economic relations and 'commodification'. A desirable response, therefore, is perhaps more likely to be a 'triple movement' that is able to combine social protection with emancipation from gender, race, and other 'identity'-based forms of dominance (Fraser, 2013).

For others still, the 'double movement' (at least at the point at which it is institutionalised in the form of a coherent social democratic response) is something to be avoided rather than sought. From this perspective, the labour movement's turn to parliamentarism and the pursuit of office represents a dampening and co-optation of what could otherwise have been a vibrant movement for radical social change. Thus, as Piven and Cloward show in the case of the United States, the turn during the inter-war years towards an institutionalised labour movement also brought with it an electoralism that undermined the movement's social power and leverage.

> Union leaders became more dependent on the Democratic Party (for prominence, not concessions) than the party was on them. Acting accordingly, union leaders promoted partisan allegiance, and by doing so, blunted the electoral impact of worker discontent. The unions became the legitimate political voice of industrial workers, and that legitimate voice spoke out repeatedly against strikers, and in support of Democratic leaders. (Piven and Cloward, 1979: 171)

Similarly, in the case of the British Labour Party, Ralph Miliband highlights the debilitating effect of entering Parliament upon the nascent workers' movement that had become energised by the General Strike and Great Depression. Thus, upon their election to Parliament, socialists and radical members of the Labour Party found themselves, 'effectively contained by their own leaders, who held that containment to be one of their prime tasks' (Miliband, 1961: 95). This need to appear electable, respectable and 'fit to govern' was also quickly internalised by the militants themselves. Indeed, as Miliband documents, the radicals found themselves in Parliament faced with a culture that acted to subdue and dampen their earlier anger and indignation. In the words of the so-called 'wild man' Labour MP, David Kirkwood, the simple, friendly and pleasant nature of opponent MPs within the House of Commons, 'pierced a link in my armour that had never been pierced before' (quoted in Miliband, 1961: 96).

The historical relationship between economic crisis and social democracy is therefore both intrinsic and far from straightforward. Whether we are likely to see a second Keynesian consensus emerge from the crisis remains moot empirically; and whether we should seek such an outcome remains contested normatively and strategically. The contributors to the present volume each contribute to these ongoing debates, especially in their empirical assessment of social democratic parties' response thus far to the crisis, and the implications this has for social democratic and broader left strategy for the future.

Social democracy during the global economic crisis

In terms of evaluating the social democratic response to the GEC, there are perhaps three (interrelated) dimensions that demand our attention: electoral performance, programmatic change, and the experience of office and/or opposition. First, in terms of electoral trends, we are interested in the response of the electorate to social democratic parties during the course of the crisis. In particular, we want to know whether the electorate has turned either towards or against social democratic parties as a result of the GEC. Second, in terms of programmatic developments, we are interested in the policies that have been advocated and/or implemented by social democratic parties in the light of the GEC. In particular, we want to understand whether policies adopted by social democratic parties have taken on a progressive character – i.e. that they potentially form an alternative to the prevailing neo-liberal consensus of the past three or four decades – or whether we see a (continued) capitulation of social democratic values. Finally, in terms of the experience of being in office and/or opposition, we are interested in how the social democratic agenda has fared in terms of parties in office and their ability to circumnavigate the constraints that unavoidably characterise the present crisis context. We seek an assessment of the degree to which being in opposition creates new opportunities for social democratic parties. We also need an analysis that is able to connect developments in each of these spheres: how does party policy (developed either in office or in opposition) translate into electoral viability for social democratic parties; what can social democratic parties achieve programmatically with strong (or weak) electoral support in the current context? Each of these questions forms the basis for the discussion of the rest of the book. However, we can nevertheless offer here our own initial (unavoidably superficial) mapping of these developments.

In terms of electoral performance, an overview suggests that social democratic parties have fared badly as a result of the GEC. As Table 1.1 highlights, in the large majority of countries in western Europe (except for France, Ireland and the Netherlands), the onset of global economic crisis has been accompanied by a decline in electoral support. Overall, we witness a decline by 4.7 percentage points in the average electoral support experienced by social democratic parties in western Europe during this period. Similarly, as we shall see, the experience of programmatic developments does not represent a source of optimism for those anticipating some kind of Polanyian 'double movement'. To an extent this varies in terms of whether the social democratic party is in office or in opposition (for details, see Table 1.2) – with those in opposition arguably being more inclined towards experimenting with a more progressive position (although note the case of Sweden, where we witness an oscillation between the left and right wings of the social democratic movement), and those in office tending towards a more acquiescent approach towards the purported logic of 'no alternative' to austerity as the so-called 'solution' to stagnation and fiscal crises. This trend is perhaps most clearly visible in the single case of the French *Parti Socialiste* and its changing programmatic agenda before and after entering office. This also possibly explains the ability of the Party of European Socialists to adopt one of the clearest moves towards a coherent and progressive alternative to neo-liberalism – i.e. that the absence of a clear partisan supranational government ensures a near-permanent experience of opposition for the PES.

While there is clear variation between countries, therefore, the current volume suggests that – at least in terms of recent empirical trends – the prospect of a reintroduction of Keynesian-style reflation, or traditional measures for redistribution, is unlikely in the foreseeable future.

Conceptualising the global crisis of neo-liberalism

Before entering into a fuller discussion of each of these themes and questions, we need also to consider and conceptualise what indeed it is that we are concerned with. In particular, in considering the impact of the global economic crisis upon social democratic parties we need first to properly conceptualise what it is that we mean when we refer to the global economic crisis. While nuanced differences obviously exist between the approaches adopted by each contributor to the book, the assumption at the centre of each of the chapters is that we are experiencing a global economic crisis of neo-liberalism. The implication, therefore, is that the crisis of neo-liberalism creates the potential to consider a shift towards an alternative socio-economic model and set of ideas. Clearly this raises further questions – what do we mean by crisis and what do we mean by neo-liberalism?

The notion of crisis has been widely discussed within the recent literature. As Andrew Gamble (2009) makes clear, the term 'crisis' has its roots in being

Table 1.1 General election results (%) of social democratic parties, 2000–13

	2007	2008	2009	2010	2011	2012	2013	2000–06 Average	2007–13 Average	Change
Austria		29.3					27.1	33.8	28.2	−5.6
Belgium	22.9			26.5				30.4	24.7	−5.7
Denmark	25.5				24.8			27.5	25.2	−2.3
Finland	21.4				19.2			24.5	20.3	−4.2
France	24.8					29.4		23.8	27.1	3.3
Germany			23				25.7	36.4	24.4	−12
Greece	38.1		43.9			12.6*		42.2	31.5	−10.7
Ireland	10.1				19.4			10.8	14.8	4
Italy**		33.2					25.4	31.2	29.3	−1.9
Luxembourg			21.6				19.2	23.4	20.4	−3
Netherlands				19.6		24.8		21.2	22.2	1
Portugal			36.6		28.1			41.4	32.9	−8.5
Spain					28.7			38.4	28.7	−9.7
Sweden				30.6				37.5	30.6	−6.9
UK				29				38	29	−9
EU-15 (average)								30.7	26	−4.7

Notes:

*Average between May and June ballots.

** Scores of the Olive Tree and Democratic Party, which are centre-left parties outside any true social democratic tradition.

Source: http://electionresources.org

Table 1.2 Social democratic parties in office and opposition in Western Europe, 2007–13

	2007	2008	2009	2010	2011	2012	2013
Austria	Office (in coalition with the Conservatives – equal partners)						
Belgium	Office (in coalition)						
Denmark	Opposition				Office (major coalition partner)		
Finland	Opposition						
France	Opposition					Office (presidency + major coalition partner)	
Germany	Office ('grand coalition')		Opposition				
Greece	Opposition		Office (in coalition since 2011, junior partner since 2012				
Ireland	Opposition				Office (junior coalition partner)		
Italy	Office (major coalition partner)	Opposition			Office (in coalition with the right and the centre)		
Luxembourg	Office (junior coalition partner)						
Netherlands	Office (junior coalition partner)			Opposition		Office (junior coalition partner)	
Portugal	Office				Opposition		
Spain	Office				Opposition		
Sweden	Opposition						
UK	Office			Opposition			

used to refer to a point of potential resolution. This has meant the point within a wider process – a disease, a play, and also of course wider historical and socio-economic processes – in which a turning point emerges. It is a turning point that takes the form of an emergency, during which the wider process has the (contingent, unforeseeable) opportunity to either recover, and thereby continue to exist, as a result of a decisive intervention; or to fail to recover and to see its existence terminated. But what, then, is the post-2007 crisis a crisis of? For Gamble (2009) it is considered a capitalist crisis. For Colin Hay (2011), in contrast, it is no crisis at all, but rather (at least in the British case) the 'accumulation of economic pathologies' that have yet to see a significant and decisive intervention or resolution. For the purposes of this book, the authors for the large part share the conceptualisation of crisis adopted by Gamble. That is, a post-2007 global economic crisis characterised by a series of economic emergencies that require a remedy that would most likely take the form of a shift away from neo-liberalism.

Nevertheless, the chapters are equally in broad agreement in their analysis that the much sought-after shift away from neo-liberalism has not yet been witnessed. We see a prolongation of the global economic crisis, therefore, in part due to the resilience of neo-liberalism (Schmidt and Thatcher, 2013). In this sense, the chapters tend to agree with Hay that there has been no decisive intervention, although we might rather conceptualise this as a perpetuation (rather than absence) of crisis.

This discussion also clearly raises the further question of what we mean in referring to 'neo-liberalism'. Discussions surrounding the meaning of neo-liberalism abound. These range from those who view it as a set of policy ideas that favour and promote the extended incorporation of the market mechanism into policy making (Hay, 2004), as well as those who view it more in terms of being something akin to an 'ideological atmosphere' (Peck, 2010: xi), through those who view it as a class project aiming to shore up the wider socio-economic relations that constitute capitalism through the commodification of forms of social life that have previously been uncommodified (Harvey, 2005), to those who view neo-liberalism as an alignment of social interests and organised social forces coalescing around a consensus (or hegemonic) view within the contemporary historical bloc (Saull, 2012). The authors of the present volume draw on each of these conceptualisations, to varying degrees focusing on the extent to which neo-liberal tendencies have been undermined and potentially reversed as a result of the crisis. In particular, we seek to assess the extent to which both social democracy (as an ideology) and (concrete) social democratic parties have been able to promote their more historic goals of redistribution, regulation and reform (for a definitional discussion of social democracy, see Bailey, 2009: 26–40). While we leave the notion of both neo-liberalism and social democracy to be defined by the chapter authors, therefore, we nevertheless seek to explore the extent to which the global economic crisis has created an opportunity for, and/or prompted, a shift between the two.

Outline of the book

The book is divided into three parts. In Part I, it explores some of the broader thematic issues underpinning questions of the political economy of social democracy during the GEC. Here we address some of the questions surrounding the implications of crisis for social democratic parties: what opportunities are opened for social democratic parties as a result of the crisis, and which are closed by the experience? How do social democratic parties interact with social movements, and how (if at all) has this interaction changed as a result of the crisis? What impact has European integration, and the euro, had upon the macro-economic policy options facing social democratic parties and social democracy, and vice versa? How in general should we expect social democratic parties to respond to economic crisis? And how should we conceptualise this process? Each of the chapters touches on one or more of these questions.

In the first substantive chapter, Fabien Escalona and Mathieu Vieira identify some of the key themes that run throughout the volume. They discuss the relationship between social democratic parties and what they claim were two 'Faustian pacts' entered into: one with European integration, and the other with the knowledge-based economy. In their attempt to respond to the ascendance of neo-liberalism, the authors argue, social democratic parties increasingly turned to European integration in an attempt to recreate the conditions for a more amenable socio-economic and political terrain. Similarly, the (especially Third Way grouping of) social democrats advocated support for the notion of a 'knowledge-based economy' as a means to promote growth, and thereby enable public authorities to (once more) advocate and fund redistributive and welfare-oriented public policies. Each of these 'Faustian pacts', however, turned out rather to constrain social democratic parties and party actors, without producing the anticipated concessions. As a result, social democratic parties find themselves unable to produce a meaningful and viable alternative programme through which to respond to the crisis of neo-liberalism.

George Ross presents in Chapter 3 a historical overview of the relationship between social movements and social democratic parties. As Ross shows, social democratic parties emerged as a political aggregator of social protest undertaken by workers, women's movements, trade unionists and anti-capitalists of various ideological positions. In adopting policy platforms that would subsequently become electable, however, social democratic party leaders also inadvertently became increasingly managerialist. It is this managerialism, Ross shows, that has subsequently produced a number of problems for social democracy. First, it disabled social democratic parties' ability to build on and represent the grievances expressed by the new social movements of the 1970s and 1980s. Similarly, it has impeded any attempt by social democratic parties to connect with the social protest movements, such as the *indignados*, that have emerged in response to the GEC. It is this disconnect, Ross points out, which raises some of the fundamental questions considered throughout this book: 'what do social democrats stand for, what do they really want to do, what can they actually do'? Without a serious response to these types of questions, social democratic parties are faced with an uncertain and potentially unsuccessful future.

In Chapter 4, Magnus Ryner identifies further limits with the European model of social democracy and especially the way it has developed over time. As Ryner highlights, the adoption of a 'Third Way' model of social democracy across much of Europe represented an acquiescence to, and increasing support for, a model of political economy built upon support for the 'Dollar–Wall Street regime'. Ultimately this represented an attempt to echo the 'success' of the US economic model, but without the advantage of being able to benefit from the seigniorage privilege available to the United States. As such, in terms of responses to the Global Economic Model, the political–economic opportunities available to European social democracy remained limited and 'when the American model entered into a deep crisis as a result of its internal contradictions, European social democracy was in no state to offer an alternative'.

Finally, in John Callaghan's chapter we turn to a discussion of the relationship between the finance sector, financial crises and social democracy. The discussion sees a detailed historical overview of this relationship as it has played itself out since the early twentieth century in the case of the British Labour Party. Here we see a history in which widespread suspicion towards the finance sector within the early Labour Party nevertheless failed to result in substantial attempts to regulate, harness or reform the City of London and its financial institutions. Thus, a deference among party leaders towards the financial elites resulted in the continued autonomy of the Bank of England following its nationalisation by the Attlee government, and similar pressures saw the Blair government granting the Bank of England independence to set interest rates over fifty years later. Any analysis of the capacity for social democratic parties to oversee and implement a coherent regulatory programme, even during the so-called 'golden age' of social democracy, therefore needs to bear in mind the sustained existence of limitations throughout the period.

In Part II of the book we turn our focus to some of the social democratic party responses that have been witnessed at the level of the nation state across Europe. We focus in particular on some of the countries with the longest tradition of social democratic and centre-left party politics, and therefore focus on western and southern Europe, with no chapters focusing on eastern European social democratic parties. In our choice of countries we do however cover a range of cases, including countries that are traditionally considered to have instituted a social democratic welfare regime (Sweden) and those with a more liberal tradition (UK), those typically considered to be located within northern Europe (Sweden, UK, Germany) and southern Europe (Spain, Greece), those that traditionally have strong links with the trade unions (British Labour Party, Swedish SAP) and those with a more autonomous relationship with the labour movement (French Socialist Party), those inside (Germany, France, Spain, Greece) and outside of the Euro-zone (UK, Sweden), and those that are more (Spain, Greece) and less (Germany, France, Sweden, UK) recently democratised. We are also able to compare the experience of social democratic parties in countries at the sharpest end of the impact of the GEC (Spain, Greece), compared with those in countries that are more able to control and lead events, potentially to their advantage (especially Germany, but also arguably France). In drawing on a range of experiences within a variety of contexts, therefore, the book provides a comprehensive overview of social democratic parties and how they have fared during the GEC.

Each chapter provides rich empirical detail regarding the experience of social democracy in each country. Yet there remains little scope for those social democrats hoping to identify sources of optimism from these empirical experiences. In each of the chapters we witness ideological confusion and/or electoral decline. Thus, in the case of the British Labour Party, Philippe Marlière identifies the absence of ideological alternatives to the TINA-logic that prevailed under the leadership of both Blair and Brown. While Brown could be argued to have implemented a neo-Keynesian package to provide short-term rescue for the banking sector, this was unaccompanied by any ideological revision of the New Labour doctrine. Equally, while the Miliband leadership that followed Labour's ejection from office might have produced a change in tone and distancing from New Labour, the underlying premise that there exists no alternative to austerity measures, an aversion to industrial action, and a pro-business macroeconomic policy, remains. Similarly, in the case of the Swedish social democrats, Jenny Andersson highlights a combination of ideological oscillation and electoral decline. With successive electoral defeats interpreted by the Social Democratic Party (SAP) in terms of a perceived weakness on issues of social discipline in 2006, and as a result of a failure to take advantage of ideological space on the left in 2010, the post-2010 period witnessed the election of an inexperienced left-oriented leader (Juholt) who was subsequently replaced by a market-oriented leader (Löfven). The failure of the Swedish social democrats to adopt a coherent programme that can unite the social democratic movement, despite being out of office for over six years, represents a significant indication of the fate of social democracy in a country that has typically been considered the site of social democracy's most impressive achievements. Similar developments are also witnessed in Ingo Schmidt's chapter on the German Social Democratic Party (SPD), where we witness the somewhat ironic electoral penalisation of the party for both its earlier implementation of austerity measures (Agenda 2010) at the beginning of the twenty-first century, and for a failure to convince the electorate that the SPD will have the economic credibility to implement necessary orthodox economic measures in the light of the current GEC.

We also see remarkably similar patterns of oscillation and ideological confusion in Christophe Bouillaud's chapter on the French Socialist Party. Thus, we witness an incoming Hollande presidency committed to the renegotiation of the EU's fiscal pact and adoption of a 75 per cent tax rate for those earning over €1 million, followed by the failure to implement either measures upon entering office. Finally, for those social democratic parties finding themselves in office during the GEC, the fate has tended to be even worse. In the case of the Spanish Socialist Party, Paul Kennedy (Chapter 10) shows how a combination of an unclear ideological message, the implementation of 'necessary' austerity measures, and an inability to connect with the party's core constituents produced the worst electoral performance for the party since the establishment of democracy and the end of the Franco regime. Similarly, in Greece, Dimitri Sotiropoulos (Chapter 11) argues that PASOK's implementation of austerity measures in an attempt to avoid a furthering of the country's economic and fiscal crisis (combined with an absence of party structure or recognisable ideological profile) resulted in the party's worst electoral performance ever – an event made more notable still by the fact that it followed a strong electoral victory only two years earlier.

The question raised by the remarkably similar experiences of social democratic parties in each of the countries studied in the book, therefore, is clearly that of how social democratic parties can rejuvenate their programme in such a way that it will enable them to be both viable as parties of government and electable as parties with a coherent ideological position that voters are prepared to support. Indeed, it remains unclear, at least on the basis of the chapters in the present volume, that such a resolution is possible (at least in the foreseeable future).

Finally, in Part III of the book we turn our attention to developments in social democracy at the supranational level. The European Union has typically had an ambiguous relationship with social democracy – at times considered a vehicle through which globalisation and the purported neo-liberal global hegemony could be challenged, at other times identified as a market-building project that has actively undermined the scope for social democratic alternatives to be promoted at both the national and supranational levels. Part III of the book therefore seeks to address these issues through a consideration of the interaction between social democracy and European integration during the GEC. Each of the chapters adopts a different perspective. Thus, Michael Holmes and Simon Lightfoot focus in Chapter 12 on the role of the Party of European Socialists (PES) group in the European Parliament, highlighting what they term the 'reactive and incremental' development of the PES position in response to the GEC. This position has become increasingly coherent as the urgency of finding a solution to the crisis has grown, although Holmes and Lightfoot see a problem in terms of communicating this message to the electorate. In David Bailey's chapter, we see a comparison between social democratic party ambitions that have developed at the EU level, and actual concrete outcomes. The mismatch between the two, Bailey suggests, can be explained by more critical approaches to social democratic parties, which tend to view social democracy's support for European integration in terms of the opportunities it provides for party elites seeking to 'conceal or obfuscate' a process of terminal social democratic decline. Similarly, in Gerassimos Moschonas's chapter, we see the development of a gradually more concrete social democratic programme to be advanced at the European level, alongside a somewhat mediocre record in terms of concrete social democratic policy outcomes. As Moschonas shows, the institutional logic of the European Union is such that transnational social democracy remains difficult to achieve, and as a result any European-level response is likely to be 'inter-partisan and intergovernmental'. While the ongoing development of a supranational form of social democracy is observed by each of the commentators in Part III, therefore, there exists a range of interpretations regarding the viability or otherwise of this emerging agenda.

In summary, the present volume does not represent easy reading for those who hope to see a revival of fortunes for social democratic parties. In order to evaluate these trends we invited Ashley Lavelle to provide a postface discussion. Lavelle is the author of a recent book (2008) that provides a compelling (and troubling, from the perspective of social democracy) analysis of the fate of social democracy, that appears in many ways to have pre-empted the findings of our present book. Lavelle therefore reflects on the current state of social democracy from a perspective that *expects* to see, in his terms, 'the death of social democracy' (Lavelle, 2008). Indeed, as with many of the other contributors to this edited collection, Lavelle sees more prospects for optimism in parties to the left of social democracy and in the social movements with which social democratic parties have thus far failed to connect. The question of whether the empirical trends observed over the past five years will be repeated in the coming years of course remains for us to see. Yet we hope with this volume, bringing together some of the leading international scholars of social democracy, that we have made an important contribution to the necessary process of rethinking, reflecting upon, and re-evaluating the strategies of social democracy – and progressives more generally – in responding to the global economic crisis that (at least at the time of writing – August 2013) appears to have no end.

References

Bailey, D. J. (2009). *The Political Economy of European Social Democracy: A Critical Realist Approach* (London: Routledge).

Bailey, D. J. and Bates, S. (2012). 'Struggle (or its absence) during the crisis: what power is left?', *Journal of Political Power*, 5(2), 195–216.

Berman, S. (2006). *The Primacy of Politics: Social Democracy and the Making of Europe's Twentieth Century* (Cambridge: Cambridge University Press).

Blyth, M. (2002). *Great Transformations: Economic Ideas and Institutional Change in the Twentieth Century* (Cambridge: Cambridge University Press).

Callaghan, J., Fishman, N., Jackson, B. and McIvor, M. (eds) (2009). *In Search of Social Democracy: Responses to Crisis and Modernisation* (Manchester: Manchester University Press).

Fraser, N. (2013). 'A triple movement? Parsing the politics of crisis after Polanyi', *New Left Review*, 81, 119–32.

Gamble, A. (2009). *The Spectre at the Feast: Capitalist Crisis and the Politics of Recession* (Basingstoke: Palgrave Macmillan).

Harvey, D. (2005). *A Brief History of Neoliberalism* (Oxford: Oxford University Press).

Hay, C. (2004). 'The normalizing role of rationalist assumptions in the institutional embedding of neoliberalism', *Economy and Society*, 33(4), 500–27.

Hay, C. (2011). 'Pathology without crisis? The strange demise of the Anglo-Liberal growth model', *Government and Opposition*, 46(1), 1–31.

Klitgaard, M. B. (2007). 'Why are they doing it? Social democracy and market-oriented welfare state reforms', *West European Politics*, 30(1), 172–94.

Lavelle, A. (2008). *The Death of Social Democracy: Political Consequences in the 21st Century* (Aldershot: Ashgate).

Miliband, R. (1961). *Parliamentary Socialism: A Study in the Politics of Labour* (London: George Allen & Unwin).

Peck, J. (2010). *Constructions of Neoliberal Reason* (Oxford: Oxford University Press).

Piven, F. F. and Cloward, R. A. (1979). *Poor People's Movements: Why They Succeed, How They Fail* (New York: Vintage).

Ryner, M. J. (2002). *Capitalist Restructuring, Globalisation and the Third Way: Lessons from the Swedish Model* (London: Routledge).

Saull, R. (2012). 'Rethinking hegemony: uneven development, historical blocs, and the world economic crisis', *International Studies Quarterly*, 56, 323–38.

Schmidt, V. A. and Thatcher, M. (eds) (2013). *Resilient Liberalism in Europe's Political Economy* (Cambridge: Cambridge University Press).

Watson, M. and Hay, C. (2003). 'The discourse of globalisation and the logic of no alternative: rendering the contingent necessary in the political economy of New Labour', *Policy and Politics*, 31(3), 289–305.

Part I

The political economy of European social democracy under global economic crisis

2

'It does not happen here either': why social democrats fail in the context of the great economic crisis

Fabien Escalona and Mathieu Vieira

Introduction

As has been mentioned in the introduction, one of the aims underpinning the present edited volume lies in addressing the following apparent paradox: notwithstanding the structural crisis that engulfed the capitalist system in a neo-liberal age (Kotz, 2009), social democracy has apparently failed to benefit from this. Given how many contemporaries are intrigued by this situation, it would be quite fascinating to see how this would affect a left-wing activist waking from a thirty-year-long slumber. This thought experiment may help us to work out a series of answers to the question that he would be obsessed with: how come the social democrats failed, for the five years that followed the outbreak of the crisis, to reverse the advances made by conservatives, and the system that they started championing in the late 1970s? In other words, while Lipset and Marks (2000) offered an explanation of 'why it [socialism] did not happen here [in the United States]', we should in turn try to shed some light on 'why it does not happen here and now either'.

The investigation undertaken by Lipset and Marks involved highlighting the obstacles to the emergence of a powerful and enduring socialist party in the United States. Qualifying the significant impact of the American political system, they focused more on the challenging cultural context and the class heterogeneity the American socialists were up against and, above all, the socialists' strategic decisions. More importantly for our purpose, their work culminated in a challenging question. Is American exceptionalism a foretaste of what is awaiting the European political scene, rather than an anomalous situation in the midst of the advanced capitalist societies? This provocative hypothesis was based on the experiences with the 'Third Way' during the 1990s but its credibility has apparently not been undermined by the present situation. Democratic socialism has seriously failed to triumph in the 'Old World', even though the workers' movement came into being there and this is where a new 'major crisis' of capitalism is making a huge impact. Quite the opposite is true, to the extent that social democracy is apparently wavering between a continuing adjustment to the constraints of neo-liberal globalisation and the search for an improbable continent-wide 'green high-tech Keynesianism'.

The purpose of this chapter is therefore to explain the reasons for this situation, focusing on the relationship social democracy has forged with the capitalist economy and the European institutions. Our discussion kicks off by looking at the defeat this political family of parties had to contend with as a result of the exhaustion of the social democratic/Keynesian project. Our key argument seeks to explain why and how social democracy made two 'Faustian pacts', thereby strengthening the neo-liberal paradigm established in the late 1970s: the conversion to the European integration process, and the enthusiasm for the knowledge-based economy. This explanation should not be confused with the 'treason trials' regularly brought against social democrats, because we do not argue that they surrendered to the new phase of capitalism for the same reasons and with the same ideas in mind as their conservative opponents. Our argument, rather, is that the Faustian pacts that have been forged continue to make it difficult for the social democratic family to offer a comprehensive and coherent alternative to the ailing neo-liberal paradigm. What we are seeing is a further headlong rush within the context of these pacts.

The question of the social democrats being unable to offer an alternative has to be separated from the issue of their return to power in the short term. Alone or as part of a coalition, they have won several general elections since the project of this book got under way. These performances have nonetheless often been mixed and their durability remains to be seen. Nor did these achievements coincide with success in recapturing an intellectual hegemony on a par with what was secured during the post-war epoch. Lastly, and logically, these returns to power have not so far led to the emergence of an egalitarian alternative to neo-liberalism. These observations may be attributed to external factors, such as the threat of speculative attacks, but also to a more basic challenge, which is related to social democracy's relationship with neo-liberalism and the capitalist economy.

In line with this argumentative thread, we will first of all return to the transition from the Keynesian–Fordist phase of capitalism to its neo-liberal one, in order to gain an understanding of the background to the forging of the 'Faustian pacts' discussed above. We will then go on to describe the nature of these pacts and their consequences. Finally, we will offer a short assessment of the social democratic response to the present crisis. The conclusion will stress how *all* the heirs of the workers' movement find themselves unable to mount an effective challenge against a system that is nonetheless shaken by its own instability.

Social democracy from its 'heyday' to its defeat

Albeit often toned down in form, the social democratic and Keynesian approaches held sway in western Europe from the post-war period to the 1970s, even when the social democrats themselves did not hold the reins of power. This situation was closely linked with the structure of capitalism that took root after the Great Depression in the 1930s and the Second World War. The economic catching-up process during the post-war epoch and Fordism's impact on the organisation of work created tremendous levels of growth and productivity culminating in a virtuous circle between mass production and mass consumption, underpinned by Keynesian-inspired macroeconomic policies and the extension of the welfare state. It may not have been the best of social democratic worlds but it was a lot like it: the annual GDP growth rates were as high as 5 per cent, living standards and profits increased at the same pace, social insecurity was on the wane and, above all, full employment was a reality in most of the advanced capitalist countries. The international context facilitated the progressive nature and effective impact of public policies. Capital controls and currency stability guaranteed the economic sovereignty of nation states to some extent, while the communist regimes were conducive to labour in its balance of power with capital.

This stage of capitalism was defined as a Fordist 'regime of accumulation' or 'productive order' (Boyer and Juillard, 1995; Dockès, 2003), or as a 'social-democratic/Keynesian compromise' (Duménil and Lévy, 2011). The capital owners had not lost their key privileges but the power and income they enjoyed in earlier times was now comparatively restricted, in favour of the working class and managers. This is why the social democrats had no need for or interest in altering the economic system or continuing to believe in the Marxist doctrine, as they were managing to achieve their key objectives – full employment and the social inclusion of the 'have-nots' – without mounting an attack against the capitalist structures of western societies. Public policies bearing the social democratic stamp were a boon not only to the movement's traditional constituencies but also to the entire political community to which it belonged. Accordingly, class interests and national interests seemed to converge (Moschonas, 2002: 63–72). In short, the social democrats' success in safeguarding workers' interests was at its height during the 'golden age of modern capitalism' between 1945 and 1973 (Crotty, 2000). The resulting spread of prosperity on a fair basis succeeded in simultaneously pleasing the social powers competing in the context of the class divide, which were therefore easier to channel than during a crisis period.

Many social democratic intellectuals and leaders made the mistake of thinking that this state of affairs would continue in the long term, when in fact the contradictions inherent in the system to which they had adapted had not gone away again and so resurfaced in the early 1970s. A key factor in the social democratic regime's destabilisation was the significantly lower increases in productivity and growth rates that have occurred since the mid 1970's (Lavelle, 2008). Keynesian policies failed to produce the anticipated successes, particularly when the end of the Bretton-Woods' system shattered the extent to which national and international regulations were compatible with each other. The social democrats found themselves helpless when faced with the champions of 'supply-side economics' which soon replaced their outmoded system (Scharpf, 1991). Any return to a kind of 'business as usual' was out of the question, owing to three major developments concentrated in the crisis of the 1970s: (1) the fulfilment of the Kaleckian prophecy that a lengthy period of full employment would end in a violent struggle between employees and employers/owners (Kalecki, 1943; Glyn, 1995); (2) the end of a new, albeit temporary, balance between the sectors where the demand of the majority of society was focused and those in which the key capitalist players found it the most profitable to invest (Husson, 2002); and (3) a return to the tendencies of mature capitalist economies to stagnate (Freeman, 2012).

These reminders help us to gain a better understanding of the appeal the European project and the knowledge-based economy had for the social democrats, as a reflection of their aim of restoring the conditions to which they owed their post-war successes. As the Keynesian approach had failed on a nationwide basis, it had to be re-established on a continental scale; and as sectors so typical of the Fordist epoch had run out of steam, emphasis was placed on new high-tech sectors. In each case this would provide a means of unleashing a new wave of growth that, in turn, would provide a tangible basis for a fresh compromise between capital and labour. These approaches serve to highlight the productivist invariant underlying social democrat thinking and the aversion to social conflict they demonstrate when the political cost of such conflict has a tendency to rise. However, our argument regarding 'Faustian pacts' also highlights the extent to which these arrangements prompted social democrats to lend their support to the core elements of the neo-liberal structure of contemporary capitalism. This new environment was not conducive to their basic principles, to say the least. The new order was in fact the incarnation of the intellectual and social revenge of the capitalist elite and their allies, who were without a shadow of a doubt the uncontested winners of this new 'social order' that emerged to the detriment of the working class (Duménil and Lévy, 2011). The hallmarks of this neo-liberal stage of capitalism were unstable growth rates, increasing inequalities, an ever-increasing number of speculative bubbles and, more broadly, the advance of productive and financial globalisation. Yet, as well as failing to undermine this new structure, the social democrats also incorporated many neo-liberal principles in their endeavours and programmes. The description of two Faustian pacts entered into by social democratic parties helps to explain how this conversion came about and why this approach scarcely changed following the onset of the 2007–08 crisis.

The first Faustian pact of social democracy: faith in European integration

Apart from a few key figures, such as the Belgian socialist Paul-Henri Spaak and socialist parties in the Benelux countries, the social democratic parties have not always been as strongly 'pro-European' historically as they are today. Underpinned by a Christian-democrat–liberal alliance, the European integration process was in the past looked down upon by social democrats, as a capitalist endeavour destabilising the foundations of the various national welfare states. Not until the early 1980s did the attitude of the social democrats change from 'ambiguity to promotion' (Holmes and Lightfoot, 2002) when it came to European integration and further integration.

What triggered this gradual conversion to European integration was undoubtedly the failure of the 'last chance' represented by the French socialist government (Ross, 1995). Mitterrand's U-turn during the 1982–83 period accordingly sealed the fate of the final 'national Keynesian' experiment in Europe. The crisis besetting the national Keynesian model in the face of globalised, financial-based capitalism hastened the European U-turn made by the social democrats in the early 1980s. The European social democratic movement became aware, first of all, that the European Economic Community (EEC) may be akin to compensation for national retrenchment, such that the reformist approach now had to be channelled through Europe (Scharpf, 1990; Ladrech, 2000) and, second, that this leap in scale, or assigning of a European dimension to the social democratic model, was required to contend with capitalism's growing international dimension. During the early 1980s, the social democrats became involved in promoting and overseeing the deepening of the European integration process in a bid to replicate the national social democratic model at the European level. However, Delwit (1994: 446) rightly stresses the 'aligned' nature or even 'constraint' inherent in this convergence.

If 'strategy' means coordinating efforts to achieve an objective, it is hard to see in this any comparison with the social democrats' conversion to the European integration process. 'Eurokeynesianism' (Aust, 2004) was more of a tactic than a strategy involving a long-term goal. The social democratic parties pinned their hopes on almost automatically regaining in Europe the leeway they had lost at the national level, but without seeking a social democratic Europe. Elisabeth Du Réau sums up perfectly the social democratic attitude by commenting that 'it was no longer a question of establishing socialism in all European countries and then, consequently, creating Europe, but to create Europe first of all and then struggle to make Europe socialist' (2001: 171). Social democracy therefore invested Europe with the ambition of conducting a social democratic policy without considering the feasibility of such a policy in the economic and institutional context of the EEC. In this sense, the slogan that the French socialist François Mitterrand coined in 1973 – 'Europe will be socialist or it will not be' – did not tally with the facts.

This is the crux of the Faustian pact that social democracy forged with the EEC (later to become the EU). As a result of upholding an economically neo-liberal and institutionally conservative European framework, the social democrats found themselves trapped by a 'deadlock' that they themselves helped to legitimise and then build. The 'magical return' (Cupérus and Kandel, 1998) in the 1990s thus appears a real missed opportunity to build a social democratic Europe, as well as laying bare a structural strategic deficit. We will consider the details of the EU Faustian pact in terms of the underlying economic and institutional policymaking principles that underpinned it.

From the Maastricht Treaty to the Treaty on Stability, Coordination and Governance: when ordoliberalism makes nonsense of social democratic economic policy

The question remains whether it is still possible to conduct a demand-led social democratic economic policy in the context of the EU, as it might be thought that the ever-increasing number of legislative and regulatory initiatives applied after 2010 in order to curb the economic crisis – what the Economistes atterrés (appalled economists) (2011) call 'the multilayered structure of the EU's "new" governance arrangements' – serves to consolidate the ordoliberal project now governing European integration. In the wake of the Maastricht Treaty and the 'social market economy' model, the EU's ordoliberal basis no longer needs demonstrating. Having emerged in the 1930s and being based on the name of the eponymous journal, this German version of neo-liberalism (Dardot and Laval, 2009)

> has no confidence in Adam Smith's cherished 'invisible hand', nor in any balanced adjustment of the markets towards equilibrium … According to this approach, market forces do not allow for any spontaneous movement towards an equilibrium. There is no 'natural harmony of interests'. The market's operations and equilibrium are dependent upon states creating and maintaining a binding institutional and legal framework allowing the market functions to operate. As the ordoliberals have faith in the wisdom of the experts it is up to them to determine the ground rules. (Les économistes atterrés, 2012: 73)

In other words, ordoliberalism is based on the principle of removing the political dimension from economic decision making. This principle was set to be the cornerstone of successive treaties, taking tangible form on the basis of three pillars: an independent central bank whose sole aim is price stability, an automatic budget policy led by the need for balanced budgets, structural reforms leading to the liberalisation of the goods and services markets, relaxing employment laws, curbing social security expenditure and public expenditure in general (Les économistes atterrés, 2012: 112).

Far from being mere observers of this ordoliberal project now guiding the EU's economic policy, the social democrats played the part of 'builders' (Scharpf, 1999: 84) of the latter. Our point of view is in line with the one Abdelal puts forward in *Capital Rules* (2007) concerning the key role played by the European social democrats – particularly the French ones (Delors, Lamy, Camdessus and

Chavranski) – in liberalising the global economy during the 1980s. A genuine 'supranational entrepreneur' (Moravcsik, 1999), Delors, the former Minister for Economic Affairs and Finance in the Mitterrand government, became a key player in favour of a political strategy for the market-led unification of Europe (Ross, 1995). As the President of the European Commission from 1985 to 1994, Delors turned the Commission into a reformist player at the instigation of the 'quiet European revolution' (Jabko, 2009: 69–88).

The impetus of a financial market on the Commission's initiative set the stage for the advent of Economic and Monetary Union (EMU). While the Treaty of Rome paved the way for the free movement of capital, the financial transactions between the member states were in reality subject to prior authorisation in the form of 'exchange rate controls'. Mindful of the inherent obstacle to the internal market, Delors and his chef de cabinet Lamy launched a process leading to financial liberalisation that was triggered in May 1986 with the publication of the Commission's 'Agenda for a Liberation of Capital Movements' (COM (86) 292, 23 May 1986). In the wake of this document, the Council proceeded in June 1988 to adopt a directive ushering in a system of unhindered capital flows.[1] The process culminated in the introduction of the Maastricht Treaty by investing free capital flows with the same status as the other internal market freedoms, with this freedom being established as a fundamental EU freedom. The abolition, on 1 January 1994, of all restrictions to movements of capital between the member states or with third countries was a reflection of the EU's policy of promoting the growing importance of financial markets in European economies.

Subsequent to the first stage of the EMU roll-out process based on liberalising capital flows, the second stage kicked off with the introduction of the so-called Maastricht 'convergence criteria'. The tough rules enacted to enforce budgetary discipline were strengthened with the adoption of the Stability and Growth Pact during the June 1997 Amsterdam European Council. Back then, the social democrats enjoyed an overwhelming majority in the Council, dominated by the Blair–Jospin pairing. Accordingly, the budgetary stability commitment was adopted at the instigation of the social democrats. The Stability and Growth Pact implied in particular that member states should keep their deficits and debts below the thresholds of 3 per cent and 60 per cent of GDP respectively. The central bank in charge of monetary policy gained its independent status in the third stage of the EMU, with the advent of the euro, on 1 January 1999. Even at the height of the sovereign debt crisis, the independence and aim of price stability have never essentially been called into question. Within a European context guaranteeing the free movement of capital, the independence of the ECB and price stability, it is not so hard to understand 'why do the social-democratic parties fail to apply social-democratic policies' (Husson, 2012b). Given this picture, it seems fair to raise the question about the compatibility of a social democratic programme with the present European framework (Schwartz, 2012).

Mechanically added to the European structure, even the adoption of a 'social treaty', as promised by the social democrats since the mid-1980s, left people feeling sceptical about the feasibility of a social democratic programme. This doubt was not dispelled by the measures adopted between 2010 and 2011 to cope with the Euro-zone crisis and which were subsequently approved via the ratification of the Treaty on Stability, Coordination and Governance (TSCG), as a further step in the process for intensifying the EU's ordoliberal venture.

The ever-closer supervision of budgetary policies has removed the member states' power to control their economies and this is in line with the 'lifelong dream of neo-liberals: the complete paralysis of budgetary policies and eliminating any discretionary authority for economic policymaking' (Les économistes atterrés, 2012: 28). The first measure in 'the multilayered structure of the EU's "new" governance arrangements' was proposed to the European Commission on 30 June 2010 and waved through at the 7 September 2010 European Council. Against the background of the 'European semester' the Commission and European Council operate an ongoing system for monitoring the member states' budgetary policies even before the parliamentary debates at the national level. During the first six months of every year, member states are required to present their budget forecasts and planned structural reforms to the Commission and European Council. In the light of the recommendations the European Council adopted in 2011 and 2012, it is hard to say a prior inspection of the member states' budgets is a tool for the upward harmonisation of social policies. On the contrary, the recommendations generally seek three aims: applying austerity measures to curb deficits, labour market reforms – or more precisely more flexible work practices – and (allegedly) support for growth through market liberalisation (Les économistes atterrés, 2012: 128). Shortly afterwards, on 29 September, the Commission stepped forwards with a set of six directives, or a '6-Pack', designed to strengthen the Stability and Growth Pact. The 'coercive' component, providing an 'excessive deficits' procedure, in fact lead to the introduction of a system where macroeconomic imbalances are monitored by the Commission and European Council. The third '2-Pack' system the Commission proposed in November 2011 significantly extends its power to control member states' budgets, including the scope for intensifying the economic and budget monitoring system for 'Member States experiencing or at risk of experiencing serious difficulties'. At the instigation of Germany and France, the Eurozone Council proceeded, on 11 March 2011, to adopt a 'Euro Plus Pact', also called the 'Competitiveness Pact'. The Pact requires the member states' heads of government and state to proceed every year to make a commitment before their peers and the Commission under various headings such as competitiveness and employment. As Weber points out, the 'hidden aim' of the Euro Plus Pact is to 'allow the European authorities to intervene more directly in two areas that normally continue to be national policymaking areas: social protection and wage negotiations' (2013: 23).

A conservative institutional system not conducive to a party-political approach
'Those opposed to a new regime start by refusing but end up accepting it in the hope of being able to turn it to good account.' The three stages outlined by Duhamel (1980: 30) to qualify the French left's response to the Fifth Republic is quite applicable to social democracy's adherence to the spirit and practices of the European institutions. And to take things a step further, it has to be recognised that while the social democrats rallied round in the hope of using the European forum to uphold their ideas, they were prevented from doing so by the EU's essentially conservative institutional framework (Moschonas, 2009). The social democrats did not realise that the institutional system was not conducive to a party-political approach enabling party politics to be introduced into the European debate and they gave even less thought to the question of what would be required in order to ensure its achievement: the creation of a genuine European party-political system.

Ever since the first European elections in 1979 and the empowerment of the European Parliament (EP), the research agenda in the EP has been focused on understanding the emergence of 'Euro-parties' and a 'European party system'. However, although the scholars who study the party phenomenon at EU level refer to the 'party system' concept, the question of the existence of such a system has never been properly examined. Without being debated, the concept of 'party system' is used for the sake of convenience to describe the partisan reality in the EP (among others, see Attinà, 1992; Lecureuil, 1996; Kreppel, 2002). In this respect, Hix *et al.* (2007) defined the system formed by the political groups in the EP as a 'two-plus several party system'. In addition, the criterion for the existence of a European party system applied by the scholars of the European Parliament Research Group, i.e. cohesion of party groups (Kreppel, 2002; Hix *et al.*, 2003), is inappropriate. We argue that rather than establishing the nature of the system formed by the European political organisations (EP groups and European federations), these researches have been trying to determine the form that it could have taken. Who seriously doubts that a party system exists in the US Congress despite the fact that intra-party cohesion is low? Moreover, some scholars have pointed out the limits of roll-call votes analysis such as the special nature of these votes, the overly direct link between party cohesion and party discipline, and the overestimation of the EP practices (Costa and Rozenberg, 2008). The cohesion of the EP groups is more the result of a rationalisation of the parliamentary work shared between the MEPs within a same group than the defence of a developed political line.

Similarly, Sartori is right to highlight that 'confusion and profusion of terms seem to be the rule' (1976: 119) concerning the research into party systems. In an earlier paper (Vieira, 2011: 8), we proposed three conditions for the existence of a party system: '(1) a set of parties (2) a parliamentary arena linked to a competitive electoral arena, and (3) a governmental arena strongly linked – designations of the representatives (i), vote of laws (ii) – to the electoral and/or parliamentary arena'. If the connection between the electoral and parliamentary arenas is a fact since the first European elections in June 1979 and the second condition is thus fulfilled, what about the other two conditions?

Since their creation at the end of the 1970s, scholars witnessed the emergence of European federations in the European public arena. These extra-parliamentary organisations have progressively organised themselves in order to ensure coordination between the actors belonging to the partisan triangle and between the various levels of powers, i.e. the coordination of the political family. The 'constitutional recognition' (Külahci, 2008) by the Maastricht Treaty of these extra-parliamentary organisations as 'political parties at European level' (art. 138A) is a decisive step in the institutionalisation process of the 'transnational party networks' (Kohler and Myrzik, 1982). This 'top-down institutionalisation' (Bartolini, 2011) of the European federations has accelerated since the introduction of financial support in 2003.[2] Despite the progressive structuring of the European federations, they cannot aspire to being labelled 'Euro-parties'. In contrast to most other scholars who employed the term 'European parties' uncritically, we argue that the analogy of words must not be taken for granted. Seiler stresses rightly that 'these unique legal items fail to meet any of the criteria political science has defined for over a century in order to develop the "political party" concept ... The political scientists prepared to regard them as parties accordingly consign Lowell, Bryce, Ostrogorsky, Michels, Max Weber and Duverger to the dustbin, i.e. the key component of the debate political science devotes to the party-political issue. They are therefore denying themselves' (2011: 281–2). Indeed, European partisan organisations do not appear in the classical definitions and typologies of political parties. Above all, European federations do not meet the traditional requirements expected from national political parties, in particular with regard to the selection of candidates. Even for the EP elections – and this situation has not changed since 1979 – the national parties distribute the investitures and not the organisations at EU level. Yet, this function was considered by Sartori as the basic definition of a political party. According to Sartori, 'a party is any political group that stands for election, and is capable of placing through elections, candidates for public office' (1976: 64). In the light of these criteria, a European partisan centre does not exist. European political organisations ensure only two genuine functions: a 'labelling function' (Sartori, 2005: 26) and a coordination function. European political organisations correspond to a *European party-political network* rather than 'European political parties' with what Sartori calls a 'legislative-electoral' profile (2005: 16). Once again, Seiler is right to suggest that 'generally, the act precedes the law, whereas in this case the law precedes the act or, more precisely, seeks to influence the act. As Paul Magnette observed, the expression "European political parties" is essentially performative' (2011: 282).

The third condition for the existence of a party system is not met at EU level insofar as the European governmental arena is not entirely connected to the parliamentary one. This disjunction between the governmental and parliamentary arenas prevents the emergence of a party system. First, the 'parliamentarisation' of the EU political system is not yet fully achieved (Magnette, 2009). Even if the parallel with the parliamentary system is appropriate in many respects considering the process of 'governmentalisation' affecting the Commission, the political power exerted by the Parliament on the Commission – which shares the executive function with the Council – remains low (Costa, 2009). Second, the legislative function is shared between the Council and the EP. In other words, the legislative function is no exception to 'institutional overlapping' (Blumann, 1995). The EP progressively becomes a 'part of the legislative body' (Blumann, 1995) and actively participates in the legislative process. The EP's legislative powers range from consultation to the co-decision procedure. The introduction of co-legislator status by the Maastricht Treaty is a sign of the increasing influence of the EP on European policy making. Nevertheless, the co-decision procedure does not concern all the EU's fields of competence. The consultation and assent procedures continue to be applied to certain policy areas. Consequently, the distribution of the legislative powers between the Council and the EP is still in favour of the Council. Although it became a legislative body, the EP somehow bears the scars of a consultative body.

Does the ratification of the Lisbon Treaty change this situation? We have pointed out the uncompleted nature of the connection between the parliamentary and governmental arenas. The Lisbon Treaty represents a move in the right direction, offering in particular a more effective separation of powers and an improvement of the EP's role in European policy making. First of all, the Lisbon Treaty introduces a change concerning the appointment of the President of the Commission. It establishes that the Council must recommend the candidate to the Commission presidency 'taking into consideration the EP elections'. Unlike the earlier procedure, it is also indicated that the candidate should be elected by the EP acting by a qualified majority of its members. The election of the President of the Commission by the MEPs aims to confer upon this official democratic legitimacy. These new measures confirm the emergence of a party-political basis to the institution that is often described as a 'technocratic apparatus', to repeat De Gaulle's expression. In addition, this new system is meant to strengthen the political responsibility of the Commission vis-à-vis the EP. The functions and the powers of control available to each institution are also clarified by the Treaty. If we bear in mind that the separation of powers in the EU is in itself different from the parliamentary or presidential system, we can appreciate that the Lisbon Treaty is a first step towards the fulfilment of the third condition for the existence of a party system. At the initiative of the Commission (TEU, art. 17), both the Parliament and the Council are now able to exert legislative power

(TEU, arts 14 and 16). The executive function is assigned to the member states and the Commission (TEU, art. 17 and TFUE, art. 291). Second, the legislative procedure is modified. The co-decision procedure is extended to thirty-four new policy areas (Ziller, 2008) to become the 'ordinary legislative procedure'. The extension of this procedure to almost all of the EU's areas of competence shows the aim of balancing the share of the legislative function and achieving a better system of inter-institutional cooperation.

In spite of the changes introduced by the Lisbon Treaty, the embryonic nature of the European partisan organisations does not allow us to speak yet of a European party system. On the one hand, the European party federations will never have the basic characteristics of political parties. On the other hand, the governmental arena is not sufficiently linked to the parliamentary one. In short, we agree with Seiler when he says that 'the addition of national party-political systems obviously does not create a system of European parties. In this case and many other cases, the whole is different from the sum of its parts' (2011: 298). Without a party-political system in common with the other parties, therefore, it was apparently pointless for the social democratic parties to seek to adjust the consensual approach inherent to the European political system (Hix, 2006).

The second Faustian pact of social democracy: faith in a knowledge-based economy

In terms of timelines, the promotion of the knowledge-based economy came after the challenge of European integration and, more importantly, did not result in equally significant institutional constraints. Yet it is equally enlightening in terms of enabling us to consider social democracy's dependence on economic growth. It also helped to give a stamp of legitimacy to public policies consistent with the continued neo-liberal structure of capitalism, where the distinguishing features are the supremacy of capital over paid employment and capital's unimpeded movement throughout the word. New information and communication technologies (NICT) figure prominently in the list of resources earmarked for these two factors. The boom and apparent successful achievements of the 'new economy' during the 1990s, particularly in the United States, made a great impression on the major part of the political elites and economies in western Europe. The social democratic leaders also fell under the sway of the new consensus that developed on the basis of the 'knowledge-based economy'.

The attraction for this latter could be described as the hope of seeing the advent of a 'new high-tech Fordism' to restore Europe's prosperity and create a tangible basis for social inclusion policies, as in the heyday of the Keynesian epoch. Several social democratic leaders or factions called for an innovation-driven economic policy and high-added-value products. These include the Third Wayers of the Labour Party in the United Kingdom, Gerhard Schröder in

Germany, Massimo D'Alema in Italy, and Dominique Strauss-Kahn in France. These stressed the importance of offering individuals as many skills as they need to become part of the global knowledge-based economy. They claimed these skills had become 'the highest form of social protection' – to quote D'Alema – and now represented the new raw material needed to take part in the competitiveness race (Jessup, 1999). In addition to the national variations on the theme of celebrating the knowledge economy, its most obvious example continues to be the Lisbon Strategy adopted by the March 2000 European Council. This entity was overwhelmingly dominated at the time by social democratic governments, while the strategy itself had been developed under the leadership of the Portuguese socialist Maria João Rodrigues. The avowed aim was to make the EU 'the most competitive and dynamic knowledge-based economy in the world', on the basis of upgrading the European social model and developing a 'learning society' (Delanty and Rumford, 2005: 106–19). A three-step approach underpinned these pronouncements: (1) social protection and public institutions had to be adjusted in order to better equip individuals and companies to take part in the competition for knowledge and innovation; (2) being well placed in terms of competitiveness would make it possible to produce a lot more wealth than in the traditional sectors of industry and services; and (3) the resulting growth could then be deployed to achieve the social democratic aims of full employment and social inclusion.

This social democratic version of the 'trickle-down' theory reflects a naive Schumpeterian economic approach, itself based on faith in the high-growth potential of NICT. Unfortunately, however, the 'knowledge-driven' phase was in fact an illusion diverting the social democrats away from the need for a consistently critical approach to neo-liberalism. Such an approach was rendered all the more impossible because those seeking to 'play along with the knowledge-based economy' ignored how much this was part of a capitalist structure that was *incompatible* with the social progress they claimed to support. To sum up, the social democrats not only overestimated the scale of the knowledge economy's growth momentum but also overestimated its progressive nature.

Certainly, the 'information revolution' and the rapid development of intangible products were indicative of a genuine technological transformation (Freeman and Louçã, 2002; Passet, 2010: 614–28). However, it was not enough by itself to define a 'productive order' as dynamic, stable and inclusive as during the post-war epoch (Husson, 2008: 66–7). This is why it was wrong to regard a knowledge-based economy as being equivalent to Fordism. First of all, the typical Fordist organisation of work was based on an unusual wage ratio and strong state and international regulatory mechanisms. Second, this institutional consistency coincided with a concentrated household demand for consumer and capital goods. By contrast, NICT were spreading against the background of deregulation and liberalisation, while employees were comparatively worse off in terms of wages. Nor should their success make us forget the more basic expansion of social needs to include human services, such as health and education.

In any event, the bursting of the dot-com bubble in the year 2000 was indicative of too much being expected of the knowledge-based economy. More importantly, this episode showed the extent to which the development of the 'new economy' was entangled with the neo-liberal phase of capitalism. The NICT 'created a system' with the financial markets, facilitating the rapid flow of capital and the amazingly intricate nature of financial products, while financial liberalisation fuelled the boom in the much-trumpeted 'start-up' sector (Plihon, 2001: 42–4). The stock market crash also revealed the basic contradiction inherent in the finance-driven accumulation regime: the profitability of productive activities cannot go on forever matching the remuneration requirements of financial assets (Lordon, 1999). This is why some observers saw the bursting of the dot-com bubble as the 'first major crisis of the neo-liberal model', especially as its resolution paved the way for the following sub-prime crisis (Joshua, 2006: 232; 2009).

'Knowledge' and the 'information revolution' are not, admittedly, neo-liberal per se and could be combined with other social systems. This is the suggestion Andersson (2010) makes in a pioneering work on the theme, where she makes a distinction in particular between New Labour's market approach and the more democratic approach of the Swedish social democrats. It should also be stressed that some features of intangible property are out of step with several facets of capitalist exploitation, as they are the outcome of work that is difficult to individualise and quantify and they may be reproduced and acquired almost free of charge after the initial investment. However, it is precisely because these non-market opportunities are such a threat that private undertakings have sought to curb them. First of all, knowledge has become increasingly beholden to the commercial sphere as a result of private intellectual property rights being extended – thanks in particular to patenting. Second, NICT have been exploited to the extent that they have made it possible to facilitate more flexible working practices and enhance the domination of shareholder sovereignty. Accordingly, knowledge and NICT have so far been reduced to 'strategic assets' to be appropriated and used for finance-dominated corporate-governance purposes (Weinstein, 2010: 135–75).

Consequently, the Third Way was the approach that prevailed out of the two singled out by Andersson. It could not have been otherwise as the non-market opportunities of the knowledge-based economy made hardly any impression on the social democrats, who did not seek to develop them, nor did they call into question the basic features of the neo-liberal structure of capitalism. On the contrary, Barker (2010) showed the extent to which social democratic governments converted European capitalism into a shareholder model of corporate governance. Meanwhile, Amable *et al.* (2009) sought to highlight the inconsistency of the 'social democratic aspirations' and the basically neo-liberal recommendations featured in the aforementioned Lisbon Strategy. This called in particular for more deregulation of the labour markets and product markets, the removal of obstacles to pension-fund investments and for public-expenditure curbs. In a nutshell, the way the knowledge-based economy was promoted by the social democrats is fairly consistent with what Zuege (2010) analysed as their search for a 'new form of corporatism' since the 1980–90 period. His criticism was levelled at the dream of 'progressive competitiveness' being doomed to defeat against the unchanged background of the global race to achieve a higher level of productivity, unless it is to remain earmarked for a tiny number of countries. In the context of the never-ending technological changes and the competition of organised labour via a fiercely polarised global market, there is nothing more to be expected from such a strategy than a 'negotiated path to austerity' (Zuege, 2000: 106).

The absence of a genuine social democratic alternative, or the relentless impact of the 'Faustian pacts'

The Faustian pacts metaphor seems to suggest that the social democrats may have sold their souls in order to revive their fortunes. 'Playing along with' the European integration process and the new economy did admittedly suggest a way out of the decline guaranteed by the commitment to a national Keynesian approach. This attitude also made it possible to cling onto the hope of reviving a social compromise in keeping with the secular aims of the social democratic family of parties. The opposing view involved submitting to the organisation of powers and institutions as characterised by the neo-liberal stage of capitalism. However, the social democratic parties seemed to have more room for manoeuvre than Dr Faust did in his dealings with Mephistopheles. They could still denounce these pacts, being accountable only to their electorate. This still left two problems to be resolved: (1) the credibility of the claim to repudiate neo-liberalism; and (2) the consistent approach to the alternative they are supposed to be championing. This section shows that these problems have not been resolved. Since the crisis broke out, the social democratic efforts and debates have continued to be confined within the pacts made earlier on, in spite of the aim of standing apart from an ailing economic paradigm.

The social democrats tried to blame the crisis on conservatives and made a genuine effort to provide a joint strategy. On the Community front, the Party of European Socialists (PES) adopted a declaration of principles in November 2011, and decided to field a candidate for the Commission presidency and present a joint programme for the European elections in 2014. Meanwhile, its foundation – the FEPS– has launched the 'Next Left' and 'Renaissance' programmes in a bid to forge a 'joint progressive vision' vis-à-vis the crisis and the challenges of the twenty-first century. As for the individual parties, the French Socialist Party and the SPD issued a joint statement, in June 2011, to uphold the progressive initiatives that might be launched by a Franco-German left-wing pairing.

The thrust of these European social democratic plans is to promote deeper European integration and a kind of 'green Eurokeynesianism'. The idea is to restore growth and job creation on the basis of a coordinated investment plan rather than continuing to charge towards austerity. The plan is also supposed to be a platform for the development of what has also been called 'green growth', 'sustainable growth' or a 'carbon-free economy'. The tax on financial transactions and 'Euro-bonds' – a system for pooling sovereign debts – would provide a means of funding the investment plan, while protecting public debts against speculative activities. The latter issue forms part of a call for tougher financial regulations (PES and S&D Group, 2010). The post-crisis venture of the European social democratic movement is therefore indicative of both an attempt to distance itself from the neo-liberal paradigm and the need to take account of environmental concerns. And yet this strikes us as being consistent with the 'Faustian pacts' forged in the past, as it is still premised on a production-based approach to progress, without including any serious questioning of the core part of the neo-liberal system. In a letter sent to the EU presidency in late 2008 the President of the PES used a discourse very similar to the one referred to earlier on: 'Only efficient and transparent financial markets will … allow long-term investments to make Europe the most competitive, knowledge-based economy in the world, based on environmental sustainability and social cohesion' (Rasmussen, 2008).

More specifically, the social democratic proposals are inherently inconsistent, as the key challenges are constantly being discussed within this party family. For example, the likes of the SPD have adopted an orthodox approach to the ECB's goals, while others, such as the French *Parti Socialiste*, are eager to reform them. Nor is there any consensus about the required limits to the devolution of power at the European level. Consequently, the joint proposals often continue to be sketchy. For one thing, it is difficult to identify the exact institutional design of the EU that the social democrats are championing. On the economic front their hostility to austerity is apparently ambiguous in so far as the Eurokeynesian tone of the resolutions is offset by convoluted assertions such as 'prospective cuts must be carefully targeted and limited, and social cuts must be avoided as far as possible' (PES and S&D Group, 2010). Moreover, the announcement of a 'green New Deal' has nothing to say about the measures left-wing government may take in the short term. The latter issue reflects the struggle the social democrats have with reconciling the national and European levels of governance. The 'salvation via Europe' they promise to their national electorates depends on completely autonomous and unpredictable decisions from the EU's other political communities. The PES therefore upholds social democratic policies at the European level, but without really thinking about how national governments could promote them, *even if they continue to be in a minority position vis-à-vis conservatives.*

This inconsistency exacerbates a more serious shortcoming: the debatable effectiveness of the social democratic proposals. For example, Euro-bonds would not be effective without an (unlikely) 'federal leap'. Moreover, the EU would remain beholden to the international financial markets to fund its public goods. The measures sought to regulate the financial markets would not call into question their supposed efficiency in earmarking resources. And yet the crisis has demonstrated that financial competition *in itself* cannot help to make a correct assessment of the value of the activities of the 'real economy' (Orléan, 2011). These examples serve to show that social democracy is still incapable of offering solutions to tackle the deep roots of the crisis. According to the regulation approach, these are to be found in the 'recommodification of labour' and the 'privatisation of credit decisions'. Hence the proposals to socialise financial institutions, reallocate power to employees in companies and curb international competition (Boyer, 2011: 188; 211–13). In a similar vein, Palley (2012) has shown that an authentically Keynesian response to the 'great stagnation' will not boil down to temporary budget stimuli but require a systemic restructuring of the 'income and demand-generating process'. That would imply full employment as a top priority of economic policy making, progressive and identical taxation for income from work and capital assets, more rights for employees and, most importantly, a return to controlling exchange rates and capital flows. EU wide, such a programme would clash with the status of the ECB, current budget rules and the 'constitutionalized' free trade (Hoang-Ngoc, 2005). However, the social democrats are not keen on altering these provisions – in any case not 'all together'.

Other more radical Marxist-oriented interpretations of the crisis even lead to the conclusion that 'there is no turning back the clock to a lost Keynesian "golden age". The fault is in the system' (Foster and McChesney, 2010). According to this approach, neo-liberalism was a response to an underlying problem *prior* to its own triumph, which is the tendency for the 'old' western economies to stagnate. Against this background, the global financial system has not interfered with the real economy but played an operational role in the new stage of capitalism. It first of all helped along the overall level of demand – which was no longer invigorated by the actual income of ordinary employees, while attracting capital not invested in the productive sphere, owing to insufficient profitability prospects (Husson, 2012a: 223–46). In other words, the social compromise in the post-war epoch, the crisis of the 1970s and the advent of neo-liberalism represent a logical sequence whose units are inextricably linked. This sequence resulted in vast pools of fictitious capital which is still waiting to be remunerated. The social democrats are not seeking their massive devalorisation, nor the artificial creation of new financial bubbles. Accordingly, they are calling for a 'return to growth' to avoid the real economy remunerating these capital amounts via increasingly harsh austerity measures. However, a sustainable expansion akin to the post-war boom is apparently unlikely (Balakrishnan, 2009), particularly as this ended at a time when the Keynesian paradigm was still dominant. Even if this kind of restoration were feasible, the growth rates would be incompatible with the need to safeguard an ecosystem that human beings can inhabit (Li, 2010). Furthermore, the dilemma specific to the capitalist economy would reappear anyway: 'if instability is averted [as was the case with Fordist regulation], profitability comes under threat. If profitability is restored [as was the case with neo-liberalism], instability reappears' (Johsua, 2009: 122).

Social democracy's historical path has not prepared it to face up to these challenges. As is demonstrated in Part II of this volume, social democratic efforts during the crisis led to orthodox economic policies rather than doctrinal and aspirational reforms. The social democrats continue to be incapable of offering a socio-economic alternative but they are likely to continue to achieve a differentiated position in terms of cultural challenges. Lipset's prediction (2001) that the European left will become 'Americanised' will then have come true to some extent. However, this scenario would be associated with a cost, as the representative system would continue to be affected by the pressures of the global crisis of capitalism.

Conclusion

The failure of the social democrats to reverse the ascendance of neo-liberalism can therefore be understood in terms of two key types of explanations. The first type refers to the consequences of what we have chosen to refer to as 'Faustian pacts'. This differs from interpretations in which social democrats are described as passive victims or traitors. According to our analysis, the scenario that has played out for thirty years is worse still, and less black and white. The neo-liberal structure of capitalism was imposed on social democracy but the latter played a part in sustaining it. In the wake of their defeat, social democrats tried to restore the conditions favourable to them in the post-war epoch. Hence the commitment to European integration and the enthusiasm for the knowledge-based economy. However, social democrats have strengthened the structure of neo-liberalism time and time again, without managing to revive the project to which they owed their 'heyday'. This contradiction was concealed by the same tactics that Streeck (2011) claims helped to reduce the conflict between the capitalist approach to allocating resources and the approach based on meeting the social needs of citizens. The present structural crisis is the result of these tactics having run out of steam. As a result, the crisis meant that the conflict between the two antagonist approaches was inevitable. It also widened the gap between what the social democrats can achieve within the current framework and the political alternative awaited by some of their electoral base (see also Bailey's contribution in this volume, Chapter 13).

At this point, a reference may be made to a second series of reasons for the lasting defeat of social democracy. The 'Faustian pacts' were nothing more than ways out of two of the contemporary dilemmas for social democracy (De Waele *et al.*, 2013). The first refers to the social democratic enterprise: is the idea of restoring the prosperity of the capitalist economy at any costs a credible proposition? If the answer is no, is human progress conceivable in a stationary economy? The latter approach would imply a level of social conflict out of all proportion to the post-war epoch, when the class compromise was helped along by outstanding growth and the 'communist rivalry'. The second dilemma is focused on European integration: is there any need to continue to respect an institutional framework that is adverse to alternatives to neo-liberalism? Or is it worth running the risk of breaking away from certain cornerstones of the European system? In the latter case, once again, it has to be realised that a serious conflict with international elites would be unavoidable. In other words, the social democrats' return to the 'primacy of politics' may be in keeping with their historical role (Berman, 2006) but it would be a tall order for this task to be accomplished in the same conditions and with the same facility as fifty years ago. The political and social costs have risen significantly and may seem exorbitant to a political family now belonging to the club of 'major governing parties'.

That said, if 'it doesn't happen here', this is not only due to the shortcomings of social democracy. The entire workers' movement has failed to recover from its historical defeat over the last thirty years, as underscored by the woes of the radical left and the trade unions. Against the background of the secular class cleavage, thirty years of neo-liberalism have been more damaging to the workers than thirty years of Keynesianism have been to the owners of capital. The 'infrastructures of dissent' (Sears, 2007) that developed after the end of the nineteenth century have been destroyed or altered. As a result, it has become more of a struggle to mobilise large sections of the population in social and political terms. The weak infrastructures of dissent are both the cause and consequence of another key issue, which is the lack of an anti-hegemonic initiative espoused by enough parties and social movements to be able to aspire to challenge neo-liberalism. This latter is kept going not only by coercion but also by cultural mechanisms making an impact on the collective imaginations. These lines of inquiry lead us to believe that the difficulties facing all of those resisting neo-liberalism are deep-seated and will be resolved only in the wake of what are likely to be painful decisions.

Notes

1 Council Directive 88/361/EEC of 24 June 1988 for the implementation of Article 67 of the Treaty.
2 Regulation (EC) No. 2004/2003 of the EP and of the Council of 4 November 2003

on the regulation governing political parties at European level and the rules regarding their funding, Official Journal of the European Union, 15.11.2003, L297/1.

References

Abdelal, R. (2007). *Capital Rules* (Cambridge, MA: Harvard University Press).

Amable, B., Demmou, L. and Ledezma, I. (2009). 'The Lisbon strategy and structural reforms in Europe', *Transfer: European Review of Labour and Research*, 15(1), 33–52.

Andersson, J. (2010). *The Library and the Workshop: Social Democracy and Capitalism in the Knowledge Age* (Stanford, CA: Stanford University Press).

Attinà, F. (1992). 'Parties, party systems and democracy in the European Union', *International Spectator*, 27, 67–86.

Aust, A. (2004). 'From "Eurokeynesianism" to the "Third Way": the party of European Socialists (PES) and European employment policies', in G. Bonoli and M. Powell (eds), *Social Democratic Party Policies in Contemporary Europe* (London and New York: Routledge), pp. 180–96.

Balakrishnan, G. (2009). 'Speculations on the stationary state', *New Left Review*, 59, 5–26.

Barker, R. M. (2010). *Corporate Governance, Competition and Political Parties: Explaining Corporate Governance Change in Europe* (Oxford: Oxford University Press).

Bartolini, S. (2012). 'The strange case of "European parties"', in E. Külahci (ed.), *Europeanization and Party Politics: How the EU Affects Domestic Actors, Patterns and Systems* (Colchester: ECPR Press), pp. 157–70.

Berman, S. (2006). *The Primacy of Politics: Social Democracy and the Making of Europe's Twentieth Century* (Cambridge: Cambridge University Press).

Blumann, C. (1995). *La fonction législative communautaire* (Paris: LGDJ).

Boyer, R. and Juillard, M. (1995). *Théorie de la régulation: L'état des savoirs* (Paris: Editions La Découverte).

Boyer, R. (2011). *Les financiers détruiront-ils le capitalisme?* (Paris: Economica).

Bryce, J. (1895). *American Commonwealth*, 2 vols (Indianapolis: Liberty Fund).

Callaghan, J. (2000). *The retreat of social democracy* (Manchester and New York: Manchester University Press).

Costa, O. (2009). 'Le Parlement européen dans le système décisionnel de l'UE: la puissance au prix de l'illisibilité', *Politique européenne*, 28(2), 129–55.

Costa, O. and Rozenberg, O. (2008). 'Parlementarismes', in C. Belot, P. Magnette and S. Saurugger (eds), *Science politique de l'Union européenne* (Paris: Economica), pp. 249–83.

Crotty, J. (2000). 'Trading state-led prosperity for market-led stagnation: from the golden age to global neoliberalism', available at: http://works.bepress.com/james_crotty/25.

Crouch, C. (1999). *Social Change in Western Europe* (Oxford: Oxford University Press).

Cupérus, R. and Kandel, J. (eds) (1998). *Social Democratic Think Tanks Explore the Magical Return of Social Democracy in a Liberal Era* (Amsterdam/Berlin: Friedrich Ebert Stiftung).

Dardot, P. and Laval, C. (2009). *La nouvelle raison du monde: Essai sur la société néolibérale* (Paris: La Découverte).

Delanty, G. and Rumford, C. (2005). *Rethinking Europe: Social Theory and the Implications of Europeanization* (London and New York: Routledge).

de Waele, J.-M., Escalona, F. and Vieira, M. (2013). 'The unfinished history of social democracy', in J.-M. de Waele, F. Escalona and M. Vieira, *The Palgrave Handbook of Social Democracy in the European Union* (Basingstoke and New York: Palgrave Macmillan), pp. 3–29.

Delwit, P. (1994). 'La gauche et l'Europe' in M. Larar (ed.), *La gauche en Europe depuis 1945: Invariants et mutations du socialisme européen* (Paris: PUF), pp. 433–50.

Dockès, P. (2003). *Les théories des crises économiques* (5th edn, Paris: La Découverte).

Duhamel, O. (1980). *La gauche et la Cinquième République* (Paris: PUF).

Duménil, G. and Lévy, D. (2011). *The Crisis of Neoliberalism* (Cambridge, MA and London: Harvard University Press).

Du Réau, E. (2001). *L'idée d'Europe au XXe siècle* (Bruxelles: Complexe).

Foster, J. B. and McChesney, R. (2010). 'Listen keynesians, it's the system! Response to Palley', *Monthly Review*, 61(11), available at: http://monthlyreview.org/2010/04/01/listen-keynesians-its-the-system-response-to-palley.

Freeman, C. and Louçã, F. (2002). *As Times Goes by: From the Industrial Revolutions to the Information Revolution* (Oxford, Oxford University Press).

Freeman, A. (2012). 'What causes booms?', paper presented at the joint conference AHE, IIPPE, FAPE, Paris, 5–7 July, available at: www.assoeconomiepolitique.org/political-economy-outlook-for-capitalism/?p=335&lang=fr.

Glyn, A. (1995). 'Social democracy and full employment', *New Left Review*, 211, 33–55.

Hix, S., Kreppel, A. and Noury, A. (2003). 'The party system in the European Parliament: collusive or competitive', *Journal of Common Market Studies*, 41(2), 309–31.

Hix, S. (2006). 'Why the EU needs (left–right) politics? Reform and accountability are impossible without it', *Notre Europe*, 'Politics: the right or the wrong sort of medicine for the EU?', *Policy Paper* 19, 1–26.

Hix, S., Noury, A. and Roland, G. (2007). *Democratic Politics in the European Parliament* (Cambridge: Cambridge University Press).

Hoang-Ngoc, L. (2005). *Refermons la parenthèse libérale!* (Paris: La Dispute).

Holmes, M. and Lightfoot, S. (2002). 'Interpreting social democracy's changing attitude to European integration', paper presented to PSA Conference, Aberdeen, 6 April 2002.

Husson, M. (2002). 'Années 1970: Les leçons d'une crise', in G. Duménil, and D. Lévy, *Crise et renouveau du capitalisme* (Laval: PUL).

Husson, M. (2008). *Un pur capitalisme* (Lausanne: Editions Page Deux).

Husson, M. (2012a). *Le capitalisme en 10 leçons* (Paris: Editions La Découverte).

Husson, M. (2012b). 'Economie politique du social-libéralisme', *Mouvements* 69, 26–33.

Jabko, N. (2009). *L'Europe par le marché: Histoire d'une stratégie improbable* (Paris: Presses de Sciences Po).

Jessup, D. (1999). 'Groping for the Third Way', New Economy Information Service, 29 April.

Johsua, I. (2006). *Une trajectoire du capital* (Paris: Editions Syllepse).

Johsua, I. (2009). *La grande crise du XXIe siècle* (Paris: Editions La Découverte).

Kalecki, M. (1943). 'Political aspects of full employment', *Political Quarterly*, 14(4), 322–31.

Kohler, B. and Myrzik, B. (1982). 'Transnational party links', in R. Morgan and S. Silvestri (eds), *Moderates and Conservatives in Western Europe* (London: Heinemann), pp. 193–223.

Kotz, D. (2009). 'The financial and economic crisis of 2008: a systemic crisis of neoliberal capitalism', *Review of Radical Political Economics*, 41(3), 305–17.

Kreppel, A. (2002). *The European Parliament and the Supranational Party System: A Study of Institutional Development of the European Parliament* (Cambridge: Cambridge University Press).

Külahci, E. (2008). *La social-démocratie et le chômage* (Bruxelles: Editions de l'Université de Bruxelles).

Ladrech, R. (2000). *Social Democracy and the Challenge of European Union* (Boulder, CO: Lynne Rienner).

Lavelle, A. (2008). *The Death of Social Democracy* (Aldershot: Ashgate).

Les économistes atterrés (2012). *L'Europe mal traitée. Refuser le Pacte budgétaire et ouvrir d'autres perspectives* (Paris: Les liens qui libèrent).

Lecureuil, C. (1996). 'Prospects for a European party system after the 1994 European elections', in J. Lodge, *The 1994 Elections to the European Parliament* (London: Pinter), pp. 183–97.

Li, M. (2010). 'The end of the "end of history": the structural crisis of capitalism and the fate of humanity', *Science & Society*, 74(3), 290–305.

Lipset, S. M. and Marks, G. (2000). *It Didn't Happen Here: Why Socialism Failed in the United States* (New York and London: W.W. Norton).

Lipset, S.M. (2001). 'The Americanization of the European left', *Journal of Democracy*, 12(2), 74–87.

Lordon, F. (1999). 'Le nouvel agenda de la politique économique en régime d'accumulation financiarisé', in G. Duménil, and D. Lévy (eds), *Le Triangle infernal: Crise, mondialisation, financiarisation* (Paris: PUF), pp. 141–59.

Magnette, P. (2009). *Le régime politique de l'Union européenne* (Paris: Presses de Sciences Po, 3rd edn).

Moravcsik, A. (1999). 'A new statecraft? Supranational entrepreneurs and international cooperation', *International Organization*, 53(2), 267–306.

Moschonas, G. (2002). *In the Name of Social Democracy: The Great Transformation: 1945 to the Present* (London and New York: Verso).

Moschonas, G. (2009). 'Reformism in a "conservative" system: the European Union and social democratic identity', in J. Callaghan, N. Fischman, B. Jackson, and M. Mcivor (eds), *In Search of Social Democracy: Responses to Crises and Modernisation* (Manchester: Manchester University Press), pp. 168–93.

Orléan, A. (2011). 'Il faut définanciariser l'économie', *Le Monde*, 6 December.

Palley, T. (2012). *From Financial Crisis to Stagnation* (Cambridge and New York: Cambridge University Press).

Passet, R. (2010). *Les grandes représentations du monde et de l'économie* (Paris: Editions Les liens qui libèrent).

PES and S&D Group. (2010). 'A progressive way out of the crisis', Joint Declaration adopted by the PES presidency and the S&D Group in the European Parliament, 10 June, www.pes.eu/en/system/files/Adopted_Declaration_Progressive_way_out_100610.pdf.

Plihon, D. (2001). *Le nouveau capitalisme* (Paris: Flammarion).

PS–SPD. (2011). 'Déclaration commune du Bureau national franco-allemand', PS–SPD Meeting, 21 June.

Rasmussen, P. N. (2008). 'Letter to the EU presidency', 6 November, available at: www.pes.eu/system/files/images/downloads/Lettre_PNR_a_Sarkozy_EN.pdf (accessed 1 April 2013).

Ross, G. (1995). *Jacques Delors and European Integration* (Oxford: Oxford University Press).

Sartori, G. (1976). *Parties and Party Systems: A Framework for Analysis* (Cambridge: Cambridge University Press).

Sartori, G. (2005). 'Party types, organization and functions', *West European Politics*, 28(1), 5–32.

Scharpf, F. (1991). *Crisis and Choice in European Social Democracy* (Ithaca, NY and London: Cornell University Press).

Scharpf, F. (1999). *Governing in Europe. Effective and Democratic?* (Oxford: Oxford University Press).

Schwartz, A. (2012). 'Une Europe de gauche est-elle possible?', *Mouvements*, 69, 62–7.

Sears, A. (2007). 'The end of 20th-century socialism?', *New Socialist*, 61, summer.

Seiler, D.-L. (2011). *Clivages et familles politiques en Europe* (Bruxelles: Editions de l'Université de Bruxelles).

Streeck, W. (2011). 'The crises of democratic capitalism', *New Left Review*, 71, 5–29.

Vieira, M. (2011). 'Does a European party system exist? A conceptual framework for analysis, *Cahiers du cevipol*, 1.

Weber, L. (2013). 'Un millefeuille pour la gouvernance économique', *Savoir/agir*, 23, 15–26.

Weinstein, O. (2010). *Pouvoir, finance et connaissance. Les transformations de l'entreprise capitaliste entre XXe et XXIe siècle* (Paris: Editions La Découverte).

Ziller, J. (2008). *Les nouveaux traités européens: Lisbonne et après* (Paris: Montchrestien).

Zuege, A. (2000). 'The chimera of the Third Way', *Socialist Register*, 36, 87–114.

3

Social democracy and social movements from crisis to crisis

George Ross

Social democracy and social protest movements have been closely related since the rise of industrial society. The social democratic story began with a congeries of anti-capitalist protest movements confronting powerful enemies that eventually coalesced into *the* dominant reformist force in democratic industrial societies. In time, however, social democracy 'normalised' into a conventional political force working within the frontiers of a capitalism it doctrinally claimed to oppose. Managerialism, to the degree to which it constrained reformism, made social democracy more vulnerable politically to protest movements. Social democratic parties today face globalisation, financial crisis, and devilishly complicated managerial puzzles and are also challenged by problems connected to the dissolution of traditional bonds with supporters. Part one of this chapter discusses ideal–typical early social democratic formations and their relationships to social movements and how these relationships changed as social democrats became reformist co-managers in democratic social market economies. Part two discusses more recent times when social democrats have had to confront the emergence of new, strong, and challenging social protest movements against a background of Europeanisation and globalisation, neoliberal policy orthodoxies and the consequences of the huge post-2008 global financial crisis.

Big tents and counter-societies

Social democracy emerged out of a nineteenth century explosion of social protest powered by indignant minorities demanding voice, votes, and rights in politics and markets, often in stridently anti-capitalist terms. Socialist activists learned important lessons from these experiences. Left to themselves, protest groups were likely to move in divergent political directions and do battle with one another, rendering progress difficult, if not impossible. Trade unionists often disagreed with political groups, anarchists struggled against statists, and religious fervour divided people who had common interests, to list but a few examples.

Limiting potential cacophony became a social democratic imperative, therefore. For social democrats to succeed it was essential to find ways to tie different social movements together around common goals. As practices evolved, social democrats thus moved toward building ideal–typical organisational models that we will call 'big tents' or 'counter-societies'. It was the German Social Democrats who first elaborated the counter-society notion and the Nordics who implemented it most successfully (Schorske, 1955; Sassoon, 1996; Berman, 2006; Bartolini, 2007). The idea was to aggregate compatible interests and movements by connecting specific demands to more fundamental policy platforms embedded in a grand narrative of hope and progress. Winning the vote, getting rights for unions and workers, constructing social protection programmes, equalising income distribution, establishing mass democratic education, and other such large reform proposals were thus assembled under a halo of the utopian socialist vision of transcending capitalism through reformist democratic politics. Mass organisations such as trade unions and membership-based political parties served as backbones, but there were also organisations for women's' rights, cultural groups, adult educational efforts, youth groups, sports teams, school and family vacation plans, and much more, all primed to march to similar socialist music. The approach was most often premised on theories that industrial capitalism created fundamental social divisions and cultural differences that counter-societies could accentuate.

The model had its problems. Insider movements like trade unions could acquire special voice and power over what social democracy could do and how its platforms were defined. Big tents, to be feasible, had to be carefully tailored out of national materials, leading to national variants that had difficulty cooperating cross-nationally despite repeated declarations of high-minded internationalism. Leaders could be tough bureaucrats who adjudicated internal conflicts with organisational power rather than creative perspicacity (Michels, 1968). The municipal socialisms that were important building blocks for many parties were often clientelistic and sometimes open to corruption for promoting cohesion. Finally, the statist bias of emerging social democracy was anathema to anarchists, who had deep roots in many places. Social democratic progress was not ineluctable, therefore. After 1917, Leninism and Third International parties, practising an authoritarian form of big-tent politics that often sought to destroy social democracy as much as transcend capitalism, changed the left political trajectory, divided progressive politics in Europe for decades, and provided opponents of the left with a new powerful anti-communist weapon. Quite as important, there were many places, particularly in anglophone countries, where model social democratisation was but partially achieved.

Social democracy has been one of the great success stories in modern political history, but the story had its ups and downs. Success led to great variations between different national movements because each lived in institutional, economic, and sociological microclimates. Usually there weren't enough workers to win elections and parties had to try to seduce support from middle classes who were often tepid about social democratic economism and workerism (Przeworski and Sprague, 1988). A few parties, particularly the Nordics, managed this by framing their reformism around 'citizens' rather than 'workers', but those who insisted on 'workerist' outlooks, programmes, and utopias had to compromise with groups that had very different concerns, a difficult job.

The post-war decades until the mid-1970s were a turning point. Social democrats emerged from the Second World War with enhanced electability. One consequence was that many of the most significant social democratic policy goals from earlier years were achieved, including deeper democratisation, the construction of welfare states, worker and union rights, governmental mechanisms for steering market economies and shaping distributional patterns to limit inequality. Widespread economic growth transformed lifestyles for entire populations. These successes had their price, however, helping to stabilise advanced capitalism and depleting social democracy's stock of policy proposals which would be very hard to replenish. Governing also made social democratic elites responsible for the management of market societies and constrained their abilities both to reward constituents and undertake more daring reforms. The post-war world of 'affluent workers' (Goldthorpe *et al.*, 1968; Goldthorpe, 1969) and 'affluent societies' (Galbraith, 1998) challenged social democrats to find policies that raised productivity and enhanced growth prospects without fuelling inflation. This involved promoting national market competitiveness and persuading big tent constituents like unions to restrain wages and enhance productivity. Supporters were not always eager to cooperate. It also turned out that nationalising industries and building big welfare states did not automatically create better, more equitable, and more efficient societies, let alone create a political dynamic towards greater reform. The British Labour Party in the 1970s provided one of the worst examples of social democrats paying dearly for unclear policy ideas and inability to bring its troops into line, in terms of IMF visits, a 'winter of discontent' and humiliating electoral defeats. Some, like the Nordics, did better, while others, in Latin Europe, had difficulty even coming to power because of authoritarian regimes and divided lefts.

Post-war social democratic managerialism distanced leaders from their supporters. Becoming more 'catch-all' electorally in order to appeal beyond traditional bases complicated political appeals. Rapid cultural and social changes in occupational structures, residential suburbanisation, the slow 'massification' of higher education and the coming of television obliged social democratic leaders to rely less on a 'big tent' model and more on new political technologies. Radical, economically risky, reforms thus came less often, even in small places like Sweden where 'encompassing' citizen organisations and intelligent elites had substantial resources and good ideas (Korpi, 1983; Pontusson, 1995). Social democracy thus gained in respectability at the cost of losing some of its radical edges and, more importantly, the credibility of its already strained utopian claims to be *the* agent for transforming capitalism. 'Revisionist' thoughts about how to reconfigure or even replace these claims, some highly creative (Mallet, 1975; Gorz, 2001; Crosland, 2006), flowered, but rarely caught fire.

The model becoming obsolete?

In this moment of transition, the 'new social movements' of the 1960s and 1970s protested for new causes. The American war in Vietnam provided the spark in the US, France had its 'May events' and Italy 'hot Autumn', with other kinds of protest in Germany and elsewhere, including central and eastern Europe. Student movements shared strident militancy and a radical, almost always anti-communist, leftism, beneath which lay specific local grievances and aspirations. The initial movements subsequently fragmented into powerful new mobilisations of feminists, environmental/ecological activists (including militant anti-nuclear power protesters), civil and human rights advocates, counter-cultural action, and new regionalisms. Scholars have come to label these multifaceted uprisings a 'cycle of protest', a contagion of rebellious energies and activism that took on an extended life of its own (Tarrow, 2011).

These diverse movements emerged outside social democratic circles and causes, focussing instead on refusing the new modernity of consumerism and bureaucratised, sometimes paternalistic, social policies, both products of the post-war marriage between Fordist capitalism and social democratic reformism, and they also rejected the adults who had made these things happen. Movement leaders announced that they were a 'New Left', which meant, to them, that the social democratic left, and the 'old' left more generally, had lost its franchise as the home of legitimate protest against the status quo. Daniel Cohn-Bendit, the rhetorical and organisational genius of France's mammoth May–June 1968 explosion, was exemplary. His strategy was to reject any firm alliances with the French left, whether socialist or communist, and his rhetoric was that the old left was *vieux jeu* with little of interest to propose.

Some analysts of the period argued that new social groups were embracing 'post-material' political attitudes (Inglehart, 1989). The new militants themselves were young and middle class, the first generations to benefit from the rapid expansion of higher education that social democrats had been important in promoting, and much more concerned with culture and identity than with issues of distribution and equality. One European authority posited that the new movements presaged a complete reconfiguration of social cleavages for a fast-arriving 'post industrial' society (Touraine, 1971).

New social movements occurred at about the moment when traditional left mass organisations like trade unions, along with social democratic parties themselves, had begun losing members. Capitalist political economies were changing rapidly. Declining union and party membership was partly a function of a relative retreat of classic blue-collar manufacturing jobs and the rise of difficult to organise service sector and white-collar work. In addition, in a few important places there were spectacular 'class struggle' defeats of labour unions that underlined changing balances of power, like the 1984 British miners' strike and Reagan's defeat of the American air controllers, both battles between strategically imprudent unions and determined neo-liberal governments that turned out very badly for the unions. Political technologies were also changing, with sophisticated polling, market research, personality-oriented campaigning, and direct approaches to potential voters through new media such as television. Armed with new approaches social democratic leaderships could map the concerns of specific social groups and target them to flexible party electoral platforms, a process that led social democrats towards ever more vague and centrist appeals. These new methods and appeals were arguably better suited than older 'big tent' methods in societies experiencing the powerful individualising effects of consumerism, new media, and mass education.

By the 1980s the neo-liberal shift was also under way. Keynesian demand management, a central component of most social democratic policy practice in post-war decades, was rapidly replaced by a new quest for price stability almost no matter the social costs. Pressure was on to trim budgets, lower taxes, lighten regulation, and in some harder-line neo-liberal places, roll back the state to free up market decision-making. The demise of Keynesianism was transnational, accompanying the progress of globalising financial markets that had the capacity to sanction national outliers. The result was that it became much more difficult to reward large national constituencies through redistribution and social programmes. Perhaps the most dramatic illustration of these processes was the policy U-turn of the Mitterrand presidency in France in 1981–83. The French left had committed itself to new nationalisations, expanded workers' rights and benefits, and strong Keynesian pump-priming. When it tried to do these things, however, heavy sanctions from international markets and the financial sector stopped them in their tracks (Ross *et al.*, 1987). The major lesson of this was that social democrats henceforth would have to exercise power within international neo-liberal constraints. The lesson was applicable to all political parties seeking to govern, of course, but because social democrats claimed to represent reform and change, they would feel these limits much more than conservatives.

The new constraints were then rapidly reinforced by globalisation, beginning with financial market globalisation, followed by new 'Europeanisation' from the EU Single Market programme and Economic and Monetary Union (ironically shepherded through the EU institutional maze by French socialist leaders

(Ross, 1995)), and more energetic market opening by the WTO in the 1990s. Globalisation also brought new competition from Asia in manufacturing sectors that western rich countries had long dominated. Rapid Europeanisation and globalisation impacted heavily on national budgeting, taxing, industrial policy prerogatives, and patterns of social stratification.

What is to be done? Big tents collapsing

The collapse of big tents, declining mass organisations, fading utopian visions, the end of the 'forward march of labour' (Hobsbawm, 1978) and a retreat of workerist identities, dramatic changes in electioneering, and revolutions in the ways that citizens obtained political information clearly loosened what had been strong ties between social democrats and citizens. Big tents had been built in part to limit a cacophony of protest from undermining the forward movement of social democratic politics during the rise of industrial capitalism and in the post-Second World War Fordist period. Changes after that opened new space for social protest more independent of social democratic and other parties left and right. Have such widened opportunities for partisan independent social protests hurt social democracy? This is the issue to which we now turn.

Movement parties poach on social democratic territory

Some new social movements, notably the Greens, had already become parties by the later 1970s and 1980s. The Greens were fortunate because environmental issues could easily be translated into a worldview about sustainable development that had broad appeal beyond activists to voters, unlike the narrower issues carried by most other new social movements. Green parties happened mainly in countries where proportional representation electoral systems allowed openings for newcomers to test their public support at the polls. Taking the party route was much more difficult in first-past-the-post and other majoritarian systems, however, where entry costs were higher and existing parties could more easily co-opt green issues.

Green parties were difficult to pin down in traditional left–right terms. Environmental positions were understood as 'progressive' but they often contradicted traditional left emphases on economic growth and redistribution. Greens nonetheless recruited support from existing lefts, particularly from younger voters with 'libertarian' propensities (see Kitschelt and Hellemans, 1990; Kitschelt, 1994). Their fortunes varied, but by the 1990s some were winning enough votes to become minority coalition partners (as happened in Finland, Ireland, the Czech Republic, France, Germany, Belgium and Sweden), often, but not always, of social democrats, and they also became important voices in the European Parliament. Green concerns also forcefully entered day-to-day political concerns across most of Europe, whether social democrats liked it or not. Most significantly, where there were Green parties, social democrats lost some potential voters to them.

The rise of Green parties previewed a reconfiguration of the traditional political spectrum due to political changes connected to Europeanisation and globalisation that fed new protest, and in many places new political parties around the emergence of new groups of winners and losers (Kriesi *et al.*, 2008; 2012). Winners were insiders in Europeanisation–globalisation processes, mainly the top of income earners – the 1 per cent in Occupy terms, and relatively protected wage earners in competitive tradable economic sectors. The losers were workers, particularly younger ones, in non-competitive industrial and the service sectors. These losers, and those with reason to think that they may become such, have often mobilised on both left and right against the real and imagined aspects of globalisation. Left 'loser' mobilisations have usually demanded new national barriers to protect jobs and rejected resisting reforms to welfare states and labour market regulations, arguing their cases in 'materialist' and nationalist terms once familiar to social democrats. Right-leaning 'loser' protests, in contrast, adopt 'populist', anti-immigrant xenophobic positions that are 'cultural' more than economic, with grievances, about threatened identities and 'us' vs. 'them'.

In the new century many left-loser movements have also become parties, following the Green model. Thus in today's Europe there are left of the left parties that seek to group the discontents of globalisation losers who might earlier have supported social democrats of younger, more 'libertarian' leftists who no longer find social democratic parties appealing, and of more traditional *gauchiste* activists (including from communist and other hard left parties seeking to recover waning appeals). These new parties seek to occupy political space they believe has been opened by social democratic moves towards the political centre (March, 2008). In today's western Europe, depending on the circumstances, they can often win enough votes to make a real difference, either becoming a potentially constraining coalition partner of social democrats, or as spoilers. They exist across the continent, again mainly in proportional representation systems, in Denmark (SF, EL), Finland (VAS), France (the PCF, the New Anti-capitalist Party, Left Front and other groups), Germany (die Linke), Greece (Syriza), Italy (PRC and PdCI), the Netherlands (SP), Portugal (PCP, Left Bloc), Spain (PCE, United Left) and Sweden (V), in addition to several parties in central and eastern Europe. Where they have broken through, social democratic parties have lost some resources.

New right populist parties and protest organisations tap sociologically similar loser groups, but with very different hard-nationalist, anti-immigrant and anti-EU appeals. Xenophobic–populist hard right parties are now well established across Europe. The French Front National, Italian Lega Nord, Belgian Vlaams Belang and Austrian FPÖ were pioneers in the 1980s and 1990s, some with roots in older crypto-fascist movements. They have been followed by the Danish

People's Party, the Pim Fortuyn list and PVV in the Netherlands, the Swiss People's Party, the Norwegian Progress Party, the True Finns, the Sweden Democrats, plus several others in central and eastern Europe. Many of these new parties now impact heavily on the actions of centre–right coalition governments (Mudde, 2007).

Social democratic parties have had major problems responding to the appeals of these new right parties (Rydgren, 2012). Social democracy has always been philosophically based on notions of equality between citizens. Compromising with arguments whose premise is that 'they' are different and less equal thus goes to the core of what being a social democrat has meant. Responses to right-loser protest parties and mobilisations, even if social democrats have not been loath to uphold and even tighten immigration laws, have almost always included policy proposals to improve the lives and situations of immigrant communities, whether in income support, housing and urbanism, education, labour market activation, public employment or civil liberties. Still, the generic social democratic answer to xenophobic mobilisation is that there should be no 'us–them' dichotomy, that this type of discourse should be taboo, and that we all owe solidarity to one another. Social democrats have also had similar, and sometimes electorally costly, responses of rejection to the personal 'security' dimensions of new populist–xenophobic appeals that demand the repression of actual and potential malefactors in minority communities – the defeat of Lionel Jospin in the 2002 French presidential elections was due, in part, to his inadequate handling of these issues. These new right-loser movements are almost always Euro-sceptic, another posture with which most social democratic parties have difficulty. The most challenging dimension of this new 'cultural' rebellion, however, is that hard-right movements and parties have been successful at recruiting support from formerly left-leaning constituencies, particularly from working-class losers in terms of income, labour market, security and life chances, who see social democrats as unresponsive to their concerns. To choose but one example, the Front National won more traditional working-class votes than the Socialists in the 2012 French presidential election cycle.

Social democrats thus are troubled in different ways by both types of Europeanisation–globalisation loser protest. Left–'materialist' mobilisations, in party form or not, expose social democratic commitments to managing Europeanisation and globalisation in conditions of neo-liberalism. And social democracy is practically defenceless in the face of populist–xenophobic cultural protests, even if some parties offer concessions despite making principled arguments against doing so.

One might still argue that left and right-leaning movements based on globalisation losers will have indeterminate overall political effects in today's 'new politics' conditions where large parties, including social democratic parties, fish for votes wherever they can plausibly be found. In fact, this has not been the case in countries with PR, rather than majoritarian, electoral systems (that is in much of Europe) where strong movements can take on party forms directly rather than trust to unpredictable patterns of indirect influence through protest. We live in an era in which incumbents have a harder time in general, meaning that it is possible for social democrats to come out ahead of centre–right rivals in any given poll, and sometimes this has happened in many different places – as recently as 1998 social democrats were in charge of eleven of fifteen EU governments, after all. And many of the factors that we have discussed affect centre-rights as well as centre-lefts. All things considered, however, there are solid indicators that social democratic voting and electoral loyalty is in slow decline practically everywhere, even if social democrats still win elections and govern (Moschonas, 2011).

Movements of crisis?

The non-party protest dimensions of left loser mobilisation have been growing and changing shape over time. In the 1990s, ATTAC, the connected World Social Forum, related protests against the G-7/8 (Porto Alegre), the WTO (Genoa, Seattle and Davos), and civil society movements against global inequalities and poverty provided examples of new forms of action, often of a transnational kind. Sometimes protest demands were sharply focused on issues such as cancelling debts of countries crippled by extreme poverty, taxes on international financial transactions, distributive justice in international trade, environmental and labour protection clauses grafted onto the rules of free trade, epidemic diseases and pharmaceutical costs, and restoration of national political power over international economic and financial flows. For a time agitation was so large and mobile that it was difficult for the world's leaders to meet together without massive police protection from screaming protesters. As movements grew, however, their demands became more diffuse and general, making their impacts on specific governmental and partisan behaviour less and less clear, even if they had to be taken seriously by social democratic elites who were constrained by the tasks of managing globalising economies. These movements also became targets of organised political groups seeking to instrumentalise the protest for partisan purposes, however, with the decline of ATTAC being one result (Ancelovici, 2002; Ayres, 2002; Della Porta *et al.*, 2006).[1]

The global financial crisis following the collapse of Lehman Brothers in 2008, including the Euro-zone crisis, has brought more new protest. So far, an important part of the story has been regional. In Greece, Spain and Portugal social democrats had intelligently embraced their countries' accession to the European Union at a moment when the political right remained discredited by association with detested authoritarian regimes. In the decades since the 1970s these southern parties were able to supplement the policy packages of other social democrats with convincing appeals for national democratisation and modernisation. As a result the post-dictatorship European south became the electoral bright spot of European social democracy, while northern counterparts had begun a slow decline.[2] Alas, southern social democrats had the bad luck of being in power when the Euro-zone mess broke.

In all three countries serious debt problems had accumulated after 2000 that anti-crisis stimulus packages exacerbated. Bond markets then became nervous about repayment. The Greek sovereign debt crisis that opened in later 2009 exposed all three, plus Ireland (where the centre-right was in power) to increased dangers of defaulting. But grudging bail-outs from Euro-zone partners followed only after May 2010, when richer northerners, led by Germany, concluded that if they did nothing they might be badly hurt. The bail-outs, when they were decided, were conditional on harsh austerity programmes overseen by the Troika (the IMF, European Central Bank and European Commission), choking off new growth and obliging cutbacks in public spending. Citizens then rejected these programmes and the politicians in power responsible for them, often in wide-spread and often innovative protest movements. Social democratic governments in all three countries lost elections as a result (Bosco and Verney, 2012).[3]

While Euro-zone leaders dithered over responding to the crisis, the Papandreou PASOK government implemented austerity programmes that threatened a wide swath of groups in a Greek society, including students and teachers, private and public sector workers, doctors and nurses, civil servants, retirees and the population more broadly. The response was outrage, and PASOK was held responsible, even if the centre-right had presided over the earlier accumulation of economic problems. The Euro-zone bail-out then obliged even more stringent cutbacks, provoking marches throughout the country and huge demonstrations in Athens's Syntagma Square in front of the Greek Parliament. An unruly mix of unions, political groups, angry young people, anarchists and *casseurs* then faced ill-disciplined and harassed police, leading to tough, sometimes violent, confron-tations, fire-bombings and several deaths (Psimitis, 2011). From this point for-ward, protests never really stopped. Most remarkable was the explosion in spring 2011 against the constraints borne by a second Euro-zone loan package. By this point Greek unemployment exceeded 17 per cent, many still employed had their salaries cut dramatically, public debt had risen to a completely unsustainable 175 per cent, young people were demoralised and misery abounded. The Greek 'Facebook May', inspired by the *indignado* movements in Spain (see below) with widespread use of social media as a mobilising tool, went on for weeks.

These protests, with little traditional union and partisan involvement, took few clear partisan positions beyond outrage at Greece's general situation, thereby letting the political chips fall where they might. They did not fall well for PASOK. After Papandreou imprudently called for a national referendum on the second Euro-zone bail-out, Germany and France had vociferously objected to his call and he resigned in favour of an EU-approved technocratic government meant to work until early national legislative elections in May, 2012. The May vote gave PASOK only 13.8 per cent, a loss of 30.74 per cent from 2009, with a new left rival, Syriza, winning 16.79 per cent, but there was no viable majority in parliament, leading to repeat elections in June. PASOK then won only 12.28 per cent, another small loss, while Syriza won 26.89 per cent (+ 10.1 per cent). This time the centre-right New Democracy party was able to form a government pledged to support EU policies, however, backed on certain policies by PASOK and Democratic Left, a new party that won more than 6 per cent. The Euro-zone crisis and the protests against its exactions thus splintered the Greek left, broke the post-dictatorship PASOK–New Democracy partisan spectrum, and PASOK had lost its position as major left claimant on government power. Worse still, extremist, anti-democratic party movements on the right, like Golden Dawn, had taken to thuggish immigrant-bashing and street brawling.

The Portugal story was different, but had similar endings. Portugal had always been relatively poor in EU terms and its sovereign debt problems were nowhere near as severe as those of Greece. However, it too had overused low EMU interest rates and overabundant capital flows from outside to grow on credit. Its social democratic government initiated austerity programmes even before Lehman Brothers, but the crisis made debt problems much worse. Portugal would be the third Euro-zone country, after Greece and Ireland, to borrow from the Euro-zone's EFSF (European Financial Stability Facility) in 2011, and the conditions attached to this made austerity much deeper, as they had elsewhere.

In response, Portugal's 12 March Movement (2011), the first *indignado*-type mobilisation in the crisis, was organised without party and union guidance and in despair about mainstream politics and parties. It used new social media skilfully, becoming the largest mobilisation since the heady days of the Portuguese anti-fascist revolution in 1974. Its success greatly contributed to the resignation of the social democratic government on 23 March after it lost a parliamentary vote on another austerity package. In the early elections of June 2011 the socialists won 28.05 per cent, an 8.5 per cent drop from 2009. The new centre-right government was led by the 'Social Democratic' party (from the old Portuguese party nomenclature that emerged from the 1974 revolution in which no one could confess to being on the right) and it quickly turned out even keener on austerity than the social democrats had been and even more closely aligned with Troika administrators of EU loans. *Indignado*-style mobilisations, supplemented by official union support, have since continued vociferously. The Portuguese social democratic electoral defeat was not as crushing as what happened in Greece, but it was serious.

Spanish Euro-zone-crisis protest events are better known, mainly because the international media highlighted the *indignado* occupation of the Puerta del Sol in Madrid much more than the unruly Greek chaos and the peripheral Portuguese movements. The Spanish crisis, like the Irish, followed directly from the collapse of an overblown real-estate bubble rather than from public financial mistakes. It became a sovereign debt problem by contagion from the private financial sector after the global collapse, fuelled particularly by overextended regional banks. As in Greece and Portugal, however, a social democratic government had to face the consequences. Under great external pressure because of the size and importance of the Spanish economy to the Euro-zone and global economy, the Zapatero government in 2010 implemented a strong austerity programme well before seeking any outside help (Royo, 2009). This programme was similar to those in other stricken EMU areas, cutting public sector wages, pensions and other benefits, and beginning major changes in Spain's unusually dualistic labour market regulations.

Spanish unions were the first objectors to object in a general strike that pulled some punches to avoid doing too much damage to an otherwise friendly government. The *indignados* in the Puerta del Sol (and elsewhere in large Spanish cities) came later, beginning in May 2011, after general unemployment had risen over 20 per cent and youth unemployment approached 50 per cent. *Indignado* protests, with young people prominent, loudly proclaimed detachment from, and distrust of, existing parties and politicians while denouncing local and international capitalism for inflicting misery indiscriminately. These issues put protesters on the left but against the social democratic government. Media notoriety followed from *indignado* tactics of occupying central public places and then establishing self-governing protest communities in them to create collectively consented order with animated constant discussion, direct democracy, and the use of new social media (Charnock *et al.*, 2011; Castaneda, 2012).

It was no accident that the *indignados* burst on the scene one a week before national elections. The movement, which closely followed and emulated the Arab spring, denounced the representational ineffectiveness, even cruelty, of existing democracy, targeting major Spanish parties, including PSOE, which had already begun to lose badly in regional elections. The centre-right won the national poll that followed, and PSOE lost 15.1 per cent of the 44 per cent that it had won in 2008. The Rajoy government that followed was even more devoted to austerity than its PSOE predecessor, confirming *indignado* contentions that voting for governmental parties would have little effect on promoting their vision of the collective good. Protest thus continued, along with a renaissance of separatist regionalism in places like Catalonia. The Spanish *indignado* example then inspired the international Occupy outbursts whose tactics and beliefs were similar but which focused most strongly on rising income inequality. In the American case, Occupy's insistence on this theme may have helped re-elect Obama.

Social democracy and social movements: brave new world?

Well over a century ago, youthful social democracy began an effort to insulate itself from disruption by centrifugal social protests by including potential protesters in broad socialist organisations that provided common identities, beliefs, policy platforms and utopian visions. Social democratic maturity and success after the Second World War brought legitimacy and modernisation but also began to undermine this older organisational pattern. Social democratic formations became 'catch-all' centre-left parties trading on reputations as credible and gently progressive governmental managers of 'social market economies' that used new approaches to campaigning structured by individualising consumerism, changes in class structures, modern media and innovative social science technologies. The post-war economic boom ended in the 1970s, bringing a set of large new changes, including the coming of neo-liberalism, Europeanisation and globalisation, which have framed the present by making governments and parties with governmental vocations, including social democratic parties, obligatorily responsive to policy imperatives coming from outside their borders.

For social democracy these processes have brought a progressive distancing from traditional bases of support and older reformist commitments (Cronin *et al.*, 2011). And, as we have argued, this distancing has been correlated with the growing salience of social protest movements and partisan groupings independent of social democracy, particularly in those places where social democracy has been strongest. 'New social movements', emanating mainly from emerging social groups and younger generations of activists who mistrusted social democrats, were influential politically – even if this influence was divided depending on whether citizens applauded or reviled their protests. They also taught lessons in protest framing and action repertoires for subsequent activists. They have been followed by a flowering of issue-oriented protests on left and right, most often unattached to party lines, sometimes in the form of energetic lobbies and NGOs, sometimes looking much like militant 1960s rebels, and sometimes even becoming parties, like the Greens. Europeanisation, globalisation and planetary financial crisis not only transnationalised policy constraints for governments, they did the same for protesters, bringing new patterns and techniques of mobilisation, helped by the internet and social media, while also nourishing new national protest movements of both left and right, and sometimes new left of the left and hard right political parties.

Reflecting generally on contemporary political parties the late Peter Mair concluded that

> governments try to solve problems, and hence parties in government try to solve problems, but they do so at an increasing remove from public opinion ... framed as the growing and potentially unbridgeable gap between responsive government and responsible government, it becomes very difficult to conceive of how the malaise might be treated or overcome... [and] ... we are dealing with a problem that can only grow worse in a period of fiscal austerity, when external constraints and financial limits become much more powerful, and when the governing parties are even less able to meet the demands of voters. (2011: 15)

Mair is here addressing dilemmas created by a reconfiguration in parties' roles. Governmental accountability and responsiveness to constituents has been partially eclipsed by their managerial responsibilities that have been greatly complicated by new Europeanisation and globalisation. He is talking about the fates of all parties, whether left and right, with a serious vocation to govern. These dilemmas impact electoral dynamics because governments that fall short of citizens' expectations will have difficulty getting re-elected and elections themselves will turn on arguments about the failures of incumbents.

Mair is reflecting on parties in general. Centre-right parties will be vulnerable to the degree that they are unable to perform managerial roles in the ways citizens expect and have to find ways to respond to xenophobic movements and hard-right party rivals. Social democrats may face an even more difficult situation, however. They still present themselves to voters as reformists who promise to make the lives of citizens better in specific ways, even if their reform proposals are now a pale shadow of what they once were and their modern technological electoralism has greatly loosened the bonds of loyalty that they once had with a wide range of constituents. Losing even more direct representational contact because of intractable international constraints on their internationally policy-making freedom can only intensify these loyalty problems, manifest, in particular by the more complex environment of independent social protest movements that no longer have confidence in social democratic pledges and capacities to deliver on them. These new vulnerabilities exploded first in the cornucopia of 1960s and 1970s 'new social movements' and have not ceased growing since.

The policy and social protest ramifications of the Great Recession and the Euro-zone crisis are likely to continue for years. The main responses to crisis, whether from national centre-rights, centre-lefts, or from European and international levels, after an initial bailout of banks and stimulus plans to stop total collapse, have been overwhelmingly neo-liberal, as if elites (including EU elites) could conceive of little else to do when things go very wrong. Even hard-line liberal organs in the financial press now worry aloud about the consequences of these growth-killing, harsh austerity policies on future social cohesion. Some commentators even read the situation as bringing a fundamental break in the social contracts of wealthy societies. Wolfgang Streeck (2011), for example, has argued that this crisis is not simply the product of an out-of-control global financial sector, but also represents the collapse of the most recent post-war reformulation of the unstable post-1945 deal between markets and democracy.

Streeck, who argues that 'democratic capitalism was fully established only after the Second World War' sees it moving through four distinct models of exchange between markets and peoples. The first, the 'golden age' of post-war redistributive reform and growth, gave way in the 1970s to a difficult, precarious and ultimately untenable moment when inflation took on the major redistributive tasks.

The third moment involved an equally untenable attempt to stem inflation while sustaining public welfare by national borrowing. The final moment, the one that ended at Lehman Brothers and the collapse of the international finance sector, brought financial market liberalisation in ways that allowed growth and a degree of citizen welfare through private consumption on credit. In the current crisis, he concludes pessimistically 'the arenas of distributional conflict have become ever more remote from popular politics' such that 'citizens increasingly perceive their governments not as *their* agents, but as those of other states or of international organisations, such as the IMF or the European Union, immeasurably more insulated from electoral pressure than was the traditional nation-state' (Streeck, 2011: 26–7). This is particularly bleak because it sees no discernible new replacement contract in the making, except neo-liberal squeezing, largely from outside national borders.

We are at the intersection of a cluster of very large, and perhaps menacing, historical changes that call for analytical humility. We have argued that social, economic and political changes over recent decades have made traditional concepts of social democratic party–constituent relationships obsolete in ways that at least theoretically free up political space for social protest in ways that challenge social democracy. Mair goes further, arguing that Europeanisation and globalisation place new managerial constraints that have been changing and diminishing the nature of partisan accountability and responsibility for all parties. Streeck adds a political economy dimension to this, contending that recent efforts at formulating a democratic social contract between markets and voters have collapsed in the advanced capitalist world with no alternative in sight. Recent *indignado* social movements proclaim that democracy itself is in crisis because elites, social democratic or otherwise, persistently ignore the needs of peoples (Kaldor and Selchow, 2012).

At the very least, citizen mistrust of politicians, including social democrats, is likely to remain high in the near future and much more social protest is likely to occur. It is also predictable that political incumbents, social democratic or not, will continue to be held responsible by these multiform protests and voters and will be unusually vulnerable. This is likely to mean that however weakened they may be, social democratic parties will profit electorally from voter efforts at 'kicking the bums out'. The recent Danish and French successes have shown, however, that it takes very little time for the very narrow limits of policy manoeuvre to appear and make clear how difficult doing progressive things has become. Until the crisis ends, social democrats are in for a rough period. Even beyond the crisis, however, big questions will remain posed. Beyond being less harsh on ordinary people than their centre-right opponents, at least in their rhetoric, what do social democrats stand for, what do they really want to do, what can they actually do and why should citizens be loyal to them?

Notes

1 On occasion, ambitious politicians within social democratic parties have instrumentalised these 'left loser' issues for their own political purposes, as in the case of the '*démondialisation*' campaign of Arnaud Montebourg in the 2011–12 French presidential campaign (Montebourg, 2011).
2 Between 1974 and 2011 Greek socialists had led governments in 21 of 37 years, in Portugal 17 of 37, and in Spain between 1975 and 2011 socialists governed 21 of 36 years.
3 In Italy, the only threatened southern Eurozone country ruled by the centre-right, the Berlusconi government, which had resisted the kinds of reforms that Germany demanded, was also replaced at practically the same moment by caretaker technocratic government led by EU insider Mario Monti.

References

Ancelovici, M. (2002). 'Organizing against globalisation: the case of ATTAC in France', *Politics and Society*, 39, 427–63.

Ayres, J. (2002). 'Transnational political process and contention against the global economy', in J. Smith, and H. Johnston (eds), *Globalisation and Resistance: Transnational Dimensions of Social Movements* (Oxford: Rowman & Littlefield), pp. 207–27.

Bartolini, S. (2007). *The Political Mobilization of the European Left, 1860–1980: The Class Cleavage* (Cambridge: Cambridge University Press).

Berman, S. (2006). *The Primacy of Politics: Social Democracy and the Making of Europe's Twentieth Century* (Cambridge: Cambridge University Press).

Bosco, A. and Verney, S. (eds) (2012). 'Electoral epidemic: the political cost of economic crisis in southern Europe, 2010–2011', special issue, *Southern European Society and Politics*.

Castaneda, E. (2012). 'The indignados of Spain: A precedent to occupy Wall Street', *Social Movement Studies: Journal of Social, Cultural and Political Protest*, 11(3–4), 309–19.

Charnock, G., Purcell, T. and Ribera-Fumaz, R. (2011). 'Indignate: the 2011 popular protests and the limits to democracy in Spain', *Capital and Class*, 36(1), 3–11.

Cronin, J., Ross, G. and Shoch, J. (eds) (2011). *What Is Left of the Left: Democrats and Social Democrats in Challenging Times* (Durham, NC and London: Duke University Press).

Crosland, A. (2006). *The Future of Socialism: 50th Anniversary Edition* (London: Constable and Robinson).

Della Porta, D., Andretta, M., Mosca, L. and Reiter, H. (eds) (2006). *Globalization From Below: Transnational Activists and Protest Networks* (Minneapolis: University of Minnesota Press).

Galbraith, J. K. (1998). *The Affluent Society* (Boston: Mariner).

Goldthorpe, J. (1969). *The Affluent Worker: Political Attitudes and Behaviour* (Cambridge: Cambridge University Press).

Goldthorpe, J., Lockwood, D., Bechofer, F. and Platt, J. (1968). *The Affluent Worker in the Class Structure* (Cambridge: Cambridge University Press).

Gorz, A. (2001). *Farewell to the Working Class* (London: Pluto).

Hobsbawm, E. (1978). 'The forward march of Labour halted', *Marxism Today*, September, 279–86.

Inglehart, R. (1989). *Culture Shift in Advanced Industrial Democracies* (Princeton: Princeton University Press).

Kaldor, M. and Selchow, S. (2012). *The 'Bubbling Up' of Subterranean Politics in Europe* (London: Civil Society and Human Security Research Unit, London School of Economics and Political Science).

Kitschelt, H. (1994). *The Transformation of European Social Democracy* (Cambridge: Cambridge University Press).

Kitschelt, H. and Hellemans, S. (1990). *Beyond the European Left: Ideology and Political Action in the Belgian Ecology* (Raleigh-Durham: Duke University Press).

Korpi, W. (1983). *The Democratic Class Struggle* (London: Routledge & Kegan Paul).

Kriesi, H., Grande, E., Lachat, R., Dolezal, M., Bornschier, S. and Frey, T. (2008). *West European Politics in the Age of Globalisation* (Cambridge: Cambridge University Press).

Kriesi, H., Grande, E., Dolezal, M., Helbling, M., Hoeglinger, D., Hutter, S. and Wueest, B. (2012). *Political Conflict in Western Europe* (Cambridge: Cambridge University Press).

Mair, P. (2011). 'Bini Smaghi vs. the parties: representative government and institutional constraints', *Working Paper* 22 (Florence: EUI).

Mallet, S. (1975). *Essays on the New Working Class* (New York: Telos Press).

March, L. (2008). *Contemporary Far Left Parties in Europe: From Marxism to Mainstream* (Berlin: Friedrich Ebert Stiftung).

Michels, R. (1968). *Political Parties* (New York: Free Press).

Montebourg, A. (2011). *Votez pour la démondialisation* (Paris: Flammarion).

Moschonas, G. (2011). 'Historical decline of change of scale? The electoral dynamics of European social democratic parties, 1950–2009', in J. Cronin, G. Ross and J. Shoch (eds), *What's Left of the Left: Democrats and Social Democrats in Challenging Times* (Raleigh-Durham: Duke University Press), pp. 50–88.

Mudde, C. (2007). *Populist Radical Right Parties in Europe* (Cambridge: Cambridge University Press).

Pontusson, J. (1995). *The Limits of Social Democracy: Investment Policies in Sweden* (Ithaca, NY: Cornell University Press).

Przeworski, A. and Sprague, J. (1988). *A History of Electoral Socialism* (Chicago: University of Chicago Press).

Psimitis, M. (2011). 'The protest cycle of spring 2010 in Greece', *Social Movement Studies*, 10(2), 191–7.

Ross, G. (1995). *Jacques Delors and European Integration* (Cambridge: Polity).

Ross, G., Hoffmann, S. and Malzacher, S. (eds) (1987). *The Mitterrand Experiment* (Cambridge: Polity).

Royo, S. (2009). 'Reforms betrayed? Zapatero and continuities in economic policy', *South European Society and Politics*, 14(4), 435–51.

Rydgren, J. (ed.) (2012). *Class Politics and the Radical Right* (London: Routledge).

Sassoon, D. (1996). *One Hundred Years of Socialism* (London: I.B. Tauris).

Schorske, C. (1955).*German Social Democracy: The Development of the Great Schism* (Cambridge, MA: Harvard University Press).

Smith, J. and Johnston, H. (eds) (2002), *Globalisation and Resistance: Transnational Dimension of Social Movements* (Lanham, MD: Rowman & Littlefield).

Streeck, W. (2011). 'The crises of democratic capitalism', *New Left Review*, 71, 5–29.

Tarrow, S. (2011). *Power in Movement: Social Movements and Contentious Politics* (Cambridge: Cambridge University Press).

4

Why the financial crisis has not generated a social democratic alternative in Europe?[1]

Magnus Ryner

The financial crisis presents us with a political paradox. The contagion effect of the US sub-prime mortgage crisis damaged global money and financial markets so severely that the very institutional foundation of the monetary system of the world economy was put in doubt. This was not only another speculative bubble that burst spectacularly (although it was that too). Given the highly complex packaging of financial products through processes of securitisation, it became impossible for buyers and sellers to sort out good debt from bad. When this resulted in shocking revelations about the balance sheets of the most iconic of 'blue-chip' financial corporations, this generated a degree of uncertainty and fear in markets that was of such magnitude that it resulted in a seizing-up of economic activity. The destruction of values was such that even the most ardent neo-conservatives, such as the former Secretary of the US Treasury, Hank Paulson, had to advocate massive nationalisations and state bail-outs. The alternative would have been no less than the collapse of global capitalism. One could not have imagined a more damning indictment of the efficient market hypothesis that had been the nodal point of decades of neo-liberal policy prescriptions. Even the sturdiest of hegemonic discourses have difficulties surviving such dissonance. When even the *Financial Times* featured articles with titles such as 'the idea that capitalism would guarantee the best outcome was wrong',[2] it seemed justified to entertain the thought that these were the dying days of a neo-liberal phase of capitalism that was ushered in thirty years ago by Reaganomics.

It is not surprising, then, that questions were raised about a possible revival of social democracy. The financial crisis would seem exactly to invite ideologies that are more conditional in their views about the market. Could one imagine a formulation that more appropriately captures the spirit of the time than that associated with the Bad Godesberg Programme:[3] 'As much market as possible; as much planning as necessary'? But it is here that we encounter the paradox: accompanying the loss of the hegemonic aura of neo-liberalism is the absence of social democracy as an effective political agent. Any illusions to the contrary were dispelled already at the 2009 elections to the European Parliament, where social democracy took a battering. Most dramatically, the Euro-zone crisis has in effect obliterated PASOK in Greece and the shambolic state of affairs of the Italian left was confirmed in the 2013 elections. In Britain, the financial crisis ruined Gordon Brown's credentials of economic competence as the Labour Party was thrown out of office in the 2010 elections, to be replaced by a coalition led by the architects of the Big Bang and the vanguard party of financialisa-tion – the Tories. While the British Conservative–Liberal Democrat coalition is deeply unpopular and divided, one is struck by the inability of Labour under Ed Miliband to offer a credible contending alternative. Similarly, in Germany the SPD had to abandon even the role as a junior partner in a Grand Coalition government in 2009, and the most that it can realistically hope for is to regain a similar junior role in coalition with a centre-right party – very much like that of the Dutch Labour Party – after the 2013 elections. Even in the sturdiest of social democratic citadels – Sweden – social democracy failed to capitalise on the financial crisis, suffering a historic second successive electoral defeat in 2010. In the few cases where social democracy has been successful in gaining office since the financial crisis it has yielded weak governments without direction and suffering from deep unpopularity. In the Danish case, the Social Democratic Party actually lost one seat in 2011 compared to the previous election and could only forge a composite coalition government because of the gains of the Radical Liberals and the Red–Green Alliance. This has turned out to be a weak govern-ment, without new ideas, and pursuing a straightforward Third Way supply-side agenda. The victory of François Hollande in the French presidential elections in 2012 relied largely on a gambit similar to that of Lionel Jospin in the 1997 legis-lative elections. A critique of EU austerity agreements ensured that the symbolic appeal to a European alternative was successful. But once in office Hollande's government essentially accepted the framework set for Euro-zone crisis manage-ment, and hence found itself caught between the rock of austerity politics and the hard place of dashed expectations of previous French governments (on social democratic symbolic EU politics, see Bailey (2005), Cafruny and Ryner (2007a: 158); on French socialism and the politics of austerity, see Clift (2003), Clift and Ryner (2013)).

This article argues that the perhaps counter-intuitive absence of social democracy as a contending political agent after the financial crisis is not a coincidence. Nor is it due to ephemeral factors such as uninspiring leadership or the cumulative effect of incumbency (although these factors are real enough and hardly helpful). The political absence of social democracy stems rather from more long-standing and organic ideological sources. Indeed, one could go so far as to argue that the financial crisis that in the 1990s and the 2000s sought to articulate high finance to increasingly commodified forms of welfare provision through retail finance is above all a crisis of the social democratic Third Way. In other words, modern European social democracy is so deeply imbricated with the system that is in crisis that it is in no position to offer an alternative to it.

In pursuit of this argument, I return to my critique of Anthony Giddens's (1998) key contribution to social democratic ideology, *The Third Way: The Renewal of Social Democracy* (Ryner, 1999, 2002: 6–54, 2003a). This should not be seen as expressing some extreme constructivist assumption that ideas by academics determine political projects. Clearly, European social democratic movements are too practical–pragmatic for this assumption to be tenable. As contending mass parties, their practical pragmatism is driven by two imperatives. The Bad Godesberg Programme is paradigmatic for the first of these. It was at Bad Godesberg, in the face of successive electoral defeats at the hands of Adenauer's CDU, that the SPD faced up to the fact that they never would become a governing party on the basis of an appeal to the industrial working class alone. Rather, the SPD would have to appeal to a broader, multifarious, composite and particularly contradictory range of political subjectivities in German civil society. In the 1950s, this meant being able to better mediate the class and confessional cleavages around an appealing national–popular hegemonic project (on overlapping cleavages in European political sociology, see Lipset and Rokkan (1967: 1–64); on the electoral dilemma facing social democracy that arises from reaching beyond the base of the industrial working class, see Przeworski (1986); the particularities of the German situation are dealt with in Lösche and Walter (1992)). This need to appeal to a heterogeneous range of subjectivities in civil society is hardly less relevant as an imperative in civil societies that have become more multicultural due to immigration, and radically plural as a result of identity politics arising from the 'postmodern condition' (see, for instance, Lash and Urry (1986)). The second pragmatic imperative concerns the need to render this plural and potentially contradictory broad range of appeal compatible with effective policy coherence. It is with reference to this balance that overt intellectual–ideological treatises under certain circumstances can play a practical role, by providing coherence and direction through a clear vision. There is plenty of evidence that Giddens served this function for European social democratic leadership in the mid 1990s (Merkel, 2000), hence engendering a euphoric momentum so that these imperatives were no longer experienced as constraining necessities in the face of the constraints posed by globalisation, but rather as an exciting opportunity to offer a hegemonic vision after a decade and a half in the political wilderness. As such, Giddens's chief treatise also reveals with more clarity than any other source exactly what the ideological rationale of social democratic politics has been since the 1990s.

Having thus identified the essence of the Third Way in the first section, I turn to the practical political economy of modern social democracy in the second section. I start with the cue offered by social democrats themselves that 'globalisation' characterised the chief condition to which they have had to respond. However, globalisation is a sanitised, idealised, and above all imprecise and fuzzy term for describing the politico-economic condition with which social democracy has found itself since the mid 1990s (Hirst *et al.*, 2009; Rosenberg, 2002). I will rather adopt Peter Gowan's term, 'Dollar–Wall Street Regime', which highlights the centrality of transatlanticism and finance in the global political economy (Gowan, 1999). This sets the stage for the third part, where I outline the attendant detrimental effects that have been corrosive for European social democracy. This includes not only the cataclysmic effects of the financial crisis itself, but also the long-standing effects of economic stagnation in the European Union (which are contrary to the promises of the Single Market) as well as the political effects arising from the disillusion of the democratic ethos that underpinned the Third Way.

The Third Way of Anthony Giddens

The key argument that Giddens advanced in *The Third Way* is summarised by two slogans: 'no rights without responsibilities' and 'no authority without democracy'. The slogan 'no rights without responsibilities' expressed the conversion to the essentials of neo-liberal economics of social democratic governments throughout Europe in the 1990s. Indeed, Giddens's argument was a rather straightforward derivative of neoclassical economic prescriptions for global competitiveness. Giddens derided 'classical' social democratic commitments to welfare state provisions that are independent of market performance and hence decommodified, as well as Keynesian aggregate demand management and industrial policy. These were seen as compromising economic efficiency, technological innovation and competitiveness. Above all, he saw social policies characterised by decommodification as a source of moral hazard. This is a term taken from the economics of insurance, and refers to the postulated paradox that insurance against a calamity increases the probability of the calamity occurring. This is because the implications of the calamity are less severe for the individual, and hence the individual engages in riskier behaviour. By extension, decommodifying social insurance affects work morale, the willingness of individuals to adjust, for instance, their vocational expectations to the market and the risk for unemployment increases. Hence, 'traditional' social democratic policy endangered productivity and output growth, employment and price stability, and was bound to frustrate the opportunities that global markets provide. Exposure to global markets would rather result in diseconomies and generate balance-of-payments deficits and capital flight.

By guaranteeing *no* rights without responsibilities, welfare and economic policy should rather expose individuals to market discipline. Third Way social democracy nevertheless differed from purer variants of neo-liberalism in that it offered supply-side policies, such as labour market training and education and tax breaks for pension savings, as enabling supports and as a quid pro quo for individuals taking their responsibility. These policies were seen as public good investments, generating positive externalities that improve economic performance

More original and interesting, but at the same time deeply problematic and flawed, was the connection that Giddens made between his rather conventional economic argument, and the developmental–democratic tradition of political liberalism (Macpherson, 1982; Held, 1987), resonating with the thinking of the New Left (Habermas, 1976; Offe, 1985). Deploying the key concept *Vergesellschaftung* ('societalisation') that can be found in the thought of Karl Marx as well as Max Weber, Giddens suggested that 'no authority without democracy' is a principle that arises out of necessity of social developments. Central in this regard is his particular reading of Ulrich Beck's (1992) *The Risk Society*. According to this reading, high modernisation resulting from the development of global capitalism is characterised by such a social transformation of the ecological environment that it makes no sense to conceive of it as an extra-social 'original nature' anymore. 'External' nature has rather been transformed and manipulated in complex ways by the contingencies of human socio-economic practices to such an extent that the effects, costs and benefits are highly complex and ambiguous. Hence, environmental impacts cannot be unambiguously and objectively established by scientists and technocrats. Rather, the merits of policies, practices and interventions with environmental impacts inevitably become subject to subjective judgement calls. In order to sustain legitimacy, citizens need to be involved in making these through an active and deliberative process.

But, not only has high modernisation transformed external nature, it has also transformed nature that is internal to the human subject itself. Self-evident norms of traditional conservative society have since the nineteenth century been progressively undermined and increasingly become subject to conscious discursive thematisation and choice. In the current juncture, the very identities of subjects have become discursively thematised, resulting in a proliferation and diversification of lifestyles. Legitimation imperatives resulting from these developments also point to 'no authority without democracy', and the inadequacy of bureaucratic steering *a la* the male (heteronormative, white) breadwinner model, characteristic of traditional social democracy. The increased engagement in NGOs and a wide range of single-issue movements at the expense of traditional political parties were seen as symptomatic of this.

The problem is not the attractiveness of Giddens's argument concerning 'no authority without democracy'. It is rather that 'no rights without responsibilities' undermine its necessary conditions, producing what we might call an 'architectonic deficit'. The importance of the architectonic functions for constructive civic engagement was apparent already in the work of Aristotle, requiring what he called 'leisure'. When assuming the subject position of citizens in the polity, to deliberate and act for the general good, individuals have to be certain that the satisfaction of basic material needs is guaranteed. Furthermore, requisite amounts of leisure are required for the nurturing of cognitive capabilities, and the capacity to affiliate with fellow citizens. Note that the last point is a relational one, requiring that *all* citizens enjoy the requisite leisure for a deliberative–democratic order to work. As Martha Nussbaum (1990) has suggested, the social democratic norms of decommodification and welfare universalism provide the modern form for providing this leisure that potentially could be provided with deliberative–democratic content. But it is exactly the forms of this publicity that Giddens would replace and hence undermine with commodification, privatisation and means testing. Giddens could only sustain his contradictory ideological construction through elisions and conflations of radically different types of 'risk management', whereby dealing with ecological risk, expressing one's own identity, being mobile on the labour market and managing one's pension fund portfolio become one and the same.

> Providing citizens with security has long been a concern of social democrats. The welfare state has been seen as the vehicle of social security. One of the main lessons to be drawn from ecological questions is that just as much attention needs to be given to risk. The new prominence of risk connects individual autonomy on the one hand with the sweeping influence over scientific and technological change on the other. Risk draws attention to the dangers we face – the most important of which we have created ourselves – but also to opportunities that go along with them. Risk is not just a negative phenomenon – something to be avoided or minimised. It is at the same time the energising principle of society that has broken away from tradition and nature. (Giddens, 1998: 62–3)

However, Giddens's prescriptions are also counter-productive from an economic point of view, since they undermine the institutional conditions for a politics of productivity, whereby technological change is generated and channelled so as to generate positive sum solutions that facilitate both healthy profit and social wage rates. I have previously demonstrated this empirically with reference to the Swedish experience in the 1980s and the 1990s (Ryner, 2002). In this chapter, I will do the same with reference to European developments as seen in the wake of the financial crisis.

The Third Way in practice

The Third Way emerged as an ideological concept of European social democracy in the mid 1990s, largely as a result of Tony Blair's ascent to leadership of the British Labour Party and his subsequent electoral victory in 1997. It is in many respects surprising that British Labour would become the beacon of social democratic renewal. After all, if one were to look at social democratic achievements in

Europe in the past one would hardly look to the British Isles. In terms of electoral success and social policy achievements, the Scandinavians were unrivalled, and as small export oriented economies they had always had to achieve their objectives while facing balance of payments constraints and competitive pressures from the international market. True, Scandinavian social democracy had faced strains as severe as anywhere else in Europe during the stagflation decade of the 1970s. But it would be grotesque to suggest that British Labour, with IMF loans, winters of discontent and all that, provided any lessons for how to deal with the 1970s crisis and its aftermath. This was rather the decade of 'Modell Deutschland', a term that became emblematic during Helmut Schmidt's tenure as Chancellor, to refer to a country that (along with Austria under Bruno Kreisky and SPÖ) continued on the seemingly evolutionary post-war path of social and economic development, while keeping inflation low and current account balances in the black.

Despite this, it was with an eye to Britain and America that Ingvar Carlsson, Göran Persson, Paavo Lipponen, Wim Kok, Gerhard Schroder and even Lionel Jospin returned social democratic parties to government in the 1990s. Global financial dynamics, much more than global competition as such, are central to any attempt to make sense of this surprising turn of the gaze to the Labour Party that, with all due respect to Harold Wilson's 'white heat', had little to show since Clement Attlee's surprise defeat of Winston Churchill immediately after the Second World War.[4] Europe's export-oriented social market economies had been developed under the permissive structures of Bretton Woods, which had resulted in a nationally segmented set of financial systems (Boyer and Hollingsworth, 1997). Bank finance ensured long-term relations between financial and productive capital and time horizons in investment, which in turn ensured *inter alia* productivity growth through technological change, corporatist bargaining, and high social wage growth, flanking full employment macroeconomic policies. The collapse of the Bretton Woods system and the cumulative growth of global financial market, starting in the currency markets, but increasingly extending into other areas first via the bond market, increasingly strained the nationally segmented systems (Helleiner, 1994; Grahl, 2001). This became clear through the capital flights from France during the first years of Mitterrand's presidency. But also in other countries, the aftermath of the collapse of Bretton Woods had corrosive effects, and as experienced by the Palme/Carlsson administrations in Sweden in the 1980s, Scandinavia was not exempt. Indeed, Mitterrand's U-turn is only the most famous of the strategic accommodations that social democratic governments made to global finance, whereby they sought to subordinate institutions and policies in their jurisdictions to the exigencies of global finance. The appeal of the Third Way in the 1990s was that it made a virtue out of this, and hence the perceived necessity was engendered with a positive vision through the embrace of the efficient market hypothesis and pragmatic monetarism (for an emblematic statement, see Balls (1998)). This became all the more urgent when the social democrats, returning to office in the 1990s, did so in a European Union that had just implemented a Single Market based on the negative–integrative principle of mutual recognition,[5] and was in the middle of completing the European Monetary Union (EMU). Financial markets were by no means exempt from this, but were rather at the centre of it all, which was confirmed by the pivotal position of the Financial Services Action Plan (FSAP) in the Lisbon Agenda (Dyson and Featherstone (1999); Story and Walter (1997); Sapir *et al.* (2004)). The FSAP was articulated with welfare policy especially through pension reforms, increasingly abandoning pay-as-you-go in favour of actuarial schemes (Clark (2002); Bieling (2006); de la Porte and Nanz (2004); Jenson and Pochet (2005)). Outside the UK, Swedish social democracy has gone the furthest in that regard. Rather than merely hollowing out existing pay-as-you-go schemes through parametric fiscal austerity and encouraging private pension savings as an auxiliary, after the 1999 reform, the core of the Swedish pensions contains decisive actuarial elements (Belfrage and Ryner (2009)). Given the pivotal position of the City of London in global finance, it is no coincidence that the epicentre of the ideas connected to the Third Way would reside in Britain, the country that most plausibly could develop an export-oriented niche strategy based on financial services. Yet, it is exactly this system that was thrown into crisis as a result of the contagion effects starting in the subprime mortgage market in the United States, and which above all has manifested itself in Europe as an asymmetric shock, dividing the mainly manufacturing-based export-oriented economies of northern Europe and the southern European so-called PIIGs that are suffering the effects induced by a one-sided adjustment to a burst real-estate bubble, which generated the Euro-zone crisis.

However, the problems and inherent limitations of this strategy for European social democracy precede the financial crisis, which merely has produced the cataclysmic and transparent manifestation of a dead end. While European social democrats looked to New Labour, it had in turn taken inspiration from Bill Clinton's New Democrats in the United States and their pursuit of welfare objectives through markets. The financial crisis has demonstrated the fallacy entailed in understanding the evident success of Clintonomics, manifested in high growth rates and low unemployment, as residing on the 'supply side' of the economy and in an optimal clearing of markets, including labour, money and financial markets, which was the premise of the Lisbon Agenda (Sapir *et al.*, 2004). A more plausible explanation, which also is more consistent with the persistence of the 'twin deficits', is to be found on the 'demand side' of the economy and in the manner in which the United States successfully managed to maintain its hegemonic position in the transnational monetary and financial system after the collapse of Bretton Woods in 1971.

Contrary to what was predicted at the time (see, for instance, Kennedy, 1988: 533–64), US monetary hegemony survived the end of Bretton Woods.

The American dollar remained pre-eminent as the reserve and vehicle currency of the global financial system, and by abandoning the peg of the dollar to gold the US actually gained rather than lost policy autonomy under the emergent flexible exchange rate system. Since US banks could accumulate liabilities in the key currency at zero-exchange risk, they augmented their competitive advantage in transnational financial affairs, which resulted in Wall Street becoming, more than ever before, the epicentre of 'global' finance. This, in turn, consolidated the capacity of the US state to shape the preferences of borrowers and lenders world-wide, engendering the US with structural power (Seabrooke, 2001). Hence, the US became the only state in the international system, characterised by flexible exchange rates, which could pursue expansionary macroeconomic policies on a consistent basis without the need of internal adjustment, because these pressures could be 'delayed' and 'deflected' to other parts of the world (Cohen, 2006). Hence, if we view matters from the more analytically precise concept of the 'Dollar–Wall Street Regime' (Gowan, 1999; on the dynamics summarised in this paragraph, see the literature that points to a remarkable emergent consensus between Weberian and Marxist scholarship, Seabrooke, 2001; Cafruny and Ryner, 2007b; Panitch and Konings, 2009), rather than the amorphous concept of 'globalisation', it becomes evident that, contrary to what Giddens contends, expansionary demand side economics remains as relevant as ever. The difference is that since the 1980s, it became the exclusive privilege of the US to pursue such policies. It is the capacity of pursuing such policies that explains the higher rates of growth and employment in the US, compared to Europe prior to the financial crisis. It should also be pointed out that, in many respects, this system is characterised by a lack of globalisation in the sense that the US can defend a mercantilist 'exorbitant privilege' (*pace* de Gaulle) by refusing international deliberation on an international reserve currency. As Leonard Seabrooke has put it, it is a system based on 'national activism and international passivity'.

Hence, over almost three decades preceding the current financial crisis, the US demonstrated an impressive capacity to convert debt into sustainable capital accumulation and growth. This capacity rested *inter alia* on three factors. The first factor is the aforementioned seigniorage privilege that made it possible to finance huge current account deficits through the differential return of US investments abroad compared to foreign investments in the US (Dumenil and Levy, 2004). The second factor was the capacity to convert debt to corporate investments via highly capitalised securities markets, which in turn depended on its institutional complementarity with the market-based system of corporate governance (Lazonick, 2010; Grahl, 2001). The third factor pertains to another institutional complementarity associated with America's residual welfare state, namely the manner in which the US system of retail finance articulated produc-tion with final consumption through consumer indebtedness. In contrast to the post-war 'Fordist' period, when this was done through negotiated wage increases tied to productivity growth, deregulated and numerically flexible labour markets meant that this no longer could be done directly through the wage relation (Aglietta, 1998). Instead, consumer debt, backed by the collateral of pension savings and increased value of mortgaged properties provided the impetus for consumption growth. This was a cornerstone to Clinton's welfare policy, which sought to extend private loans and home ownership to broader segments of the population through the sub-prime market. The privatisation of the New Deal housing policy institutions Freddy Mac and Fanny Mae, making them dominant interlocutors between the mortgage market and securities market were corner-stones in that regard (Schwartz, 2009).

The Third Way of European social democracy was based on the premise that it was possible to copy the American model. However, since the essence of its dynamism was not based on the postulated liberal supply-side principle of optimal market clearing, but rather on a mercantilist principle of debt-finance demand expansion, this was not the case. By contrast, European social democracy locked itself into a self-limiting institutional architecture, resulting from the EMU and the Lisbon Agenda. First, contrary to the stance of the US Treasury and the Federal Reserve, the European Central Bank and EU national governments have pursued highly restrictive macroeconomic policies. This is in part a question of deliberate action. However, it is also due to institutional design and the structurally subordinated position vis-à-vis the US in which the EMU was forged. As Benjamin Cohen (2003) has argued, the Euro suffers from an 'anti-growth bias'. European bond markets are fragmented. There is no European equivalent to the US Treasury Bill. Furthermore fragmentation and lack of depth of these and other capital markets in the Euro-zone means that the cost of doing business in Euros remains high compared to the US. Further, Cohen points to the 'persistent inertia' in monetary behaviour, which in many respects is another way of pointing to the dominance of US denominated actors in financial sectors. This also means that the Euro is unlikely to enjoy the seigniorage privileges[6] in world financial markets that the US enjoys, and if the Euro were to challenge the dollar it would seriously undermine one of the central pillars behind its success.

Uneven development has proven to be a central feature of this self-limiting European structure of capital accumulation (Stockhammer, 2008; Bellofiore *et al.*, 2011). Economies in northern Europe that still have a significant high-value-added manufacturing base (such as Germany and the Scandinavian countries) are articulated with US-centred finance-led capital accumulation through export-oriented growth strategies. Third Way politics has facilitated 'competitive corporatism' where wage increases remain below productivity growth. These economies recovered rather well after the relative stabilisation of the world economy after the London G-20 summit in 2009, largely because of demand–pull from emerging markets. At the same time, they remain very vulnerable on the fortunes of export markets at a time when the capacity of the US economy to remain the consumer and clearer of external account of last resort is uncertain, and when it is unlikely that Asian markets can take over that role. However, for now this has prevented the opening of policy space for considering economic alternatives, since it has become possible to obscure the real sources of the financial crisis and blame the financial crisis on the deficit countries in the Euro-zone. This brings us to the other side of Europe's uneven development coin in southern (and eastern) Europe, which was articulated to US-centred finance-led growth not via export orientation but through peripheral financialisation. Peripheral financialisation is a form of dependent development where dominant, mainly external financial institutions, make speculative investments in what is considered undervalued assets (Raviv, 2008; Becker *et al.*, 2010). The elimination of exchange rate risks proved to promote such investments causing a housing-bubble in southern Europe, but without productive investments and with deteriorating terms of trade vis-à-vis northern Europe. It is against the backdrop of these asymmetries and a monetary union without fiscal federalism that one can make sense of the protracted Euro-zone crisis (Lapavitsas *et al.*, 2010; Stockhammer, 2011; Becker and Jäger, 2012).

Corrosive effects

One of the key effects has consequently been economic stagnation in Europe. One indicator of this is GDP growth in the Euro-zone (Table 4.1). Contrary to the promises that have been made since the Single Market Programme was launched in 1985, rates of GDP growth have continuously stagnated over the years, and they have become outrightly disastrous since the outbreak of the financial crisis. This hardly constitutes a sound material foundation for a political ideology, such as the social democratic one, whose acceptance of capitalism is based on it being a system that generates growth, which then can be distributed.

Furthermore, uneven development has been debilitating for developing a coherent social democratic vision of Europe and has increasingly given way to national parochialism. The spat between Peer Steinbruck and Gordon Brown

Table 4.1 GDP annual average in the Euro-zone (1973–2013)

Year	Average annual GDP: Euro-zone
1973–79	2.7
1984–94	2.5
1994–98	2.3
1999–2003	2.1
2004–08	1.8
2009–13	−0.5

Source: OECD, 2013

about 'crass Keynesianism' at the height of the financial crisis in the end of 2008 was a rather unedifying expression of this, and in marked contrast to the joint Blair–Schröder Paper a decade earlier.[7] Rather than being an exception, subsequent Euro-zone crisis management has confirmed these divisions with northern European social democracy operating within the framework of nations-based competitive corporatism, pitted against southern European parties.

If the tendencies towards a social democratic alliance in the late 1990s have eroded at a European level, the same is also the case within countries. Stagnating output and productivity growth does not constitute a propitious terrain for sustaining the composite social alliances that mass parties must sustain, and for which the Third Way sought to provide a formula. As the Schröder government in Germany, for instance, committed itself to the Third Way formula, it continuously struggled to maintain support among its traditional working-class voters and employees working in the public sector, and eventually collapsed. Similar problems can be observed elsewhere. The failure to sustain such alliances in the wake of decades of stagnation and austerity has generated a crisis of representation, which has provided fertile ground for other parties, Syrizia in Greece, the Five Star Movement in Italy, Trotskyites and the National Front in France, the Left Party and the Pirate Party in Germany, and more often than not for extreme right parties such as the Sweden Democrats, the True Finns, the Danish People's Party, the PVV, the FPÖ, the PZÖ and the Golden Dawn.

Concomitant with the corrosion of the Third Way social alliances has been the exposure of the Giddens equation of 'no rights without responsibilities' with 'no authority without democracy' as a charade, or perhaps a cheap marketing trick akin to infamous New Labour spin-doctoring. If Ulrich Beck has identified the necessity for progressive politics to counter the condition of high modernity with more democratic forms of politics, the Third Way, by prioritising 'no rights without responsibilities' has an abysmal record in delivering on that score. Over the last years, in the run-up to the war in Iraq, through the curtailing of liberties in the wake on the war on terror, and with a propensity to wanting to meddle in every detail in citizens' lives while shielding political elites from accountability, 'modern' social democracy in Europe has been associated with an increasingly authoritarian form of politics, rather than with a democratisation. Rather than building on the potentials of welfare universalism, and filling it with democratic and pluralist content (on the potentials of which, see Rothstein, 1997), social democracy increasingly turned to the liberal model of welfare residualism and means testing, which has amplified all the problems of governability and legitimation crisis that Habermas and Offe warned against already in the 1970s and the 1980s.

Hence, when the American model entered into a deep crisis as a result of its internal contradictions, European social democracy was in no state to offer an alternative. When it proved impossible to bridge the pent-up overproduction of the world economy (on which, see Brenner 2005) through the extension, in the last instance, of ever more risky forms of debt to the precariously employed American working poor, the speculative bubble eventually collapsed. Far from Europe being delinked from the US through macroeconomic prudence and microeconomic efficiency (following years of flexibility reforms), export orientation and subordinate financial imbrication ensured that the crisis quickly spread to Europe. Given the extent to which European social democracy had put its bets with US-led neo-liberalism, despite being dependent on an entirely different social base, it is not surprising that it is one of the primary political casualties of the crisis. The tragedy is that in a situation where the radical right is moving forward its positions, Europe truly needs an agent capable of pursuing the Bad Godesberg formula in pursuit of a politics of 'no authority without democracy'.

Notes

1 This is an expanded and updated version of 'An obituary for the Third Way: the financial crisis and social democracy in Europe', *Political Quarterly* (2010), 81(4), 554–63. It is reprinted here with the kind permission of Wiley Publishers.

2 See the special issue of the *Financial Times* on 'The future of capitalism', 12 May 2009. Other articles include a reassessment of Adam Smith: 'the pioneer of economics recognised that markets required controls' and another by Paul Kennedy which rehabilitates Keynes and Marx as two of the four 'great thinkers' on capitalism (together with Smith and Schumpeter).

3 The Bad Godesberg Programme was adopted by the German Social Democratic Party, the SPD, in 1959. Confirming the SPD's aspiration to achieve its aims with a 'social market economy', as opposed to through socialist transformation, it has generally been seen as an expression of the political pragmatism that ultimately made Willy Brandt and Helmut Schmidt West German chancellors. By the standard of the Third Way, however, the document seems decidedly left-wing.

4 Clement Attlee famously defeated Winston Churchill in 1945, ensuring that the first British post-war government would be a Labour government. Although, this government is known for the social reforms it introduced, most notably the National Health Service, comparative social policy history generally regards its social democratic achievements as modest. Struggling with reconstruction of a country exhausted from the war effort, high levels of indebtedness, an unsympathetic anti-socialist US ally, a prolongation of austerity and rationing marred this government, which contributed to the reaffirmation of the Tories as the natural party of government. 'White Heat (of technology)' refers to the defining policy theme of the Labour government of Harold Wilson 1964–70, and its embrace of state-led industrial policy, which never came to play the role that it did in, say, France or Japan.

5 Mutual recognition is the key norm that underpins the Single European Market. Initially formulated in a key ruling by the European Court of Justice in 1979 (the *Cassis de Dijon* case) it became the central plank of the agreement at the Milan European Council Summit in 1985. Mutual recognition refers to the principle that,

upon entering the EC (later the EU), member states mutually recognise the validity of each other's legislation on what, how and for whom to produce. In other words, it is in principle illegal within the EC/EU to prohibit the import of a commodity that has been legally produced in another member state. Hence, by adopting the Milan agreement, member states authorised the Commission to commence a 'bonfire of controls' or member state regulations that contravened such mutual recognition. This is referred to as negative integration as the adoption of this principle leads to market integration through the doing away with regulations that contravenes it. This should be contrasted with the more cumbersome process of 'positive integration', which is based on member states agreeing upon common regulation or a common policy. The dynamics of mutual recognition led to concerns of competitive pressures leading to a lowering of labour, social and other standards through 'social dumping'.

6　Seigniorage privileges refer to the lower interest rates that the issuers of legal tender currency enjoy should they wish to borrow money. The reason why markets lend them at lower rates is that the risk of such loans defaulting is comparatively low, indeed next to nil. In the last instance, such borrowers can simply print more money.

7　The spat was triggered by the nominally social democratic British Prime Minister Brown addressing the economic downturn in the instinctively Anglo-Saxon neo-liberal style through tax cuts (requiring cutbacks in future social expenditure). This prompted an instinctively German and monetarist reply by the nominally social democratic German Finance Minister Steinbruck, who even at this stage of economic collapse was offended by the possible implications for fiscal balance and inflation. An alternative was formulated in the early months of the German Red–Green government in 1998–99 by then SPD Party Chairman and Finance Minister Oskar Lafontaine, based on a broadening of the tax base and a Franco-German sponsored renegotiation of the EMU (and, by extension, in alliance with Japan, the transnational financial) settlement along social-Keynesian lines. I have argued elsewhere that this alternative also was part of an alternative strategy to cement a broad based progressive social alliance around the Red–Green mass party coalition (Ryner, 2003b).

References

Aglietta, M. (1998). 'Capitalism at the turn of the century: regulation theory and the challenge of social change', New Left Review (old series), 232, 41–90.

Bailey, D. (2005). 'Obfuscation through integration: legitimating "new" social democracy in the European Union', Journal of Common Market Studies, 43(1), 13–35.

Balls, E. (1998). 'Open macroeconomics in an open economy', Scottish Journal of Political Economy, 45, 113–32.

Beck, U. (1992). The Risk Society (London: Sage).

Becker J. and Jäger, J. (2012). 'Integration in crisis: a regulationist perspective on the interaction of European varieties of capitalism', Competition & Change, 16(3), 169–87.

Becker, J., Jäger, J., Leubolt, B. and Weissenbacher, R. (2010). 'Peripheral financialization and vulnerability to crisis: a regulationist perspective', Competition & Change, 14(3–4), 225–47.

Belfrage, C. and Ryner, M. (2009). 'Renegotiating the Swedish social democratic settlement: from pension fund socialism to neoliberalization', *Politics & Society*, 37(2), 257–88.

Bellofiore, R., Garibaldo F. and Halevi, J. (2011). 'The global crisis and the crisis of European neomercantilism', in L. Panitch, G. Albo and V. Chibber (eds), *The Socialist Register 2011: The Crisis This Time* (London: Merlin Press).

Bieling, H. J. (2006). 'EMU, financial integration and global governance', *Review of International Political Economy*, 13(3), 420–48.

Boyer, R. and Hollingsworth, J. R. (1997). 'From national embeddedness to spatial and institutional nestedness', in Hollingsworth, J. R. and Boyer, R. (eds), *Contemporary Capitalism: The Embeddedness of Institutions* (Cambridge: Cambridge University Press), 435–8.

Brenner, R. (2005). *The Economics of Global Turbulence* (London: Verso).

Cafruny, A. and Ryner, M. (2007a). 'Monetary union and the transatlantic and social dimensions of Europe's crisis', *New Political Economy*, 12(2), 141–65.

Cafruny, A. and Ryner, M. (2007b). *Europe at Bay: In the Shadow of US Hegemony* (Boulder, CO: Lynne Rienner).

Clark, G. (2002). 'European pensions and global finance: continuity or convergence?', *New Political Economy*, 7(1), 67–91.

Clift, B. (2003). 'The changing political economy of France: *dirigisme* under duress', in A. Cafruny and M. Ryner (eds), *A Ruined Fortress? Neoliberal Hegemony and Transformation in Europe* (Lanham, MD: Rowman & Littlefield), pp. 173–200.

Clift, B. and Ryner, M. (2013). 'The Euro-zone crisis, Franco-German relations and the new politics of austerity', paper presented at 'The Hollande presidency one year on', Reuters Institute for the Study of Journalism, University of Oxford, Oxford, 3 May.

Cohen, B. (2003). 'Can the euro ever challenge the dollar', *Journal of Common Market Studies*, 41(4), 575–95.

Cohen, B. (2006). 'The macrofoundation of monetary power', in Andrews, D. (ed.), *International Monetary Power* (Ithaca, NY: Cornell University Press), pp. 31–50.

de la Porte, C. and Nanz, P. (2004). 'The OMC – a deliberative–democratic mode of governance? The case of employment and pensions', *Journal of European Public Policy*, 11(2), 267–88.

Dumenil, G. and Levy, D. (2004). 'The economics of US imperialism at the turn of the 21st century', *Review of International Political Economy*, 11(4), 657–76.

Dyson, K. and Featherstone, K. (1999). *The Road to Maastricht: Negotiating Economic and Monetary Union* (Oxford: Oxford University Press).

Giddens, A. (1998). *The Third Way: The Renewal of Social Democracy* (Cambridge: Polity Press).

Gowan, P. (1999). *The Global Gamble* (London: Verso).

Grahl, J. (2001). 'Global finance: the challenge to the euro', *New Left Review* (new series) 8, 23–47.

Habermas, J. (1976). *Legitimation Crisis* (Boston: Beacon Press).

Held, D. (1987). *Models of Democracy* (Stanford, CA: Stanford University Press).

Helleiner, E. (1994). *States and the Re-emergence of Global Finance* (Ithaca, NY: Cornell University Press).

Hirst, P. Thompson, G. and Bromley, S. (2009). *Globalization in Question* (3rd edn, Cambridge: Polity).

Jenson, J. and Pochet, P. (2005). 'Employment and social policy since Maastricht: standing up to the European monetary union', in R. Fishmane and A. Messina (eds), *The Year of the Euro: The Cultural, Social and Political Import of Europe's Common Currency* (Notre Dame: University of Notre Dame Press), pp. 161–85.

Kennedy, P. (1988). *The Rise and Fall of Great Powers* (London: Fontana Press).

Lapavitsas, C., Kaltenbrunner, A., Lindo, D., Michell, J., Painceira, J. P., Pires, E., Powell, J., Stenfors, A. and Teles, N. (2010). 'Euro-zone crisis: beggary thyself, beggar thy neighbour', *Journal of Balkan and Near Eastern Studies*, 12(4), 321–73.

Lash, S. and Urry, J. (1986). *The End of Organized Capitalism* (Madison: University of Wisconsin Press).

Lazonick, W. (2010). 'Innovative business models and varieties of capitalism: financialization of the US corporation', *Business History Review*, 84, 675–702.

Lipset S.M. and Rokkan. S. (eds) (1967). *Party Systems and Voter Alignments: Cross National Perspectives* (New York: Free Press).

Lösche, P. and Walter, I. (1992). *Die SPD: Klassenpartei, Volkspartei, Quotenpartei* (Darmstadt: Wissenschaftlige Buchgesellschaft).

Macpherson, C. B. (1982). *The Life and Times of Liberal Democracy* (Toronto: University of Toronto Press).

Merkel, W. (2000). 'Die dritten Wege der Sozialdemokratie', *Berliner Journal für Soziologie*, 10, 99–124.

Nussbaum, M. (1990). 'Aristotelian social democracy', in B. R. Douglas, G. Mara and H. S. Richardson (eds), *Liberalism and the Good* (London: Routledge), pp. 203–52.

OECD (2013). *Economic Outlook* (Paris: OECD).

Offe, C. (1985). *Contradictions of the Welfare State* (Cambridge MA: MIT Press).

Panitch, L. and Konings, M. (eds) (2009). *American Empire and the Political Economy of Global Finance* (Basingstoke: Palgrave).

Przeworski, A. (1986). *Capitalism and Social Democracy* (Cambridge: Cambridge University Press).

Raviv, O. (2008). 'Chasing the dragon east: exploring the frontiers of western European finance', *Contemporary Politics*, 14(3), 297–314.

Rosenberg, J. (2002). *The Follies of Globalization Theory* (London: Verso).

Rothstein, B. (1997). *Just Institutions Matter* (Cambridge: Cambridge University Press).

Ryner, M. (1999). 'Die neue Diskurs über den dritten Weg', in H. J. Bieling and J. Steinhilber (eds), *Die Konfiguration Europas* (Münster: Westfälischen Dampfboot), pp. 243–75.

Ryner, M. (2002). *Capitalist Restructuring, Globalisation and the Third Way: Lessons from the Swedish Model* (London: Routledge).

Ryner, M. (2003a). 'What is living and what is dead in Swedish social democracy?', *Radical Philosophy*, 117, 23–32.

Ryner, M. (2003b). 'Disciplinary neoliberalism, regionalization and the social market in German restructuring', in A. Cafruny and M. Ryner (eds), *A Ruined Fortress? Neoliberal Hegemony and Transformation in Europe* (Lanham, MD: Rowman & Littlefield), pp. 201–27.

Sapir, A. *et al.* (2004). *An Agenda for a Growing Europe: The Sapir Report* (Oxford: Oxford University Press).

Schwartz, H. (2009). *Subprime Nation: American Power, Global Capital and the Housing Bubble* (Ithaca, NY: Cornell University Press).

Seabrooke, L. (2001). *US Power in International Finance: The Victory of Dividends* (Basingstoke: Palgrave Macmillan).

Stockhammer, E. (2008). 'Some stylized facts on the finance-dominated accumulation regime', *Competition & Change*, 12(2), 184–202.

Stockhammer, E. (2011). 'Peripheral Europe's debt and German wages: the role of wage policy in the euro area', *International Journal of Public Policy*, 7, 83–96.

Story, J. and Walter, I. (1997). *Political Economy of Financial Integration in Europe: The Battle of the Systems* (Cambridge, MA: MIT Press).

5

Social democracy in the light of capitalist crises: the case of British Labour

John Callaghan

Introduction

The striking feature of the recent British political debate about reform of the financial sector since 2007 has been its timidity; in 2013 we are still waiting for the implementation of such modest reforms as have been agreed. This reflects the extent to which the political elite had contributed to the idea that the financial sector was a shining example of dynamic, innovative, globalised, wealth creation, protected by its own expertise and self-policing from dysfunction. In Labour's case it also reflects the extent to which it abandoned critical thinking about 'free markets' in the 1990s and gave up any pretence to an industrial policy. The future lay in services and the best of these were financial. The financial sector contributed 14 per cent to UK GDP, according to its advocates (*Telegraph*, 2010), who continued to press its case even after taxpayers had bailed out the UK banks – producing massive state deficits, recessionary conditions and the prospect of many years of austerity. There has been no coherent, let alone radical, reform discourse in Parliament. Some suspect that this is because all mainstream political parties essentially see the City as one of the UK economy's comparative advantages. The German Finance Minister, Peer Steinbrück, for example, who accepted the large claims for the importance of Britain's financial sector quoted above, complained in September 2009 that UK and US resistance to German and French demands for tighter restrictions on banks – and hedge funds in particular – was explicable in the British case because of its greater dependency on the financial sector, which contributed 15 per cent to GDP, compared to the 6 per cent of its German counterpart.[1] Two years later the British government made it clear that it would not countenance any version of the 'Tobin tax' on financial transactions, when the German and French finance ministers proposed its adoption to the European Commission (Parker, 2011).

One might not guess from this recent history that the British Labour Party, in common with other social democratic parties, has a long history of regarding the finance sector as a problem, even an enemy. The City of London was an object of socialist protest even before the Labour Party was formed. In 1886 the Marxist Social Democratic Federation (SDF) organised a demonstration to protest against the City's extensive privileges of self-government and tax avoidance/exemption, its riches and greed and its great companies that were 'without conscience or soul [and] do evil continuously' (Torr, 1956: 233–8).[2] The growing importance of finance capital was also analysed in important theoretical works that were influential on the left in the first decade of the twentieth century (Hobson, 1902; Hilferding, 1910; Bukharin, 1915; Lenin, 1916). It is fair to say, however, that these studies were devoid of practical advice for politicians seeking to manage a capitalist system.

Special role of finance in Britain

The Labour Party, in fact, showed little understanding of how the City worked and was bereft of policies for dealing with British financial institutions until the 1930s, that is, until after the collapse of the second minority Labour government in 1931. Britain's financial system had acquired many of its most important and most enduring features by the middle of the eighteenth century and had operated successfully on a political–institutional basis that united commercial, financial and imperial strategy for well over a century before the Labour Party came into existence. Britain's imperial, mercantile, naval and financial expansion began under a leadership drawn from the old landed elite and the *nouveaux riches* of the City and largely stayed under this leadership. The Bank of England, a de facto gold standard, the national debt, the development of specialist merchant banks, the rise of the stock exchange, the growth of marine insurance, the market in mortgages and the use of bills of exchange; all these elements of the 'financial revolution' were established under the auspices of a ruling bloc composed of aristocratic, mercantile and financial elites which overlapped with those that permeated the higher reaches of the state (Clark, 1956: 61–2).

The integration of 'the world of 'acceptable' business [and] that of elite politicians and ... their perceptions of the national interest' was undoubtedly cemented by success, initially in the seventeenth century wars against the Dutch, then those of the eighteenth century against France, culminating in the defeat of Napoleon' (Cain and Hopkins, 1993a: 13). The most important figures in the City were accustomed to obtaining privileged information 'principally from contact with those who controlled the machinery of the state' (Cain and Hopkins, 1993a: 26). New industrial wealth was absorbed into the dominant system in the nineteenth century on the basis of free trade imperialism. Industrial, commercial and financial growth in the nineteenth century appeared as aspects of a single totality, free from tensions between the constituent parts until anxieties about Britain's industrial competitors raised doubts about the dominant cosmopolitan policies from the 1880s. But Britain's financial and imperial role in the world remained pre-eminent until 1914 and even though the First World War permanently ended that global financial hegemony 'the City of London retained its independence and its central position in British economic life throughout the inter-war period ... its priorities continued to imprint themselves on economic policy and on the empire, as they had done before the war' (Cain and Hopkins, 1993b: 5).

Serious concerns that British manufacturing industry was losing its competitive edge grew from the 1880s but the most potent political case for protectionism took the form of Joseph Chamberlain's scheme for imperial preference and this was defeated at the general election of 1906. The arguments generated by Chamberlain's campaign led some of its participants to identify finance capital as a specific interest that could prosper even as British industry declined; and observers could see the leadership of the City in the defence of Free Trade (Semmel, 1960). Traditional priorities, conforming to the dominant interests of the City, survived and though interrupted by the First World War, they were reasserted by committees of bankers even before the war came to an end, as the basis of a return to the pre-war normal.[3]

The wisdom of a speedy return to the gold standard was virtually taken for granted in 1918, while devaluation of sterling was rejected without argument. The abrupt economic slump of 1921 and chronic mass unemployment in the years that followed made no difference to these judgements. The protests of the Federation of British Industries against the deflationary policies being pursued so that sterling could return to its pre-war parity against the dollar were to no avail. Individuals associated with the Labour Party – such as H. N. Brailsford and G. D. H. Cole – added their voices to the protests and the Labour conference in 1924 demanded nationalisation of the Bank of England. But Labour professed no alternative policy and Philip Snowden made clear to the House of Commons that the party only questioned the speed with which the return to gold was being implemented, not the goal itself (Adams Brown Jr, 1970). These objectives entailed the restoration of confidence in sterling as a reserve currency, the preservation of the City's role in overseas investment and in facilitating international loans. The return to gold in 1925 came after four years of deflation and stagnation and the overvalued pound (£1= $4.86) necessitated further deflationary policies and a concerted attempt in the export industries to recover competitiveness by driving down wages and shedding labour. When the world economic crisis came Britain was one of the first countries to be attacked by global speculative capital in 1931 and the gold standard was abandoned in September of that year by the national government formed in the wake of Labour's second period in office (Pollard, 1970: 2–3).

The world economic crisis, begun in October 1929 by the financial crash on Wall Street, affected Britain far less than Germany or the United States. Indeed the 1930s saw British economic recovery on the basis of closer imperial economic integration and growth in the relative importance of intra-imperial trade, especially after the Ottawa Agreements (1932) adopted a system of imperial preference and the Sterling Area (1937) was created on the basis of both the Empire and countries heavily involved in trade with Britain (such as Argentina and Denmark). The City remained globally oriented, as it always had been, and though the Macmillan Committee of 1930 complained of its lack of investment in domestic industry, nothing changed in this regard. The political–economic elite also remained recognisably aristocratic–financial, public school and Oxbridge educated. The Conservative Party was by now the undisputed representative in Parliament of a broad coalition of the propertied under a leadership congenial to the City. Indeed the intimacy between the City and the Conservative Party was such that it could 'effectively "veto" candidates which it deemed unsuitable for the role of Chancellor of the Exchequer' (Cain and Hopkins, 1993b: 30). Even in the 1930s the City 'remained the headquarters of the largest commercial and financial bloc in the world, the Sterling Area' (Cain and Hopkins, 1993b: 31). It was, according to the Labour Party leader Clement Attlee, writing in 1937, 'another power than that which has its seat at Westminster ... a convenient term for a collection of financial interests ... able to assert itself against the Government of the country' (179).

The road to 1945 and the first majority Labour governments (1945–51)

Attlee's words convey something of the unhappiness that Labour leaders felt about this state of affairs. The proximate cause is not hard to locate; 'The 1931 crisis and demise of the Labour government stimulated a radical reappraisal of Labour's whole approach to policy, especially economic policy' (Tomlinson, 1997: 147). The deliberations of the Macmillan Committee, 1929–30, had helped to educate trade unionists like Ernest Bevin by among other things raising anew the old questions about the hegemony of the sectional interests of self-governing financial institutions and their intimate relationship with the Bank of England and the British government. In financial and monetary policy Labour's thinking was informed by the conviction that the crisis which had destroyed the second Labour government was partly the result 'of the malevolence of financial institutions' as well as Labour's lack of understanding of those institutions. Accordingly the institutional structure necessary to control the banking and financial systems was 'the main economic preoccupation of Labour party conferences and policy subcommittees' by the mid 1930s (Durbin, 1985: 162). Leading figures in the party attended meetings of the informal XYZ Club, which was set up so that they could learn how the financial institutions worked. Yet the striking feature of the Attlee governments of 1945–51 was that these debates – which assumed that radical reform of the financial system was required – had little impact on policy in the mid to late 1940s. In explanation Sidney Pollard suggested that 'the vision of a planned industry directed to social ends was as divorced, and as distracting, from reality in the 1930s as the less distinct visions of socialism had been in the 1920s' (1970: 158).

By the mid 1930s Labour had accepted that the Bank of England would be nationalised. Many on the left of the party had argued for the nationalisation of the joint stock banks, while other targets sometimes included the acceptance houses, the discount houses, the insurance industry, the building societies and investment houses. 'The House of panics' – as the stock exchange was dubbed in one Labour debate – was also an occasional candidate for nationalisation. Most of the participants in these debates agreed that a socialised banking system was necessary for the regulation of both the amount of savings and the amount and direction of investment, while a National Investment Board (NIB) was favoured by others to determine investment priorities without the necessity of joint stock bank nationalisations. The participants in these debates could not agree on what should be nationalised or the form and powers of the institutions to be taken into public ownership. But they all agreed on the necessity of increasing state control of industry and of the need to adopt a system of planning. Differences arose in the detail of how these objectives could be realised (Toye, 2003: 83). Under Hugh Dalton's leadership, however, Labour's policy statements argued by 1935 that only an NIB and a nationalised Bank of England were required to achieve the party's three main purposes – controlling internal and external panic, curing unemployment and exercising power over investment (Durbin, 1985: 215–16). This became party policy (Attle, 1937: 179–81). For all the talk of socialist planning in the 1930s and during the Second World War, Labour also remained committed to other priorities, seemingly removed from economic management that necessarily influenced what they could achieve in that field. Among these was the Westminster system of politics itself and of equal importance was Labour's fidelity to a conventional foreign policy which gave priority to Britain's global imperial role. Any economic planning that accepted the framework of the Westminster system would be implemented by committees of government ministers, ultimately responsible to Parliament, rather than the autonomous Supreme Economic Authority of the sort Labour debates often referred to in the 1930s. Planning in Britain would also have to coexist with capital exports, maintenance of the sterling area, a stable and strong pound and global responsibilities for the colonial and informal empire; all of which would put pressure on scarce resources and the balance of payments and help to determine the priorities of policy.

Socialist planning

Planning was Labour's central economic idea and it remained so until the 1960s, resurfacing again in the 1970s and early 1980s. As Ritschel points out, 'the new concept was suddenly embraced by nearly the entire Labour movement as the missing collectivist key to the transition from capitalism to socialism' (1997: 100–1). But the same author is clear that 'it never succeeded in fashioning an agreed definition of the sort of planned economy a socialist government would put into place' (Ritschel, 1997: 101). For many it served rather as 'a powerful but vague ideological myth'. The leadership of the party, carrying most of the organisation with it, could never accept the left's highly centralised version of socialist economics inspired by the Soviet model of comprehensive state owner-ship. The party leadership instead adopted Herbert Morrison's model of the autonomous public corporation managed by experts who would themselves be governed by market disciplines in the quest for economic efficiency. Such public corporations would be adopted in a limited number of industries and allowed to operate free from political diktat. This was settled on by 1937. There was no evidence provided in Labour policy documents to suggest that manage-ment methods in the industries affected would change very much and the same was true of the modus operandi of a future nationalised Bank of England. Hugh Dalton did refer to the need for a Supreme Economic Authority, as some sort of coordinating body, but as early as *Practical Socialism* (1935) it was obvious that this vaguely conceived body would also be free of state direction. The same was true of his idea of a National Investment Board. This would largely ignore the private sector – except for licensing new public issues in the capital market – and confine itself to the coordination of investment plans in the public sector. It would be managed by experts free of state interference but they would have no power to raise capital or manage the national income in the manner advocated by John Maynard Keynes.

In the event the nationalised Bank of England remained the spokesman of the City of London in government and never became an active agent of either macroeconomic management or of microeconomic planning. The treasury and the government were left without strong controls over the Bank to determine monetary policy and clearing bank behaviour. The Governor of the Bank could not be dismissed by the government; he remained a guardian of the interests of the City of London, from whose leading personnel the Bank's employees were normally recruited. The work of the Bank remained opaque to Government but this was temporarily obscured by the mood of the moment, which was more favourable to planning the UK economy than it had ever been before. In practice planning amounted to cooperation between government, industry and the unions in the form of tripartite discussions on bodies like the National Joint Advisory Committee and the Economic Planning Board, bodies that were largely confined to disseminating government information rather than wielding power of their own.

Similarly the NIB, which was promoted at times in the early 1930s as an essential element in future planning, was only a peripheral and unimportant body by the time it came into existence, a marginality that can be traced back to its original conception, even though the manifesto of 1945 imagined that it would be able to 'determine social priorities and promote better timing of investment'. Contemporary critics, however, observed that seven-eighths of investment in Britain was generated by the profits of companies. Once the war-time physical controls over investment were abolished, as everyone assumed they would be when shortages were overcome and rationing was no longer necessary, Labour's physical controls over the economy would diminish enormously. When Dalton introduced the NIB in government he made clear that its role was only advisory. The Cabinet would remain responsible for economic and financial planning, but while planning rhetoric remained enthusiastic and vague, leftish elite opinion was moving to Keynesianism by the late 1940s.

The golden age

Planning nevertheless continued to fascinate Labour politicians and many looked back on the 1945–51 governments as evidence of its success. Some lead-ing Labour politicians also continued to believe that the City was too powerful in its ability to determine economic policy compared to an elected Labour government. One result of this power, as perceived by critics of Britain's relative economic decline in the 1950s – an economic decline which Labour stressed in the early 1960s – was the neglect of the domestic economy, as the global perspec-tive of the City tended to predominate when policy makers had to make critical choices (Shonfeld, 1965). British industry, on this reading, was starved of invest-ment as funds flowed to the richer parts of the Sterling Area in the late 1940s and early 1950s. Policy, it was claimed, remained obsessed with the strength of sterling and not enough concerned with the condition of British manufactur-ing. Yet the reserve currency status of sterling – a consistently defended object of policy – made the pound vulnerable to speculation, as balance-of-payments deficits were turned into sterling crises. Economic growth, it was argued by the later 1950s, was sacrificed for the benefit of a stable currency. The external ori-entation of City institutions also made them irrelevant, when not obstructive, to the task of raising investment in home industry (Tomlinson, 2004: 175). While many of these critics of British economic policy could be found in the Labour Party, both Hugh Gaitskell (leader from 1955 to 1963) and his successor, Harold Wilson, believed that British economic rejuvenation would take place within the Commonwealth, rather than the Common Market, and both sup-ported Britain's global colonial, military and financial role. These considerations made them more supportive of the Sterling Area than others within the party until Wilson reappraised the option of joining the Common Market in 1966. By this time Labour's assumption that the City benefited from a strong pound was also in need of revision as it became clear that its 'offshore' status allowed it to operate successfully with dollars and other currencies and was no longer dependent on maintenance of the Sterling Area (Tomlinson, 2004: 189).

The golden age saw an unprecedented period of full employment but it was not a time of social democratic success in government for most of western Europe and welfare reforms in the period, including some of the more generous (Schwarz, 1997: 224–8), were often introduced by centre-right parties (Kohl, 1981). The presumed efficacy of Keynesian macroeconomic management in the 1950s and 1960s (Giddens, 1994: 74; Vandenbroucke, 1998: 50) is in important ways a myth created by theorists of globalisation such as Anthony Giddens (Vandenbroucke, 1998: 50), though one shared by enthusiastic Keynesians from the time (Crosland, 1952; Jay, 1962; Stewart, 1969: 9), and 'all socialist revisionists throughout Europe in the 1950s [as]...a necessary part of their new vision' (Sassoon, 1996: 245). It seemed 'perverse' to Douglas Jay, for example, when considering the correlation of full employment and the Keynesian consensus, to resist the 'rational and cheering inference that the application of the remedy has had something to do with the cure' (1962: 134). This is an interesting judgement given the experiences of the Labour governments of 1945–51, 1964–70 and 1974–79. All of these were preoccupied by crisis management as they grappled with events beyond their control. Attlee might have been amused by the notion that his governments had 'steered' the economy. Wilson expressed himself dismayed when he discovered that his own governments were 'blown off course' by more powerful financial forces than he had perhaps bargained for, even though, as Ben Pimlott pointed out, 'Labour had always been conscious of the fear it created on the money markets and of the expectation, which was likely to be self-fulfilling, that a Labour victory would mean a financial panic' (1992: 351). Thomas Balogh, Wilson's Keynesian economic adviser, counted ten major balance-of-payments crises in Britain in the period 1918–63 – 'all with the same pattern and lesson' (1963) – and the Labour governments that followed in 1964–70 were plagued by short-term movements of speculative finance in the context of the chronic balance-of-payments problem that Balogh was alluding to (Tomlinson, 1981: 121).

Some observers thought they saw 'The most protracted and open struggle between the two major forms of capital in Britain occurred during the 1960s' (Ingham, 1984: 201). By then the familiar elements of the critique of finance were associated both with the Labour Party and (briefly) the Confederation of British Industry (CBI), while various economic analysts and academics supplied their own versions of it, generally stated with renewed vigour in the light of what was taken to be evidence of Britain's relative economic decline. As leader of the Opposition (January 1963–October 1964) Harold Wilson argued that Britain's sluggish economic growth derived from underinvestment in domestic industry, the failure to plan effectively, an elitist educational system and a cult of amateurism that pervaded the boardroom and the civil service. Others pointed more directly at what Sidney Pollard called 'the considerable apparatus of Government economic power' which had been mobilised for the benefit of finance and against the interests of domestic economic growth (Ingham, 1984: 209). Wilson proposed to establish a Department of Economic Affairs (DEA) to oversee a National Plan which would bring cumulative economic growth of 25 per cent over a five-year period. The DEA would be a rival power base to the Treasury and the Bank of England in the determination of economic policy inside Whitehall.

But, as Tomlinson points out, 'Almost the whole period from 1964 to 1970 saw the government lurching from crisis to crisis as it grappled with short-term macro-economic problems, mostly arising from external problems. The period began, as it was to continue, with a foreign exchange crisis' (2004: 49). The Treasury and the Bank of England continued to tender advice which gave priority to the defence of sterling, constraints on public expenditure, and the need to correct the balance-of-payments deficits. Devaluation was ruled out by Wilson for political reasons – the damage it would do domestically to Labour's credibility as an economic manager, and the fear of competitive retaliatory devaluations which might lead to events 'bringing down the whole international financial system' – an imagined prospect which Wilson appears to have shared with the Treasury and the US administration of President Lyndon Johnson. Wilson also argued that for devaluation to be successful it would necessitate deflationary policies, which he wanted to avoid. In the event deflationary policies were employed *instead* of devaluation and the National Plan target of 25 per cent growth in GDP between 1964 and 1970 was soon completely subverted. Devaluation was delayed until November 1967, sterling's role as a reserve currency was ended in 1968 and decisions were taken to reduce Britain's military role in the Gulf and South Asia. But as Tomlinson says 'many of Britain's foreign exchange problems of the 1960s had little to do with the current account, but related to shifts in capital flows, which were extraordinarily difficult to predict, and often hard to understand, even in retrospect' (2004: 60). Thus even after devaluation there was increased uncertainty about the future of the Bretton Woods system 'and this tended to encourage flows between currencies, from all currencies into gold, and especially out of those perceived to be weak'. The crisis of March 1968, another post-devaluation scare, was, according to Cairncross writing in 1996, 'more frightening than in the run-up to devaluation, perhaps more than in any crisis in the last twenty years' (Tomlinson, 2004: 60). Speculation against the pound continued even after the balance of payments situation radically improved in the summer of 1969. Relations between the government and the Bank of England and the City were often tense in this period. The City nevertheless had the upper hand. Nothing was done by government to change the 'off-shore' status of a growing volume of its activities. Yet these were a major source of volatile flows of the 'hot money' that blighted the experience of Wilson's governments.

When Labour left office in 1970 there had been no measures taken to weaken the City; the Treasury had survived the challenge of the DEA; and the civil service endured only minimal reforms. Only after the pound's devaluation in 1967 did it become clearer to the government that the fortunes of the City were no longer dependent on the reserve currency status of the pound. The City had been taking advantage of the burgeoning 'off-shore' Eurodollar market since the late 1950s and the Bank of England had decided – without any reference to a Labour government – that 'London's almost absolute economic freedom to engage in wholesale monetary transactions' (a condition that had been maintained throughout the 1950s to foster invisible earnings and maintain confidence in sterling) could be further enhanced by taking no steps to regulate, much less curb, the Eurodollar market (Ingham, 1984: 207). All that Labour could do was complain pitifully of the 'gnomes of Zurich' – that is foreign speculators – when in reality one of the major source of its problems was under its nose.

After 1973

The collapse of the Bretton Woods system in 1973 can be used as a convenient marker to denote the beginning of a period of growing financial volatility, slower rates of economic growth, higher rates of inflation and growing unemployment. All West European countries were adversely affected, though the impact varied, as did the policy response. Britain was among the countries which experienced the highest rates of unemployment, averaging just over seven per cent of the workforce in the years 1974–82 (Norway and Sweden, at the other extreme, averaged around 2 per cent). In the 1970s British Labour's debate and policies on the economy were dominated by the Alternative Economic Strategy (AES). The financial sector did not feature strongly in Labour's Programme 1973, though it asserted that the power of financial institutions was excessive and the TUC even voted for nationalisation of banking in that year. In 1975 Labour and Industry proposed setting up an investment fund and in later documents there was talk of a National Investment Bank. In 1976 Banking and Finance featured nationalisation of the four largest clearing banks, the seven largest insurance companies and one merchant bank – the purpose being to change investment patterns. Though the Labour conference supported the proposal to nationalise banking, which reappeared in Labour's Draft Manifesto in 1980, it was strenuously opposed by the banking trade unions. At the end of 1980 Labour's research department admitted 'As yet we have no policy on how to deal with the various crises in the financial markets; and our policies on the financial institutions are clearly unacceptable, as they stand … to many of our major affiliates' (Wickham-Jones, 1996: 65–6). By 1982 nationalisation of the banks was demoted to a reserve position – something that might be invoked in the event that stricter controls on banks and a NIB failed to achieve the redirection of investment that was deemed necessary. In *New Hope for Britain*, the manifesto of 1983, Labour pledged to create an NIB 'to put new resources from private institutions and from the government – including North Sea oil revenues – on a large scale into our industrial priorities. The bank will attract and channel savings, by agreement, in a way that guarantees these savings and improves the quality of investment in the UK.' It said it would 'Exercise, through the Bank of England, much closer direct control over bank lending. Agreed development plans will be concluded with the banks and other financial institutions.' It would also create a public bank operating through post offices, by merging the National Girobank, National Savings Bank and the Paymaster General's Office and set up 'a Securities Commission to regulate the institutions and markets of the City, including Lloyds, within a clear statutory framework'. It would also 'expect the major clearing banks to co-operate with us fully on these reforms, in the national interest. However, should they fail to do so, we shall stand ready to take one or more of them into public ownership' (Labour Party, 1983).

Taking the period 1978–97 as a whole, official unemployment in Britain averaged two million people or 8.9 per cent of the workforce – almost five times the average for the golden age, twice as high as the average pre-1914 figure and close to the inter-war average (Matthews, 1968: 555). Employers made increasing use of part-time workers and trade union membership declined in this adverse economic context. By 1994 Labour Force Survey data showed that only 48 per cent of employees belonged to workplaces in which unions were recognised, varying from 34 per cent in the private sector to 86 per cent in the public sector (compared with 60 per cent and over 90 per cent respectively in the early 1980s) (Farnham, 1996: 591). Six Acts of Parliament concerned with trade unions were introduced between 1980 and 1993, having the combined effect of enforcing pre-strike postal ballots; outlawing secondary strikes, unofficial strikes and the closed shop; and rendering strikers vulnerable to dismissal. The unions had lost five million members by 1992. The number of days lost through strike action fell to 528,000 in 1992 compared to an annual average in the 1970s of seven–ten million. Multi-employer bargaining was by 1990 'the main basis for pay increases for only 19 per cent of manual employees in private manufacturing and for only six per cent of non-manual employees' (Lecher, 1994: 39). Pollard's judgement on this 'experiment' is that it was by 1990 one of 'unmitigated failure'; Britain still had the highest rate of inflation of the advanced economies; the highest interest rates, high unemployment, large-scale bankruptcies of firms in all sectors of the economy, falling output, declining national income and the largest deficit on the current balance of payments in its history (1992).

New Labour

The years of economic growth 1992–97 changed this perception in the parliamentary Labour Party. It was now thought that the Thatcher reforms had reinvigorated the British economy and restructured it to succeed in conditions of globalisation. Success was all the shinier for the fact that Germany was struggling economically after reunification and the Japanese economy was stagnant. One common economic experience, however, concerns the activities of the financial institutions. The growth in financial intermediation was outstripping the growth of economies. The trend accelerated from the early 1980s and was even faster in the 2000s. The largest 1,000 banks in the world reported aggregate pre-tax profits at $800 billion in fiscal year 2007–08, almost 150 per cent higher than 2000–01, equating to annualised returns to banking of 15 per cent. In the UK, banks' assets had flatlined at 50 per cent of national income until the 1970s; they then rose, accelerating in the 2000s to over 500 per cent of national income, though even this figure underestimates the real situation because of the practice of keeping 'certain exposures off-balance sheet' (Haldane, 2010). If there was recognition of a problem – the massive growth in bank-generated digital money (debt representing 97 per cent of all money in the UK by 2007), much of it in home ownership – it was marginalised by the rhetoric of awe at the powers of 'the financial markets' and the narrative of the UK's desirable passage to post-industrial prosperity.

It was under Thatcher that exchange controls were removed in October 1979 and a variety of deregulatory measures taken which opened the City and released many financial institutions on to world markets. The intention was to maintain the City's reputation 'as the most liberal and deregulated [financial] centre', in the face of US competition for this position (Hellheiner, 1994: 151). Other countries followed the deregulatory path soon after. Self-regulation had been official doctrine in the UK throughout the twentieth century and after 1986 it was institutionalised in the Securities and Investment Board (SIB) and later the Financial Services Authority (1997). Throughout the 1980s and 1990s the financial services sector was celebrated as a shining success story which fulfilled in practice what the reigning free market ideology promised to all sectors of the economy, once they became sufficiently competitive. The fact that so much of British manufacturing failed to live up to this prospectus only served to empha-sise the financial sector's importance to the UK economy.

We saw that the Bank of England had chosen to regard the Eurodollar and Euro-bond markets as 'offshore' from the time of their first emergence. This meant that the UK had abdicated its regulatory role on activities centred in the City of London. Thus a 'regulatory vacuum' had been created in respect of busi-ness linked to a network of tax havens, many of them British Overseas Territories like the Cayman Islands (Shaxson, 2011: 88). Financial institutions operating from the City were able by these devices to keep a growing volume of transac-tions off their books. By the end of 1960 the market in Eurodollars was worth a billion dollars; by 1970 it was worth $46 billion; by 1988 $2.6 trillion. Banks from other jurisdictions took part in this trade as the market grew and came to embrace all the leading currencies. American attempts to control financial outflows by taxing interest on foreign securities in July 1963 merely prompted American companies to make greater use of the London offshore market, where taxes did not exist. Eventually the US permitted offshore activities of its own but Washington's tolerance of the market in Eurodollars was also influenced by its control of the printing of dollars, which had the beneficial effect of enabling the American state to spend more than the ailing American economy could afford. The volume of credit generated by this market was not held back by any of the precautionary principles that constrain normal banking, precisely because it was not regulated. This growing volume of credit could move with great speed (as 'hot money') in response to economic indicators, destabilising entire economies as Wilson's Labour governments discovered between 1964 and 1970.

Policy change in the Labour Party from 1987 demonstrated an accelerated retreat from state planning and a redirection towards celebration of the efficacy of markets. The industries for which planning proposals had been conceived had either gone or shrunk. Labour's last experience of government had been an unhappy one. The return to mass unemployment in the 1970s, coupled with stagflationary conditions, balance-of-payments deficits and heavy government borrowing, had been predictably constraining during the years 1974–79. The French Socialists (PS) ran into the same difficulties, with unemployment around two million, inflation at 13 per cent and persistent balance-of-payments problems by the end of the 1970s. By 1981, when the PS took office and tried to reflate the economy, an international recession was deepening, governments in the United States, Britain and West Germany were committed to deflationary policies, and steps had already been taken to deregulate financial markets. Like Leon Blum in 1936, Mitterrand entered government at a time of international deflation, chronic deficits on current account, currency speculation, financial disorder, capital flight and the explicit hostility of business (Ambler, 1985: 19–20; Halimi, 1996: 86). Much of this can be attributed to the decisions of western policy makers determined to resolve the economic problems of the 1970s in ways congenial to holders of money and capital. Agencies such as the IMF, OECD, World Bank and GATT/WTO had been transformed in the 1980s into proselytisers for a raft of neo-liberal policies designed to stifle inflation, deregulate markets and institutionalise new trading regimes (Callaghan, 2000). The Mitterrand experience – a rapid U-turn and the collapse of much of the Socialists' reform programme – soon became annexed to the thesis that social democratic governments were faced with more or less permanent constraints attributable to a new stage in the evolution of the global economy, rather than those deriving from specific policies and the economic problems of a particular conjuncture (Fox-Piven, 1995; Carney, 1996).

As late as 1989 in *Meet the Challenge, Make the Change*, the Labour leader Neil Kinnock could still denounce the Conservatives as 'the party of the City', while depicting Labour as 'the party for industry' (Labour Party, 1989: 6). By 1992 the remnants of an industrial policy were barely visible in the general election manifesto which talked about state support for businesses, education, science and skills. The emphasis was increasingly supply side. In the mid-1990s the need for a revolution in education and skills was increasingly attached to the theme of globalisation, after the manner of Bill Clinton's Secretary of State for Labour, Robert Reich, but without the radicalism of his *The Work of Nations* (which advocated steeply progressive taxation and the elimination of corporate subsidies). Labour invoked globalisation to conjure a picture of intensified competition and severe punishment of those who tried to 'go-it-alone' as 'billions of dollars' flowed back and forth at the command of punitive financial markets (Labour Party, 1994: 13). Nothing could be done to reign in these forces. Policy now favoured devices such as public–private partnerships in infrastructural projects, as well as in health, childcare and training which were contrasted with 'the old national levers of demand management', rendered obsolete by globalisation. Rapidly growing world trade, footloose companies and fast-moving markets were presented as the facts of life. But government could encourage economic growth, New Labour insisted, by securing stable and low rates of inflation and other aspects of a 'business-friendly' environment such as light business regulation.

Industrial policy soon disappeared altogether from Labour policy documents and as the British economy expanded in the 1990s and 2000s the growth of services, particularly financial services, was taken as evidence of successful transition to the future. Occasionally a problem was adumbrated that policy might address. In 1995 it was the need for 'more effective regulation and supervision of currency and financial markets to ensure that the growth of derivatives and other financial instruments does not destabilise world capital markets' (Labour Party, 1995: 17–18). Gordon Brown promised to end tax evasion by the rich in 1993. But the party's City spokesman, Alistair Darling, ruled out 'draconian measures' against the City on the grounds, as journalists reported, that it 'would simply lead to a mass exodus of investment to financial centres with a lighter regulatory framework'. Voluntary self-regulation would therefore continue under Labour government (Elliot and Kelly, 1994). The pre-manifesto of 1996, *New Labour: New Life for Britain*, stressed the 'change in the political balance of power' signified by the trillion dollars a day traded on the financial markets. Blair's introduction to the manifesto of 1997 argued that Labour would strive to facilitate even faster economic change than already existed by 'enhancing the dynamism of the market', rather than curbing it (Labour Party, 1997: 3). Gordon Brown repeated this analysis in *Labour's Business Manifesto* in the same year, emphasising the redundancy of the 'old national economic policies' and the inevitability of rapid, incessant change. Blair told Japanese business leaders in 1996 that 'a country has to dismantle barriers to competition and accept the disciplines of the international economy'. He also invoked the punishment meted out by the financial markets on governments that deviated from sound money policies, or which kept taxes too high. Later that year in Singapore he announced that the old redistributory tax and benefit policies were also obsolete. The same analysis was repeated at Newscorp International headquarters in Australia, when he visited Rupert Murdoch, and again at a gathering of the German employers' federation (BDI), where the Labour leader stressed the evils of over-regulation (Callaghan, 2000: 161–2).

Far from abolishing the Corporation of the City of London, which Labour promised in opposition, Prime Minister Blair reformed it by enlarging the business vote which already controlled its affairs. Gordon Brown, the Chancellor, made a virtue of light regulation of the City by publicly questioning 'the old assumption' that it would lead to irresponsible behaviour (Shaxson, 2011). Labour gave the Bank of England independence to set interest rates in 1997 and allowed the Financial Services and Markets Act (2001) to stipulate that the FSA would not prevent, or even discourage, the creation of new financial instruments. The FSA was also told to avoid creating regulatory barriers that would damage the UK's competitiveness.

New Labour clearly believed that Britain's comparative economic advantage lay in flexible markets, an open economy, low taxes and light regulation of business. This formula for success was now taken to the EU as the new Prime Minister campaigned against the disease of 'Eurosclerosis' – defined as excessive business regulation, rigid labour markets, high taxes and overly generous welfare arrangements. Deregulation and flexible labour markets would create jobs in Europe, Blair insisted, as they had in Britain. The East Asian financial crisis, which began within months of Labour's general election victory, slightly altered this rhetoric for an interval and stimulated other centre-left parties to call for reforms. The PES–ECOFIN report *The New European Way* in October 1998 demanded a 'governance framework for the global economy', involving a 'new code of conduct' for market operators, and greater transparency in both public and private sectors, which would increase the resilience of the international financial system and improve multilateral surveillance of national policies. An Economic Security Council operating within the UN framework could be created to address global issues such as the stability of exchange rates. Gordon Brown cheerfully joined in the chorus, demanding a 'new institutional architecture' for global finance. But Brown was doing nothing more than copying the empty rhetoric of the US Treasury and the International Monetary Fund, both of which believed that only minor changes were needed (Stiglitz, 2002: 233). Dominique Strauss-Kahn, Lionel Jospin's Socialist Minister for Economy, reflected this consensus when he publicly stated that the Asian crisis occurred because the liberalisation of the economies concerned had not proceeded far enough (Shaxson, 2011: 166).

Contradictory messages were transmitted from the 'social democratic family'.

In preparation for the 1998 Bundestag elections, for example, the SPD talked about controlling some of the effects of globalisation by transferring power to transnational political organisations such as the EU, so that binding regulations might be enforced. The party's manifesto also referred to the elimination of tax havens, the prevention of welfare dumping, and compulsory regulations to address tax evasion, while EMU was held out as a possible answer to globalised financial markets. The Belgian, Swedish, Norwegian and French Socialists flirted with the Tobin tax as a measure to dampen financial speculation. Oskar Lafontaine briefly championed majority voting within the EU on issues such as the harmonisation of business taxes, the elimination of corporate tax avoidance and tax havens. But Gordon Brown quickly announced, in response, that he would veto any such efforts, while the London *Observer* pointed out, in explaining Brown's position, that 'the strength of the City of London ...depends on investors' intent on tax evasion' (*Observer*, 1998). In 2011 it was reported that ninety-eight of the leading FTSE 100 companies made extensive use of tax havens, with the banks most heavily committed to them (*Independent*, 2011). Blair and Schröder, however, had issued a joint statement in December 1998 opposing a unified European system of corporate taxation and rejecting any measures leading to a higher tax burden for business. Talk of taxing financial transactions never entered the public agenda in Britain. Four years of austerity after the financial crisis and successive party conferences had passed without a single leading politician demanding support for the transactions tax proposed by the European Commission.

Broken eggs and the national interest

It was wryly observed that the consequences for the financial institutions and managers who caused it were remarkably modest in the UK; 'Someone threw an egg at Fred Goodwin's[4] house. That's it. There are no consequences in London' (Shaxson, 2011: 250). The Labour Party's attempts over the course of the twentieth century to place finance at the service of industry and society look like a series of broken eggs pitched against an immovable granite wall. Emerging from a position of suspicion and ignorance about the City, Labour's opportunity to reform the financial sector came after many years during which the motivation to curb the City had grown and the Second World War had provided the political basis for action. Labour achieved little. The national interest was taken to involve the maintenance and development of the Empire–Commonwealth, the preservation of the Sterling Area and the freedom of the Bank of England to continue operating in the old way as a custodian of the City's interests acting within the state. On none of the subsequent occasions when Labour formed a government did the party show that it had either an understanding of the City's current operations or any appetite for reforming it, though there was talk in Opposition, from time to time, of the necessity for such reforms. In 1997–2007 successive Labour governments behaved as its uncritical supporters.

The City of London Corporation remained as independent of UK governance structures in 2011 as it had been in 1886 when the SDF attempted to disrupt the Lord Mayor's Show. It continued to act as an immensely wealthy lobby for what we now call neo-liberalism. With a workforce of 350,000, four-fifths employed in financial services, the City, by the time New Labour entered office in 1997, 'accounted for half of all international trade in equities, nearly 45 per cent of over-the-counter derivatives turnover, 70 per cent of Eurobond turnover, 35 per cent of global currency trading and 55 per cent of international public offerings … making London the world's biggest international – and offshore – financial hub' (Shaxson, 2011: 247). Since the late 1950s it has attracted financial institutions based in foreign jurisdictions seeking to evade their domestic regulations. The effects of its unregulated status also include providing arguments for deregulation elsewhere, on precisely the grounds that business flees to London unless the authorities elsewhere replicate its advantages. It provides channels for money beyond the control of tax authorities and law enforcement agencies in other countries, allowing pariah states to evade international sanctions and connecting tax havens across the globe in ways which infect local jurisdictions and siphon money out of regulatory and law-enforcement systems. On top of these benefits, Britain's tax laws attract foreign tax evaders who have the right to be resident in London without paying tax on their global income, while Britain's libel laws assist them in their ability to suppress unwanted investigations of their financial activities. Meanwhile British society has become one of the most unequal in the developed world. A more complete subversion of social democratic objectives would be hard to construct.

Notes

1 BBC website, 'UK blocking tough finance rules', 23 September 2009, http://news.bbc.co.uk/1/hi/8270404.stm (accessed 8 November 2011).
2 Herbert Morrison of the London Labour Party called attention in 1917 to the square mile of 'entrenched reaction' represented by the City (see Shaxson, 2011: 260).
3 Interim Report of the Cunliffe Committee, 15 August 1918, full text available at: http://freetheplanet.net/articles/106/interim-report-of-the-cunliffe-committee-1918.
4 Goodwin was chief executive of the Royal Bank of Scotland which recorded a loss of over £24 billion in October 2008.

References

Adams Brown Jr, W. (1970). 'The conflict of opinion and economic interest in England', in S. Pollard (ed.), *The Gold Standard and Employment Policies between the Wars* (London: Methuen), pp. 44–67.

Ambler, J. S. (1985). 'Is the French left doomed to fail?', in J. S. Ambler (ed.), *The French Socialist Experiment* (Philadelphia: Institute for the Study of Human Issues).

Attlee, C. R. (1937). *The Labour Party in Perspective* (London: Gollancz).

Balogh, T. (1963). *Planning for Progress* (London: Fabian Society).

Bukharin, N. (1915 and 2003). *Imperialism and World Economy* (London: Bookmarks).

Cain, P. J. and Hopkins, A. G. (1993a). *British Imperialism: Innovation and Expansion* (London: Longman).

Cain, P. J. and Hopkins, A.G. (1993b). *British Imperialism: Crisis and Deconstruction* (London: Longman).

Callaghan, J. (2000). *The Retreat of Social Democracy* (Manchester: Manchester University Press).

Carney, L. S. (1996). 'Globalisation: the final demise of socialism', *International Journal of Politics, Culture and Society*, 10(1), 41–71.

Clark, G. (1956). *The Later Stuarts 1660–1714* (Oxford: Oxford University Press).

Crosland, A. (1952). 'The transition from capitalism', in R. H. S. Crossman (ed.), *New Fabian Essays* (London: Turnstile Press), pp. 33–68.

Dalton, H. (1935). *Practical Socialism* (London: Routledge).

Durbin, E. (1985). *New Jerusalems: The Labour Party and the Economics of Democratic Socialism* (London: Routledge).

Elliot, L. and Kelly, R. (1994). 'Labour admits City is needed', *Guardian*, 4 October.

Farnham, D. (1996). 'New Labour, the new unions, and the new labour market', *Parliamentary Affairs*, 49(4), 584–98.

Fox-Piven, F. (1995). 'Is it global economics or laissez-faire', *New Left Review*, 213, September–October.

Giddens, A. (1994). *Beyond Left and Right* (Cambridge: Polity Press).

Haldane, A. (2010). 'The contribution of the financial sector: miracle or mirage?' paper given at the Future of Finance Conference, 14 July, available at: www.bankofengland. co.uk/publications/speeches/2010/speech442.pdf (accessed 8 November 2011).

Halimi, S. (1996). 'Less exceptionalism than meets the eye', in A. Dayley (ed.), *The Mitterrand Era: Policy Alternatives and Political Mobilization in France* (London: Macmillan), pp. 83–96.

Hellheiner, E. (1994). *States and the Re-emergence of Global Finance* (Ithaca, NY: Cornell University Press).

Hilferding, R. (1910). *Finance Capital: A Study in the Latest Phase of Capitalist Development* (Vienna: Wiener Volksbuchhandlung).

Hobson, J. A. (1902 and 1988). *Imperialism: A Study* (London: Unwin Hyman).

Independent (2011). 'British firms attacked for routine use of tax havens', 11 October.

Ingham, G. (1984). *Capitalism Divided? The City and Industry in British Social Development* (Basingstoke: Palgrave Macmillan).

Jay, D. (1962). *Socialism in the New Society* (London: Longman).

Kohl, J. (1981). 'Trends and problems in post-war public expenditure development in western Europe and North America' in P. Flora and A. J. Heidenheimer (eds), *The Development of Welfare States in Europe and North America* (New Brunswick: Transaction), pp. 307–44.

Labour Party (1983). *New Hope for Britain* (London: Labour Party).

Labour Party (1989). *Meet the Challenge, Make the Change* (London: Labour Party).

Labour Party (1994). *Rebuilding the Economy* (London: Labour Party).

Labour Party (1995). *A New Economic Future for Britain* (London: Labour Party).

Labour Party (1997). *New Labour: New Life for Britain* (London: Labour Party).

Lecher, W. (1994). 'The current state of the trade unions in the EU member states: Britain', in W. Lecher (ed.), *Trade Unions in the European Union: A Handbook* (London: Lawrence & Wishart), pp. 129–233.

Lenin, V. I. (1916 and 1996). *Imperialism: The Highest Stage of Capitalist Development* (London: Pluto).

Matthews, R. C. O. (1968). 'Why has Britain had full employment?', *Economic Journal*, 78(3), 555–69.

Observer (1998). Editorial, 29 November.

Parker, G. (2011). 'Germany rebukes UK over Tobin Tax opposition', *Financial Times*, 15 November.

Pimlott, B. (1992). *Harold Wilson* (London: Harper Collins).

Pollard, S. (1970). 'Introduction', in S. Pollard (ed.), *The Gold Standard and Employment Policies between the Wars* (London: Methuen), pp. 1–26.

Pollard, S. (1992). *Development of the British Economy, 1914–1990* (4th edn, London: Edward Arnold).

Reich, R. (1992). *The Work of Nations* (New York: Vintage).

Ritschel, D. (1997). *The Politics of Planning: The Debate on Economic Planning in Britain in the 1930s* (Oxford: Oxford University Press).

Sassoon, D. (1996). *One Hundred Years of Socialism* (London: I.B. Tauris).

Schwarz, H.-P. (1997). *Konrad Adenauer: German Politician and Statesman in a Period of War, Volume II, Revolution and Reconstruction* (Oxford: Berghahn).

Semmel, B. (1960). *Imperialism and Social Reform* (London: Allen & Unwin).

Shaxson, N. (2011). *Treasure Islands: Tax Havens and the Men Who Stole the World* (London: Bodley Head).

Shonfeld, A. (1965). *Modern Capitalism* (Oxford: Oxford University Press).

Stewart, M. (1969). *Keynes and After* (London: Penguin).

Stiglitz, J. (2002). *Globalization and Its Discontents* (London: Penguin).

Telegraph (2010). 'Editorial', 1 December.

Tomlinson, J. (1981). *Problems of British Economic Policy, 1870–1945* (London: Taylor & Francis).

Tomlinson, J. (1997). *Democratic Socialism and Economic Policy: The Attlee Years 1945–51* (Cambridge: Cambridge University Press).

Tomlinson, J. (2004). *The Labour Governments 1964–70* (Manchester: Manchester University Press).

Tomlinson, J. (2004). 'The Labour Party and the City', in R. Michie and P. Williamson (eds), *The British Government and the City of London in the Twentieth Century* (Cambridge: Cambridge University Press), pp. 174–92.

Torr, D. (1956). *Tom Mann and His Times* (London, Lawrence & Wishart), pp. 235–8.

Toye, R. (2003). *The Labour Party and the Planned Economy, 1931–51* (London: Boydell).

Vandenbroucke, E. (1998). *Globalisation, Inequality, and Social Democracy* (London: Institute for Public Policy Research).

Wickham-Jones, M. (1996). *Economic Strategy and the Labour Party* (Basingstoke: Palgrave Macmillan).

Part II

National responses to crisis

6

Coping with TINA:
the Labour Party and
the new crisis of capitalism

Philippe Marlière

Introduction

Relying heavily on its financial services, the British economy has been one of the hardest hit in Europe by the collapse of the banking industry. The credit crunch, aggravated by the bursting of a decade-old house price bubble, has taken a severe toll on the economy. For many commentators, the banking crisis of 2008 marked the end of New Labour economics. The Keynesian style reaction to the crisis by the Gordon Brown government and, subsequently, the election of a new leader eager to turn the page on the New Labour era seem to have opened up the possibility for a renewal of ideas and policy in the Labour ranks. Now in opposition, the Labour Party has a chance to reflect on the meaning of the crisis. The current situation also offers an opportunity to seek an explanation for the financial meltdown and assess New Labour's responsibility in the debacle.

'There is no alternative' – TINA – was the sound bite which Margaret Thatcher, the Conservative Prime Minister, once famously used. This acronym has come to signify that 'there is no alternative' to economic liberalism, that free markets, free trade and capitalist globalisation are the best and only way for modern societies to develop. This has been the Conservative mantra over the past thirty years, but it has also been to a large extent that of New Labour between the mid-1990s and 2008.

Yet, one of the defining characteristics of traditional social democracy in Europe had always been a critique of capitalism. From its origins as a revolutionary political movement in continental Europe (notably in Germany), social democracy has gradually become a force integrated within the capitalist order. This integration has been so effective that social democracy is now one of the central pillars of liberal–capitalist societies (Marlière, 1999: 1). It would therefore be tempting to assess the extent to which the 2008 crisis has forced the Labour Party to rethink its more recent pro-market philosophy and policies.

In order to achieve this, I first attempt to understand the impact of the new major 'crisis of capitalism' on the British economy, the third one since the beginning of the twentieth century. Second, I examine how the Brown government tackled the crisis from 2008 onward. Third, I discuss the extent to which Ed Miliband, the New Labour leader, is committed to breaking away from TINA. Susan George, a prominent critic of neo-liberal globalisation, once opposed TINA by saying: 'There Are Thousands of Alternatives' – TATA (Lees-Galloway, 2009) – which also refers to a political slogan of the alter-globalisation movement that came out of the World Social Forum. So, is TINA on the way out for Miliband's Labour Party? If it is, is new economic thinking being progressively formulated?

The third crisis of capitalism

In September 2008, stock markets around the world started to falter and plummet. A number of banking, mortgage and insurance companies failed. The problems appeared in the American financial system, spread quickly to Britain and later to mainland Europe. This 'contagion effect' (Preston, 2009: 507) prompted the historian Eric Hobsbawm to write that the world was facing the 'most serious crisis of the capitalist system since 1929–33' (2008: 28). Six years later, the crisis still has not receded.

The United Kingdom is presented as a 'liberal market economy' (Hall and Soskice, 2001). A 'liberal market economy' has a 'small state', shuns labour market regulations, and minimises state intervention in the economy through low taxation and modest welfare spending. The liberal state plays the role of a neutral arbiter concerned essentially with keeping open, competitive markets. Labour relations are decentralised and individualistic and trade unions are relatively weak. The state does not try to coordinate labour-management relations. In the United Kingdom, the influence of the City weighs heavily on policy making. 'Financialisation' characterises the British economic system. It aims to make all citizens financial subjects, able to bear the risks and accept responsibility for their own lifestyle decisions. People are ready to take much higher levels of debt to fund those decisions, and therefore in need of the services that 'a rapidly expanding financial services sector could supply' (Gamble, 2009a: 453–4).

To fully appreciate the current political situation in Britain today, it is helpful to briefly examine the political impact of the conservative victory in 1979. From the early 1980s, the 'hard right' was in power in the USA and in the UK. Ronald Reagan and Margaret Thatcher gradually contributed to bring about a new policy paradigm based upon neo-liberal ideas. Those policies were in turn exported to a large number of countries all over the world. They designed a 'smaller state' and they were associated with privatisation, deregulation and supply-side policies. 'Financialisation' was a growing sector of employment in the United Kingdom and was making a major contribution to exports. The success of the financial services meant that the City came to wield increasing political power. From 1986 onward, new regulatory legislation swept away existing rules to attract foreign banks to the City of London and to make it a leading financial centre in the world (Moran, 1990).

In 1997, the Blair government was as much willing to work alongside the City as the Conservatives in office had been. Keeping London as a major financial centre came to be seen as a priority. Brown, the Chancellor, was the zealous supporter of deregulated financial services (Lee, 2007). New Labour also took great pride in presenting itself as the party and government of 'light' financial regulations. This is what Brown was saying in his annual speech at Mansion House as late as June 2006:

> The message London's success sends out to the whole British economy is that we will succeed if, like London, we think globally … if we advance with light touch regulation, a competitive tax environment and flexibility … And just as two years ago we promoted the action plan for liberalising financial services across Europe, I can tell you that the Treasury is now working with Charles McCreevy [European Commissioner for International Markets and Services] and with you to ensure that the forthcoming European financial services white paper signals a new wave of liberalisation … In 2003, just at the time of a previous Mansion House speech, the Worldcom accounting scandal broke. And I will be honest with you, many advised me that we were right not to go down that road which in the United States led to Sarbanes–Oxley, and we were right to build upon our light touch system through the leadership of Sir Callum McCarthy – fair, proportionate, predictable and increasingly risk based. (2006).

After the traumatic exit of the pound from the Exchange Rate Mechanism following Black Wednesday in 1992, the British economy grew steadily for the next sixteen years. This performance contrasted with Britain's post-war experience of 'boom and bust', in which periods of growth were punctuated by sharp contractions, often associated with sterling crisis and balance-of-payments problems. Although elected on a platform to end British economic decline, the Thatcher government had presided over a sharp recession in the early 1980s with unemployment rising to over three million. After implementing severe austerity policies, the Conservatives managed to restart the economy, but the boom was short-lived. By the end of the 1980s, there was another deep recession and a rise in inflation. This recession undermined the position of sterling and led directly to the crisis in 1992. The economic fluctuations between 1979 and 1992 seemed to indicate that the British economy was caught in a permanent cycle of 'boom and bust'.

In office, Chancellor Brown proclaimed the end of 'boom and bust', and boasted that Labour had found the secret of non-inflationary growth (Gamble, 2009a: 451). However, viewed in the international context, the British economic performance was anything but exceptional as there was non-inflationary growth throughout the international economy. Some European countries experienced recessions (notably following the bursting of the dot.com bubble in 2000–01) but, overall, this was a time of prosperity for almost everyone. This period allegedly marked the success of neo-liberal ideas associated with the Washington consensus, notably in the Anglo-American world (Gamble, 2009b).

When the 2008 debacle occurred, proponents of laissez-faire economics argued that these events were purely of a financial nature, and therefore the remedy should be of a technical, not political, order (Garrett, 2011: 281). A majority of commentators have described the recent events as a 'financial crisis'. Others, who are in the minority, believe that things are much more serious than a 'financial crisis'. Some are of the view that we are facing a 'crisis of capitalism' (Gamble, 2009b). This terminology helps emphasise the fact that the current crisis is exceptional, and for that reason that it is inherently political in nature. This crisis creates 'the conditions for the rise of new forms of politics and policy regimes … A crisis of capitalism does not mean the end of capitalism, or even the beginning of the end. It is rather a period when capitalism is reorganised' (Gamble, 2009b: 7). According to this line of reasoning, one can identify two such crises in the past century: the Great Depression of the 1930s and the stagflation of the 1970s (Casey, 2010). Both crises led to dramatic transformations of capitalist economies. The 2008 crisis would thus represent the third crisis of capitalism. If this argument is at all valid, one should wonder what kind of structural, organisational and ideological transformations have been brought about by the 2008 financial meltdown. Did the crisis create a policy shift similar to that from Keynesianism to monetarism in the UK in the 1970s? Did it inspire a new 'policy paradigm' (Hall, 1993: 279)?

The British Labour Party offers a fascinating case study because this party was in office when the banking crisis occurred (2008–10). Furthermore, it is also interesting to see where the party stands on these issues now that it has been back in opposition with a new leader (since September 2010).

The New Labour government and the crisis

The most striking element of continuity in economic policy since 1979 has been the emphasis on controlling inflation (Hodson and Mabbett, 2009: 1044). Thatcher governments identified inflation as a priority to create growth and prosperity. Brown, as Chancellor and as Prime Minister, agreed on that ground with his Conservative predecessors (Brown, 1999). The Labour government followed the Conservative approach of achieving the target by announcing an inflation target and publicising the advice of the Bank of England on the appropriate settings for monetary policy. Policy transparency was intended to influence inflation. The Blair government changed an important aspect of the institutional framework: it granted the newly created Monetary Policy Committee (MPC) operational control over monetary policy. This meant that the Chancellor could no longer go against the Bank's advice in setting the interest rates, as was the common practice prior to 1997. The transfer of the power to set and control interest rates to the Bank of England was seen by commentators as a way to secure an immediate vote of confidence from the markets (King, 1997: 81–97).

The Blair–Brown governments were therefore largely comfortable with the neo-liberal agenda (Hay, 1999; Heffernan, 2001; Marlière, 2008). As Hall put it, the New Labour experiment was essentially neo-liberal, but it contained a 'subaltern programme, of a more social democratic kind, running alongside' (Hall, 2003: 19). In terms of policy *objectives* (as opposed to policy *means*), an element of the old Labour 'ethos', which Blair and Brown accepted, endured. It obliged New Labour to fund and provide public services and social welfare in an effort to reform, in some measure, the socio-economic situation that they had inherited from the Conservatives. For instance, the minimum wage, family credits, indirect use of tax revenues to redistribute resources to the poor and fund increased expenditure on public services (Heffernan, 2011: 166). According to Hay, New Labour 'ceased effectively to be a social democratic party, committed as it had by then become to pervasive neoliberal economic orthodoxy and to a basic acceptance of the legacy of the Thatcher years' (1999: 42). Others, like Heffernan, argued that what was unusual about New Labour was not the endorsement of neo-liberalism, but the use of market instruments to promote reformist goals (2011: 165). New Labour pro-market philosophy was particularly evident in its attitude towards the financial industry. From 1997 onward, Blair's government was keen to celebrate the City of London and promoted deregulation of the financial activities by setting up a 'light-touch regulation system' (Beech, 2009: 529).

Labour's spending plans were largely dependent on the economic growth generated by the financial markets. It was revenues generated by economic growth, and not income or resource redistribution that financed the increase in public expenditure. This procedure was completely in line with the Thatcherite philosophy, according to which economic prosperity can only come from the proceeds of the competitive free market. This model unravelled in the wake of the economic recession prompted by the banking collapse of 2007–08.

On 13 September 2007, Alistair Darling, the Chancellor, took a leading role as the financial crisis unfolded. The Bank of England was then providing emergency support to Northern Rock, one of the country's leading mortgage providers. Northern Rock was a former building society that had demutualised in the 1990s and adopted an aggressive model which involved high leverage and high risk. At some point, the bank was offering 125 per cent mortgages (Gamble, 2009a: 455). Interestingly, in the first weeks of September, only Vince Cable, for the Liberal Democrats, was calling for the immediate nationalisation of Northern Rock. The Labour government clearly did not want to become involved in running banks because it did not want to damage the markets' confidence in the City (Gamble, 2009a: 456).

On 14 and 17 September, long queues formed outside Northern Rock's branches. Panic was only diffused when the government declared that it would guarantee all deposits in the bank. The government provided capital to Northern Rock, and the bank was eventually nationalised. The Brown government, while intervening in order to prevent a complete default and to guarantee the funds of depositors, persisted for many months in trying to find a private sector solution for Northern Rock.

The government's stand on Northern Rock exposed worrying deficiencies in the existing institutional framework, whereby the Financial Services Compensation Scheme provided a 100 per cent guarantee on only the first £2,000 deposits. On 1 October 2007, the Financial Services Authority (FSA) raised this limit to £35,000 and subsequently to £50,000. Shortly after this, the government committed itself to guaranteeing all retail-bank deposits in the UK (Hodson and Mabbett, 2009: 1051).

In the wake of Lehman's collapse, Lloyds TSB, with direct support from the Brown government, purchased HBOS, the largest mortgage lender in the UK until then. A couple of weeks later, the government nationalised Bradford & Bingley. On 8 October 2008, Brown and Darling announced a massive bank bail-out, including £50 billion of cash for equity swaps, £100 billion in short-term loans from the Bank of England, and another £250 billion in loan guarantees. Five days later, the government announced that the Royal Bank of Scotland, Lloyds TSB and HBOS would receive £37 billion between them in exchange for equity stakes of roughly 60 per cent for RBS and 40 per cent for the merged Lloyds TSB and HBOS. The government would also have a say in how the nationalised banks were run (Casey, 2010: 14).

The Labour government was also slower than its US counterpart to recognise that the credit crunch required a change of interest rate policy. The Bank of England cut its interest rate, but it did so more cautiously than the Federal Reserve. A majority of members on the Bank's Monetary Policy Committee believed that the greatest danger was from inflation not recession (Gamble, 2009a: 456).

Having averted the collapse of the banking sector, the Labour government was willing to revive growth, and it pursued massive stimulus packages from November 2008 onward; Darling approved a £21 billion pound stimulus package. The bulk of the stimulus came through a reduction of VAT from 17.5 per cent to 15 per cent. The threat to the British economy was avoided, although at the cost of soaring budget deficits (Quinn, 2011: 406).

The net result of fiscal and monetary stimulus has been mixed. After a sharp recession in 2009, anaemic growth – largely a jobless one – has returned in 2010 and 2011. These results were obtained at a terrible cost for the public finances.

Deficits reached 11.3 per cent of GDP in 2009. In the UK, GDP dropped around 8 per cent and unemployment rose by 8 per cent (Casey, 2010: 16).

In the aftermath of the financial meltdown of 2007–08, the Labour Party found it hard to adjust to the new political and ideological landscape. The financial sector was badly damaged and the neo-liberal ideas which sustained it had been discredited. Bankers became hate figures, on a level with estates agents, journalists and politicians (Gamble, 2009a: 457). However, nothing seems to have changed since 2008: bankers continue to operate as they did before the beginning of the crisis. For instance, more than 100 bankers at RBS were paid more than £1 million and total bonus payouts reached nearly £1 billion in 2010, even though the bailed-out bank reported losses of £1.1 billion for 2010. Len McCluskey, the General Secretary of Unite, declared: 'Taxpayers will be baffled as to how it is possible that while we own 84 per cent of this bank [RBS], it continues to so handsomely reward its investment bankers. This is an institution in which over 21,000 front-line and support staff has been sacked' (Treanor, 2011: 7).

However, some commentators have argued that the sharp increase in government borrowing and the suspension of the fiscal rules constitute an ideational or even a paradigmatic shift at the heart of New Labour, and away from monetarism. The strongly interventionist stand of the Labour government since the start of the crisis has signalled, for some, a shift towards a rather radical Keynesian agenda. Proponents of this thesis argue that 'Brown and his Chancellor, Alistair Darling, have rediscovered the political economy of ... Keynes' (Lee, 2009: 30). Commentators – notably in the Murdoch press – presented these measures as marking the end of New Labour. The *Sun* newspaper argued that New Labour had finally succumbed to 'socialism' (Fielding, 2012: 657).

Others – among whom one finds the majority of academic commentators – have argued that there is indeed little evidence to suggest that the New Labour government did revert towards a more Keynesian paradigm based on expenditure of goods and services or increasing transfer payments. More than half of the deterioration in the fiscal balance has occurred as a result of the financial crisis (Hodson and Mabbett, 2009: 1053). These expenditures did not directly help raise household income or boost the demand for goods and services. The bailouts were essentially intended to revive the supply of credit.

In the case of monetary policy, the instrument of quantitative easing was ad hoc policies in order to address pressing financial problems, but they did not alter the relationship between the government and the banks. As for fiscal policy, the borrowing government rose sharply in response to the global financial crisis, but this change had more to do with the costs of the bank bailouts than with the Chancellor's rather modest stimulus package. When it comes to the financial sphere, the Northern Rock financial crisis prompted the Brown government to introduce a new policy instrument with the creation of a special resolution

regime. However, the government did not introduce macro-prudential regulatory instruments that might have helped reduce the ability of the City to profit
from the next boom (Hodson and Mabbett, 2009: 1058).

The crisis has exposed the flawed economic policies and beliefs at the heart
of New Labour: the lack of attention to financial stability and concerns over
the ability of existing instruments to deliver asset price stability. New Labour
reckoned that fiscal discipline would bring about balanced economic growth and
steadily raising investment. This belief has been profoundly shaken as a result of
the crisis.

By the end of 2009, Alistair Darling and Peter Mandelson felt that the most
effective way to win back lost voters was to demonstrate the government's
economic competence. They argued that Labour had to be open about the
need for massive cuts given that public spending was set to account for 53 per
cent of GDP by 2010. Gordon Brown and Ed Balls, then Secretary of State for
Children, Schools and Families, wanted to promise some future spending in
health and education (Fielding, 2012: 658). In March 2010, in his Pre-Budget
Report, Darling announced that a re-elected Labour government would cut
spending on a scale 'deeper and tougher' than under Thatcher, and would halve
the deficit by the end of the next parliament. This was a deliberate attempt to
sound like the Conservatives on the issue of deficit (Fielding, 2012: 659). Yet
differences between the two parties remained. Darling intended to start the cuts
in 2011 in order to allow the economy to recover. He also planned to tax the
wealthier classes and to raise £6 billion by increasing the National Insurance
on higher earners. A survey carried out in May 2010 showed that there was
no majority in favour of making major cuts in spending and public services to
reduce the debt: 45 per cent were in favour, against 46 per cent who supported
raising taxes broadly and cutting spending and services less (Greenberg Quinlan
Rosner Research, 2010).

The political consensus on cuts and austerity proved disastrous for both the
Labour and conservative parties. Faced with an absence of choice, the electorate failed to give a majority to any of the two major parties. It was clear that
with 29.1 per cent of the share of the votes – its worst electoral result since
1918 – Labour had lost the 2010 general election. Voters blamed Labour for the
economic crisis and were of the view that the recession had destroyed Labour's
reputation for economic competence (Quinn, 2011: 403–11).

New leader, new ideas?

According to Katwala, then General Secretary of the Fabian Society, neither
Blair nor Brown ever attempted a 'frank audit' of Thatcherism (2009: 11).
This amounts to an acknowledgement by this party insider that although New
Labour had a mandate for some important policy shifts, it neither achieved, nor

attempted a deep realignment of British politics. Would Ed Miliband be a post-New Labour leader, and challenge Thatcher's TINA mantra?

In the run-up to the campaign for the leadership of the Labour Party, Ed Miliband was, of all the main contenders, the most vocal critic of New Labour (Jobson and Wickam-Jones, 2010: 525–48). He was the one who presented himself as the true alternative to New Labour and its pro-market philosophy. This is arguably an ironic claim from someone who had been so deeply embedded in New Labour governments. First, Ed Miliband was an adviser to Brown and later as a New Labour cabinet minister between 2005 and 2010.

Ed Miliband's leadership campaign revolved around three main ideas: (a) he proposed a Keynesian-style approach to deficit reduction; (b) he committed himself to combat social inequalities; (c) he promoted an interventionist state; that is, a state in charge of regulating market capitalism and of stimulating economic growth and social justice. Miliband was critical of the coalition's programme of deficit reduction and cuts in public spending. The Labour leader argued that those cuts would harm the most vulnerable in society. Instead of severe spending cuts aimed at halving the public deficit in four years, the new Labour leader proposed a living wage, a graduate tax to replace the unpopular tuition fees and a progressive approach to taxation (Hasan and Macintyre, 2011: 227).

During the party leadership contest, Ed Balls, another candidate and a former close ally of Brown, had argued that the thrust of both the Coalition's and Darling's deficit plans were 'too deep and too fast' (Wintour, 2010: 6). By appointing Balls as shadow Chancellor, Ed Miliband could have encouraged a more 'left-wing' approach than the austerity choice made by Darling. Miliband eventually chose Alan Johnson, a Blairist who had supported Darling's stand over the deficit (Watt, 2010: 8). Moreover, Johnson was lukewarm about the top rate of income tax which had been introduced by the Brown government. When Johnson unexpectedly resigned in January 2011, Miliband eventually appointed Balls, a choice that marked a slight shift towards a more 'Keynesian' style approach to secure future growth.

The newly elected leader insisted that it was time to go 'beyond' New Labour. He said in a speech in Gillingham on 27 November 2010, and announced a two-year review of Labour Party policy. These reviews allegedly aim to rethink the assumptions that guided New Labour (Prabhakar, 2011: 32). In the first speech following his election as party leader in September 2010, Ed Miliband attempted to set out a new agenda for the Labour Party. He distanced himself from New Labour on policy issues and he detached himself from Brownite 'boom and bust' (Jobson and Wickham-Jones, 2010: 526).

In a speech at the Fabian Society in January 2011, Ed Miliband spelled out his economic vision in more detail and was also very critical of New Labour in power (Miliband, 2011a). He argued that New Labour had failed on three counts. First, he said that it was important to understand why the economy had stopped working for the people, and how Labour could offer a new economic model. Second, Miliband recognised that New Labour managerialism took the government away from the 'instincts and values of the broad progressive majority in Britain'. He argued that New Labour came to be seen as the 'people who put markets and commerce before the common good'. Third, he admitted that New Labour did not manage to build a 'broad, open progressive majority'. Ironically, the Labour leader attacked the 'Conservative fallacy that markets always know best', failing to acknowledge that this had been Blair–Brown thinking over the past 15 years. He then moved on to attack bankers: 'I want us to articulate the frustration of people who are fed up with bankers taking vast public subsidies and then rewarding themselves for failure while the rest of the country struggles.' This was a comment that neither Blair nor Brown would have contemplated making. However, this is also a fairly safe point to make today given the profound unpopularity of bankers among the British public. Furthermore, Miliband acknowledged that the New Labour government did not get 'banking regulation rights'. With him, taxing high earners and bonuses was no longer a taboo subject. Miliband called on the government to extend a £3.5 billion tax on bankers' bonuses for another year (Stratton and Wintour, 2011: 5). This measure was a step down from an earlier claim that the government's one-off tax on bankers' bonuses should be made permanent (*The Independent*, 2011: 9). Later, the Labour leader led the chorus of critics who forced Stephen Hester, the RBS boss, to abandon his plan to take a £1 million bonus (84 per cent of the bank is now owned by the government after being rescued by taxpayers' money in 2008). After criticising Network Rail directors for seeking large bonuses, Miliband broadened his attack on the Coalition by calling a Commons vote and by urging an end to the 'bonus culture'. In February 2012, Ed Miliband argued that 'all companies must show responsibility, but banks have a particular responsibility, because they are either directly or indirectly supported by the taxpayer' (Wintour, 2012: 28). He called for 'one nation banking', claiming that 'if banks do not change their ways, the only result will be further isolation from society, greater public anger, and an economy which does not pay its way'. This did not mean a condemnation of bonuses in theory on his part, but he warned that 'exceptional rewards for exceptional performance means that the kind of huge bonuses which have caused such controversy recently should not be handed out for just doing your job. They should not be a one-way bet' (Wintour, 2012: 28).

In stark contrast with New Labour, the new party leader has signalled his support for the European Commission's proposals to introduce a financial transaction tax. This very modest tax would see a 0.1 per cent charge on stock and bond trading and 0.01 per cent on derivatives contracts. The European Union predicts that it would raise £50 billion a year (Tolley, 2011). Later, Miliband seemed to change his mind on the proposed tax, saying that it was unfeasible (Beckett, 2012: 14).

Turning his back on over a decade of New Labour policies, Ed Miliband has asserted that 'free markets combined with "light-touch" regulation were sold to Middle Britain on the basis that they would guarantee economic freedom, rising living standards and a fair reward for the hard-working majority'. Following the banking debacle, Miliband seems to have given up on a number of New Labour ideas and policies. He thinks that after eleven years of a Labour government, the 'squeezed middle' is not better off, as people have become 'too reliant on personal debt and financial services'. Today, wealth creation and social justice 'need to be built into the way our economy works'.

Miliband dismissed Conservative thinking on the causes of the crisis. He objected to the idea that it 'was high levels of public borrowing that caused the crisis'. The Labour leader conversely argued that it was the 'crisis that caused high levels of public borrowing' and denied that the solution to the crisis should consist of cutting back spending completely.

Miliband argued that the New Labour tradition which embraced markets 'is also important for [people's] future and for creating wealth'. He nonetheless believes that his party would also need to draw on 'that other tradition based on mutualism, localism and the common bonds of solidarity'.

'Responsible' capitalism

Together with a Keynesian approach to deficit reduction and a concern with rising inequalities, Ed Miliband launched an attack on 'predatory capitalism' and called for 'responsible capitalism'. He first coined the expression at the 2011 Labour Party annual conference (Miliband, 2011b). The speech was seen by some as a major shift in Labour policy. Seumas Milne, a left-wing *Guardian* columnist, wrote that it was the most radical speech by a Labour leader for a generation as it signalled an 'unmistakeable break with the corporate consensus of the past three decades and the model of unfettered market capitalism this has enforced' (2011: 24). In an essay subsequently published on the topic, Miliband essentially described 'responsible' capitalism not as an 'economy based on predatory, short-term speculation', but one in which there is 'a more active role for government in making the market economy work' (2012a).

Ed Miliband is said to be receptive to Glasman's ideas. Glasman, a London-based academic, has coined the expression 'Blue Labour' ('Blue' as in small-c conservatism) to mark an intellectual and political break with the New Labour experiment. According to Glasman, Ed Miliband's Labour needs to value tradition a bit more to relearn some of the lessons of its pre-1945 past. Back then, the party was allegedly more concerned about solidarity and community, and it was not comfortable with the 'filthy rich' (as Mandelson famously once put it).

He also believes that 'Old' labour was 'worse', as it was 'entirely disengaged from democracy in the economy'. For Glasman, 'Blue Labour' is about rediscovering the Labour tradition and its critical relationship with capitalism (Glasman *et al.*, 2011). He argues that Labour politics should be rooted in the democratic resistance to the commodification of human beings. The Labour Party should promote local communities and stress the importance of human association, of relationship building, and of solidarity: 'Labour must establish those conversations that broker a common good within party organisations such as Progress, the Fabians, Compass and the Christian Socialist Movement and build a common programme' (Glasman, 2011: 32). Glasman is critical of Blair and Brown who 'were recklessly naive about finance capital and the City of London and relentlessly managerial in their methods. [Blair's] concept of modernisation [verged] on the demented: a conception of globalisation understood entirely on the terms set by finance capital' (Glasman, 2011: 32). Glasman's views on the banking system are bolder and more demanding than Ed Miliband's: 'The control of the City of London in regional investment must be broken and local banks established that could enable people to have meaningful jobs and live closer to their parents.'

In line with 'Blue Labour' thinking, Ed Miliband sees in our current circumstances a 'quiet crisis that is unfolding day by day in kitchens and living rooms in every town, village, and city up down this country' (Harvie and Milburn, 2011: 16). The Labour leader describes a crisis of 'social reproduction' – that is, a breakdown in the ability of individuals, families and communities to educate and care for one another, and to develop. These, Miliband argues, are the consequences of more than three decades of neo-liberal policies (privatisations and marketisation). However, when it comes to new ideas and new policies, Miliband seems as bereft of new thinking as other political leaders.

At the 2011 Labour Party conference in Liverpool, Miliband reckoned that British voters are ready to break from what he calls 'the old settlement' established by Thatcher and largely continued by Blair and Brown:

> I think there is a new centre ground in politics. And this is where I am moving on from New Labour. The old centre ground said you would demand responsibility at the bottom, but you do not talk about it at the top because there are vested interests that are too powerful to take on ... There's a new centre ground about saying inequality is not just a problem because of the gap between the rich and the poor, but between the rich and everybody else. (quoted in Rawnsley and Helm, 2011: 24)

Miliband blamed the 'economic system', and called for a 'new economy' that rewarded 'producers' and not 'predators', or 'wealth creators' instead of 'asset strippers'. The Labour leader hinted at the direction he might like to take: government intervention to reshape the corporate sector, as well as employee representation on top paying committees.

Miliband and Balls have promised to use the proceeds from selling RBS and Lloyds to pay down debt. It remains a very modest contribution to solving the credit crisis. It, for instance, ignores the case for turning the part-nationalised banks into public investment banks to drive recovery. This is an idea which has been floated by Adam Posen, a member on the Bank of England's Monetary Policy Committee, or the *Financial Times* journalist, Brittan (2011: 18).

Interestingly, these comments were accompanied by others more in line with the New Labour legacy. Miliband reminded the audience in Liverpool that a 'generation ago a Labour leader came to the Conference to condemn the behaviour of a Labour Council in Liverpool'. The Militant tendency, the 'Hard Left' of the Labour Party, played a leading role in the Liverpool City Council between 1983 and 1987. He warned that a future Labour government will not be able to reverse 'many of the cuts this government is making', adding that if the Coalition in office 'fails to deal with the deficit in this Parliament, we are determined to do so'. Miliband also underlined important elements of continuity with Thatcherism and Blairism: he argued that Thatcher was 'right to change the rule on the closed shop, on strikes before ballots'. Furthermore, Ed Miliband denounced the public sector workers' strike at a union rally in London in June 2011 against the cuts in public services (Wintour, 2011: 7). He reiterated his anti-strike stance before the delegates at the TUC annual congress' and he went on to back the Hutton report on pensions (Mulholland and Milmo, 2011: 6) which angered the unions for increasing the amount of pension contributions and for further delaying the retirement age (TUC, 2010).

Miliband asserted that Labour remains 'a party that understood wealth creation as well as its distribution, that we needed for economic prosperity as well as social justice, and that solving our society's problems could not be done without a partnership between government and business' (2010). These are words which could have directly come from the New Labour playbook. Critics have also stressed that it is virtually impossible for the current Labour leadership – notably Ed Balls – to be critical of the current economic situation, as it was complicit in the regulatory failures of the 2000s (Cohen, 2011: 37).

All these things considered, one may point out notable rhetorical differences between the Labour Party and the Coalition government. Ed Miliband, for instance, supported – albeit cautiously – the Occupy movement at St Paul's Cathedral in London, arguing that it represented a 'challenge to the Church, to business and also to politics' (Miliband, 2011c). He has also insisted that the deficit 'had to be reduced, but in a steady and balanced way' (Miliband, 2012b).

This being said, it is rather hard to find major policy disagreements between the Labour Party and the Coalition. For instance, Labour has accepted every spending cut being imposed by the Coalition and has endorsed George Osborne's public sector pay freeze. Balls has even admitted that it might need to continue beyond the end of the current parliament (Batty, 2012: 8). Len McCluskey, the general secretary of Unite union, declared on that occasion that this was 'the last gasp of New Labour's neo-liberalism which led to 2008'. He added that 'Ed

Balls's sudden embrace of austerity and the public sector pay squeeze represents a victory for discredited Blairism at the expense of the party's core supporters' (McCluskey, 2012). McCluskey also condemned Balls's 'fallacy that increasing the wages of the low-paid risks unemployment' and reminded that 'the view that deficit reduction through spending cuts must be a priority in order to keep the financial speculators onside has been the road to ruin for Labour chancellors from Philip Snowden to Denis Healey' (2012).

Conclusion

In the end, did the 2008 crisis bring about a paradigmatic shift from monetarist policies to Keynesian style policies? In other words, is the blind belief in TINA being eroded in Labour ranks?

As we have seen, the Brown response to the crisis fell short of real economic realignment. There was indeed an increase in government borrowing and the fiscal rules were suspended. This constitutes an unorthodox move from monetarist orthodoxy. That said, it does not represent an ideational or even a paradigmatic shift away from monetarism. There is little if no evidence at all to suggest that the Labour government's intentions were to permanently revert to a more Keynesian style paradigm based on expenditures on goods and services or increasing transfer payments. The expenditures incurred by the government were an ad hoc reaction in order to revive the supply of credit and to prevent the complete collapse of the banking sector. The injection of cash did not directly help raise household income or to boost the demand for goods and services.

Ed Miliband's personal handling of the crisis has so far been patchy and vague. He has made several harsh comments on the 'bankers' greed' or on the free markets in a number of speeches. The Labour leader has also committed his party to somewhat restricting the power of 'unfettered markets' (tax on bankers' bonuses or on financial transactions), but these words have not yet translated into party policy. Furthermore, they seem very moderate in scope, and do not mount a comprehensive challenge against the neo-liberal world and the TINA narrative.

Under 'Red Ed', the Labour Party does not seem intent on challenging the economic ideology and the political narrative which have so dramatically wrecked the world economies and impoverished entire populations. Yet even proponents of neo-liberalism acknowledge that people have had enough with free market ideology. As a leader of the *Financial Times* put it in October 2011: 'A month ago the disparate band of protestors who set up camp in downtown Manhattan's Zuccotti Park to decry the excesses of capitalism were seen as little more than idealistic youth, doing what youth tend to do. Today only the fool-hardy would dismiss a movement reflecting the anger and frustration of ordinary citizens from all walks of life across the world' (*Financial Times*, 2011: 12).

References

Batty, D. (2012) 'Ed Balls lays out Labour plan to regain economic stability', *Guardian*, 14 January.

Beckett, A. (2012). 'Ed Miliband: keep calm and carry on?', *Guardian*, 14 January.

Beech, M. (2009). 'No new vision: the gradual death of British social democracy', *Political Quarterly*, 80(4), 526–32.

Brittan, S. (2011). 'Use the UK's state bank holdings to speed a recovery', *Financial Times*, 23 September.

Brown, G. (1999). 'The conditions for full employment', Mais Lecture, Cass Business School, City University, London.

Brown, G. (2006). '2006 Mansion House speech', full text, 2 June, www.guardian.co.uk/business/2006/jun/22/politics.economicpolicy.

Casey, T. (2010). 'The end of the affair? Free Market Capitalism in the US and the UK after the financial crisis', paper prepared for 'The UK and US in 2010: transition and transformation', American Political Science Association Annual Conference, George Washington University, Washington, DC, 1 September.

Cohen, N. (2011). 'Labour's wretched lack of backbone over banks', *Observer*, 11 September.

Fielding, S. (2012). 'Labour's campaign: things can only get…worse', *Parliamentary Affairs*, 63(4), 667–88.

Financial Times (2011). 'America wakes to the din of inequity', 16 October.

Gamble, A. (2009a). 'British politics and the financial crisis', *British Politics*, 4(4), 450–62.

Gamble, A. (2009b). *The Spectre at the Feast: Capitalist Crisis and the Politics of Recession* (Basingstoke: Macmillan).

Garrett, M. (2011). 'Britain. Social work in a "broken society"', *European Journal of Social Work*, 14(2), 281–6.

Glasman, M. (2011). 'My blue Labour vision can defeat the coalition', *Guardian*, 24 April.

Glasman, M., Rutherford, J., Stears, M. and White, S. (eds) (2011). *The Labour Tradition and the Politics of Paradox*, available at: www.lwbooks.co.uk/ebooks/labour_tradition_politics_paradox.html.

Greenberg Quinlan Rosner Research (2010). 'UK post-election questionnaire', 7–9 May, available at: www.greenbergresearch.com/articles/2445/5674_ukeu050910fq.uk.pdf.

Hall, P. A. (1993). 'Policy paradigms, social learning, and the state: the case of economic policymaking in Britain', *Comparative Politics*, 25(3), 275–96.

Hall, P. A. and Soskice, D. (eds) (2001). *Varieties of Capitalism: The Institutional Foundations of Comparative Advantage* (New York: Oxford University Press).

Hall, S. (2003). 'New Labour's double-shuffle', *Soundings*, 24, 10–24.

Harvie, D. and Milburn, K. (2011). 'Ed Miliband's "quiet crisis" is down to capitalism', *Guardian*, 27 September.

Hasan, M. and Macintyre, J. (2011). *Ed: The Milibands and the Making of a Labour Leader* (London: Biteback).

Hay, C. (1999). *The Political Economy of New Labour: Labouring Under False Pretences?* (Manchester: Manchester University Press).

Heffernan, R. (2001). *New Labour and Thatcherism: Political Change in Britain* (Basingstoke: Palgrave Macmillan).

Heffernan, R. (2011). 'Labour's New Labour legacy: politics after Blair and Brown', *Political Studies Review*, 9(2), 163–77.

Hobsbawm, E. (2008). 'The £500bn question', *Guardian*, 9 October.

Hodson, H. and Mabbett, D. (2009). 'UK economic policy and the global financial crisis: paradigm lost?', *Journal of Common Market Studies*, 47(5), 1041–61.

The Independent (2011). 'Ed Miliband: "We need to raise taxes for the better-off"', 30 August.

Jobson, R. and Wickham-Jones, M. (2010). 'Gripped by the past: nostalgia and 2010 Labour Party leadership contest', *British Politics*, 5(4), 525–48.

Katwala, S. (2009). 'In Maggie's shadow', *Public Policy Research*, 16(1), 3–13.

King, M. (1997). 'Changes in UK monetary policy: rules and discretion in practice', *Journal of Monetary Economics*, 39(1), 81–97.

Lee, S. (2007). *Best for Britain? The Politics and Legacy of Gordon Brown* (Oxford: Oneworld).

Lee, S. (2009). 'The rock of stability? The political economy of the Brown government', *Policy Studies*, 30(1), 17–32.

Lees-Galloway, I. (2009). 'There are alternatives to explore', *Transnational Institute*, May, available at: www.tni.org/archives/media_manawatu0509.

McCluskey, L. (2012). 'Ed Miliband's leadership is threatened by this Blairite policy coup', *Guardian*, 16 January.

Marlière, P. (1999). 'Introduction: European social democracy in situ', in R. Ladrech and P. Marlière (eds), *Social Democratic Parties in the European Union: History, Organization, Policies* (Basingstoke: Macmillan), pp. 1–15.

Marlière, P. (2008). *La social-démocratie domestiquée: La voie blairiste* (Bruxelles: Editions Aden).

Miliband, E. (2010). 'Speech to the Confederation of the British Industry', 25 October, available at: www.cbi.org.uk/pdf/20101025–cbi-ed-miliband-speech.pdf.

Miliband, E. (2011a). 'Speech to the Fabians', London, 15 January, available at: www.newstatesman.com/blogs/the-staggers/2011/01/labour-government-politics.

Miliband, E. (2011b). 'Speech to the 2011 Labour Party conference', available at: www.labour.org.uk/ed-milibands-speech-to-labour-party-conference.

Miliband, E. (2011c). 'Aspects of business, finance and politics seem out of touch with 99% of people', *Observer*, 6 November.

Miliband, E. (2012a). 'Building a responsible capitalism', *Juncture*, 25 May, available at: www.ippr.org/juncture/171/9200/building-a-responsible-capitalism.

Miliband, E. (2012b). 'Speech on the economy', OXO Tower, London, 10 January, full transcript, *New Statesman*, 10 January, available at: www.newstatesman.com/uk-politics/2012/01/labour-government-money.

Milne, S. (2011). 'Now Ed Miliband's challenge is to put his stamp on the Labour Party', *Guardian*, 28 November.

Moran, M. (1990). *The Politics of the Financial Services Revolution: The US, the UK and Japan* (Basingstoke: Palgrave Macmillan).

Mulholland, H. and Milmo, D. (2011). 'Miliband heckled after telling TUC pension strikes were mistake', *Guardian*, 13 September.

Prabhakar, R. (2011). 'What is the legacy of New Labour?', in S. Lee and M. Beech (eds), *The Cameron–Clegg Government. Coalition Politics in an Age of Austerity* (Basingstoke: Palgrave Macmillan), pp. 75–88.

Preston, P. (2009). 'The other side of the coin: reading the politics of the 2008 financial tsunami', *British Journal of Politics and International Relations*, 11(3), 504–17.

Quinn, T. (2011). 'From New Labour to new politics: the British general election of 2010', *West European Politics*, 34(2), 403–11.

Rawnsley, A. and Helm, T. (2011). 'Miliband launches his vision for "New society and new ethics"', *Observer*, 25 September.

Stratton, A. and Wintour, P. (2011). 'Ed Miliband calls on government to extend banker bonus tax', *Guardian*, 10 January.

Tolley, S. (2011). 'Miliband gives support in financial transaction tax', *MoneyMarketing*, 6 October, available at www.moneymarketing.co.uk/politics/miliband-gives-support-on-financial-transaction-tax/1039021.article.

Treanor, J. (2011). 'RBS bankers get £950m in bonuses despite £1.1bn loss', *Guardian*, 24 February.

TUC (2010). 'TUC response to Hutton review', TUC, 7 October, available at www.tuc.org.uk/economy/tuc-18609-f0.cfm.

Watt, N. (2010). 'Alan Johnson backs Alistair Darling's deficit reduction plan', *Guardian*, 8 October.

Wintour, P. (2010). 'Darling and Balls clash over Labour's deficit plans', *Guardian*, 27 September.

Wintour, P. (2011). 'Ed Miliband booed at Union rally after attacking public sector strikers', *Guardian*, 30 June.

Wintour, P. (2012). 'Ed Miliband to call Commons vote on bonuses', *Guardian*, 2 February.

7

Losing social democracy: reflections on the erosion of a paradigmatic case of social democracy

Jenny Andersson

Introduction

Swedish social democracy has long since lost its hegemonic position in domestic politics. Depending on how we draw the historical time line, the party has been in trouble since at least 2002, in other words well before the 2006 election, when it lost to the Swedish right, and the 2010 election, when it scored its worst result in parliamentary elections since 1914. In fact the party has not been truly hegemonic in Swedish politics since the late 1960s, and its crisis is therefore not merely a question of recent developments but should be historicised and understood over a much longer period.

Nevertheless, the situation since 2006 is itself relevant to our understanding of the way that social democracy's capacity of action in the present suffers from a series of historical mistakes that it has performed over time, and particularly in the restructuring process of the 1990s. The main argument of this chapter is that the consequences of these mistakes are today actively circumscribing social democracy's capacity for reformism on the strategic as well as on the ideological level. Some of these consequences, I propose, have long-term effects and effectively hinder social democracy's current capacity for reformism. While my explanation of social democracy's crisis is therefore *endogenous* in the sense that I see it as arising from strategic and ideological miscalculations within social democracy, I also argue that the consequences of these calculations are now acting as structural constraints on social democracy. In other words, it could be proposed that the ideological legacy of the Third Way is exerting a heavy influence on social democracy's capacity to respond to crisis. The chapter considers three dimensions to this: first, there is the question of ideology and world-view and particularly the way that social democratic ideology has, since the 1990s, been oriented around market making and the middle-class subject; second, there is the question of institutional change and the privatisations and financialisation of the Swedish model; and, third, an issue that is not dealt with specifically in the chapter but is part of the background, there is the question of the many conflicts and factions that run through social democratic party organisations today so that one might even ask the question whether they are really one organisation or several competing ones. These fractures are legacies of the 'modernisation' embarked on in the 1980s and 1990s. While I think that these things apply to social democracy in Europe on a more general level, I propose that the paradigmatic role played by Swedish social democracy in the history of European labourism makes the case particularly illustrative for our current understanding of what social democracy is.

I will begin this chapter with a short description about key events in party life since 2006 and I will use the rest of the chapter to argue what I think is the real meaning of what may seem, on the surface, to be a series of power struggles and scandals.

Events since 2006

In Swedish politics, the lost election in 2006 meant the end of 'the long 1990s', the decade marked by the recession in the beginning of the 1990s and by the rise to political power of Göran Persson, former party leader, Minister of Education and then Finance under Ingvar Carlsson, and Prime Minister from 1996 to 2006. When Persson came to power in 1996, the SAP had firmly adopted the Third Way since the writing of the so-called 'Crisis programme', which paved the way for its return to governmental politics in 1982, but which also signalled the end of Keynesianism and the beginning of a long series of new public management reforms in the public sector (SAP, 1981). In fact the apparently successful transformation of Swedish social democracy, from its traditional functional socialism into a liberal leaning market embracing centre left party, was a fundamental influence on the European Third way, as it took form more than a decade later under Blair and Schröder (Andersson, 2006, 2009, 2010). Under Persson, changes were implemented not only in Sweden's social model but also in the party organisation that had enduring effects. Important parts of the party's traditional elite were marginalised and lost voice, making certain key advisers (later Minister of Finance Per Nuder, Jens Henriksson, Margareta Andersson, both with close links to New Labour) directly influential. While the party had already entered into a fundamental conflict with the trade unions over its first attempt at monetary policy after 1982, this was now a further sidestepping of the party's traditional apparatus. In particular, the trade union economists that had been highly influential in the development of social democratic economic and social policy in Sweden since the immediate post-war period were marginalised as the party started depending on its own advisers for economic and social analysis. These microeconomic architects and advisers continued the process of reforming the public sector, particularly by the overseeing of the budget process including the golden rule and the pursuit of key supply-side orientations in employment and social policy. Active labour market policies were effectively replaced with activation, as part of new efforts to tackle persisting unemployment after 1996. Activation, however, was a measure built on significantly different values from the old 'model'. Other reforms, in particular the radical pension reform in 1994, were decidedly market oriented, and intended to restore international confidence in the Swedish welfare state, but would also turn out to have important consequences for future pension levels.

The election loss in 2006 was first interpreted as a general fatigue with Persson, and second, as having been lost over two vital issues – jobs, in other words, persisting problems with long-term unemployment particularly among the young, and the question of the urban middle class. Important parts of the party elite interpreted the lost election as being due to a too soft approach to benefits and work. The route back to power, according to this analysis, was through the toughening up of party discourse, including themes of obligation and duty in the labour market, and order and discipline in schools. The new leader Mona Sahlin, from 2006, therefore embarked on a political strategy, which consisted of being tough. She was supported by young social democrats on the party's right with good connections to the media and to some of the key PR firms and think tanks. Subsequently, in 2010, when Sahlin lost a second election to Fredrik Reinfeldt's Alliance and was pushed to step down, it seemed that the left flank of the party might be gaining an upper hand. This impression was strengthened not only by international developments, including Ed Miliband's election as Labour Party leader in the UK, but also by the outcome of the election. The 2010 election changed the political landscape to the extent that there was now a real cost associated with being in the centre, since other parties were delighted to play the opposition. The elections saw the arrival into Parliament of the radical populist right, Sverigedemokraterna (SD), and a second term for the right-wing alliance led by Fredrik Reinfeldt's conservative Moderate Party. Meanwhile the SAP was now a much smaller party than before, meaning it could no longer very credibly behave like the natural party of government. While old players like the left (Vänsterpartiet), the Christian Democrats (Kristdemokraterna), the Liberal Party (Folkpartiet) and Centerpartiet were increasingly weak, the Greens (Miljöpartiet) and the Sweden Democrats (Sverigedemokraterna, SD) seemed poised to become major actors. Both these parties are successful rivals to social democracy, for middle-class votes (the former) and blue-collar and senior votes (the latter), they are unsure of their left–right alliances, and ready to bargain for ministerial posts and influence with whoever is in a position to form a government.

If the 2006 election, then, meant that Swedish social democracy was faced with a credible and surprisingly solid governmental alternative on the right in the shape of the so-called Alliance, the 2010 election now meant that the political landscape became volatile, due to the size of previously small parties and particularly to the growing influence of SD. This context, past the 2010 election and with falling popularity numbers for Prime Minister Reinfelt, could have presented an opportunity for the party, and several observers argued that an electoral space seemed to be opening up on the left. To some extent the party did move to the left, in the leadership disaster that began with the appointing (in a closed committee) of the formerly rather marginal figure of Hakan Juholt. From the Juholt debacle, some of the fragility of the SAP in the present became very clear. Juholt was an impulsive leader with inexperienced advisers, who were largely young members of the left of the party. He underestimated the hold of the party apparatus by certain Stockholm elites, and he also underestimated the links between these groups and the media. He also made several very clumsy volte faces on key political issues. The left's main tabloid *Aftonbladet* could therefore quickly dismiss him as having a political compass 'spinning like crazy' and Juholt also quickly became the target of a media orchestrated campaign in which he was accused of misuse of public money, while no serious offence was proved (Kielos, 2011). After the media had laid siege to the SAP party headquarters, and after a series of damaging text messages detailing party deliberations had been mysteriously leaked, Juholt had to step down, a year into his mandate. In this year, he tried to tackle virtually every high-stake issue: Swedish participation in the intervention in Libya, the promise to restore pensions to pre-pension reform levels, the voucher schools, the in unemployment insurance, and the preservation or not of the so-called 'RUT-avdrag' reform (the tax deductions introduced in 2007 for domestic services). In other words, he made bold statements on all the issues that have, since the 1990s, effectively split the party in two factions, with modernisers and the Stockholm elite on one side, and trade union and older members on the other, only to then have to back-pedal.

Juholt's year in power made it quite clear that the left of the Swedish Social Democratic Party did not have the capacity to lead the party, and there was, again, the appointment in a closed committee of a compromise candidate, Stefan Löfven, this time clearly on the moderniser wing of the party. Löfven's election as party leader witnessed the re-emergence of a number of the faithful policy architects of the Persson years, particularly Magdalena Andersson. A decidedly market-oriented strategy continued. The party economic programme was presented to the public as the 'business plan' for Sweden (Löfven and Andersson, 2012). When, in the summer of 2012, a public scandal erupted over the private care corporation Carema (one of the biggest actors in the Swedish welfare sector), the SAP's response was very feeble. The Carema scandal came in a series of newspaper stories, published by the liberal daily *Dagens Nyheter*, about the large profits made in the welfare sector by a small number of large corporations who make their profits from receiving public subventions and cutting the cost on the care provided. Such profits benefit from lax regulation, and several of the corporations are registered in tax havens in the English Channel (Hökerberg, 2012). The public outrage was such that all other political actors more or less unanimously called for the introduction of regulation, with the one exception of the SAP which instead defended the role played by the market and by private providers in the Swedish welfare state.[1]

Politics against markets

The varied responses from social democratic parties to the ongoing crisis makes one thing very clear: the relationship between social democracy and capitalism has changed decisively. One of the central ways of understanding social democracy is through the classical vision of a movement that uses parliamentary power to intervene into the structures of capitalism in order to recreate a common good that is understood to have been destroyed or impeded by market forces (Stephens, 1986; Sassoon, 1996; Moschonas, 2002). Historically, social democracy in general, and Swedish social democracy in particular, have been organised around notions of the destructive nature of capitalism and the role of the social democratic state in restoring efficiency and harmony in economic and social relations. In Sweden, this was the essence of the functional socialism that became the party's response to the Depression (Tilton, 1991). It was economic crisis in the 1930s that led to the SAP's calls for mobilisation in the name of the common good, and crisis helped the SAP represent itself as the responsible carrier of the national future and of the interests of all the people (Berman, 2002; Andersson, 2006).

In the work that laid the basis for much of how we think of social democracy, indeed for the very definition of social democracy that influenced the social sciences from the 1980s onwards, Gösta Esping Andersen wrote that social democracy is a movement which attempts, through the use of parliamentary power, to build institutions that protect citizens against the market (Esping Andersen, 1985). Drawing on work carried out in collaboration with Walter Korpi, Esping Andersen argued that the use of the welfare state was to build principles of social citizenship, that is to say institutionalised forms of solidarity, capable of building historical compromises between the working class and the middle classes.

Esping Andersen's and Korpi's interpretation became a blueprint for thinking about social democracy and also laid the basis for many descriptions of Swedish social democracy as an ideal type model of social democracy. Virtually all classical works on SAP stressed the same aspect, the ideological and strategic use of welfare institutions to build a social democratic society through the reciprocal mechanisms of solidarity built into those institutions. When pulled into the institutions of the welfare state, the middle class would change their political preferences and understand themselves as part of the social democratic project.

The working class had thus successfully replaced the bourgeois, repressive state with the welfare state, and transformed the state from a body of class interest to a neutral agent of class compromise (Rothstein, 1996, 1998). But as the Carema example demonstrates, defining social democracy as an actor against the market is today not very meaningful and makes it hard to understand what kind of political agent social democracy really is when the distinction of market and politics itself is blurred in its ideological articulations as well as in its policy applications.

Social democrat policy makers in Sweden and elsewhere have, at least since the 1990s, understood the market as a central vehicle for politics and for the active building of middle-class values and individual preferences. As the decommodifying content of central forms of welfare policy evaporated by their increasing market orientation in the same period, the fundamental characteristic of the social democratic welfare state, to protect workers from the market and to gradually transform society, has also been fundamentally weakened. As institutions of the welfare state no longer promote collective solidarity and redistribution, but rather seek the personal insurance of risk, individual advancement and freedom of choice, the reciprocal mechanisms built into the institutions of the welfare state have also changed. The welfare state today promotes individualism and, to a much lesser extent, forms of collective solidarity. Whatever special link existed between social democracy and the welfare state has thus been lost, also making it much more difficult for social democracy to use the institutions of the welfare state as part of its reformist politics.

In fact we can understand social democracy as directly engaged in a contemporary process of market making. An early body of literature on the Third Way was focused on the question of whether it was neo-liberal or not, and to what extent social democracy's turn to the Third Way was a fundamental break with its historical traditions (Hay, 1998; Ryner, 2002). A number of studies saw for instance New Labour as a mere continuation with Thatcherism. To my mind, much of this literature was based on a much too optimistic account of social democracy's past, and it neglected the extent to which some aspects of Third Way policies drew on disciplinarist and productivist strands that existed historically in social democracy (Andersson, 2010). This is not to say that the Third Way was not as such a break with other, more radical, egalitarian and democratic traditions in social democracy that virtually disappeared in the 1990s (Shaw, 2007). More recent studies have argued that policies such as social investment strategies, asset-based welfare, the financialisation of pension funds or the creation of a virtual market for education and the commercialisation of cultural policy can actually be understood as being part of an active process of market making, in which the social agenda is crucial (Bewes and Gilbert, 2000; Belfrage, 2008). We could thus understand social democracy's reform agenda in the 1990s and 2000s as a 'capitalisation of the social' or, as a number of other studies now suggest, a

Polanyian embedding of market values in social life (Andersson, 2010; Le Galès and Faucher-King, 2010). The purpose of means such as standards, audits, baby bonds, and ILAs in the UK, and free schools, vouchers and privatised pension funds in Sweden, was to set market mechanisms in place in sectors previously defined by the absence of market norms. Some of these reforms were flagship policies of the right, some of them were bipartisan or cross-parliamentary such as the 1994 pension reform in Sweden, and some of them originated in social democratic initiatives. Whatever their ideological origin, however, these policies have either been actively embraced by social democratic leaderships and taken on board as parts of social democratic policy, or silently accepted, in both cases often at the cost of internal fracture. From this perspective, the long Third Way era, and the historic importance of the fundamental ideological reorientation carried out by European social democracy in the mid-1990s, can be understood as the historic marriage between social democracy and neo-liberalism, resulting in an active forging of a market economy in fields that were previously protected from the market – for instance culture, education, welfare.

This active promotion of the market in previously protected domains of social life was not a simple capitulation to neo-liberalism, but it did take huge political effort. First, it required a substantial transformation of ideological postulates. The general appraisal of market mechanisms which underpinned European social democracy's transformation in the period from the 1970s onwards has been described more than once so there is no need to do it again, but it might be stressed that the 1990s saw a fundamental depoliticisation of the idea of the market in social democrat rhetoric and ideology. Through key ideological shifts such as the Clause IV debate, or the rewriting of the SAP party programme in 2001, the market was reconceptualised as a neutral political instrument, a mechanism for resource allocation, and a vehicle for individual and collective advancement. The Swedish party programme even separated the market and capitalism. We are against capitalism, the programme says, because it is a system of exploitation, but for the market, because it is a 'mechanism of resource distribution', and does some things more efficiently than the state. The market was thus neutral (SAP, 2001).

These programmatic changes were contested, and significant political capital went into ensuring their status. The violent reactions of 'third wayers' and modernisers to any attempt from party lefts to shift the ground away from third way positions is indicative of their conviction that a crucial electoral ground was conquered through this shift, and that this was a crucial but fragile victory. The Third Way can and I think should, be understood as an active process of ideology building – in other words, it came with a set of beliefs on how the world should be organised, and in order to defend these beliefs other things became taboo. The belief that the market is neutral created, for instance, a taboo of speaking critically of either the market or of capitalism. Over time, such ideological beliefs have become ontological – in other words they have become central elements in how party elites see reality.

Second, such ideological postulates served a key function, namely that of legitimising central changes in policy and institutions. These policy changes, in turn, have a life of their own because establishing market mechanisms in fields where such mechanisms had been absent was a deliberate way of changing individual and organisational behaviour, including the creation of new forms of interests, but also electoral preferences and class positions that in turn affect social democracy's capability of reform. I would propose that Sweden is a very good example of this, as demonstrated by changes in a number of key areas of the welfare state.

Politics for the market: the rise of welfare capitalism in Sweden

The origins of what is known in Swedish as *friskolor* and in English as voucher schools, of which many are also faith based and community schools, are complex. They were introduced by then Prime Minister Carl Bildt, neo-liberal leader of the conservative Moderate Party, in 1992. This was directly inspired by the attempts of Margaret Thatcher to create a market for education in the UK, as well as by the debate on school vouchers in the US. Social democracy was, in the 1990s, against the reform and swore to undo it on its return to government. However, the SAP had already in its previous period in government decentralised the school system to the municipal level, de facto opening the door for what would become huge differences in school standards across the country. The party has also never acted to undo the reform or propose any form of regulation. Schools are one of the fields that, since the 1980s, have been identified by party elites as a key issue where the middle-class desires more diversity and freedom of choice (*valfrihet*), a concept that became a founding principle of social democratic policy in the mid-1980s when it was looking for ways to compete with the neo-liberal concept of freedom (*frihet*). In the 1980s, under the leadership of Olof Palme and Ingvar Carlsson, *valfrihet* became the guiding star of a series of reforms to introduce decentralisation and privatisation, which targeted the often clumsy bureaucracy of the welfare state, but in the 1990s and 2000s, such principles of diversity became linked ideologically to principles of social mobility, based on a familiar critique of the comprehensive system as blocking the kind of choice that allows for middle-class parents to pursue their aspirations. Hence voucher schools became understood as a central instrument for enabling individual advancement as well as being an application of the market mechanism in promoting individual freedom and therefore something which social democracy cannot be against.

These ideological postulates contrast starkly with social reality, and there is ample evidence to suggest that free schools have detrimental effects in terms of segregation and social mobility for important groups of the population. Today the free schools operate as a de facto schools market for about 20 per cent of Swedish high school students, often times recruiting good students meaning that there are important detrimental effects on the remaining public schools. Through the use of standards, audits, national tests and assessment of teachers and schools, the price mechanism of the market is substituted and parents and pupils are encouraged to act as rational consumers comparing value for money. Schools advertise their brand in the Stockholm subway, and some providers are, in fact, multinational corporations with a complicated ownership structure that includes hedge funds such as Wallenberg Invest. A recent study suggests that about 60 per cent of these schools are shareholding companies, in other words profit-making entities, while about 30 are faith-driven charter schools. About 30 per cent of these schools are owned by ten big corporations, of which one of the biggest, Academia, is owned by another hedge fund, EQT. Other financial actors in the Swedish school sector are the Norwegian hedge fund FSN Capital and the Danish Axcel (Vlachos, 2011).[2] Sweden is the only country in the EU where there are no restrictions on free schools' ability to make profits or indeed reduce costs per pupil and distribute the surplus to shareholders, the occurrence of which is now a demonstrated fact (Vlachos, 2011). Media reports suggest that actors in other privatised areas of schooling and welfare do the same thing, from preschools to elderly care. This strategy, along with the absence of regulation and efficient tax regimes, explains the truly surprising profit margins that exist within the welfare sector.

This discussion needs to be located within a Swedish context, in which the public in general is very strongly in favour of public welfare state arrangements, indicating that there would appear to be a significant gap between the public and party positions (Svallfors, 2004). It could be proposed that this gap is something that party analysts have disregarded in their focus on the urban middle class, and that that constitutes a strategic error. Whether this is or is not the case depends on future developments, but this is currently moving ground. In 2011, a first independent inquiry into the consequences of welfare privatisations in Sweden, written by SNS (a highly respected think tank with links to the Swedish employers) came to the rather humble conclusion that more empirical research should be devoted to the question (Hartmann *et al.*, 2011). This was enough for violent reactions from key actors from the Swedish right, among them Pejje Emilsson, the former creator of the conservative PR consultancy Kreab and director of Kunskapsskolan AB, which has 10 per cent of the schools market in Sweden. The SNS director was forced to resign after it emerged that he had tried to censure the report and stop its researchers from publicising their results.[3] This caused a first public scandal, followed by the Carema scandal in the summer of 2012 and repeated reports on the profits of the welfare industry since.

The question of profits in the welfare sector is therefore now becoming politicised in a way that it has not been before. This puts the party in a difficult position, due to the fact that since 2006 it has identified the role of the market in welfare services as a key issue in securing middle-class support and gone to considerable lengths to assure the public that social democracy respects the market mechanism in public services. For instance, when, in the run-up to the 2010 election campaign, key voices on the left of the party (such as that of the Stockholm leader Carin Jamtin) advocated the introduction of regulation to stop free schools from distributing the profit made from public subventions to private shareholders, they were immediately accused by figures such as Kjell Olof Feldt of trying to abolish the principle of profit in public services and thereby jeopardising middle-class support for the party (Feldt, 2009; Jamtin, 2009). At the party congress in 2009, Mona Sahlin hoped to silence the debate once and for all and pushed through congress a decision that formally approved the principle of profit in schools (SAP, 2009). Yet, the fact that schools and social services in Sweden have become a high-stakes game for actors in a market with very beneficial terms has become increasingly obvious to the Swedish public, thereby putting the party, or at least its leadership, on the spot.

Moreover, while newspaper reports have highlighted the degree of collusion between market actors and right wing politicians in securing welfare contracts, in 2012, another scandal erupted which appeared to identify direct links between key social democratic advisers and PR firms and lobbyists acting for capital interests in the welfare industry (Suhonen, 2010). If the fundamentals of the 'prime scandal' are true, then welfare capitalism has its ties firmly within the party itself. By welfare capitalism we would then have to understand, not the historic attempts to use the welfare state in order to intervene into the market, but the transformation of the welfare state into a series of new markets and interests through strategic alliances between financial and political capital, including social democracy.

The long-term effects of welfare capitalism on the scope of reformism

The fundamental changes in welfare state structures, of which the free schools discussed here are one example and of which could also be mentioned the important pension reform of 1994, have changed risk and opportunity structures, and through this class positions and patterns of social segregation. Privatisation has also created what can only be described as vested interests, not only in shareholding value, but in those groups whose opportunities for social mobility are positively boosted by market choice. Free schools are a case in point – they allow parents with children in underprivileged areas to break their kids out of underperforming public schools, hence reinforcing vicious circles of segregation. The institutional shifts in the Swedish welfare state have been accompanied by a massive shift in resources, and in some cases important speculative effects. In Sweden, as in the UK, the deregulation of credit markets and the privatisation of housing markets have led to the emergence of a substantial property owning, but sometimes highly risk exposed, middle class, which has a direct interest in maintaining low interest rates and high property prices (Finansinspektionen, 2010). In the UK, the creation of such a house-owning middle class was a strategic political calculation, partly to do with an ideological agenda of ownership, and partly to do with the idea that accumulated housing wealth would compensate for the erosion of public pensions. As Matt Watson has recently put it, the privatisation of housing is no less than the political creation of a middle-class constituency of monetary conservatives, who will defend low interest rates even at the social cost to the rest of the community (2008). The political backing of this particular interest comes at the clear expense of those who lack assets, and hence contributes to the creation of what will arguably be a key dimension of social conflict in the wake of crisis. To undo such a shift in wealth once it is in place is just short of a revolution.

Marketisation and financialisation therefore changes the goalposts of reformism by introducing important feedback effects (Soss and Schram, 2007). The reforms discussed here were not temporary austerity reforms. They were reforms which aimed, explicitly, to pin down change for a long time coming, including actively changing the values of the electorate and locking in institutional change over time. The consequences of these measures are arguably yet to be appreciated. In other words, there is a key task for the social sciences in terms of analysing the shift of risk and interest that has taken place in recent decades and in terms of establishing who are the winners and the losers of these changes (Hacker and Pierson, 2010). In Sweden, such analysis is complicated by the fact that we are still lacking substantial conclusions regarding the consequences of privatisations. This lack of knowledge is arguably in itself a problem for a socially reformist party.

Nevertheless, certain hypotheses may be called for and it is here useful to revisit the classical social science literature on social democracy as a strategic agent. The cited literature on the relationship between social democracy and the welfare state that influenced social science in the early 1980s argued that social democracy used the institutions of the welfare state in order to entrench certain values of redistribution among the electorate, build class alliances around working and lower middle-class interest, and create forms of institutionalised solidarity as a way of building power resources for working-class interests over time. From another perspective, Przeworski and Sprague (1986) argued that reformist social democratic politics transform working-class interest, so that they end up undercutting the working-class constituency and lock themselves into trade-offs and dilemmas which eventually result in their becoming dependent on strategic decisions to seek alliances with the middle class, thus eroding their own class base. Both theories emphasised the causal link between what social democracy does, the institutions that it uses, and the way that its constituency changes over time – in other words, social democracy's advertent or inadvertent role in creating a, social democratically disposed or not, middle class.

It would be timely to revisit this literature. Many welfare reforms in recent decades have come about with the purpose of freeing the middle class from the welfare state, and, contrarily, in order to use the welfare state to build middle-class values by shaping social institutions capable of reproducing these over time. It could be suggested that welfare reform has created vested interests that act contrary to social democracy's traditional reform agenda, and contribute to restrained policy positions; (see, for instance, Blyth and Katz, 2005; Blyth *et al.*, 2010). Choice accommodates individualism as a dominant value, but it also forces people to behave as individualists. Welfare systems based on capitalisation push people to behave as capitalists. If we look at it from this perspective, social democracy in the present can be understood not only as reacting to middle-class demands, but also as deeply involved in changing preferences through a complex system of policy and bureaucracy (Le Galès and Faucher-King, 2010). The creation of new forms of vested interests in housing markets, school reform and a multitude of other examples, seems to lock-in social democratic politics to positions which it is uncomfortable with and which also may be increasingly electorally risky as the interests being created as such depend on an anticipation of future outcomes which are increasingly uncertain due to the economic crisis. In essence the creation of these new social interests mirrors what Jacob Hacker (2004), for instance, has described as the privatisation of social risk in the process of welfare state change. In backing contentious issues such as those discussed, social democracy runs the risk of critically widening fissures between traditionalists and modernisers within its own organisational structure (such as in the backbencher revolts over education in the UK or the divide between party elites and trade union grass roots in Sweden), of further alienating a disenchanted part of its more traditional electorate, and of inadvertently creating a kind of middle-class backlash when what constituted choice and opportunity for social mobility in one era turns into risk and insecurity in another. Meanwhile, the risk associated with choice could be the basis for new forms of political alliances between a choice-fatigued and risk-averse middle class, and a working class excluded from real choice through the effects of segregation. Their interests might be intrinsically different – but it might also be that the role of successful social democratic politics historically was to bridge such difference by building forms of institutional solidarity over time.

Neglecting this represents a significant risk for social democracy, particularly since for historic reasons a Swedish middle-class electorate could be more prone to take out its frustration with the transformations of the welfare state on social democracy, rather than on parties on the right. Voters can sanction social democratic parties for not being social democratic. In this light, developments since

2002 would need a different interpretation from that established by the party leadership. It could thus be the case that the decrease in social democratic voters since 2002 is not an expression of unrealised aspirations for more choice, but the expression of a latent frustration with social democracy for selling out the welfare state. In other words, election data since 2002 could be interpreted as a punishing social democracy for not being social democratic enough. The far right party (SD) systematically exploits such a feeling within the electorate.

Whose crisis? Concluding remarks

The SAP is of course not the only social democratic party to be in a troublesome electoral position and it is also not the only party of the European left to be having a tough time with renewal. But from having been a party of great consensus, compared with how other social democracies in Europe have been torn apart by internal factions, today the SAP stands out as highly divided. In the UK, the contest for the leadership of the Labour Party meant that the alternative strategies of the candidates were made relatively clear. In France, infighting stopped at least temporarily with the successful primaries, which also sought to recreate a connection between the party and the French public. The SAP's leadership affairs have, on the contrary, been tremendously damaging for its public image, and have further stifled attempts at internal debate, contributing to an isolation of the party elite from the rest of the party.

The divisions within social democratic parties in Europe today are the result of the Third Way years, which for some represented a process of modernisation which made social democracy electable again, at the necessary cost of jettisoning some labour values that (to this section of the party elite) were in any case mainly symbolic. To others, it was a process of betrayal in which the values of social democracy were lost and in which social democratic leaders lost remaining connections with the working class. This is by no means a new conflict or dilemma in the history of social democracy; it is in a sense the classic dilemma of reformism. However, the situation has changed significantly since the 1990s. The crisis that hit the world in 2007 has brought back austerity politics and has at least to some extent repoliticised fundamental economic and social questions. In some countries, such as the UK, crisis has pushed social democratic positions forwards and re-enabled a certain critique of the market. This is not the case in Sweden. Partly this is to do with the fact that crisis itself is astonishingly virtual. In other words, the economic management of Anders Borg is apparently successful. While the krona has remained strong in the Euro-zone, unemployment is at 8 per cent (which is high not only in Swedish but also in European terms) and there are indeed disturbing signs of a housing bubble there is nevertheless still no real crisis debate. Crisis, therefore, does not play the same role in Sweden as it does in the UK. The absence of a renewed critique of the market and capitalism is also a result of the fact that the electoral statistics are slowly shifting in favour of social democracy – Reinfeldt's popularity is falling, and Löfven is climbing in the polls as an effect of this; meaning that the party chooses, when it can, not to rock the boat. But the contestation and controversy arising over private actors' role in the welfare state is a crucial issue, because it puts the party to the test. Just how much market action is the party able to tolerate? Who will be the interpreter of some of the most radical inequality trends in the EU, if it is not social democracy? If it does not change strategy, the party could find itself in a situation for 2014 where it becomes the central scapegoat for thirty years of privatisation in the Swedish welfare state – at which point there are only two winners, either the Sweden democrats or the former communist party, Vänsterpartiet.

Notes

1 See for instance Stefan Löfven in TV interview in SVT Agenda (26 August 2012).
2 Other studies give mixed empirical conclusions about the impact on segregation, etc. See for example Lindbom (2008).
3 SNS is a well-renowned institution in Sweden, with origins from the 1940s. It has produced a number of well-regarded inquiries into the functioning of the Swedish welfare state and its research led reports are usually very well regarded. A number of well-established academics have now left their positions in SNS research council or ceased to collaborate with the institution.

References

Andersson, J. (2006). *Between Growth and Security: Swedish Social Democracy from a Strong Society to a Third Way* (Manchester: Manchester University Press).

Andersson, J. (2009). *När framtiden redan hänt* (Stockholm: Ordfront).

Andersson, J. (2010). *The Library and the Workshop: Social Democracy and Capitalism in an Age of Knowledge* (Palo Alto, CA: Stanford University Press).

Belfrage, C. (2008). 'Towards universal financialisation in Sweden', *Contemporary Politics*, 14(3), 277–96.

Berman, S. (2002). *The Social Democratic Moment* (Cambridge, MA: Harvard University Press).

Bewes, T. and Gilbert, J. (eds) (2000). *Cultural Capitalism: Politics after New Labour* (London: Lawrence & Wishart).

Blyth, M., Hopkin, J. and Pelizzo, R. (2010). 'Liberalization and cartel politics in Europe: why do centre-left parties adopt market-liberal reforms?', paper presented at the 17th Conference of Europeanists, Montreal, 15–17 April.

Blyth, M. and Katz, R. (2005). 'From catch-all politics to cartelization: the political economy of the cartel party', *West European Politics*, 28(1), 33–60.

Esping-Andersen, G. (1985). *Politics against Markets* (Princeton, New Jersey: Princeton University Press).

Feldt, K. O. (2009). 'Friskolornas vinster utmanar inte skolan', *Dagens nyheter*, 4 August.

Finansinspektionen (2010). 'Den svenska bolånemarknaden och bankernas kreditgivning', December.

Hacker, J. (2004). 'Privatizing risk without privatizing the welfare state: the hidden politics of social policy retrenchment in the United States', *American Political Science Review*, 98, 243–60.

Hacker, J. and Pierson, P. (2010). *Winner-Take-All Politics: How Washington Made the Rich Richer and Turned Its Back on the Middle Class* (Cambridge, MA: Harvard University Press).

Hartmann, L. (ed.) (2011). *Konkurrensens konserkvenser. Vad händer med svensk välfärd?* (Stockholm: SNS).

Hay, C. (1998). *The Political Economy of New Labour* (Manchester: Manchester University Press).

Hökerberg, J. (2012). 'Så granskade vi Carema', *Dagens nyheter*, 15 May.

Jamtin, C. (2009). 'Därför misslyckades vi', *Dagens nyheter*, 28 July.

Kielos, K. (2011). 'Juholts politiska kompass snurrar hej vilt', *Aftonbladet*, 8 October.

Korpi, W. (1983). *The Democratic Class Struggle* (London and New York: Routledge).

Le Galès, P. and Faucher-King, F. (2010). *The New Labour Experiment: Change and Reform Under Blair and Brown* (Stanford, CA: Stanford University Press).

Lindbom, A. (2008). 'Friskolorna och framtiden. Segregation, kostnader och effektivitet', Skolverket and Uppsala University.

Löfven, S. and Andersson, M. (2012). 'Vi presenterar en ny affärsplan för Sverige', *Dagens nyheter*, 24 September.

Moschonas, G. (2002). *In the Name of Social Democracy. The Great Transformation: 1945 to the Present* (London: Verso).

Przeworski, A. and Sprague, J. (1986). *Paper Stones: A History of Electoral Socialism* (Chicago: University of Chicago Press).

Rothstein, B. (1996). *The Social Democratic State: The Swedish Model and the Bureaucratic Problem of Social Reform* (Pittsburgh: University of Pittsburgh Press).

Rothstein, B. (1998). *Just Institutions Matter: The Moral and Political Logic of the Universal Welfare State* (Cambridge: Cambridge University Press).

Ryner, M. (2002). *Capitalist Restructuring, Globalisation and the Third Way: Lessons from the Swedish Model* (London and New York: Routledge).

SAP (1982). *Framtid för Sverige* (Stockholm: Socialdemokratiska arbetarepartiet).

SAP (2001). Party programme.

SAP (2009). Party congress debate, 30 October.

Sassoon, D. (1996). *One Hundred Years of Socialism: The West European Left in the Twentieth Century* (London: I.B. Tauris).

Shaw, E. (2007). *Losing Labour's Soul: New Labour 1997–2007* (Basingstoke and New York: Palgrave MacMillan).

Soss, J. and Schram, S. (2007). 'A public transformed? Welfare reform as policy feedback', *American Political Science Review*, 101(1), February.

Stephens, J. D. (1986). *The Transition from Capitalism to Socialism* (Chicago: University of Chicago Press).

Suhonen, D. (2010). 'En trojansk häst i arbetarrörelsen', *Aftonbladet*, 20 December.

Svallfors, S. (2004). 'Class, attitudes and the welfare state: Sweden in comparative perspective', *Social policy and administration*, 38(2), 119–38.

Tilton, T. (1991). *The Political Theory of Swedish Social Democracy: Through the Welfare State to Socialism* (Oxford: Clarendon Press).

Vlachos, J. (2011). 'Friskolor i förändring', in L. Hartmann (ed.), *Konkurrensens konsekvenser* (Stockholm: Studieförbundet näringsliv och samhälle, SNS).

Watson, M. (2008). 'Constituting monetary conservatives via the savings habit: New Labour and the British housing market bubble', *Comparative European Politics*, 6, 285–304.

8

German social democracy: a popular project and an unpopular party

Ingo Schmidt

The welfare state enjoys great popularity in Germany, whereas the existing market system is increasingly seen as a source of injustice (TNS Emnid and Bertelsmann Stiftung, 2012). These should be ideal conditions for social democrats that have a long history advocating the political regulation of market economies (Berman, 2006). Embedded markets, social democrats argued against nineteenth-century liberals and their neo-liberal successors in the late twentieth century, allow the realisation of market efficiencies without the distributional conflicts and inequalities produced by unregulated markets. This basic idea was couched in the Marxisant language of organised capitalism in the 1920s and was the core of the Keynesian welfare state after the Second World War. It was adjusted to the postmodern civil society discourse of the 1990s when it was presented as a Third Way beyond Keynes and Hayek.

Today, Social Democrats in Germany (*Sozialdemokratische Partei Deutschlands*, SPD) should be particularly eager to embrace the popularity of the welfare state as a way to regain some of the support they lost on their Third Way trip. Indeed, this was a trip that started with the tailwind of the 'New Economy' euphoria of the late 1990s, but then turned to drastic cuts of social standards and spending in the wake of the 2001 stock market crash and the subsequent economic stagnation from 2002 to 2005 (see Table 8.1). These cuts, announced by then Chancellor Schröder in 2003 under the label, 'Agenda 2010', were much deeper than anything the conservative Christian Democrats (*Christlich Demokratische Union*, CDU) – frequently labelled as neo-liberals by Social Democrats – had done to roll back the welfare state during their time in office from 1982 to 1998 (Schröder, 2003; Camerra-Rowe, 2004; Merkel *et al.*, 2006: 172–87). Moreover, these cuts stood in sharp contrast to earlier tax cuts that had one-sidedly benefited rich households and large corporations (Harlen, 2002). Taken together, economic policies under Schröder led to a massive increase in income inequality and insecure and low-wage jobs (Bispinck and Schulten,

Table 8.1 GDP growth, 2000–06

	2000	2001	2002	2003	2004	2005	2006
Germany	3.1	1.5	0.0	−0.4	1.2	0.7	3.7
Euro-Zone	3.9	2.1	1.2	1.3	2.4	1.9	3.1

Source: European Commission

2011). Contrary to their expectation that this would enable the SPD to attract new voters, by demonstrating a willingness to energetically restructure the welfare state, voter approval for the SPD plunged with every round of cuts. After the federal elections in 2005, the SPD had to accept the role of junior partner to the Christian Democrats in order to stay in power. With only 23 per cent of the vote in the 2009 election they fell to their all-time low in the history of the Federal Republic. Despite some recovery since 2009, approval rates are still more than 10 percentage points below the 40.9 per cent with which they took office in 1998 (see Table 8.2).

Rather than distancing themselves from the deeply unpopular 'Agenda 2010' policy and seizing the opportunity to reinvent themselves as defenders of the welfare state in times of economic crisis, however, leading Social Democrats still praise this policy as the pre-emptive measures that protected Germany from the worst effects of the Great Recession and the Euro crisis (Schröder, 2012). Sticking to a set of policies that is not only unpopular but has arguably contributed massively to the Euro crisis by undercutting wages in other countries and boosting German export surpluses (Schmidt, 2013a), may seem futile. A look at The Left (Die Linke), the 2007 merger of East Germany's Party of Democratic Socialism (PDS) and Social Democratic dissidents opposing Agenda 2010 policies (Fülberth, 2008), indicates that the embrace of policies that put social equality over international competitiveness and profits isn't a recipe for success either. The Left tried to fill the vacuum left by the Social Democrats after their Third Way turn and cater to widespread tastes for the welfare state – but to little avail. After a short increase in voter approval after its founding, The Left fell back to the levels that the PDS had reached in the past and also to its reliance on voters in East Germany. The political winner of the Euro crisis is clearly Angela Merkel's CDU (see Table 8.2). Merkel faces resentment in the crisis-ridden debtor states of the Euro-zone for prescribing them an overdose of Schröder-style policies in collaboration with the European Central Bank, the EU Commission and the International Monetary Fund. At home, though, she is widely credited for avoiding contagion. In short, she earns the credit the Social Democrats think they deserve for making the German economy safe from the challenges of international competition. Regardless of whether Merkel deserves this credit, however, these developments point (along with declining support for The Left

National responses to crisis

Table 8.2 Election results in (West) Germany, 1949–2013

	Social Democrats	PDS/ The Left	Greens	Liberals	Christian Democrats	Others	Voter turnout
1949	29.2	—	—	11.9	31.0	27.9	78.5
1953	28.2	—	—	9.5	45.2	16.5	86.0
1957	31.8	—	—	7.7	50.2	10.3	87.8
1961	36.2	—	—	12.8	45.3	5.7	87.7
1965	39.3	—	—	9.5	47.3	3.6	86.8
1969	42.7	—	—	5.8	46.1	5.4	86.7
1972	45.8	—	—	8.4	44.9	0.9	91.1
1976	42.6	—	—	7.9	48.6	0.9	90.7
1980	42.9	—	1.5	10.6	44.5	0.5	88.6
1983	38.2	—	5.6	6.9	48.8	0.5	89.1
1987	37.0	—	8.3	9.1	44.3	1.3	84.3
1990	33.5	2.4	5.0	11.0	43.8	4.3	77.8
1994	36.4	4.4	7.3	6.9	41.4	3.6	79.0
1998	40.9	5.1	6.7	6.2	35.1	6.0	82.2
2002	38.5	4.0	8.6	7.4	38.5	3.0	79.1
2005	34.2	8.7	8.1	9.8	35.2	4.0	77.7
2009	23.0	11.9	10.7	14.6	33.8	6.0	70.8
May 2013 (Polls)	26.0	7.0	15.0	4.0	40.0	8.0	

Note: 1949–87: West Germany; 1990–2010: Germany including the former German Democratic Republic.
Source: Infratest Dimap

since the Great Recession) to a fundamental contradiction in German politics. Even though the welfare state is highly popular, its actual provisions are subordinated to world market success. Austerity is thus, however grudgingly, accepted as necessary in order to defend or regain international competitiveness. Many of those who suffer the most from such measures would rather abstain from voting than supporting a party such as The Left, which aims to realise a genuine social democratic project.

This 'export consensus' developed in Germany during the post-war era, when the welfare state advanced in tandem with export-led growth. It is a consensus that still impacts upon politics in today's world of recurrent economic crises and poses a major problem for the SPD, which is expected to pursue a welfare state-oriented agenda despite many who support such an agenda believing that this is not possible during times of weak economic growth or outright crisis (Schmidt, 2008). This is, of course, exactly what Third Way strategists had argued before the current period of crises. In their view the Keynesian era, in which governments had sufficient sovereignty to manage aggregate demand

and employment levels and raise taxes to pay for the welfare state, had withered in the light of unregulated world markets. This was a context, they argued, in which every attempt at political regulation would cause a downward spiral of capital flight, devaluation, inflation and recession (Scharpf, 1991). Theoretically, they claimed, global civil society could regain some of the regulatory capacities that nation states had lost (Held, 2004). More practically, they thought that the institutional framework of the European Union would allow the transposition of welfare states into a European Social Model (Schmidt, 2009). Yet, even when the movement for an alternative globalisation was at its height from the late 1990s to the early 2000s, it was quite obvious that this lagged significantly behind the power that neo-liberal globalisation had amounted. The war on terror, beginning in 2003, and the economic crises beginning with the Great Recession, threw the alter-globalisation movement further back. The problem for Social Democrats, who had half-heartedly supported the moderate wing of this movement, was that they considered civil society to be another countervailing power to markets after states had allegedly lost the capacity to regulate market activities due to the increasing mobility of capital. Social Democrats did not think of states and civil society as necessary complements to markets, without which capital could neither reproduce nor accumulate. This wasn't much of a practical problem in times of economic prosperity when welfare state expansion could be financed without cutting into company profits. In times of crisis, though, distributional conflict sharpens and the power of capital that is institutionalised in the state and articulated in civil society is readily available to support the forces of capital.

Social Democratic responses to the current crises illustrate this all too well. Accepting the imperatives of capital accumulation, they abandon the idea of states or civil society as countervailing powers to market rule, and with it the social democratic project of balancing market efficiency and social equality. The result is that they lose voters who had supported them in the past because of their welfare state policies. At the same time, many of these voters, or anyone else with a taste for such policies, lose their political representation. The economic crisis leads to a political crisis of social democracy and a crisis of representation of the subordinate classes who, for the time being, haven't found other ways to voice their interests. This is, of course, what The Left is trying to cope with. On the one hand, The Left tries to reinvent the original social democratic project of reinstituting the primacy of politics over markets, no matter how little room for compromise between labour and capital the crisis has left and how illusory the hope for a return to prosperity and class compromise may be. On the other hand, The Left struggles with the invention of a new socialist project after the failure of Soviet communism and its East German offshoot (Schmidt, 2012). One major obstacle in this respect, and this is true for The Left, the SPD and anyone else seeking greater social equality, is the continuing acceptance of the imperatives of capital accumulation, taking the form of an export consensus in Germany which is shared even by many of those who express political preferences for the welfare state.

Economics: from export promotion to Euro crisis

German politics, from the Great Recession to the Euro crisis, has been profoundly shaped by the export-oriented growth that accompanied welfare state expansion during the post-war era. The experience of economic prosperity based on world market integration contrasted sharply with the economic and political catastrophes under the Nazi regime. Moreover, the fact that the standard of living in capitalist West Germany grew faster than in state-socialist East Germany was widely seen as proof of the superiority of free market economies over any kind of state intervention. It didn't matter that, in actuality, West Germany's economic success greatly benefited from the preferential treatment it received from the US government in its efforts to build an anti-communist bloc. What mattered was the common belief that this success was built on hard work in a free market society. This belief not only confirmed negative images of state-socialist East Germany; it also impeded the social engineering advocated by Keynesian theorists and policy makers (Allen, 1989).

The export consensus developed during the long post-war boom was reinforced during the economic and political crises of the 1970s. During that decade, a mix of New Lefties, left-wing Social Democrats, unionists and Euro-Communists suggested to extend the regulatory powers of the existing welfare states as a first step towards socialist transformation. This idea didn't have much practical impact. Once in office, governments that were elected on a platform of some kind of alternative economic policies, as in Britain in 1974 and France in 1981, quickly turned to austerity to curb inflation and budget deficits (Schmidt, 2011). However, debates about these policies were particularly heated in countries where inflation and deficits were especially high and labour conflicts seemed to paralyse the entire economy. This coincidence of severe economic problems and intense political conflict and debate was effectively used by right-wing Social Democrats in Germany to present '*Modell Deutschland*' as a haven of stability in a sea of economic and political turmoil (Esser *et al.*, 1980; Gebauer, 2005). One of the main reasons the right wing won the strategic debate against the left wing of the party was that the latter were presented as the ones who would bring turmoil to Germany if ever allowed to attain cabinet seats. These hints invoked memories of the Weimar Republic and its collapse into the Nazi regime and implied that the left, who were summarily dismissed as Soviet henchmen, had to be contained in order to avoid repetition of those developments. In this respect, they could build on the anti-communism that had developed as a corollary to West Germany's export consensus (Hofmann, 1967: 131–67).

Inflation scare and export growth

In addition to the fear that the left wing of the SPD were associated with political turmoil, right-wing Social Democrats also successfully built on deep-seated fears of inflation (that were themselves a legacy of the hyper-inflation and currency reforms that had followed both world wars) to highlight the inflationary consequences of alternative economic policies. At the same time, the right of the SPD could rally popular support for the priority they were giving to fighting inflation. Practical support for the fight against inflation came from the metal workers' union, IG Metall. A substantial share of the members of IG Metall (by far the largest union in Germany) work in highly export-dependent sectors, such as automobiles, electronics and machine building. Despite its sometimes militant rhetoric, IG Metall leaders (and even more so its negotiators) tried everything they could to keep wage pressure on prices at a level that would ensure inflation in Germany was below average compared with other industrial countries. This strategy aimed to secure world market share for Germany's export industries, and contributed to current account surpluses at a time when most other industrial countries ran deficits. Ironically, these current account imbalances would deliver something that looked like proof of the shortcomings of Keynesian policies. At the G-5 meeting in 1978, German Chancellor Helmut Schmidt was under pressure from the governments of deficit countries, notably US President Jimmy Carter, and agreed to expansionary fiscal policies that would boost domestic demand, including imports, and thus contribute to the balancing of the world economy (James, 1997: 167–73; Notermans, 2000: 175–91).

However, before the Keynesian multiplier effects had worked their way through the world economy the 1979 oil price hike occurred. Though it was clearly triggered by plunging oil production and political instability following the revolution in Iran, the coincidence of Keynesian measures and accelerating inflation shifted the balance between Keynesianism, let alone its more radical variants, and neo-liberalism further towards the latter (Altvater *et al.*, 1979: 324–41). This shift at the end of the 1970s finished off the attempts by the left wing of the SPD to pull its policies towards a new kind of socialist reformism with which that red decade had begun. However complete the victory of the right wing over its inner party rivals was, it was just one part of a general shift to the right. Another part of the shift was the Liberal Party's change of partners. They had been in a coalition government with the SPD since 1969 and switched to the CDU in 1982. A year later, this new coalition was endorsed in a federal election.

Electoral success during boom periods

References to Germany's export successes and the failure of interventionist policies abound in today's policy debates. In this sense, historical experiences from the 1950s to the early 1980s and the way these are enshrined in collective memories is a relevant frame for present policies. But this is not the only way in which these histories matter. A more specific look at the fortunes and misfortunes of social democracy reveals striking parallels between the two periods during which they were in office, 1966–82 and 1998–2009. The only difference is that they started the first period as junior partner in a grand coalition with the CDU before taking the driver's seat after the 1969 election, while they were elected to that leading role directly when they took office again in 1998 but ended their government tenure as the Christian Democrats' junior partner from 2005 to 2009. Other than that, parallels prevail over differences.

The Social Democrats rode into office on a wave of economic growth in both periods. Expectations that this growth would last forever, which were as common during the long post-war boom as they were during the much shorter New Economy upswing of the 1990s (Bronfenbrenner, 1970; Weber, 1997), were disappointed while the SPD were in office. The world economic crisis of 1974–75 and 2001, respectively, prompted austerity measures both times (Polster and Voy, 1991; Camerra-Rowe, 2004; Merkel *et al.*, 2006). The cuts that the government under Helmut Schmidt decided upon in November 1975, when the economic recession was already nearing its end, were marginal compared to Gerhard Schröder's Agenda 2010 but were nevertheless highly symbolic. They were the first cuts in welfare state spending in the history of the Federal Republic and thus marked the turn from welfare state expansion to retrenchment. Though often accepted as unavoidable measures to regain international competitiveness, they were unpopular in both the 1970s and the 2000s and cost the SPD electoral support in both cases; and things would only get worse.

Austerity policies in periods of crises

The 'Volcker Shock' (Panitch and Gindin, 2012: 163–93) tore the German economy down from 1980 to 1982, the response to which by the Schmidt government was further austerity measures. The political outcome was a loss of voters and government power. In the 2000s, the deeply unpopular Agenda 2010 resulted in the downgrading of the SPD's role in government to junior partner after the 2005 election. In the next election, held in the middle of the Great Recession, the SPD scored, as already mentioned, an all-time low in the history of the Federal Republic. Voters they had lost in 2005 due to the Agenda 2010 policies had no reason to vote SPD four years later. Moreover, whereas Merkel took credit for being an effective crisis manager, the Social Democrats were perceived as either ineffective or overly interventionist by many voters. That the Social Democratic Minister of Finance, Peer Steinbrück, designed considerable parts of Merkel's crisis management didn't matter to these perceptions. Junior partners in a grand coalition don't call the shots in federal elections (Bytzek, 2011; Zohlnhöfer, 2011).

Most explanations of the 2009 election results focus on the capacities of the competing parties to mobilise their voters around headline issues. They also assume that such mobilisation is dependent on highly volatile short-term perceptions of such headline issues in the media. What these explanations conceal are the economic and social changes that impact expectations and behaviour over the long term. When the Christian Democrats replaced the Social Democrats in government in the early 1980s, many people were hoping for a return to the kind of long-term prosperity they had experienced between the mid-1950s and the early 1970s. In fact, one of the main reasons for the Christian Democrats' return to office in the early 1980s was that they had successfully convinced voters that the economic crises of the 1970s were caused by Social Democratic interventionism and that prosperity would make a comeback once markets were freed from red tape and the inflated income claims represented by organised labour and the welfare state. Yet, even when the economy came out of recession in 1983, the year the Christian Democrats were elected into office, things weren't the same as they were before the 1974–75 crisis.

The longer the neo-liberal wave of accumulation was dragging on with sluggish growth and recurrent government appeals to further belt tightening, the more the long post-war boom appeared as a mystical 'golden age' (Hobsbawm, 1996: 225–402), while the present ushered into an 'age of diminished expectations' (Krugman, 1997), at least for the majority of the population that had to sell their labour power to make a living and/or was reliant on one kind of welfare state support or another. In sharp contrast to the neo-liberal ideology that kept on trumpeting economic prosperity as a result of the next round of deregulations and cuts, the neo-liberal era saw the establishment of a long-term trend of diminishing expectations, only briefly interrupted by capitalist euphoria over the collapse of Soviet communism in the early 1990s and hopes for a New Economy in the late 1990s. Eventually, popular protests against Schröder's Agenda 2010, the formation of The Left and the sharp decline in voter approval for the SPD from 1998 to 2009, brought underlying fears about economic and social futures to the fore again. Since the Great Recession, polls consistently show that a majority of the population expects that the worst is still to come. This is the context in which Merkel established her reputation as an effective crisis manager and kept the Social Democrats at bay.

Beggar-thy-neighbour policies and the Euro crisis

Working-class expectations diminished in all rich capitalist countries during the neo-liberal era. In Germany this development was accompanied by a growing pride in world market success, a reflection of growing current account surpluses, and a complementary rise of fears about drowning in world economic turbulences. These contradictory perceptions, in combination with the diminished expectations and fears that were mentioned above, became a major factor in German politics after the Great Recession was transformed into the Euro crisis.

In Germany, the recession was deeper than in other rich countries because its economy is more dependent on exports than most others. Despite the depth of the recession, job losses were kept at a minimum while other countries saw unemployment rising significantly (see Table 8.3). Moreover, the rebound of the German economy after the recession was also stronger than elsewhere so that unemployment rates that kept lurching upwards in other countries declined between 2009 and 2012. A key reason for the low number of jobs lost during the recession was the government's decision to extend the period during which workers on short-time work could receive supplementary short-time allowances from the employment office. This measure, marking a temporary but significant departure from neo-liberalism, allowed companies to retain their permanent workforces without extra costs and workers to retain their expenditure levels. Keeping permanent workforces on their payrolls also allowed German export industries to regain their dominant position in European and world markets, respectively, as soon as the recession came to an end. Employment growth during those years, which was soon heralded as a 'German labour market miracle' in the media (Burda and Hunt, 2011), was largely driven by casual and low-paying jobs enabled by the SPD's Agenda 2010 policies. From the Great Recession to the onset of the Euro crisis and beyond, the German economy maintained significant current account surpluses and thus shifted parts of the burden of the crises, notably in terms of unemployment and debt-financed fiscal stimulus packages, on to other countries. In fact, Germany's beggar-thy-neighbour policies are a key factor explaining the transformation of the Great Recession into the Euro-crisis (Lapavitsas *et al.*, 2010; Schmidt, 2013a).

Individual people experienced these macroeconomic developments between 2008 and 2012 in contradictory ways. On the one hand there was a widespread relief about the fact that the crisis had been much deeper elsewhere, with some scholars even suggesting that there was a 'crisis without crisis consciousness' (Dörre *et al.*, 2009). On the other hand, there were growing fears that contagion would eventually lead to the explosion of unemployment and impoverishment as had been witnessed as a result of the Euro crisis in the southern periphery of the Euro-zone. These fears are likely to grow because the last quarter of 2012 saw the entire Euro-zone, including its creditor countries, slipping back into recession (BBC News, 2013). Relief and fear were accompanied by a growing discontent with increasing inequality and distrust in the political system, notably focused on the institutions of the EU (Scharpf, 2011), and a concern to keep Germany safe from crisis contagion.

Merkel was very successful in transforming these contradictory perceptions into domestic support for the austerity packages imposed onto crisis-ridden members of the Euro-zone and, by doing so, gaining popularity at home. Although the SPD eventually supported every rescue measure that Merkel negotiated at the European level, they did not receive any credit for their support. The reason for this was not only that, as an opposition party, the SPD could not

Table 8.3 Macroeconomic indicators, 2007–12

	GDP growth (%)		Unemployment rate (%)		Budget deficit (% of GDP)		Government debt (% of GDP)		Current account (% of GDP)	
	Germany	Euro-zone	Germany	Euro-zone	Germany	Euro-zone	Germany	Euro-zone	Germany	Euro-zone
2007	3.3	3.0	8.7	7.1	0.2	−0.8	65.2	60.7	7.5	0.3
2008	1.1	0.0	7.5	7.2	−0.1	−2.4	66.8	64.8	6.2	−0.3
2009	−5.1	−4.3	7.8	9.8	−3.1	−6.9	74.5	77.0	6.0	0.2
2010	4.2	2.1	7.1	9.6	−4.1	−6.5	82.5	82.9	6.1	0.2
2011	3.0	1.4	5.9	9.7	−0.8	−4.5	80.5	86.2	5.6	0.3
2012	0.8	−0.4	5.5	10.7	−0.2	−3.7	81.7	89.9	5.7	0.6

Source: European Commission

provide the same kind of leadership that Merkel has exercised as legal representative of the Federal Republic at international meetings, but also because Merkel has unequivocally articulated what she considers to be Germany's national interests (whereas Social Democrats have been more ambiguous about these interests). Social Democrats share with Merkel the dedication to promoting German export industries, but they are also more committed to European integration as an end in itself (SPD, 2000) and show some understanding of the potentially devastating effects, economically and politically, of the aggressiveness with which Merkel embraces forced austerity in other countries as part of Germany's beggar-thy-neighbour policies (Lehndorff, 2012). Indeed, these policies have helped to transform long-existing fears, that European integration could overburden the German economy, into a creditor chauvinism that undermines the legitimacy of any kind of European integration (Hartleb, 2012; Wiegel, 2011).

In the face of these developments, the Social Democrats find themselves in a paradoxical position. On the one hand, they took the heat for rolling back the welfare state in the aftermath of the 2001 recession and thus laid the groundwork for Germany's export success during the Euro crisis, a success for which Merkel gets the credit simply because she is in office. On the other hand, they recognise the fault lines of a kind of European integration built on German current account surpluses and political dictates. To people who translated their fears of economic and social insecurities into a creditor chauvinism that holds a lack of work ethics and wasteful government spending in the debtor countries responsible for the Euro crisis, social democratic pleas for a more balanced approach towards European integration, for example through the issuing of Euro-bonds and mutual liabilities among EU member states, are nothing short of treachery. While sharing the export consensus that still shapes German politics to a significant extent with the Christian Democrats, the Social Democrats seem to be the specialists for unpopular measures while the Christian Democrats get whatever credit can be earned by maintaining export-oriented accumulation strategies. Is this just a question of hiring incapable spin doctors and of poor policy management or are there other reasons that can explain why one of the outcomes of economic crises in Germany are crises of social democracy? The economic conditions under which Social Democrats and Christian Democrats pursue their policies and that are, in turn, reproduced by these policies are the same for both parties. Therefore, one would assume that the reasons for Christian Democrats' popularity and Social Democratic unpopularity in times of economic crisis are political.

Politics: workers without representation and a party with a reduced following

The founding of The Left represents a major challenge for the SPD (Schmidt, 2012). In the 1970s, the SPD had alienated many activists in the then new

social movements with their top-down policies and their unconditional commitment to economic growth and new technologies, notably nuclear energy. This
alienation helped to establish the Greens (*Die Grünen*) (Klein and Falter, 2003).
In the 1990s, they decided to build their own party structures from scratch
in East Germany rather than trying to win over members from the PDS, the
successor of East Germany's former ruling Socialist Unity Party (Sozialistische
Einheitspartei, SED). By doing so, they helped the PDS to establish itself as a
regional party in a united Germany (Behrend, 2006). Although the Greens and
the PDS also attracted some support from other parties, most of their support
came from potential SPD voters. Stiffer competition for votes notwithstanding,
the SPD learned fairly quickly to cooperate with these new parties. In 1985,
the Social Democrats formed their first coalition government with the Greens
in the West German state of Hesse, and from 1998 to 2005 these two parties
formed the federal government. The PDS supported a minority government
between the SPD and the Greens from 1994 to 1998 in the East German state
of Saxony-Anhalt and in 1998 the first coalition was formed between the SPD
and the PDS in Mecklenburg-West Pomerania. Out of the cooperation with
the Greens on the state level grew federal election platforms around the issues
of ecological modernisation and the embedding of the world market in global
governance structures. Cooperation with the PDS in East Germany lacked such
socio-philosophical superstructures but proved to be an effective way for the
SPD to establish itself as a governing party in East Germany, which would not
have been possible without support from the PDS.

Coming to terms with The Left was a different matter, though. In this case,
the Social Democrats could not hope to reach out to new voters by collaborat-
ing with the Greens or expand regionally through coalitions with the PDS.
The question was rather whether they could, or should, try to regain members,
activists, and voters they had lost to The Left through collaboration. Assuming
that the SPD, like any other party, aims at maximising votes the answer to this
question is clearly 'yes' but this is not the way things went. When the Social
Democrats tried to define their position towards The Left they quickly found
themselves in intense conflict. One of the reasons for this was personal. The Left
is essentially a merger between the PDS and the Electoral Alternative for Labour
and Social Justice (Wahlalternative Arbeit und Soziale Gerechtigket, WASG),
a group of party members that had left the SPD in opposition to the Agenda
2010 (Nachtwey, 2007). This split within the SPD had destroyed many personal
relationships and left many in the party feeling bitter and betrayed. The fact
that Oskar Lafontaine, who had been SPD chairman from 1995 to 1999 and
Minister of Finance under Schröder, a position he left after a year in opposition
to Schröder's aggressive pursuit of neo-liberalism, played a key role in the founding of The Left also didn't help communications between the two parties.

However, bad chemistry wasn't the only reason why the Social Democrats

had such a hard time defining their relationship with The Left. Equally important were concerns that collaboration in West Germany, where the PDS had
only played a marginal role, would make The Left presentable and thus might
help The Left rather than the SPD in attracting voters. Moreover, right-wing
Social Democrats who were bitter about the split with the WASG also felt relief
over the weakening of the party's left wing. They thought collaboration with
The Left would only lead to the same kind of strategic debates between the
parties that they had won within the party prior to the formation of the WASG
and The Left, respectively. True to their anti-communist convictions, right-
wingers in the SPD also thought that The Left was under the control of unre-
pentant communists coming out of the PDS and its predecessor SED (Leonhard
and Leonhard, 2009). Considering that many former Social Democrats found
themselves arguing with pragmatists coming out of the PDS in much the same
way they had argued with Third Wayers in the SPD (*Sozialismus*, 2011),[1] such
suspicions seem pretty misplaced but certainly had a significant impact on
inner-party discussions. At the other end of the party spectrum, the left wing,
which had been significantly weakened by the formation of the WASG, aimed at
rebuilding what they considered to be the original red–green project, an environmentally enlightened social democracy committed to international cooperation
rather than free markets and great power politics. Things came to a head after
the 2008 state election in Hesse (Broughton, 2009; Reinhardt, 2011: 159–62).

Confronting The Left

Prior to the 2008 state election in Hesse, then chairman Kurt Beck had pushed
the SPD to leave the decision to collaborate with The Left to the party branches
in each state. His intention was to avoid the kind of inner-party conflict that
unfolded after the Hesse elections, which ended with a stalemate between the
Social Democrats and the Christian Democrats though the former had won 7.6
per cent compared to the previous elections while the latter had lost 12.6 per
cent. Neither of them was interested in a grand coalition and thus needed small
party support to form a government. The Social Democrats had the Greens on
board but were still one vote short of a majority. Before the election, they had
declared that they would not form a coalition government with The Left and
would rather work with the Liberals. Yet, the latter declined. After months of
internal discussion, a Social Democratic convention voted 98 per cent in favour
of forming a minority government with the Greens, which The Left had said it
would support without taking any government positions. This decision triggered
a media campaign charging the SPD with breaking its campaign promise of not
forming a coalition with The Left and opening the way for communist subversion in West Germany. Shortly before the new government should have been
elected in Parliament, four SPD MPs, all tied into networks of the party's right

wing, declared that they wouldn't vote for the government the party convention had almost unanimously decided upon. This cabal (Zastrow, 2009) forced new elections in early 2009 that ended with a crushing defeat for the Social Democrats who lost 13 per cent of their vote and scored a record low of 23.7 per cent in a state where they had won over 50 per cent in the 1960s.

Later that year, the SPD could have formed a government in Thuringia led by The Left party, which scored 27.4 per cent compared to the SPD's 18.5 per cent, but eventually decided to be a junior partner in a Christian Democrats-led government rather than accepting that role 'under' The Left (Jou, 2010). However, when they came first in the Brandenburg elections a few weeks later, reaching 33 per cent compared to The Left's 27.2 per cent, they did not hesitate to take The Left on board as a junior partner. In 2010, they even formed a minority government with the Greens that was supported by The Left (i.e. exactly the same constellation that had aroused SPD right-wingers so much in Hesse) following elections in North Rhine-Westphalia (by far Germany's most populous state and, due to its large industrial centres along rivers Rhine and Ruhr, a Social Democratic heartland since the party's early days). When polls indicated that the SPD might be able to form a majority government without support from The Left, they called a snap election in 2012.

The pragmatic stance towards The Left in North Rhine-Westphalia, compared with the bitter conflicts in Hesse, does not indicate a programmatic turn to the left. Although rhetoric during election campaigns is geared towards social protection and fairness, Social Democratic priorities are firmly established on the side of international competitiveness and the consolidation of public households. The 'danger' of realignment between the left wing of the SPD and The Left that seemed to be possible after the latter's founding, has been successfully warded off by the former's right-wingers. Right-wing dominance within the party was confirmed when Franz-Walter Steinmeier, a close aide of former Chancellor Schröder, and Peer Steinbrück, who was Minister of Finance under Merkel and responsible for bank deregulations in North Rhine Westphalia where he held cabinet posts between 2000 and 2005, decided on Steinbrück as frontrunner in the 2013 federal elections. Another right-wing cabal that completely bypassed democratic selection processes within the party and was an offence to Sigmar Gabriel, SPD chairman since 2009, who had also shown an interest in running for chancellor.

Contrary to Steinmeier and Steinbrück, who don't deviate one inch from the neo-liberal course adopted under the chancellorship of Schröder, Gabriel has tried to reconcile these hard right-wingers with the left wing of the party in order to re-establish it as a catch-all party of the left that would be able to regain the voters it lost while travelling the Third Way (Gabriel, 2008). Gabriel's vague notions of progressiveness certainly help to sell the current brand of social democracy without over-emphasising its unpopular commitment to neo-liberalism. At the same time, Steinbrück builds his campaign around the notions of fair taxation (SPD, 2013) and financial market regulations (SPD, 2012). These topics pick up widespread discontent with increasing inequality and the power of finance capital and translate them into fairly vague policy proposals that don't imply the undoing of any of the neo-liberal reforms the SPD had pushed through during their time in office, alongside a careful avoidance of commitments to welfare state expansion.

The role of the working-class vote

Neither economic crises between 2008 and 2012, nor the decline in voter approval from 1998 to 2009, prompted a change of political direction for the SPD. The attempts towards such change that left-wing Social Democrats undertook after the 2005 election were successfully warded off by the party's right wing and weren't repeated after the 2009 election, even though the electoral rewards earned by the Third Way candidate Steinmeier were so disastrously low that everyone in the party, regardless of political persuasion, would have had a reason to pursue more appealing policies. The fact that this didn't happen led some observers to suggest that social democracy has lost its character as a catch-all party, or, in German political parlance: a people's party. Third Way social democracy, the argument goes, is no longer able to amalgamate different interests, namely those of working-class and middle-class voters into a coherent programme (Walter, 2010a; see also Allen, 2009). It only protects the interests of those who benefited from welfare state expansion in the past, particularly the new professional middle classes that developed over the course of the twentieth century (Howe, 1992), but has nothing to offer to the traditional working class or the working poor, the 'precariat' and the excluded whose ranks swelled massively under the reign of neo-liberal capitalism (Castel and Dörre, 2009; Standing, 2011).

This interpretation of Social Democratic misfortunes at the ballot box gives a twist to older arguments about the decreasing significance of the working-class vote (Kitschelt, 1994). According to these arguments, which were developed and popularised from the 1980s to the 1990s, social democracy had two choices. It would either wither away with the manufacturing working class, which had been its core constituency since the rise of social democratic mass parties in the late nineteenth century but was sent to the dustbin of history by the rise of post-industrial society. Alternatively, it was suggested, social democracy could embrace the post-material values that would replace class as a key determinant in post-industrial societies. However, it wasn't social democracy but the Greens who picked up such arguments most enthusiastically to brand themselves as a distinguishable, and increasingly indispensable, player in a political system in which the dominance of the SPD and the CDU has been considerably weakened over the last two decades (see Table 8.2). Social Democrats, deeply rooted in the productivism of the industrial revolution and committed to competitiveness and growth, found it harder to embrace the post-material agenda. Trying to reconcile the conflict between class politics and post-materialism, they picked the 'new middle', the term used in the 1998 election campaign (Hombach, 1998), as their preferred voter reservoir. Essentially, this was an attempt to update the strategy with which they had been successful in the 1960s and 1970s. Employment shares had been shifting from manufacturing workers to service sector, white- and pink-collar workers since the 1950s. These changes in employment struc- tures were driven by above-average productivity growth in manufacturing and the expansion of corporate bureaucracies and public services. Adopting the then fashionable notion of industrial modernity, the Social Democrats were able to build an electoral alliance between waged and salaried workers that led them to unprecedented electoral success.

Yet, the 1990s rerun of this strategy, couched in the language of the increasing importance of knowledge workers, failed after its initial success in 1998. Many of these knowledge workers swelled the ranks of the new 'precariat' and felt uncom- fortably close to the working poor and socially excluded whose numbers were also sharply increased due to recurrent economic crises and welfare state retrenchment. Moreover, private sector workers who still had decent jobs came under increasing pressure from temporary workers, and public sector workers were confronted by downsizing and privatisation efforts. Rather than finding themselves in a strong and growing new middle, increasing numbers of workers found themselves part of a new underclass or feared they would soon join its ranks. These social realities also left their mark on electoral politics. Contrary to the 'post-material values trumps class'-hypothesis en vogue in the 1990s, class cleavages still have a significant impact on voting behaviour (Elff, 2007; Elff and Rossteutscher, 2011). Yet, since the interests articulated by classed-based votes aren't effectively represented in Parliament, let alone at cabinet tables or at the meetings of international organisa- tions, more and more people, particularly at the low end of the social hierarchy, abstain from voting altogether (Lijphart, 1997; Schäfer, 2009).[2] As a result, the SPD is losing parts of its core constituency, and at the same time working-class interests lose much of their voice in the political system.

Working-class representation today may be as weak as it was during the times of Eduard Bernstein who had argued that Social Democrats, if they wanted to win elections, needed to reach out beyond their working-class supporters to the middle class (Bernstein, 1991). Based on the long boom following the Second World War, they were successful in following his advice, but the turn to slower growth since the early 1980s, not to speak of current crises, eroded the economic basis of this success. Attempts to restore economic growth through a redistribu- tion from wages to profits failed and led to even deeper social divisions so that the representation of working-class interests is more urgent today than it was during the heyday of welfare capitalism in the 1970s. However, the measures that helped capitalists roll back social standards – automation, reorganisation of companies and relocation of work – also led to an unmaking of the working classes as we knew them since the late nineteenth century. The networks of working-class neighbourhoods with their sports and cultural clubs, union, and party branch meetings that were so crucial in building social democracy has been largely undone. As a class in itself, the working class is alive and kicking, in fact with each round of crisis and austerity measures it receives a boost, but as a class for itself it is somewhere between dead and dormant (Schmidt, 2013b).

And this is not the only class that represents a problem for the Social Democrats. Faced with economic crises, the middle class turns more and more against redistribution through the welfare state in an attempt to defend its economic and social status compared with the working class. The electoral success of the Liberals and the Greens since the beginning of the crisis illustrates this turn against the welfare state. Unlike the, however transformed, catch-all parties of the SPD and CDU, the Liberals and Greens are distinct parties of the middle class that don't need to reconcile conflicting social interests among their voters (Walter, 2010b). At the height of the recession, polls found the Liberals at 17 per cent, way above their long-time average; and the election in September 2009 saw them win a record high of 14.6 per cent. Polls in June 2011 saw the Greens with 24 per cent, only one point of percentage behind the SPD. These successes are, however, anything but stable. Since June 2010, the Liberals have been at or below 5 per cent, which is the threshold needed to gain a seat in the federal and state parliaments in Germany, and the Greens have failed to stay above 20 per cent for any substantial length of time. What this suggests is that the middle class is not only determined to defend its privileges, but also that it feels threatened by the crisis. Increasing middle-class support for far-right views, which, unlike in most other European countries, haven't coalesced around a populist or far-right party, is another indication of middle-class angst (Decker *et al.*, 2010).

Where does this leave the SPD? In the face of a working class that loses interest in electoral politics and an inward-turning middle class there appears to be little room for the kind of electoral alliance that carried it to success between the 1960s and 1970s. Crises and austerity may usher in a remaking of the working class as a political agent but this, if it happens at all, would be a lengthy process for which parties facing the next election cannot wait. In the meantime, the SPD will be caught by the short-time fashions of medial and electoral cycles. This may even be sufficient to achieve occasional electoral victories; but it is certainly nothing from which anything like the social democratic hegemony of the post-war period, when even Christian Democratic parties had to support the welfare state if they wanted to be elected, can be built. The social democratic project remains popular but doesn't find a political force willing to attempt to once more put it into practice. Attempts to do so in this new age of austerity may lead to the conclusion that reconciliation between conflicting social interests is no longer possible and therefore that the pursuit of social democratic ideas will lead to the search for socialist alternatives (Lebowitz, 2010; Veltmeyer, 2011). But this is a search and learning process one shouldn't expect from the old social democratic parties, but rather from new left parties, such as The Left in Germany, extra-parliamentary movements, and labour activists willing to overcome the corporatist traditions that still dominate union practices today.

Notes

1 See the articles in the special section.
2 See also the column 'Voter turnout' in Table 8.2.

References

Allen, C. (1989). 'The underdevelopment of Keynesianism in the Federal Republic of Germany', in P. Hall (ed.), *The Political Power of Economic Ideas: Keynesianism Across Nations* (Princeton: Princeton University Press), pp. 263–89.

Allen, C. (2009). 'Empty nets: social democracy and the catch-all party thesis in Germany and Sweden', *Party Politics*, 15(5), 635–53.

Altvater, E., Hoffmann, J. and Semmler, W. (1979). *Vom Wirtschaftswunder zur Wirtschaftskrise* (Berlin: Olle & Wolter).

BBC News (2013). 'Eurozone recession deepened at end of 2012', 14 February, www.bbc.co.uk/news/business-21455423.

Behrend, M. (2006). *Eine Geschichte der PDS – Von der zerfallenden Staatspartei zur Linkspartei* (Cologne: ISP Verlag).

Berman, S. (2006). *The Primacy of Politics: Social Democracy and the Making of Europe's Twentieth Century* (Cambridge: Cambridge University Press).

Bernstein, E. (1991). *The Precondition of Socialism* (Cambridge: Cambridge University Press, originally published in German in 1899).

Bispinck, R. and Schulten, T. (2011). 'Trade union responses to precarious employment in Germany', WSI Diskussionspapier, Düsseldorf.

Bronfenbrenner, M. (1970). *Is the Business Cycle Obsolete?* (New York: Wiley).

Broughton, D. (2009). 'Seconds out for the second round: the *Landtagswahl* in Hessen, January 2009', *German Politics*, 18(2), 265–9.

Burda, M. and Hunt, J. (2011). 'What explains the German labor market miracle in the Great Recession?', *Brookings Papers on Economic Activity*, spring, 273–314.

Bytzek, E. (2011). 'The zero-sum game of governing together? Effects of Merkel's grand coalition on the results of the 2009 German federal election', *German Politics*, 20(2), 260–72.

Camerra-Rowe, P. (2004). 'Agenda 2010 – redefining German social democracy', *German Politics and Society*, 22(1), 1–30.

Castel, R. and Dörre, K. (2009). *Prekarität, Abstieg, Ausgrenzung: Die soziale Frage am Beginn des 21. Jahrhunderts* (Frankfurt and New York: Campus).

Decker, O., Weißmann, M., Kiess, J. and Brähler, E. (2010). *Die Mitte in der Krise. Rechtsextreme Einstellungen in Deutschland* (Berlin: Friedrich-Ebert-Stiftung), available at: http://library.fes.de/pdf-files/do/07504-20120321.pdf.

'Die Linke – Auf Kurssuche' (2011). *Sozialismus*, 38(5), 7–31.

Dörre, K., Behr, M., Eversberg, D. and Schierhorn, K. (2009). 'Krise ohne Krisenbewusstsein?', *Prokla*, 39(4), 559–76.

Elff, M. (2007). 'Social structure and electoral behavior in comparative perspective: the decline of social cleavages in western Europe revisited', *Perspectives on Politics*, 5(2), 277–94.

Elff, M. and Rossteutscher, S. (2011). 'Stability or decline? Class, religion and the vote in Germany', *German Politics*, 20(1), 107–27.

Esser, J., Fach, W. and Simonis, G. (1980). 'Grenzprobleme des 'Modells Deutschland'', *Prokla*, 10(3), 40–63.

Fülberth, G. (2008). *Doch wenn die Dinge sich ändern – Die Linke* (Köln: Papy Rossa).

Gabriel, S. (2008). *Links neu denken – Politik für die Mehrheit* (Munich: Piper).

Gebauer, A. (2005). *Der Richtungsstreit in der SPD: Seeheimer Kreis und Neue Linke im innerparteilichen Machtkampf* (Wiesbaden: VS Verlag für Sozialwissenschaften).

Harlen, C. M. (2002). 'Schröder's economic reforms: the end of Reformstau?', *German Politics*, 11(1), 61–80.

Hartleb, F. (2012). 'European project in danger? Understanding precisely the phenomena "Euroscepticsm, populism and extremism" in times of crisis', *Review of European Studies*, 4(5), 45–63.

Held, D. (2004), *Global Covenant – The Social Democratic Alternative to the Washington Consensus* (Cambridge, MA and Malden: Polity).

Hobsbawm, E. (1996). *The Age of Extremes: A History of the World 1914–1991* (New York: Vintage).

Hofmann, W. (1967). *Stalinismus und Antikommunismus – Zur Soziologie des Ost-West-Konflikts* (Frankfurt: Suhrkamp).

Hombach, B. (1998). *Aufbruch. Die Politik der neuen Mitte* (Munich and Dusseldorf: Econ).

Howe, C. (1992). *Political Ideology and Class Formation. A Study of the Middle Class* (Westport, CT and London: Praeger).

James, H. (1997). *Rambouillet, 15. November 1975. Die Globalisierung der Wirtschaft* (Munich: Deutscher Taschenbuch Verlag).

Jou, W. (2010). 'The 2009 Thuringia Landtagswahl: exploring a new coalition formula', *German Politics*, 19(2), 222–9.

Kitschelt, H. (1994). *The Transformation of European Social Democracy* (Cambridge: Cambridge University Press).

Klein, M. and Falter, J. W. (2003). *Der lange Weg der Grünen* (Munich: Beck).

Krugman, P. (1997). *The Age of Diminished Expectations* (Cambridge, MA and London: MIT Press).

Lapavitsas, C., Kaltenbrunner, A., Lindo, D., Michell, J., Painceira, J. P., Pires, E., Powell, J., Stenfors, A., Teles, N. (2010). 'Eurozone crisis: beggar thyself and beggar thy neighbour', *Research on Money and Finance*, occasional report, March.

Lebowitz, M. (2010). *The Socialist Alternative: Real Human Development* (New York: Monthly Review Press).

Lehndorff, S. (2012). 'German capitalism and the European crisis: part of the solution or part of the problem?', *transform! European network for alternative thinking and political change*, November, available at: http://transform-network.net/journal/issue-112012/news/detail/Journal/german-capitalism-and-the-european-crisis-part-of-the-solution-or-part-of-the-problem.html.

Leonhard, E. and Leonhard, W. (2009). *Die linke Versuchung – Wohin steuert die SPD?* (Berlin: be.bra Verlag).

Lijphart, A. (1997). 'Unequal participation: democracy's unresolved dilemma', *American Political Science Review*, 91(1), 1–14.

Merkel, W., Egle, C., Henkes, C., Ostheim, T. and Petring, A. (2006). *Die Reformfähigkeit der Sozialdemokratie. Herausforderungen und Bilanzen der Regierungspolitik in Westeuropa* (Wiesbaden: VS Verlag für Sozialwissenschaften).

Nachtwey, O. (2007). 'Im Westen was Neues. Die Entstehung der Wahlalternative Arbeit und Soziale Gerechtigkeit', in T. Spier, F. Butzlaff, M. Micus and F. Walter (eds), *Die Linkspartei. Zeitgemäße Idee oder Bündnis ohne Zukunft?* (Wiesbaden: VS Verlag für Sozialwissenschaften), pp. 155–84.

Notermans, T. (2000). *Money, Markets, and the State: Social Democratic Economic Policies Since 1918* (Cambridge: Cambridge University Press).

Panitch, L. and Gindin, S. (2012). *The Making of Global Capitalism: The Political Economy of the American Empire* (London and New York: Verso).

Polster, W. and Voy, K. (1991). 'Von der politischen Regulierung zur Selbstregulierung der Märkte', in K. Voy, W. Polster and C. Thomasberger (eds), *Marktwirtschaft und politische Regulierung, Band 1* (Marburg: Metropolis), pp. 205–8.

Reinhardt, M. (2011). *Aufstieg und Krise der SPD – Flügel und Repräsentanten einer pluralistischen Volkspartei* (Baden Baden: Nomos).

Schäfer, A. (2009). 'Wahlbeteiligung in Deutschland: Die soziale und räumliche Kluft wächst', unpublished ms (Cologne: Max-Planck-Institut für Gesellschaftsforschung).

Scharpf, F. W. (1991). *Crisis and Choice in European Social Democracy* (Ithaca, NY and London: Cornell University Press).

Scharpf, F. W. (2011). 'Monetary union, fiscal crisis, and the preemption of democracy', *London School of Economics*, 'Europe in Question' discussion paper series.

Schmidt, I. (2008). 'Wirkungsmächtige Illusionen: Export – Gerechtigkeit – Wachstum', in I. Schmidt (ed.), *Spielarten des Neoliberalismus* (Hamburg: VSA-Verlag), pp. 123–46.

Schmidt, I. (2009). 'New institutions, old ideas: the passing moment of the European Social Model', *Studies in Political Economy*, 84, 7–28.

Schmidt, I. (2011). 'There were alternatives: lessons from efforts to advance beyond Keynesian and neoliberal economic policies in the 1970s', *Working USA*, 14(4), 473–98.

Schmidt, I. (2012). 'The Social Democratic Party in Germany: Caught between the fall of the Berlin Wall and the rise of The Left', in B. Evans and I. Schmidt (eds), *Social Democracy After the Cold War* (Athabasca: Athabasca University Press), pp. 235–70.

National responses to crisis

Schmidt, I. (2013a). 'Unmaking neoliberal Europe: capitalist crisis and the search for alternatives', *Perspectives on Global Development and Technology*, 12(1–2), 41–62.
Schmidt, I. (2013b). 'Geschichte und Sozialismus', in I. Schmidt (ed.), *Rosa Luxemburgs 'Akkumulation des Kapitals – Die Aktualität von ökonomischer Theorie, Imperialismuserklärung und Klassenanalyse* (Hamburg: VSA-Verlag, forthcoming).
Schröder, G. (2003). 'Regierungserklärung zur Agenda 2010', Berlin, 14 March.
Schröder, G. (2012). 'Agenda 2010: the key to Germany's economic success', *Social Europe Journal*, 23 March, available at: www.social-europe.eu/2012/04/agenda-2010-the-key-to-germanys-economic-success.
SPD (2000). Grundwertekommission beim Parteivorstand der SPD, *Der Globalisierung ein europäisches Gesicht geben* (Berlin), available at: http://library.fes.de/pdf-files/netzquelle/01780.pdf.
SPD Bundestagsfraktion (2012). *Vetrauen zurückgewinnen: Ein neuer Anlauf zur Bändigung der Finanzmärkte*, 25 September, available at: www.spdfraktion.de/sites/default/files/konzept_aufsicht_und_regulierung_finanzmaerkte.pdf.
SPD Pressemitteilung (2013). *Braunschweiger Erklärung für mehr Steuergerechtigkeit*, 14 January, available at: www.spd.de/presse/Pressemitteilungen/85640/20130114_braunschweiger_erklaerung.html.
Standing, G. (2011). *The Precariat – The New Dangerous Class* (New York: Bloomsbury).
TNS Emnid and Bertelsmann Stiftung (2012). 'Kein Wachstum um jeden Preis', July, available at: www.bertelsmann-stiftung.de/cps/rde/xbcr/SID-123E9105–1459E333/bst/xcms_bst_dms_36359_36360_2.pdf.
Veltmeyer, H. (2011). *21st Century Socialism – Reinventing the Project* (Halifax and Winnipeg: Fernwood).
Walter, F. (2010a). *Vorwärts oder abwärts? Zur Transformation der Sozialdemokratie* (Frankfurt: Suhrkamp).
Walter, F. (2010b). *Gelb oder Grün? Kleine Parteiengeschichte der besserverdienenden Mitte* (Bielefeld: Trancript).
Weber, S. (1997). 'The end of the business cycle?', *Foreign Affairs*, July–August, 65–82.
Wiegel, G. (2011). 'Right-wing populism in Germany too? A European trend and its special German features', *transform! European network for alternative thinking and political change*, September, available at: http://transform-network.net/journal/issue-092011/news/detail/Journal/right-wing-populism-in-germany-too-a-european-trend-and-its-special-german-features.html.
Zastrow, V. (2009). *Die Vier – Eine Intrige* (Berlin: Rowohlt).
Zohlnhöfer, R. (2011). 'The 2009 Federal Election and the economic crisis', *German Politics*, 20(1), 12–27.

9

The French Socialist Party (2008–13): not revolutionaries, not luminaries, just 'normal' guys amidst the tempest

Christophe Bouillaud

Introduction

With François Hollande's election to the presidency on 6 May 2012, the *Parti socialiste* (PS) seized national power after ten years in opposition in the middle of an economic crisis presented by French media as being by far the worst the western world has known since the Great Crisis of the 1930s.

Seizing power in such a desperate situation was not something new for the French socialists. In 1936, the direct ancestor of the PS, the SFIO, had been called for the first time to head a Third Republic government in the middle of another Great Crisis. Léon Blum, leader of the SFIO, was nominated in June 1936 Président du Conseil. The left alliance (SFIO, Radical Party and French Communist Party (PCF)), called the *Front Populaire* (Popular Front), had won the parliamentary election of April–May 1936. Ranging from moderate left-of-centre radical party to Stalinist communists, its large electoral victory was in part a result of the ill-fated deflationary economic policies of Pierre Laval's right-of-centre government. Aimed at preserving the external value of the franc while enabling French products to compete on international markets through the reduction of nominal wages, wage reductions through legal orders outraged many middle and working-class voters, shifting the balance of the overall electorate to the left. In 1981, François Mitterrand was the first French socialist leader to be elected President of the Fifth Republic, also taking advantage of the ill-fated economic policy of the incumbent power. After an unsuccessful Keynesian stimulation, the *relance*, under his first Prime Minister, the neo-Gaullist Jacques Chirac, the liberal President elected in 1974, Valéry Giscard d'Estaing, had chosen from 1976 onwards to shift his overall economic stance in the direction of a 'monetarist' approach aiming to curb double-digit inflation. Raymond Barre, as the new 'independent' Prime Minister and Minister of the Economy and Finance, had conceived a *politique d'austérité* (austerity policy), launched through comprehensive anti-inflation programmes (*Plan Barre*). Since then, austerity became an infamous expression in French political speech. No French government would ever acknowledge that its own policy is tuned in such a way. In fact, Barre, a former university economics professor and Economy and Finance European Commissioner (1967–73), aimed to curb inflation through the reduction of overall demand, which implied a sharp rise in unemployment and many bankruptcies and plant closures for out-of-date industrial sectors – a policy that the British Prime Minister Margaret Thatcher would apply only a few years later with far more success. This austerity policy was rejected by Mitterrand as he was candidate to the 1981 presidential election. Nevertheless, after less than two years of Keynesian 'relance' under Pierre Mauroy's premiership, President Mitterrand chose to shift back to a 'monetarist' policy. It was the famous *tournant de la rigueur* (austerity turn) of 1983, which remains to date the milestone of any thinkable socialist economic policy in France. In 1997, Lionel Jospin won a parliamentary majority – called at the time *Gauche plurielle* ('plural left') since it regrouped socialists, communists and greens – in a snap early election called by President Jacques Chirac, also in a middle of a crisis that French media called at the time, exactly like in 2007–12, the worst by far the western world had known since the great crisis of the 1930s. Jospin's government once again helped French capitalism to get through a crisis without too much damage.

So everyone having some historical memories of the PS's governmental action in similar disastrous situations could draw the overall shape of Hollande's future presidency: stirring words against 'money' and 'finance' during the campaign to win the election, but even stronger deeds to modernise French capitalism thereafter – i.e. the scenario already played in 1981 and 1997. To regroup all left-oriented voters, the candidate had to revivify some classical slogans of the French left in general: 'Change is now', claimed Hollande during his campaign. Ben Clift rightly describes the rhetorical move of the PS before 2012 as 'a more radical, maximalist direction in the three important areas of financial and bank regulation, redistributive taxation and revitalising industrial policy' (2013: 108). The two most striking examples of this outspoken radicalisation were when Hollande declared in January 2012 during a huge meeting at Le Bourget near Paris in front of overheated sympathisers: 'My enemy is the world of finance' and when he announced a few weeks later his aim to tax at a 75 per cent level all activity revenues over €1 million. In the same vein, to win back the many left-oriented voters dubious about EU fiscal consolidation policies, Hollande pleaded for a renegotiation of the 'Fiscal Compact' (TSCG), still at the time of the May 2012 presidential election to be ratified by France, and more generally for a radical shift towards a growth agenda for Europe.

In fact, this lip-service to traditional values of the French left did not impress informed observers even before the May 2012 election. Emmanuel Todd, heterodox economist and historian pleading for 'European protectionism', coined an expression to describe the unthinkable during the campaign: 'revolutionary hollandism'.[1] Hollande, the 'normal President' as he presented himself at this moment in contrast with Nicolas Sarkozy's incumbent 'hyper-presidency', might have no choice other than reinvent himself as a 'Chavez-style' revolutionary leader to save his future presidency from a full disaster. According to Todd, Hollande would eventually change course under pressure from his core electorate, the educated middle classes (that is to say not the working-class constituency that had been the case in the 1970s).[2] Todd was widely derided, since the track record of the PS and of Hollande himself pointed exactly in the opposite direction. Hollande was a young counsellor in Mitterrand's presidential administration in the 1980s, and he was, later in his career, in charge of the direction that the PS took at the very time that Jospin was Prime Minister (1997–2002). In fact, many other commentators, mostly liberal oriented, tried to assess whether Hollande would have enough political 'courage' to reform France in the same vein as his fellow socialist comrade Gerhardt Schröder in Germany after 2003. At the time of writing – nearly one year after Hollande's election to the presidency – it seems that these second generation of observers were prescient: France is heading slowly in this very direction in the name of *socialisme de l'offre* ('supply-side socialism'). Once again, the PS has decided to adapt the French economy to the perceived necessities of global competition, but without any clear-cut discourse able to justify this option to French public opinion.

This choice is reinforced by the PS's full commitment to the EU. One of the very first decisions Hollande took in June 2012, during his first European Council as French President, was to endorse the 'Fiscal Compact' as it has been agreed by Sarkozy, without any renegotiation of any kind, and with no real reorientation of European economic policies towards growth. Without much disagreement among the rank-and-file deputies and senators, the 'Fiscal Compact' was endorsed in October 2012 by the two socialist-dominated Chambers of the French Parliament, and gave way to an 'organic law'[3] on the matter constraining future budgets to obey the old and new European fiscal rules and create a new 'independent authority', the *Haut Conseil des finances publiques* (HCFP), to monitor French budgetary process. The new treaty implied that France should have a null 'structural deficit' ('golden rule') and should reduce its overall public national debt – both far less than optimal rules advocated by critical economists (Les économistes atterrés, 2012). Accordingly, when both the European Commission and 'northern' European partners instructed France in 2011–13 to abide by the treaties – that is written commitments to fiscal austerity – it was impossible for the PS not to accept the application of the very principles that it had fully endorsed in the past, and that it has just approved again with the 'Fiscal Compact'.

From the early days of Hollande's presidency – and even before his election – the question was to understand how these medium-term commitments of the PS to free-market global capitalism and to the EU were to be articulated with the pressing demand by the French electorate of an economic policy able to fight unemployment, to raise living standards and to preserve the 'French way of life'. All other non-economic 'societal' reforms such as 'gay marriage', voting rights for non-European foreigners at local elections, and changing attendance hours for children in primary education, were therefore considered from the start as far less crucial for the success or failure of the socialist presidency (Dupin, 2012). This mood of French public opinion was fully taken into account in Hollande's presidential campaign when he repeated relentlessly that fighting unemployment would be his foremost preoccupation as president if he were to be elected, and that by the end of 2013 the job-market situation would get better.

Since economic policy is the only aspect that both the general public and the commentators are focusing on in judging the PS actions in office, this chapter will first present an overview of the first year of economic policy experienced by the new socialist presidency, focusing especially on the following questions: what is to be done to tackle the economic crisis? How does the presidency intend to fight ever-increasing unemployment? How will it preserve industrial bases in the French economy and so prepare the basis of future growth? The chapter then turns to an explanation of the responses witnessed by Hollande's presidency: the internal dynamics of the PS itself; and the nature of the electoral competition in France. We will conclude with a more general reflection on what remains of national economic policy and of national choices in a time of accelerated 'Europeanisation through crisis'.

French economic policy during the first year of Hollande's presidency

Monetary policy: fully delegated to the European Central Bank

One must take into account that France, as a member of the Euro-zone, voluntarily – and completely – relinquished its monetary policy in 1999. Any 'normal' incoming president therefore has no choice but to accept this state of affairs, in the case of Hollande this is especially so given that his own party took this historic decision. President Mitterrand's socialist administration negotiated and ratified the Maastricht Treaty. Today, the French government can only influence the formation of the ECB's policies through its remaining prerogative to nominate some members of its Governing Board. Of course, it still can choose freely the Governor of the Banque de France, the French central bank, and can push for its own candidate to the ECB's Executive Board or even to ECB's presidency. Christian Noyer, Governor of the Banque de France since 2003, saw his own mandate renewed for six years in 2009. Alas for Hollande, however, the new head of the ECB, Mario Draghi, was chosen by the European Council prior to Hollande's election in May 2012, and will remain in office until 2019. The only French member of the ECB Directorate, Benoît Cœuré, a brilliant young French economist with a strong experience in the French Ministry of Finance under conservative governments, took up his new role on 1 January 2012, and will be in charge until 2020. A committed federalist, Cœuré declared his view – to be faithful to Maastricht's statutes of the ECB – that inflation constitutes the primary evil for the poor in any country, thereby underlining his refusal to support any proposal for the ECB to adopt a Keynesian monetary policy.[4]

Although the monetary policy was clearly out of the control of the new French socialist administration, therefore, the very low level in historical terms of leading interests rate set by the ECB in 2012–13 (0.75 per cent) did not give rise to much criticism during the first months of Hollande's presidency. Draghi's choice, announced at the very end of July 2012 in a press conference, to ensure the existence of the Euro-zone 'whatever it takes', was clearly approved of by the new French administration, and so was the new device of ECB's intervention on financial markets, called Open Monetary Transactions (OMT), which implemented it. Because the French public debt benefited from a 'fly to quality' effect since the beginning of the crisis of European public debts in 2009–10, the interest rate set by international financial markets were in 2011–13 lower than ever (sometimes less than 2.5 per cent on ten-years bonds), and their 'spread' with the new German debt remained low. But, if – contrary to other countries of southern Europe – France's deficit financing did not result in high interest rates at the time, liberal economists nevertheless warned that financial markets could easily change their view from one day to the next and that credible medium-term austerity measures were therefore necessary to preserve this (undue?) advantage. The new Minister of Finance, Pierre Moscovici, clearly accepted this line of thinking in his early declarations, and the nomination of the new Budget Minister, Jérôme Cahuzac, a former Chairman of the National Assembly's Finance Commission during the previous legislature (2007–12), indicated the will of the presidency to cut overall French public spending. In fact, Cahuzac had built his political reputation through his sharp and informed reviews of the UMP majority's budgets.[5]

The French socialist government, chaired by Jean-Marc Ayrault, only became critical of the exchange rate of the Euro in 2012. The Euro's rise against other values – including the dollar and the yen – was considered a risk for French industry, which itself faced difficulties. In fact, this question of the exchange rate of the Euro pointed more towards an opposition between France and Germany than it did between France and the ECB. Germany's governments defend stiffly a 'strong Euro' corresponding to the needs and possibilities of the German 'export machine', while France's new government declared itself astonished by the deterioration of the French commercial balance sheet during the last decade and committed itself to the renewal of French industry.

Overall, the new government seemed to be satisfied with the ECB's general stance at this stage of the European crisis. The role of the ECB, according to the new French government, would even extend further in the near future, since

France was one of the countries pleading for a 'Banking union' at the European level in which all European 'systemic banks' would be monitored directly by the ECB. One might argue that a European monitoring of France's greatest banks proved itself an objective necessity since the socialist majority – as had been the previous conservative majority – seemed to be captured by the French banking industry's lobby. The reform of the banking law, which was supposed to protect the banks from their own hubris on the global financial markets, was clearly so limited in scope that two economists of opposite faiths, the liberal Elie Cohen and the Marxist Frédéric Lordon both considered it unclear, especially when comparing it to other post-2007 financial crisis banking reforms in other western countries (Cohen, 2013; Lordon, 2013) – so much, then, for the fight against 'finance'.

If the new socialist government accepts its obvious lack of influence over the setting of the ECB's monetary policy, and does not wish to get into trouble with the French banking industry, it nevertheless does not wish to let market forces determine the financing of the economy. The government therefore tried to engineer a better way to finance emerging economic activities. One of the pledges of Hollande during his campaign was to establish a new publicly owned bank in charge of financing investments in new future-oriented economic sectors. Of course, creating such a publicly owned bank to finance investment, or a special institution to finance and monitor strategic industrial sectors, does not represent a new idea in French economic history. In fact, this new bank, called the *Banque publique d'investissement* (BPI), is merging several financial institutions already created in the last fifteen years by both conservative and socialist governments[6] and hopes to capitalise on their experience, while extending their scope of action. One could ask why the French socialist government feels the need to create such an institution which is supposed to remedy market failure, particularly when one considers that France has one of the most developed and diversified finance industries in the world. Since 2008, none of the 'universal banks' (including Banque Nationale de Paris, Société générale and Crédit agricole) were destroyed by the financial crisis, and only banks that played no role in terms of industry financing (including Dexia and Crédit immobilier de France) had failed. Anyhow, intellectually, BPI is a mix of beliefs in old-style 'colbertism', in 'Schumpeterian' supply-side economics as embedded in the European 'Lisbon Strategy', and in 'creative territories'. It is supposed to be able to invest no less than €44 billion – a huge amount by any standards – although it remains to be seen if it will be able to really help launch a new wave of innovative industries, which would also retain their productive plants on national French territory and not only their R&D departments and other high-skilled departments. In fact, the official aim of the BPI is not only to create new economic ventures, if possible at the edge of the technological frontiers, but also to help create jobs for ordinary workers. Since the French regions (nearly all politically dominated by the PS since the 2004 and 2009 elections) are associated with the venture, there is also a clear risk of petty clientelism.

Budgetary policy: under the realm of old and new European rules

The budgetary policy of Ayrault's government is no less constrained than its monetary policy. Having endorsed on the eve of his five-year mandate, the 'Fiscal Compact', and all the new European rules set on national budgetary matters since 2010 ('European Semester', 'Six-Pack', and so on), Hollande has had no choice but to follow the general mood in European decision circles, and the mood was not much in favour of the 'Keynesian' growth option. Moscovici clearly wished to become the new chairman of the 'Eurogroup' to replace the time-serving Luxembourg's Prime Minister and Economy and Finance Minister, Jean-Claude Juncker. He was however defeated without much debate by another socialist, the new Dutch Finance Minister, Jeroen Dijsselbloem. The Dutchman was without any international experience, contrary to his French rival who could praise himself for having negotiated in 2000 the Nice Treaty as European Affairs Minister, but Dijsselbloem had as a citizen of the 'serious North' much clearer credentials in term of austerity steering.

As a new president, Hollande was tireless in repeating his campaign mantra of growth and jobs in any public French or European occasion, including in front of the European Parliament. But, to date, he only obtained a 'European Growth Plan' of €130 billion at the same June 2013 European Council meeting, during which he accepted that he would have to abandon his attempt to renegotiate the 'Fiscal Compact'. Looking at the details of the €130 billion Growth Plan, most commentators were rapidly convinced that it was a non-event, engineered only to save face for Hollande. The results of the European Council's decision on the new European six-year budget (2014–20) in February 2013 proved again that no European intergovernmental majority was to emerge on a renewed Keynesian-style view of the EU's role.

At the national level, in an already rapidly deteriorating economic environment in Europe, and in France, as a result of the austerity turn of 2010–11, Ayrault's government had no choice but to come to terms with the official European objectives of public debt (60 per cent of GNP) and public deficit (3 per cent of GNP). Overall, since it was the easiest way to try to balance the 2012 annual budget, the government raised taxes (mostly on higher middle-class wage earners and on capital owners). Since 2010, under European pressure, the former UMP's conservative government had already chosen to raise taxes on these very same categories after their sharp reduction in previous years. The measures of the new Socialist-led government were only a little sharper, but triggered very irritated reactions from young entrepreneurs, who called themselves by derision '*les Pigeons*' (the suckers). A whole debate developed in the press on entrepreneurs' flight and more generally of capital owners' flight from this new French 'socialist hell'. Gérard Depardieu, the world-famous actor, sought Russian nationality to protest against the French government, and became the symbol of fat cats' refusal to pay more taxes, even at the cost of leaving France. The implementation of the tax at 75 per cent on salaries of more than €1 million per year proved itself to be far from straightforward. It was so ill-conceived by Finance Minister Cahuzac – or, it might be said, so *cleverly* ill-conceived? – that the French Constitutional Court deemed it in December 2012 unconstitutional. At the end of March 2013, Hollande made clear during a TV interview that the burden of the 'special tax' will be not on the individual receiving such a high level of pay, but on the enterprise employing him.

Still, while having to raise taxes and/or cut expenses, the government sought at the same time to show that social justice was at the centre of its action. As promised in Hollande's electoral programme, the government cancelled the tax hike of VAT prepared by the former government for 1 October 2013, leaving it unchanged at 19.6 per cent, and even reduced the level of indirect taxation on automobile fuel during the last months of 2012 to help drivers' budgets. The government raised the amount of some very visible social allocations – among them the Special September Grant for families having children at school (+ 25 per cent). It even keeps Hollande's promise to allow those persons who began work very early in life to draw on pensions at 60 years again, albeit on very restrictive conditions. Having already registered the negative impacts of austerity in other European countries, the PS-dominated government declared at this very early stage of its own economic and social policy that it was well aware of the necessity of not killing internal consumption by a rise in taxes on the less privileged citizens – quite the contrary, giving them a little more money through fiscal redistribution was presented at this early stage as a means to maintain overall consumer demand.

The tone of the first full-year budget was set in the autumn 2012 budget. Pledging to respect 'in any case' the 3 per cent threshold of overall state deficit, there was no alternative in agreeing the new budget but to try to stabilise expenses as much as possible in a piecemeal manner (as, already clearly overvalued, growth estimates for 2013 were in place). Some traditional leftist-defended ministerial departments, such as the Culture Ministry – chaired by a young woman Aurélie Filipetti (former socialist MP and novelist) – suffered much, while the Education Ministry (chaired by an older socialist leader Vincent Peillon) received more financial attention.

Overall, the Ayrault government's first budget did not undertake to make significant change, such as that which would have radically changed the great equilibriums of French public finance and would have clashed with entrenched public or private interests. To give only two examples, while seeking to close income tax loopholes, the 2013 budget retained a tax loophole linked to investments in the French Outremer (overseas territories) – where the PS and more generally the left has a clear electoral majority and in which it appeared difficult to cut subsidised and inefficient private investments (although this also helped to dampen the effect of the new rise in taxation for those on higher incomes). By the same token, to help build private housing for renting, the famous 'Scellier' tax loophole was replaced by a new one, the 'Duflot' tax loophole. This was despite the fact that this kind of tax loophole had proved itself incapable of solving the housing problem in France over the last thirty years, prompting disappointment at its resurrection under Cécile Duflot, the new 'Green' Minister of Housing.

To respond to growing fears about the future of French industry, Ayrault asked Louis Gallois – former CEO of a number of major French corporations – to prepare a white paper on the topic. The resulting 'Gallois Report' (Gallois *et al.*, 2012) recommended thirty-five measures to save French industry, and was fully endorsed the next day by Ayrault's government under the name of *Pacte national pour la croissance, la compétitivité et l'emploi* (Pact aiming at growth, competitiveness and job creation) – or, for the French press, '*Pacte pour la compétitivité*'. The Gallois Report and the measures it justified were a typical example of supply-side rhetoric. The most salient aspect of the measures, taken at the same time the 2013 budget was passing through Parliament, was to introduce a huge *crédit d'impôt* (tax break) in 2013 and 2014 for all French enterprises: €10 billion in 2013 and €20 billion in 2014. For each firm, the tax break – 4 per cent in 2013 and 6 per cent in 2014 – would be calculated on the whole amount of salaries below two-and-a-half times the minimum wage. The aim was to reduce by the same amount of the tax break the cost of work in France – not really a new kind of measure by French standards (Askenazy, 2011). Ayrault's government had in fact devised a proxy to an internal devaluation – similar to that in other southern European countries under the pressure of German competitiveness – without having to reduce directly the net earnings of wage earners of the private sector. The leader of the biggest representative organisation of business, the MEDEF, Laurence Parisot, was clearly pleased with this outcome. Ayrault's government has chosen to finance part of this tax break for the private sector through a VAT hike, to take place on 1 January 2014, on most ordinary consumption and also through a further reduction in state spending.

In any case, Ayrault's government is committed to reducing the nominal deficit of France in 2017 to 0 per cent, and to reducing further the structural primary deficit as calculated by the European Commission. The government wishes at the same time to subsidise further the private sector through a huge tax break. At this point, one might wonder which 'structural reforms' might come in the near future to finance this epochal downsizing of the French public deficit. A new bureaucratic process of reviewing the state's expenses has been announced under the acronym MAP (Modernisation of Public Action), and seems to be exactly the same kind of bureaucratic process as the former well-known RGPP (General Review of Public Policies). It was launched in 2007 on the eve of Sarkozy's presidency and aimed at the same goal of cutting inefficient state expenses. In 2007–12, RGPP was duly criticised by the left in general and the PS in particular for its blindness to social needs, to working conditions in the public sector, to simple economic rationality, and so on. RGPP was largely considered inefficient. The Public Administration Minister, Marylise Lebranchu, repeated many times that MAP would be cleverer and fairer than RGPP, without making clear how such a bureaucratic miracle would happen. As the early months have shown, Ayrault's government does not seem to be ready to enter into significant conflict with any entrenched interests, and, for the time being, we are in the early stages of MAP.

Structural reforms: according to the European 'one best way', but carefully
Since the monetary and budgetary policies are under strict European constraints, which economic tools remain available to the French socialist government other than those which have already been alluded to? Of course, the government remains free to choose its own 'structural reforms', as long as they remain in line with the European 'one best way' defined jointly by the European Commission, the ECB and the northern states of European Union. To achieve such a 'structural reform' of the labour market in a painless fashion, Ayrault's government has chosen to let the 'social dialogue' between organised business and representative trade unions decide. After some months of negotiation, reformist labour unions (CFDT, CFTC and CFE–CGC) and business organisations (MEDEF, CGPME) signed a joint document on 11 January 2013. According to this *Accord national interprofessionnel* (ANI),[7] French firms will be able to fire people more easily or force workers to accept worse economic conditions when a firm's economic situation is deemed difficult; workers will enjoy more social protection when at work and when unemployed, and large firms will have more say in business strategy. It remains to be seen, however, whether this structural reform – completely in line with European orthodoxy on the matter – will change the dynamics of the French labour market in the medium term.

To cope with rising unemployment, Ayrault's government has also reinvented – again – two particularly noxious special labour contracts: the *contrat d'avenir* (contract for the future) for undereducated youngsters and the *contrat de génération* (generational contract) to subsidise in the same movement the employment of too young and too old workers (on the noxiousness of these contracts, see Askenazy, 2011). Overall, after nearly one year, not much has been done. To give only one example, professional training during working life has long been considered by all French specialists to be a complete financial, organisational and human failure. It is true that the mainly Socialist-led regions are supposed to be officially in charge of professional training – which is not in fact the case – yet the whole system is far too complicated and intricate. At this stage, starting from scratch would be the only rational solution, but it is also self-evident that no 'normal' French government will have the political clout to decide to kill all these (inefficient if not corrupt) existing structures and to go against all the vested interests of this sector, including those strongly linked with trade unions, business associations and local authorities of any kind. Hollande waited until March 2013 to announce reforms of this sector – to be discussed with all stakeholders until the end of 2013 – exactly like his predecessor, Sarkozy, who also claimed to be attempting to reform the sector (without real effect).

To give some French 'populist' touch to this very classical 'supply-side' and 'austerity' policy mix, there is also in Ayrault's government a Minister for Productive Recovery, Arnaud Montebourg. Montebourg has been the rising star of the left of the PS since the late 1990s, and also most critical of Europe and of globalisation during the 2000s and 2010s, and yet found himself in charge of saving French industry. Present in the media every time an industrial plant – with many, mostly male and middle-aged, workers – was about to be closed by irrational or greedy private owners, Montebourg tried to find economic solutions to save the workplaces. Sarkozy, as Minister of the Economy in 2004–05, had enacted with some success the same drama. Montebourg in an even less rosy economic situation had some minor successes and also major failures – as in the symbolic case of Arcelor Mittal's plant in Florange, where the local trade unions called him at the end of the 'rescue process' a liar and a traitor to the 'working class'. From the scale of globalised capital, the letter Montebourg received from Maurice Taylor, the boss of Titan, the Australian tyre company which he had solicited to save a Goodyear's plant and its thousand workers in Amiens, was a perfect rebuttal – and, since it was disclosed by a daily newspaper (*Les Echos*, 2013), it was considered to be a lesson of international political economy for everyone. From a more medium-term perspective, Montebourg champions in the European public sphere the option according to which the EU should become less naive in international economic relations, and should make use of both a new 'European protectionism' and a new 'European industrial policy' to save its industrial basis from emerging economic powers – such as China, India and Brazil. This unorthodox message, coming from a junior minister of a state facing huge economic difficulties, remained to date – as far as we know – without direct influence over European policies. France even agreed, in the early months of Hollande's presidency, to open the preliminary discussions for the establishment of a free trade area between the United States of America and the EU. Many could then wonder how long Montebourg would continue to be willing to appear as the leftist guarantor of this so obviously 'social–liberal' government.

Overall, the economic policy of the first year can be summarised as follows. On the one hand, the government is searching for a 'supply-side' solution to French economic woes. Still committed to the European 'Lisbon Strategy', conceived in the last years of the last century, with the PS back in government, the government sees no other solution for the French economy in an open free-market world economy than to regain a 'technological edge' for French products on European and world markets through innovation. The BPI is to date the main symbol of this hope for the coming decades. This solution is congruous, as we will see, with the aspiration of its new core social base in the great metropolitan cities of France (Escalona and Vieira, 2012). On the other hand, to cope with more mundane and immediate problems, Ayrault's government seems to be committed to 'normal' economic policies. These 'business as usual' policies remain the same as they were in the 1970s (Askenazy, 2011): they are economically inefficient, but are deemed by all successive governments as necessary tools to maintain some calm in the country – and Ayrault's government is no exception. Furthermore, Ayrault's government is committed for budgetary reasons to 'structural reforms', still to be finalised at the time of writing. If possible, these reforms should be approved by stakeholders, or should be implemented in a piecemeal manner, so as to exhaust any kind of opposition. The downsizing of the old-style welfare state should proceed, if possible, without prompting excessive levels of protest. The Socialist-dominated government claims here a big advantage over the former conservative government since it can neutralise at least part of the trade unions and left-oriented civil society.

First explanation: the internal dynamics of the PS

More than ever a middle-class party

One may wonder at this stage of this discussion why Hollande chose this economic policy, leading in the short run to a very high level of unemployment by French standards (more than 10 per cent) and in the medium term to the destruction of many *acquis sociaux* (social rights) and to the downsizing of the welfare state, both elements of social life a socialist party is supposed in theory to care for.

First, one has to remember that the PS has not for decades been a party with strong links with the 'working class' in any meaningful sense of the word. Most members of the party are members of the middle classes. According to the last inquiry on the topic published by the *Revue socialiste* (Rey, 2011), no less than 64 per cent of socialist militants have a university diploma: among them, 10 per cent are alumni of *grandes écoles* (the French equivalent of 'Oxbridge' or 'Ivy League' universities). For the younger generations (under 40), the proportion with a university diploma increases to no less than 81 per cent! This is not exactly an accurate representation of ordinary French citizens of the same generation. Manual workers are, like in any other major political party in France, under-represented among the militants, if not totally absent (3 per cent), whereas they still constitute a little more than 20 per cent of the French workforce. Many militants are older men, many of whom already draw on their pensions, therefore not facing directly the vagaries of the French labour market. Further, among the younger militants, most of them enjoy a stable and well-paid job, well in line with their high level of education. The linkage with the trade unions through militancy, even with reformist trade unions like CFDT, also seems to be fading rapidly for the younger generation of militants.

The overrepresentation of public sector employees among the militants, very clear in the 1980s, has diminished (Rey, 2011): 50 per cent of the militants who joined the PS after 2008, when active, are employed by the private sector, but, still in 2011, only 44 per cent of militants of working age were active in the private sector. It has also long been remarked by analysts that the PS is in fact little more than a national association of elected local officials (Lefebvre and Sawicki, 2006; Lefebvre, 2011). Mayors of great cities or local 'barons' are the true masters of the party. Research has even shown that socialist 'militants' are in fact produced by the socialist control of locally elected institutions (Juhem, 2006), and not the other way round: ambitious people wanting to make it in the local spoil system, or simply people wanting to have a job in the local administrations. This very territorial nature of the PS can be well observed in the present reluctance of many Socialist deputies and senators to pass a law which would stop them having at the same time national parliamentary responsibilities and local elective responsibilities, although such a strict interdiction of *cumul des mandats* (occupation of several elected posts at the same time) was an integral part of the presidential programme of Hollande and was previously endorsed by an overwhelming vote of socialist militants in 2009.

Stronger than ever in local administrations

After the defeat of Jospin in the 2002 presidential election, each new round of local elections has seen victories for the PS, mainly against the more moderate part of the right wing of the political spectrum, and most of all in the western part of France. The PS now controls most of the regions, a majority of departments, and most major French cities. After the last round of municipal elections (2008), only Marseille and Bordeaux among the great cities remained under a UMP mayor. In consequence, at the Senate elections of October 2011, the PS and its leftist allies (Communists, Left Radicals and Greens) were able to change the political orientation of the Second Chamber for the first time since the early days of the Fifth Republic. A new senatorial majority was formed through the election at the Second Chamber presidency of Jean-Pierre Bel, a rather unknown local socialist politician. From this perspective, with the PS as the party dominating the local authorities, it appears quite logical that Hollande – himself Mayor of Tulle (2001–08) and President of the General Council of the Corrèze department (2008–12) – has chosen Ayrault – long-time serving mayor, first of Saint-Herblain (1977–89) and then of Nantes (1989–2012) – as his first prime minister.

Most of these 'barons' have excellent relations with the businesses of their own sphere of territorial influence. On their own small scale – a town, an agglomeration, a department, a region – they are all supply-siders seeking private enterprises to invest in their 'realm' to create jobs to satisfy potential wage earners and to expand their business tax base to alleviate the burden to local taxpayers. In fact, their relation to the general public seems to be dual natured: on the one hand, they speak person to person with distinguished members of the local, national or international business community, or with their own kind in the vast realm of French public administration; on the other hand, they take care, some-times directly and sometimes through the local social services they are managing, of the 'losers' of economic globalisation in their own 'realm'. So they remain socialist if the word means having a special interest for 'social problems', such as poverty, old age and urban delinquency, and a desire to change society (Dargent, 2011; Rey, 2011). While this kind of (mostly legal) 'clientelism' – or 'care' in a more polite wording – may ensure that some PS members have a solid electoral standing, it nevertheless provides few insights into the real working conditions in the private sector of the French economy in this late stage of capitalism.

The 'renovation' of the PS (2008–11): changing everything not to change anything
Apart from these medium-term considerations for the sociological composition of the PS, one has to consider that the internal politics of the PS since 2005 have ensured a complete domination of a moderate view of the economy among the PS's leadership. As the reader might know, when asked to choose which position to adopt on the European Constitutional Treaty (ECT), the PS opted to ask its militants directly to endorse a position. The party vote subsequently split, with a majority choosing to accept the ECT, and the PS recommending that the national electorate vote yes. During the 2005 referendum campaign, however, while some of the leaders of the internal 'no' vote remained silent and therefore loyal to the democratic choice of the party, others decided to put their voice behind the 'no' campaign. The 'traitors' to party discipline, as they were called at the time by their fellow-comrades, had understood the growing sentiment for a 'no' vote among the PS's natural electorate, that it is to say workers and lower middle classes. The most prominent among these 'traitors' was Laurent Fabius – former Prime Minister (1983–86) during Mitterrand's presidency. The outstanding victory of the 'no' vote in the French referendum was therefore a blow to the party's internal majority, and especially to Hollande, its chief at the time. The division of the party over the European question was evident, but the socialist 'no' campaigners had ensured that at least a part of the PS was on the side of the 'no' majority of the French people.

In November 2008, the congress at Reims, which aimed to reorganise the party after its severe defeat at the 2007 presidential election, reaffirmed the exist-ence of a clear pro-European majority. The left of the party (called Un monde d'avance) which wanted to push a new vision of Europe, under the direction of

Benoît Hamon, was clearly defeated with the support of less than 20 per cent of the mandates. The bitter fight during and after the Reims congress for the direction of the party between Ségolène Royal, former candidate to the 2007 presidential elections, President of Poitou-Charentes region since 2000, and Martine Aubry, former Minister for Work and Solidarity (1997–2000), Mayor of Lille since 2000, had little to do with their economic or European positions. Both women were for the 'yes' in 2005, and they had not much to say about this topic. Finally, following the militants' final vote, Aubry won by a narrow margin. This was not without some cheating in some federations on both sides.[8] The pro-European direction of the PS did not marginalise the politicians who had opted for the 'no' option in 2004–05: Hamon was now the speaker of the PS, and Montebourg was in charge of renovating the party. Still, some partisans of the 'no' vote seized the occasion of the Reims congress to secede from the PS. Jean-Luc Mélenchon, a senator, and Marc Dolez, a deputy, both considered that the PS's majority remained so oriented towards a benign view of Europe and of capitalism that nothing more could be achieved politically by remaining inside it, and therefore organised the scission. They created immediately a new organisation, called *Parti de gauche* ('Left Party') to underline the PS's contradictory nature. It regrouped these (few) PS dissidents and (even fewer) dissidents of other left parties. The new Left Party immediately joined force with the old PCF and other fringe left organisations to fight under the (old-fashioned) umbrella name of *Front de gauche* (Leftist Front). This split of some of the PS's left leaders (Mélenchon, Dolez) and the co-optation of other minority parties' leaders (Montebourg, Hamon) resulted in internal critical leftist voices being weaker than ever within the PS.

The European elections of June 2009 witnessed disappointing results for the 'renovated' PS. With only 16.5 per cent of the national vote, the PS suffered both from the concurrence of the clearly new pro-European list *Europe-Ecologie-les Verts* (16.3 per cent) and the more Euro-sceptic list Front de gauche (6 per cent). Nevertheless, due to the enduring unpopularity of Sarkozy, the 2010 regional election was a great success for the PS, which was able to retain the dominant position it had won at this level of government in the previous 2004 regional election. So, when the time came on the eve of 2011 to choose the PS's presidential candidate for 2012 through a primary election – as in 1995 and 2007 – there was no doubt that a pro-European social–liberal candidate would be appointed. At the beginning of 2011, most commentators speculated on the exact time of return in the French political arena of 'DSK', Dominique Strauss-Kahn, former Minister of the Economy (1997–99), Chairman of the IMF since 2007. After his defeat in the 2007 PS primary, at the hands of Royal, and following the rout of his primary's opponent in front of Nicolas Sarkozy, DSK accepted the new president's offer to be the French candidate to the IMF's chairmanship. From Washington, he clearly prepared his image as the new 'wise man' for France. DSK's 'Sofitel scandal' of May 2011 changed everything. As the process of candidate selection was planned by Montebourg as 'Secretary to the Renovation' – even before DSK's scandal – this time the PS's primary election would be made open to all self-declared left-oriented voters, taking inspiration both from the traditional American and more recent Italian models. Of course, with the loss of the 'evident candidate', the primary failed to become a popular endorsement, and rather, became a real competition in which the whole of public opinion was mobilised. Royal, Aubry and Hollande were the main candidates. On the right side of the PS, Manuel Valls, a mayor in the suburbs of Paris, was to represent the 'New Labour' French-style option – liberal on economy and tough on crime and immigration. On the left side of the party, Montebourg was to propose an alternative to the 'business-as-usual' left-of-the-centre social–liberal mix of the PS majority. He published with some public success a book on the topic of *démondialisation* ('deglobalisation') (Montebourg, 2011). The book was prefaced by Todd and therefore focused mostly on European protectionism. Montebourg had sought to radicalise the discourse of the 'euro-critical socialists' (such as himself) during the 'no' campaign in 2004–05 (Heine, 2009). In the primary contest, he won a 17 per cent share of the 2.6 million voters in the first round, which was considered a surprisingly good result and which gave him a new political standing. In the second round, he opted officially to remain neutral between Hollande and Aubry, although he voted for Hollande, thereby leaving some of his own first-round supporters amazed given that Hollande's positions seemed at the time even more conservative on economic and social issues than those of Aubry. Montebourg clearly intended to climb on the bandwagon whatever the ideas of the frontrunner.

In sum, apart from some lip-service to left classical slogans around 'change', 'justice', 'the fight against unemployment', and so on, and much discussion of the 'renovation of the party', the internal dynamics of the PS remained clearly on the side of continuity. Hollande's orientations as a candidate in the presidential election mirrored the general orientation of public policies during the PS' previous period in office (1997–2002). Many observers noted, even during the presidential campaign itself, that Hollande had no flagship socio-economic reform to defend in front of the electorate – contrary to 1997, when the general working time reduction to fight unemployment (the '35-hour-working week') was mainly used as a tool to win the electorate's attention, but similarly to 2007 where this void of propositions led to defeat. The proposal of Hollande, which was not even present in his own primary campaign, to tax at 75 per cent people earning more than €1 million a year, can be seen in retrospect as a communication tool to change this impression.

Second explanation: the trend to bipartism of the political system and the dynamics of public opinion

While the PS continued on a similar trajectory to that established during the 1990s, the years 2008–12 also witnessed a process of renewal for the PS in terms of public opinion. In particular, from 2008, the PS won every local election. As the main opposition party in a two-round majoritarian electoral system (Grunberg and Haegel, 2007), it had a clear positional advantage in a situation where the conservative government was unpopular. Only a few months after his election in May 2007, Sarkozy became unpopular and remained so until the end of his term in office. By a simple pendulum's movement, the PS gained ground without much effort. In this dual system, to vote PS was for most ordinary voters the best way to condemn the UMP's action.

The real problem facing the PS was the fact that the party was unpopular among working-class workers. The severe defeat in the 2002 presidential election was largely due to the fact that workers abandoned the PS. In the 2007 presidential election, the result improved, but was not enough to ensure victory. A think tank, Terra Nova, even published – in preparation for the 2012 presidential campaign – a document suggesting abandoning altogether the conquest of the (male) (French-born) working class (Ferrand *et al.*, 2013). The document argued that, authoritarian by nature, these workers were a lost cause for the PS. To win the election, the PS would need to concentrate on a 'rainbow coalition'. It would be made of women in the workplace and outside the workplace, descendants of recent (Muslim) immigrants in the suburbs, sexual (gay) minorities and the educated middle classes. Of course, other left intellectuals, among whom Laurent Bouvet (2012) was most prominent, were highly critical of this option.

In practical terms, Hollande decided not to abandon the workers' electorate to his opponents, to either his right or left. He praised during his campaign the many virtues of industry, and took advantage of Sarkozy's earlier (ineffective) promises made in 2007 on the same topic. The closure of a steel plant, in Florange, by Laskhi Mittal's multinational firm (Arcelor Mittal in France), was central to this strategy.

Ultimately, this approach proved to be a good investment for Hollande: in the first round, he retained the vote of 27 per cent of workers (the National Front candidate, Marine Le Pen, was first with 29 per cent of workers' vote) and 28 per cent of employees (the other candidates were not able to retain the vote of more than 22 per cent of these latter) (IPSOS, 2012a); and, in the second round, he obtained 58 per cent of workers' vote and 56 per cent of employees' vote. Among the whole electorate, in the second round, 100 per cent per cent of those locating themselves close to a party of the left voted for him (IPSOS, 2012b). *Le peuple de gauche* were back.

A few months after his election, Hollande was already confronted with the fact that, according to opinion pools, he had already lost most of the support he gained in May 2012 among workers and employees. It was a rational attitude from this part of the population, since many industrial plants were closing in the aftermath of his election and, more generally, as unemployment was booming in these early months of the new presidency. No important social or economic reforms – which could have improved the daily life of wage earners – was implemented in the early days and months of Hollande's presidency, or even discussed. The contrast was sharp with previous socialist experience – 1981, 1988, 1997, not to speak of 1936 – or even with the early days of Sarkozy's presidency. The former president had passed in the summer of 2007 a law referred to by its acronym TEPA. It ensured that overtime work would no longer be the subject of direct taxation. TEPA was a direct application for wage earners of Sarkozy's slogan during his campaign: 'working more for more pay'. In contrast, no such symbolical decision was even taken by Ayrault's government. Even the official national minimum wage (SMIC) was not significantly raised. The disappointment was great. Change was not even now!

For many observers, this development in the sphere of public opinion was unsurprising. The real analytical question was to understand why (some) low-skilled wage earners were still ready to believe that the PS was more aware of their immediate needs than was really the case. The three previous socialist 'experiences' (1981–86, 1988–93, 1997–2002) during the Fifth Republic had always the same epilogue, with the core of the (male) working class experiencing that, even when the PS was in charge of national affairs, it failed to act as their best advocate – at least, not the best advocate of their immediate interest in the sense of ensuring that they kept their jobs. The closure of traditional industrial plants of old industrialised regions continued undisturbed during the 1980s and 1990s without the PS making much difference – even facilitating the closure of many industrial plants with its links with moderate trade unions. Since one can easily observe a strong continuity in terms of personnel between all of these former governmental episodes and all the frontrunners to the 2012 Socialist Primaries – DSK, Aubry, Royal, Hollande – one can ask oneself whether there exists a strong *myopia* or even *self-delusion* of this part of the electorate. One may also underline, again, that in the French majoritarian political system the only short-term relevant option to 'get the bastards out' is to vote for the PS when the UMP is in charge, and for the UMP when the PS is in charge. Investing in a lost vote for another party – extreme left, centre, extreme right – supposes a longer time horizon.

According to the opinion pools, the popularity of Hollande and Ayrault is rapidly declining to record lows: 31 per cent of satisfied respondents for the president and his prime minister in March 2013 according to IPSOS political barometer (IPSOS, 2013). This fall in popularity is most marked among workers and employees. Rightist and centrist voters are not pleased, a third of leftists likewise. The choice of European-led austerity under Hollande is refused with outrage by the same social groups which voted 'no' to the European Constitution in 2005: the less privileged part of the population. Only the core of the PS's electorate – middle classes working for the public sector – continue at the time of writing to approve of the majority of decisions made since May 2012.

A last element must be underlined to understand how French public opinion was able to accept the PS's mild proposals made during the presidential campaign. Contrary to many other European countries since 2008 having to fight against budget deficits – due to a banking crisis (Ireland), a fiscal crisis (Greece) or both (Spain) – Sarkozy's government did not choose to *directly* cut public wages, state pensions or social allocations. The basic rise in pay for public wages has been duly frozen since 2010, and new social contributions were to be paid by public employed wage earners. But the careers of public wage earners continued, with the continued possibility of increased earnings. Fewer new persons were to be engaged (only one person for two retirements) by the state, so that working conditions became difficult in many public-organised sectors, such as education or health, but the overall situation was not as desperate as in other European southern countries. The local authorities still had the option of hiring new employees. From our point of view, the mild nature of Sarkozy's choices during the early stage of the European crisis – which led to an outburst of French public debt and made French internal demand the 'consumer of last resort' for the whole of Europe in 2009–11 – explained why the electoral base of the PS was not entirely aware of developments in the rest of Europe. Being 'against European austerity' and being 'for jobs and growth' does not have exactly the same practical meaning when wages continue to grow, compared with when they are reduced overnight by 5, 10 or 25 per cent – or when you are simply laid off by your public employer.

Since Sarkozy was greatly unpopular for the greater part of his five-year mandate, and since neither he nor his majority wanted to enter into a full-scale 'Thatcherite-style' conflict with French trade unions, he did not indulge in 'structural reforms'. For instance, the right while in power did not dare to change the legal working hours – which remains at 35 hours per week – and the reform of pensions of 2011 was relatively mild by today's European standards. Of course, the whole left and the trade unions were critical of the public policies of the right, but Sarkozy took great care not to appear to be the butcher of social rights, knowing through his experience as minister of the interior – in 2005 during the riots in the French suburbs and during the demonstrations in 2006 against a special labour contract for youngsters – that the French streets can be dangerous for a conservative government. No more 1968 please!

Some even noted, in 2011, that France was quiet, whereas elsewhere in Europe or in America, mass demonstrations against capitalism took place, around *indignados* or Occupy Wall Street movements – which were inspired by a pamphlet written by an old figure of the French left, Stéphane Hessel. The PS, which was endorsed by the same Hessel, seemed at the time to be heading for victory in the next presidential election, and many otherwise unsatisfied electors were waiting for such a victory, hoping to see a significant change. Street protests were not necessary, since the PS should solve everything once in power.

What it means to govern under European rule

Nearly a year after his election, Hollande's situation is already ironical, and might soon become tragic. The PS has a long-term commitment to European integration. The PS has endorsed every European treaty since 1992, and now according to the European rules the PS has no apparent choice but to cut drastically public budgets and go for dramatic structural reforms. For the fiscal year 2013 the European Commission will surely admit in the name of the European recession that the level of French public deficit is to remain well above the 3 per cent red line (3.7 per cent at the time of writing). Alas, in the coming fiscal years, if no economic miracle happens, no solutions other than more taxes and more cuts will be the order of the day. This 'taxing and cutting' obligation will last until the end of Hollande's presidency. Since the core of its own electorate is dependent on a high level of public spending, the situation will be even more intricate for the PS. More generally, all economic policies seem to be only the French application of a European 'one best way'. No national debate can change this 'one best way'. As an escape option, a 'normal' government can only procrastinate when lacking courage in front of vested interests defending the national status quo. Any national government is expected to apply the wished-for EU common recipes to the country over which it is in charge. This kind of politics is then more about management of public (bad) feelings than (ambitious) goal-setting.

Historically, the French PS wanted to build Europe for a number of reasons, since it considered Europe to be the more accurate level at which to protect the French people from the impact of globalisation and to build a new kind of welfare state. Montebourg, as Minister for Industrial Recovery, retains this line of thinking and hopes for a more protectionist Europe. Moscovici thinks he can still defend a more balanced approach to debt sustainability. More generally, Hollande and his government are still asking for more pro-growth European policies, but what does this mean? Obtaining 'euro-bonds' from Germany and other creditors' member states? Asking Germany to reduce its own internal demand for consumer goods in order to help French exporters? Having less fiscal austerity in southern Europe? Creating a European (or Euro-zone) 'federal budget' to stabilise the demand fluctuations in Europe, alongside the monetary policy of the ECB – such a federal budget which would require more than 5 to 15 per cent of GNP to be devoted to Europe according to some economists? As far as we know today, it remains difficult to imagine how the French government will be able to change *alone* the direction of the European policy mix. The last decisions on the European budget add to this pessimistic analysis. A diversified EU at 27 countries cannot be managed by the French *volonté politique* (political will) as it was the case in a European Economic Community at 6, 9 or even 12 countries. The present generations of French socialist leaders seem to have difficulties to accept this new low-profile status of France, and to act accordingly.

If it fails to achieve these goals of growth and protection through the choice for Europe, the French PS will appear to have chosen a flawed long-term strategy for France. The FN and the whole rightist *souverainistes*, of course, have been saying this for decades, as are, on the other side, the Front de gauche and some intellectuals like Todd. The UMP, the main party of the right, is still silent on this topic, but some conservative voices are already heard to criticise the naive European stance of the PS. The next years could be a dead end for French socialism, like the Algeria War (1954–62) was for its ancestor, the SFIO – or, if all ends well, a lasting triumph for the generation which chose Europe in 1983.

Notes

1 In an interview with Eric Aeschimann and Hervé Algalarrondo, journalists for the left-of-centre news magazine *Nouvel Observateur*, published on 1 March 2012 (http://tempsreel.nouvelobs.com/election-presidentielle-2012/20120304.OBS2872/ emmanuel-todd-je-parie-sur-l-hollandisme-revolutionnaire.html (accessed 14 March 2013).

2 Since the 1980s, the level of unemployment and job insecurity for low-skilled workers is far higher in France than for the educated middle classes, which as a matter of fact did not suffer much from the economic downturn. During downturns, the state was always able to create public jobs for middle-class aspirants, while accepting a high level of long-term unemployment for workers, even more so when socialists were in charge (Chauvel, 2006; Davezies, 2012).

3 'Loi organique n° 2012–1403 relative à la programmation et à la gouvernance des finances publiques' (17 December 2012).

4 During a public roundtable, on 'the ECB in the Eurocrisis', organised at 'Les Journées de l'Economie', Lyon, Bourse du Travail, 9 November 2012.

5 Cahuzac had to resign in March 2013 since an online media, Mediapart, had discovered a few months before that he had for many years held bank accounts, first in the Swiss Confederation, and then in Singapore, to cover his fiscal evasion activities.

6 Oseo, CDC Entreprise and FSI (Fonds stratégique d'investissement).

7 'Accord national interprofessionnel du 11 janvier 2013 pour un nouveau modèle économique et social au service de la compétitivité des entreprises et de la sécurisation de l'emploi et des parcours professionnels des salariés'.

8 In a first count, Aubry had only 42 votes more than Royal, and, in a second count, only 102, on more than 134,000 votes for the second round cast by militants. Accusations of cheating were rife on both sides. Two journalists gathered one year after the psychodrama which agitated French socialists in November 2008, with many

indications tending to prove these accusations (André and Rissouli, 2009). Royal alluded again in 2012 to the fact she had had victory stolen from her in 2008.

References

André, A. and Rissouli, K. (2009). *Hold-uPS, arnaques et trahisons* (Paris: Editions du Moment).

Askenazy, P. (2011). *Les décennies aveugles: Emploi et croissance (1970–2010)* (Paris: Editions du Seuil).

Bouvet, L. (2012). *Le sens du peuple: La gauche, la démocratie, le populisme* (Paris: Editions Gallimard).

Chauvel, L. (2006). *Les classes moyennes à la dérive* (Paris: Editions du Seuil).

Clift, B. (2013). '*Le changement?* French socialism, the 2012 presidential election and the politics of economic credibility amidst the eurozone crisis', *Parliamentary Affairs*, 66, 106–23.

Cohen, E. (2013). 'Les banques: une réforme bien modeste', *Telos*, 25 February, available at: www.telos-eu.com/fr/globalisation/finance-mondiale/banques-une-reforme-bien-modeste.html (accessed 1 April 2012).

Dargent, C. (2011). 'Les adhérents socialistes: attitudes, valeurs et ancrages idéologiques', *La Revue socialiste*, 42, 135–42, available at: www.revuesocialiste.fr/2011/05/06/les-adher ents-socialistes-attitudes-valeurs-et-ancrages-ideologiques (accessed 14 March 2013).

Davezies, L. (2012). *La crise qui vient. La nouvelle fracture territoriale* (Paris: Editions du Seuil).

Dupin, E. (2012). *La victoire empoisonnée* (Paris: Editions du Seuil).

Les Echos (2013). 'Goodyear: la lettre de Titan à Montebourg', 19 February.

Les économistes atterrés (2012). *L'Europe mal-traitée. Refuser le Pacte budgétaire et ouvrir d'autres perspectives* (Paris: Les liens qui libèrent).

Escalona, F. and Vieira, M. (2012). 'La social-démocratie des idéopôles. Une illustration française de la dissociation entre électorat populaire et électorat socialiste', in J.-M. de Waele and M. Vieira (eds), *Une droitisation de la classe-ouvrière en Europe?* (Paris: Economica), pp. 121–41.

Ferrand, O., Jeanbart, B. and Prudent, R. (2013). *Gauche: quelle majorité électorale pour 2012?*, Terra Nova, available online at: www.tnova.fr/essai/gauche-quelle-majorit-lectorale-pour-2012 (accessed 14 March 2013).

Gallois, L., Lubin, C. and Thiard, P.-E. (2012). *Pacte pour la compétitivité de l'industrie française*, Commissariat général à l'investissement, Rapport au Premier Ministre (Paris: La Documentation française), available at: www.economie.gouv.fr/competitiv ite-rapport-louis-gallois (accessed 14 March 2013).

Grunberg, G. and Haegel, F. (2007). *La France vers le bipartisme?* (Paris: Les Presses de Sciences Po).

Heine, S. (2009). *Une gauche contre l'Europe?* (Bruxelles: Editions de l'Université de Bruxelles).

IPSOS (2012a). 'Tour de l'élection présidentielle. Comprendre le vote des Français', available at: www.ipsos.fr/ipsos-public-affairs/actualites/2012-04-22-comprendre-le-vote-des-francais (accessed 14 March 2013).

IPSOS (2012b). 'Tour de l'élection présidentielle. Comprendre le vote des Français', available at: www.ipsos.fr/ipsos-public-affairs/actualites/2012-05-06-comprendre-vote-francais (accessed 14 March 2013).

IPSOS (2013). *Le baromètre de l'action politique IPSOS/Le Point*, available at: www.ipsos.fr/ipsos-public-affairs/actualites/2013–03–11–nouveau-decrochage-popularite-l-executif-notamment-gauche (accessed 14 March 2013).

Jeanbart, B., Ferrand, O. and Prudent, R. (2013). *Gauche: quelle majorité électorale pour 2012?*, Terra Nova, available at: www.tnova.fr/essai/gauche-quelle-majorit-lectorale-pour-2012 (accessed 14 March 2013).

Juhem, P. (2006). 'La production notabiliaire du militantisme au Parti socialiste', *Revue française de science politique*, 56(6), 906–41.

Lefebvre, R. (2011). *Les primaires socialistes. La fin du parti militant* (Paris: Editions Raisons d'Agir).

Lefebvre, R. and Sawicki, F. (2006). *La Société des socialistes. Le PS aujourd'hui* (Bellecombe-en-Bauges: Editions du Croquant).

Lordon, F. (2013). 'La régulation bancaire au pistolet à bouchon', *La pompe à phynance, Blog du Monde diplomatique*, 18 February, available at: http://blog.monded iplo.net/2013-02-18-La-regulation-bancaire-au-pistolet-a-bouchon (accessed 1 April 2013).

Montebourg, A. (2011). *Votez pour la démondialisation!* (Paris: Flammarion).

Rey, H. (2011). 'Les adhérents au parti socialiste: permanence et changement', *La Revue socialiste*, 42, 125–33, available at: www.revuesocialiste.fr/2011/05/06/les-adherents-socialistes-permanences-et-changements (accessed 14 March 2013).

10

Back to the drawing board: the PSOE after the 2011 general election

Paul Kennedy

Introduction

When the Spanish Socialist Workers' Party (PSOE) comfortably won the March 2008 general election, gaining a vote even higher than the previous historic peak obtained when the party entered office in 2004, there was ample reason for satisfaction. With Spanish economic growth outpacing the EU average since the mid-1990s, unemployment had been brought down to 8 per cent and the party's programme for the 2008 general election contained a pledge to create two million new jobs so as to secure full employment within four years (PSOE, 2008). During the bulk of the party's first term in office (2004–08) Spain had enjoyed a budget surplus, and public sector debt was among the lowest in the EU. At the end of the previous year, the EU's statistical office, Eurostat, had announced that Spanish per capita income had overtaken that of Italy for the first time, leading the Spanish Prime Minister, José Luis Rodríguez Zapatero, to suggest that France might provide the next realistic target.[1] In his inauguration speech following the PSOE's victory, Zapatero (2008) claimed that the successive surpluses in the public accounts would enable the economy to absorb the impact of the downturn in economic activity which was already becoming apparent, and to ensure that there would be no need to resort to either increased taxation or cuts in social provision. Furthermore, the government had implemented a number of important reforms in the area of civil and gender rights which were among the most progressive in Europe. Four months after the election, 98 per cent of delegates at the party's 37th congress endorsed Zapatero's leadership. It is therefore understandable that Zapatero was able to establish a degree of control over the party and government even greater than that enjoyed by Felipe González, who had led the PSOE during its previous period in office between 1982 and 1996.

At the November 2011 general election, the PSOE obtained under seven million votes, almost 4.5 million fewer than in 2008, and almost four million behind the victorious Popular Party (PP). The PSOE captured just 29 per cent of the vote, compared to the PP's 45 per cent, and its capture of just 110 of the 350 parliamentary seats, a loss of 59, gave the party its lowest total since the establishment of democracy following Franco's death. While the PP's vote increased by just over 0.5 million votes compared to 2008, it won 186 seats and a comfortable overall majority.

The fate suffered by the Spanish Socialist government at the 2011 general election provides a case study of a government effectively rendered unelectable by the impact of the economic crisis. Stating that he would put in place all economic reforms considered necessary to stave off the kind of bail-out required by Greece, Ireland and Portugal, 'whatever the personal cost', Zapatero implemented a severe austerity package, prominent among whose measures was an average 5 per cent reduction in civil servants' salaries, the slashing of public sector investment, the freezing of pensions, and the extension of the retirement age from 65 to 67. Moreover, he presided over a vertiginous increase in unemployment, which affected almost five million people, 22 per cent of the active population – the highest level in fifteen years. This statistic, which was the highest in the Eurozone, included almost half of under-25s. The prime minister announced in April 2011 that he would not be standing for a third term and that the task of leading the party into the general election, which he had brought forward in November 2011, four months earlier than expected, was entrusted to the former interior minister and first Deputy Prime Minister, Alfredo Pérez Rubalcaba. Given this legacy, it is unsurprising that Rubalcaba struggled to gain a hearing from an electorate angered by the government's apparent impotence in the face of the challenges posed by the economic crisis.

Following the election, the PSOE struggled to come to terms with the scale of its defeat, and it prepared to analyse the reasons for the collapse in party support as well as proposing a way forward in opposition. The party's 38th congress, held in February 2012, constituted the first step in this process, although opinions within the party were mixed as to whether the decision to go ahead with the election of a new leader within three months of such a historic defeat was overly hasty. Given that the PSOE faced the prospect of a long time in opposition, some felt that the party should take a considered approach in order to ensure that the right person was selected, rather than being unduly concerned about a temporary power vacuum within the leadership. After such a crushing defeat, it was incumbent upon the PSOE to carry out a process of renewal capable of 'detoxifying' the PSOE 'brand' and re-establishing its credibility as a party of government. The party's most recent experience of opposition between 1996 and 2004 provided lessons in this regard. During José María Aznar's first term in office between 1996 and 2000, the PSOE had turned in on itself and squandered the regenerative opportunities offered by opposition, before the poor result obtained in 2000 forced the party to carry out a process of generational, ideological and programmatic renewal which served as the basis for the general election victories of 2004 and 2008. However, this process would be complicated by the fact that those who had served in Zapatero's government and who were viewed as potential leaders of the PSOE had seen their own credibility undermined by association. Throughout the 2011 general election campaign, Rubalcaba was constantly reminded that he had been a key figure in a government which had presided over the transformation from boom to bust. Furthermore, in 2000, unlike in 2012, the election of a leader did not take place within the context of an international economic crisis which called into question the very foundations of Spain's socio-economic model.

The following questions will be considered during the course of this chapter. How are we to account for this slump in the PSOE's fortunes over such a relatively short period of time? How accurate is it to suggest that the economic crisis was the sole reason for the PSOE's poor showing at the 2011 general election? Finally, how has the party fared in opposition under the leadership of Rubalcaba?

The chapter is structured as follows. The first section considers the situation in which the Socialist government found itself after its re-election in 2008 with respect to its main achievements and challenges. The following section covers the government's reaction to the economic crisis during its second term in office 2008–11, most particularly after the onset of the Greek sovereign debt crisis in May 2010, and briefly considers the party's record in opposition since its crushing defeat at the 2011 general election. The conclusion then seeks to provide an appraisal of the PSOE's performance, together with an attempt to identify its chief failings.

On the edge of the precipice: the PSOE government in 2008

Given the innovative nature of many of its policies throughout its first term in office between 2004 and 2008, the economy was the one area which was notable for continuity, rather than change, with respect to the policies of the previous PP government under Aznar between 1996 and 2004. Although it was the withdrawal of Spanish troops from Iraq within weeks of the PSOE entering office which attracted international attention, it is significant that the first item of legislation passed by Zapatero's government was concerned with the issue of domestic violence, given Zapatero's decision to prioritise gender rights throughout his period in office. Women occupied half of the seats in cabinet, while María Teresa Fernández de la Vega was appointed First Deputy Prime Minister, the first time in Spanish history that a woman had occupied the post. Further proposals included a Law on Equality between Men and Women. Despite the vehement opposition of the Catholic Church, legislation was passed which allowed marriage between persons of the same sex and which gave gay couples the right to adopt. A Law concerning the Recovery of Historic Memory was approved which honoured the memory of those who had suffered repression at the hands of the Franco dictatorship, with financial support being provided for those still searching for family members' remains (Kennedy, 2007).

Beyond the area of civil and gender rights, the government also made use of the surplus in the public accounts to pass a Dependency Law aimed at providing support for those requiring or providing care. Described by the government as the 'fourth pillar' of the welfare state, joining existing provision in health care, education and pensions, the initiative was perhaps the most important piece of legislation of Zapatero's entire premiership, with over 700,000 people who had previously received no state aid benefiting. Moreover, the initiative led to the creation of 260,000 jobs in the care sector and can be considered the government's most prominent redistributive measure. A further indication of the government's social democratic policy credentials was the fact that those on the lowest incomes enjoyed the largest percentage decrease in their income tax contributions between 2004 and 2008, while social expenditure accounted for half of the 2008 budget.

Zapatero was nevertheless keen to stress that he was not minded to put at risk economic stability. Interviewed in 2006, he commented that his social-ism was not of the old 'tax and spend variety, where there is unlimited public spending paid for by tax increases … Public finances should be managed rigorously' (Calamai and Garzia, 2006: 83). The previous year he had argued, 'a modern left programme is based on a well-managed economy with public accounts in surplus, moderate taxes and a limited public sector' (Girauta, 2010: 226). Endorsement of the government's economic policy was provided by the Organisation for Economic Co-operation and Development, which highlighted fiscal prudence and beneficial structural reforms as explanatory factors for the economy's robust performance in terms of growth, employment and public finances (OECD, 2007: 1).

The PSOE's first term in office had also been notable for the wide-ranging reform of the statutes which govern the responsibilities enjoyed by Spain's sev-enteen autonomous regions. Although the process – particularly as regards the Catalan statute – was one of the most controversial elements in the government's programme, it did not prevent the PSOE from gaining re-election in the 2008 general election. Any criticism of the process by the PP was undermined by the fact that several of the regions taking advantage of the opportunity to update their statutes were governed by the PP.

The continuation of the economic boom, which stretched back to the mid-1990s, was nevertheless the key element in the PSOE's re-election in 2008. The broad parameters of economic policy had been put in place by Aznar's PP gov-ernments between 1996 and 2004, and, with Spanish economic growth easily outpacing the EU average, there appeared to be little incentive for the Socialists to reject an economic growth model based on the construction sector. With the budget in surplus, public sector debt below 40 per cent, and unemployment falling to below the EU average, any major deviation from an economic growth model which appeared to provide economic stability appeared unnecessary.

With the benefit of hindsight, it was clear that the model favoured by both the PP and PSOE governments contained the seeds of its own destruction. While Spain created 40 per cent of new jobs in the Euro area in the fifteen years up to 2007, many of these jobs were linked to the construction sector, which accounted for 10 per cent of GDP by 2007, well above the 5 per cent average figure of Spain's EU partners (Chislett, 2008; O'Kean, 2010: 19). Employment in the construction sector rose from 1.2 million in 1996 (9 per cent of the labour force) to 2.7 million (13 per cent of the labour force) in the second quarter of 2007. This meant that there were almost as many people employed in construction as there were in the whole of the industrial sector in 2007 (Salmon, 2010a: 46). At the heart of the property boom lay the low interest rates maintained by the European Central Bank since the turn of the decade. Banks, companies and households took on increased levels of debt as real interest rates, that is to say nominal interest rates minus inflation, effectively became negative between 2002 and 2006 (Juan, 2011: 23–4).

Given that the fate of Zapatero's government was, ultimately, to be inexorably linked to the economy's dependence on the construction sector, and related high levels of indebtedness, it is noteworthy that the PSOE's programme for the 2004 general election identified the dangers inherent in such reliance. Reference was made to the 'cult of bricks and mortar'; the 'escalation of private sector indebtedness, of both families and companies'; and 'the current risks concerning the Spanish economy, which is highly indebted and geared towards bricks and mortar' (PSOE, 2004: 103–4). Moreover, Miguel Ángel Fernández Ordóñez, Governor of the Spanish Central Bank from 2006, and Miguel Sebastián, Industry Minister throughout Zapatero's second term in office, both warned as early as 2003 against the dangers of excessive debt, the fallout from an eventual drop in demand within the construction sector, and the fact that construction was crowding out investment in other areas, such as high-tech activity sectors of the economy (Juan, 2011: 32–3). Addressing the parliamentary finance committee in June 2011, Fernández Ordóñez claimed that the Bank of Spain's warnings had been ignored by successive governments: 'If more attention had been given to what the Bank of Spain had been saying for a long time, for example during the property bubble, when different governments and opinions suggested that there was nothing to worry about . . .' (*El País*, 2011a)

In addition to this dependence on the construction sector, the economy displayed a number of important weaknesses, including a current account deficit that reached 10 per cent of GDP in 2007, the second largest quantitative amount in the world after the United States, indicating the Spanish economy's dependence on external funding (Andrés *et al.*, 2011: 70). Particularly affected was the private sector in the form of businesses and households. The economy also suffered from low levels of productivity, weak indicators related to the knowledge economy, a high degree of dependence on imported energy, and a dual labour market in which one-third of the labour force was employed on short-term contracts with little or no protection, whereas the other two-thirds were protected by measures which made it expensive for companies to adjust to changing labour market conditions (Salmon, 2010a: 40). All these factors would contribute towards the steep increase in unemployment in the period after the 2008 general election.

The PSOE's victory in that election was nevertheless never in doubt, given that the very buoyancy of the economy had the effect of dampening debate on economic policy. However, once the election was out of the way, Zapatero's government proved to be singularly ineffective in recognising the seriousness of the economic downturn, acknowledging its own errors, and acting with sufficient alacrity to put in place an effective response to the crisis – failings which will be considered in the next section.

The PSOE and the economy from 2008 to 2011: into the abyss

Whereas the swift deterioration in Spain's economic situation in the period after the 2008 general election presented Zapatero with a number of daunting challenges, his reaction to the economic downturn – particularly during its early stages – did much to erode his credibility as prime minister, and that of his party. Initially playing down the gravity of the situation, Zapatero rejected the term, 'crisis', favouring 'economic slowdown', and his ministers were forced to follow his lead, even when the depth of the downturn was becoming clear. A year after the general election, in March 2009, Zapatero claimed, 'We're amongst those suffering least from the crisis and we're going to come out of it first. The unemployment and deficit figures will be sorted out and the most vulnerable won't suffer' (Girauta, 2010: 228). Moreover, Zapatero made further pledges which he was ultimately unable to fulfil. Austerity measures which he had previously emphatically ruled out were later implemented in an even more rigorous form than when first mooted, as policy appeared to be made on the hoof, devoid of any strategic vision. The impression was one of ineffectiveness, improvisation and, ultimately, impotence as even those sectors of the population which had previously been sympathetic to the PSOE were left feeling confused and disillusioned.

Addressing the PSOE's Federal Committee a month after the 2008 election, Zapatero taunted the Popular Party that even the most pessimistic forecasts for unemployment still indicated a figure below the lowest level of unemployment – 11 per cent – achieved under Aznar's PP government between 1996 and 2004. Later in the same speech, Zapatero commented, 'now we're going to see why it was so important for us to have managed our public accounts so brilliantly'

(*El País*, 2008). The relative health of the public finances certainly did provide the government with a margin for manoeuvre with respect to providing a fiscal stimulus for an economy which had slipped into recession in the latter half of 2008. Despite Zapatero's boast, unemployment increased to 14 per cent by the end of 2008, underlining the speed of the downturn.

The initial response of the international economic community to the economic and financial crisis, as illustrated at the G20 meeting of finance ministers that was held in Washington in November 2008, was to boost growth via fiscal and monetary measures. The Spanish Socialist government's economic policy response should be seen within this context. In relative terms, its fiscal stimulus package was one of the largest implemented by governments seeking to address the economic crisis, reaching €42 billion between 2008 and 2009, and equivalent to 4 per cent of GDP, approximately 2 per cent for each year (Presidencia del Gobierno, 2010: 12; 41). Measures included increased funding for local authority infrastructure projects to the tune of €13 billion between 2008 and 2009; support for small businesses in the form of government sponsored loans; and help for vulnerable social groups, including the unemployed and those experiencing difficulties repaying their mortgages (Salmon, 2010b: 84–5). The decision to give a €400 rebate to all of those paying income tax – regardless of their income – was a further component of the package. The fact that this latter measure was announced in the run-up to the 2008 election laid Zapatero open to charges of populism. A further measure which attracted much criticism when the economy began to experience difficulties was the government's decision to launch a scheme in July 2007 whereby all those giving birth to, or adopting, a child – once again, whatever their financial circumstances – were given €2,500 from public funds. The initiative was withdrawn at the end of 2010.

With the public deficit rising steadily throughout 2009, disagreements emerged within the government over the direction of economic policy. The Governor of the Bank of Spain, Fernández Ordóñez, who was appointed by the Socialists in 2006, called for a thorough reform of the Spanish labour market and, in particular, of the country's system of collective bargaining, but was snubbed by Zapatero, who refused to countenance a reduction in the costs associated with laying people off (Chislett, 2009). Similar disagreements led to the replacement of Pedro Solbes, Finance Minister since Zapatero entered office, with Elena Salgado, in April 2009. He had been at odds with Zapatero for expressing misgivings about the relaxation of budgetary restraint linked to the funding of fiscal stimulus measures favoured by the prime minister.

Interviewed on the radio in September 2009, Zapatero claimed that the worst of the crisis was already over (Zavala, 2010: 219). It would have been more accurate to have acknowledged that, by the autumn of 2009, the scope for discretionary spending had diminished considerably, as the financial markets began to reflect concerns over the scale of public sector deficits, forcing governments across the EU to draw up austerity measures. In Spain, pressure was building for the government to identify a strategy to contain public expenditure and to reduce the public sector deficit, which had reached 11 per cent of GDP by the end of the year, mainly due to the sharp decrease in tax revenue, the rise in the number of people requiring unemployment benefit, and the cost of the fiscal stimulus measures. As early as February 2009, the European Commission, in accordance with the excessive deficit procedure of the Stability and Growth Pact, had issued a warning to Spain over the size of its deficit, necessitating a shift from fiscal stimulus measures to cuts across the public sector, in pay, employment and investment, so as to meet the target figure of 3 per cent of GDP by 2013 (Salmon, 2010a: 43).

The relative timidity of the measures contained in its Sustainable Economy Bill, unveiled in November 2009, which attempted to establish a new economic model to replace the discredited construction-based approach, gave the impression that the government was starting to be overtaken by events. The initiative consisted of a package of measures aimed at securing a more competitive model of production which would be more economically and environmentally sustainable. Concerned with measures on the transparency of pay packages for the directors of publicly quoted companies, sustainable tourism, the streamlining of the convoluted process of setting up a business, and ensuring that local and regional governments make more prompt payment to suppliers in an effort to prevent further business failures, the package was generally viewed as falling far short of its stated objectives. Most notably, it failed to provide the structural reforms required in such areas as the labour market, education, and the country's energy model and pensions, all of which would have to be addressed in order to produce a genuine change in the economic growth model (Abellán, 2009).

The shock engendered by the release of worse-than-expected economic indicators in January 2010 and revelations concerning the Greek sovereign debt situation served to prompt the government into taking further action on the economy. With the number of unemployed totalling 4.3 million, just under 19 per cent of the labour force, the government announced an ambitious austerity plan which aimed to reduce the deficit to seven per cent of GDP in 2011, a cut of more than €50 billion over a three-year period, €10 billion of which would be contributed by local and regional governments. Most prominent among the proposals was the decision to increase the retirement age from 65 to 67 in order to guarantee the sustainability of the public pensions system.

With the Greek sovereign debt crisis coming to a head in May 2010, the entire financial and economic crisis took a turn for the worse, which, for Spain, marked a turning point, and, for Zapatero and his government, a point of no return. Previous attempts to play down the scale of the crisis, allied with Zapatero's claims that Spain was well placed to withstand its most harmful effects, were now viewed by many throughout Spain as evidence of a government which had, at best, been mistaken, and, at worst, been in denial over the gravity of the situation. Zapatero thenceforth had little option other than to announce a new round of austerity measures on 12 May as market pressures intensified due to concerns about the growth prospects of the Spanish economy and the effect on its capacity to meet its deficit reduction targets. President Obama added his voice to the European Commission's demands for robust action from Zapatero.

Interviewed by the Spanish newspaper, *El País*, in November 2010, Zapatero indicated that he had been left with little choice other than to intensify the economic austerity programme. Had he not done so, 'the following day market instability and doubts about sovereign debt, including our own, would have placed us in a difficult situation ... the markets were capable of placing our solvency in question'. At this stage, therefore, the crisis developed from being largely linked to the downturn in the construction sector to centring on Spain's sovereign debt. In the same interview he ruefully recalled how, in the period before the economic crisis, he had been criticised for having run successive budget surpluses, 'because a Socialist Government should invest and increase public spending ... in the markets, the perception of our public accounts was excellent' (*El País*, 2010).

The government agreed to reduce the deficit by 1 per cent of GDP more than had been agreed only four months before; that is to say, from 7 per cent to 6 per cent by the end of 2011. This necessitated a further package of cuts, which included an average 5 per cent reduction in civil servants' salaries in 2010, followed by a pay freeze in 2011; a pensions freeze in 2011, albeit exempting those in receipt of the minimum pension; an extra saving of €1.2 billion by local and regional governments; a €6 billion reduction in public sector investment; and a €600 million cut in development aid between 2009 and 2010. Moreover, limits were placed on the coverage of the Dependency Law. The aim was to save a further €15 billion over the period 2010–11. The measures obtained the approval of Parliament by a single vote.

The response of public sector workers was to hold a strike in June 2010 to protest against the austerity package. The threat of a strike did not prevent the government from proposing further measures the same month, including a reduction in the amount of redundancy pay received by those on permanent contracts. This initiative was viewed by some as being a missed opportunity to carry out a more thorough reform of the labour market. Relations between the government and trade unions had by now deteriorated to such an extent that a general strike was held in September 2010, although the strike was generally viewed to have been only moderately successful. The trade unions nevertheless claimed that the strike contributed towards the government agreeing to sign a tripartite agreement with the trade unions and employers' organisations, the *Social and Economic Agreement*, in February 2011. Although the agreement retained a retirement age of 65 for those who had worked for 38 years, it set a marker for an extensive reform of the collective bargaining system, whose rigidities hampered the ability to respond to periods of economic downturn. Zapatero's government nevertheless failed to follow through with a thorough reform of the labour market, and the issue was effectively pushed back until after the general election.

By the autumn of 2010, the government's situation was looking sufficiently perilous for there to have been some doubts as to whether it would be able to gain parliamentary approval of its 2011 budget, although a deal was eventually struck with the Basque Nationalist Party (PNV) and the Canary Coalition (CC). This support was necessary because the failure to approve the budget may have forced the government to bring forward the general election.

Any satisfaction enjoyed by the government quickly dissipated when the Catalan branch of the Socialist Party, the Partit dels Socialistes de Catalunya – PSC, which had been in office since 2003 as part of a centre-left coalition, obtained its worst ever result at regional elections in November 2010, gaining just 18 per cent of the vote, a fall of 9 per cent compared to the last regional elections in 2006. The result was particularly worrying for Zapatero as support in Catalonia had been a vital element in his general election victories in 2004 and 2008.

Six months later, the PSOE obtained its worst results ever in local and regional elections, gaining just 28 per cent of the vote, almost exactly the percentage it would subsequently obtain in the general election of November 2011, and almost 10 per cent behind the Popular Party, which obtained over two million more votes. Only the national level of government currently eluded the PP, which was now able to consider the realistic prospect of achieving an overall majority at the general election.

One month before the local and regional elections, in April 2011, Zapatero had announced that he would not be standing for a third term as premier. By now viewed as a liability to his party and government, he agreed to remain prime minister only until the general election, which, in July, he declared would take place on 20 November 2011, four months earlier than expected. The former Interior Minister and First Deputy Prime Minister, Rubalcaba, accepted the difficult task of leading the party into the election in June, the month after the only other candidate with a realistic chance of beating Rubalcaba in any primary election for the leadership, Carme Chacón, the Defence Minister, declared she would not be standing.

Any Socialist hopes that the economic situation might stabilise in time for the election were thwarted by a deterioration in the Euro-zone crisis in August 2011, when the European Central Bank had to step in to buy Italian and Spanish bonds as yields increased. An indication of the pressures which the European Union was exerting upon Spain was provided the same month, when Zapatero unexpectedly announced that Article 135 of the Spanish Constitution would be amended so as to include a clause limiting the budget deficit and the level of public debt. Payment of the deficit would be prioritised over all other considerations. This development proved to be a foretaste of the agreement reached at the Brussels European Council meeting in December 2011 on the tightening of rules concerning the maintenance of balanced budgets. The initiative obtained the support of the opposition PP, which claimed that it had long advocated such a move, and was pushed through within a matter of weeks. So hastily was the measure adopted that there was very little public debate over this key development. Moreover, Rubalcaba's task of differentiating the PSOE from the PP in the run-up to the election was also complicated by the proposal. Once again, the imperatives imposed by the economic crisis contributed towards the impression of incoherence within the PSOE leadership.

Although, throughout the general election campaign, the PSOE made much of Rubalcaba's credentials as a safe pair of hands in difficult times, the deterioration of Spain's economic situation, most graphically illustrated by unemployment edging inexorably towards five million, effectively meant that the PSOE's candidate faced an impossible task. Although Zapatero was notable by his absence throughout virtually the entire campaign, his baleful legacy was all pervasive in a country which appeared to be at the mercy of the bond markets as confidence in Spain's capacity to cover its debts evaporated. The government's refusal to acknowledge the seriousness of the impact of the crisis on Spain and to take the necessary steps to allay the effects of the downturn – a denial which lasted for well over a year – together with pledges not to make the kind of cuts that eventually proved to be necessary in order to address the public sector deficit, as well as a marked reluctance to accept responsibility for what had happened, meant that the PSOE entered the campaign under the most challenging of circumstances. The fact that, under the Socialists, Spain had not required a bail-out similar to that requested by Greece, Ireland and Portugal, was a victory of sorts, but was hardly the kind of achievement likely to attract votes.

Given that the PSOE's results were almost uniformly disappointing throughout Spain, even in what had long been considered the Socialist strongholds of Catalonia and Andalucía, the party was faced with having to come to terms with a vastly diminished status as a political force. The PSOE has traditionally experienced greater difficulty in maintaining the loyalty of its voters than the Popular Party, which has been able to obtain around ten million votes at all general elections since its victory in 1996. The PSOE vote has been more volatile, with the party obtaining fewer than eight million votes in 2000, and as we have seen, fewer than seven million in 2011. The mobilisation of its vote has therefore been more of a challenge for the PSOE than for the Popular Party. According to analysis of opinion polls that were carried out by the polling organisation Metroscopia for the Spanish newspaper, *El País*, just 60 per cent of those who voted for the PSOE in 2008 remained loyal in 2011, while around 90 per cent of those voting for the PP in 2008 did so again in 2011, together with over two-and-a-half million new voters, one-and-a-half million of whom had voted for the PSOE in 2008. Moreover, the austerity measures announced by Zapatero in May 2010 provoked a steep fall in support for the PSOE. The difference in voting intention between the PSOE and the PP in March 2010 was an average of 3.4 per cent; by the time of the general campaign in 2011 the difference had increased to an average of 13.4 per cent, which proved to be below the actual difference of almost 16 per cent between the two parties, a new record since the establishment of democracy after Franco's death. Altogether, 3.9 million people who had voted for the PSOE in 2008 transferred their vote to other parties in 2011, while half-a-million former PSOE voters abstained (*El País*, 2011b).

Defeat at the 2011 general election did not appear to mark the PSOE's nadir, as the party met with a series of disappointing results in regional elections under the leadership of Rubalcaba throughout the course of 2012. Although the party was able to remain in government in Andalucía following elections in March, it was only able to do so by reaching an agreement with the Communist-led United Left (Izquierda Unida – IU). The PSOE lost 9 of the 56 seats it had won at the previous election in 2008, gaining 655,000 fewer votes. The PP obtained 3 more seats than the PSOE – 50 to the PSOE's 47 – and over 40,000 more votes. The PSOE's showing in Galicia and the Basque Country in October, and in Catalonia the following month, was even more disappointing, with the leadership of Rubalcaba being placed in doubt just months after he had been appointed PSOE general secretary in February 2012. There appeared to be no light at the end of the tunnel, with the party failing to gain support at the expense of a PP government engaged in implementing a seemingly never-ending series of cuts within the context of an unemployment rate nudging 26 per cent.

Conclusion

Speaking the week after the general election, Zapatero addressed the party's Federal Committee and argued that the economic crisis had been the key factor in the PSOE's poor performance. He also acknowledged that the government had made mistakes both in its handling of the crisis, as well as in its failure to communicate to the public the reasons behind the many difficult actions it had been forced to take. In particular, no comprehensive, coherent narrative had been produced to explain the need for an intensification of the government's austerity programme after May 2010. He stressed, nevertheless, that the government had done what had been necessary and that, given how difficult the conditions had been, there had been no alternative (Zapatero, 2011).

While any analysis of the decline in support suffered by the PSOE between 2008 and 2011 must award a central role to the effects of the economic crisis, it would be a mistake to suggest that the crisis was the sole reason for the resounding defeat suffered by the party at the November 2011 general election. If the PSOE is to re-establish its status as a party worthy of being returned to government, it will have to carry out a far more thorough process of self-criticism. Ever since Zapatero was elected to the post of general secretary at the PSOE's 35th congress in July 2000, he was able to impose a level of dominance over the party which not only discouraged criticism from within the party's ranks, but which, during his first term, led him to display a level of self-confidence which proved fatal once boom turned to bust during his second term. Precious time was lost when, instead of acknowledging the intensification of the crisis, the government instead sought to deny that any such crisis existed, despite ample evidence to the contrary.

Although, when the PSOE entered office in 2004, it rightly criticised the economic growth model's excessive dependence on the construction sector, and expressed concerns about the excessive levels of debt taken on by both households and businesses, it failed to produce an alternative model. In particular, the government could have taken steps to prick the property bubble but chose not to. Initiatives such as the €400 tax rebate – announced just weeks before the 2008 general election – also laid the government open to charges of engaging in gimmicks geared towards bribing the electorate at a time when it was already becoming clear that the economy was running out of steam.

During its first term in office the party had also been more concerned with civil and gender rights, rather than with correcting weaknesses within the Spanish economy. While it would be wrong to suggest that genuine achievements were not effected during this period – the legalisation of gay marriage and adoption, and the Law on Equality between Men and Women are just two of the measures which deserve to be acknowledged as being genuinely progressive – it was nevertheless the case that the government was also guilty of making proclamations which had little relevance to people's daily lives. At the same time, the government, which, after all, was a social democratic government, failed to award the same level of prominence to its redistributive credentials. This is not to say that the government did not have a number of notable redistributive achievements to its credit – the Dependency Law was quite rightly viewed as establishing the welfare state's 'Fourth Pillar', adding to existing provisions in health care, education, and pensions. Conversely, Zapatero was guilty of comments which appeared to contradict the party's centre-left essence. Addressing the PSOE's Federal Committee in September 2005, he had claimed that, 'lowering taxes is a left-wing policy'.

Another criticism in the economic arena is that the devolution of power to Spain's autonomous regions, which progressed considerably during the PSOE's first term in office in the form of the reform of several regions' autonomy statutes, served to complicate the government's efforts to control the public deficit, given many regions' reluctance to rein in spending. In this connection, it is important to recall that the local and regional levels of government are responsible for half of public spending, with the regions now having responsibility for education and health care.

Many also felt that, in promoting regional interests via the reform of autonomy statutes, Zapatero had at times neglected the national interest. Zapatero had famously remarked that he would support any proposal for reform of its statute which was approved by the Catalan Parliament. In actual fact, the Spanish Parliament in Madrid introduced extensive amendments to the draft agreed in Barcelona before the final, somewhat diluted, version became law in 2006. A further indication of the sensitivity of the regional question was the fact that Chacón's possible candidacy for the post of PSOE general secretary was criticised after the general election by the former Deputy Prime Minister, Alfonso Guerra, and the former President of the lower house of Parliament, José Bono, who claimed that, as a Catalan, and a prominent member of the PSC, she would have difficulty speaking on behalf of Spain.

The neglect of the party's natural supporters, who had been badly hit by the crisis, is a further criticism which can be made. Given the scale of the economic crisis, it is understandable that the government was not always able to maintain its ideological coherence, but it is nevertheless the case that many natural PSOE supporters were left confused and dismayed by the government's actions. The government failed to explain clearly why it acted as it did, why it believed its actions to be in the national interest, and what the consequences of its failure to act would have been. In this respect, Felipe González had been far more effective than Zapatero in explaining his government's actions both to the PSOE and to the broader electorate during his period in office, including important shifts in policy, such as the U-turn on Spanish membership of NATO during Gonzalez's first term in office between 1982 and 1986. In particular, he had been adept at stressing that the national interest would always come before the party's interest. Zapatero was never able to develop a similar narrative, although it is important to stress that he was leading the country during its worst economic crisis in many decades.

Like many other political parties, the PSOE was also accused of having lost touch with the electorate. Although by no means a unique case, prominent socialist figures were accused of being 'professional politicians' divorced from the average citizen and unfamiliar with the day-to-day struggles of people whose income barely stretched to the end of the month. As the party looked to its statutes and resolutions in preparing for the election of a new leader in the aftermath of its general election defeat, the electorate felt alienated from byzantine procedures which appeared to have little to do with their own concerns. In essence, the PSOE had become too inward-looking, and it needed to be receptive to the views and concerns of those within the population who had traditionally looked to the party to bring about a progressive process of modernisation underpinned by a sense of fairness and freedom.

One of the most worrying aspects of the PSOE's decline was the loss of support within the younger members of the electorate. With almost half of under-25s being unemployed, it is hardly surprising that the party struggled to obtain the youth vote. Many young people had been alienated from the entire political process, and the protests which started in Madrid on 15 May 2011, before spreading throughout the country, reflected the view of many young people that neither the PSOE nor the PP truly represented them. Recapturing a significant proportion of the youth vote will be one of the PSOE's biggest challenges over the coming years.

Mistakes had also been made during the general election campaign. Although Zapatero maintained a low profile throughout the run-up to Spain going to the polls, the fact that he remained, in addition to being prime minister, general secretary of the party, served to undermine Rubalcaba's authority as the PSOE's candidate at the election. Zapatero's decision to push through changes to the Constitution above the heads of the electorate, apparently causing friction between him and Rubalcaba, was a particular case in point. The overall effect was to add a degree of ambiguity concerning Rubalcaba's status which was reminiscent of the uneasy Aznar–Rajoy tandem which reacted so ineffectively to the terrorist attacks that dominated the final days of the 2004 general election campaign. The refusal to apologise for the errors made in government during the campaign further undermined his party's capacity to attract votes. Furthermore, any attempt to present the PSOE as a more progressive alternative to the PP was hampered by the electorate's all-too-fresh memories of the cuts imposed by Zapatero.

Given the scale of the PSOE's defeat it is clear that the project put in place by Zapatero following his election to the post of PSOE general secretary in 2000 has run its course, and the party faces the prospect of a long period in opposition. In order to re-establish its credentials as a party of government, the PSOE must construct a credible narrative which starts from the basis of acknowledging the many errors committed under Zapatero, before setting the foundations for a new project which responds to the demands of a population which has been left feeling vulnerable and insecure. With no end to the economic crisis in sight, and the PP government having to intensify its austerity measures, it is by no means certain that Mariano Rajoy will be any more adept than Zapatero at retaining his popularity and that of his party. Yet, as the PSOE's disappointing results at regional elections throughout the course of 2012 indicate, it is by no means inevitable that the PP government's falling approval ratings will translate into increased support for the PSOE. It remains to be seen whether the PSOE, which has historically displayed remarkable powers of recovery, is capable of carrying out the kind of profound transformation which offers the only route back to office. The prospect of irrelevance awaits the party unless it rises to this challenge.

Note

1 Diario de Sesiones del Congreso de los Diputados, No. 309, 19 December 2007, p. 15380.

References

Abellán, B. (2009). 'El Gobierno deja de lado las grandes reformas en la Ley de Economía Sostenible', *El País*, 28 September.

Andrés, J., Boscá, J. E., Domènech, R. and Ferri, J. (2011). 'Job creation in Spain, productivity growth, labour market reforms or both?' in J. E. Boscá, A. Díaz, R. Domènech, J. Ferri, L. Putch and J. Varela (eds), *The Spanish Economy: A General Equilibrium Perspective* (Basingstoke: Palgrave Macmillan), pp. 69–96.

Calamai, M. and Garzia, A. (2006). *Zapatero* (Barcelona: Península).

Chislett, W. (2008). *Inside Spain*, 48, Madrid, Real Instituto Elcano de Estudios Estratégicos.

Chislett, W. (2009). *Inside Spain*, 53, Madrid, Real Instituto Elcano de Estudios Estratégicos.

El País (2008). 'Zapatero: La peor previsión sobre el paro será major que la que tuvo el PP', 27 April.

El País (2010). 'Entrevista al Presidente del gobierno', 21 November.

El País (2011a). 'Si hubiesen escuchado al Banco de España...', 22 June.

El País (2011b). 'El PP debe la mayoría absoluta más al colapso del PSOE que a su resultado; Las medidas anticrisis y la fidelidad a la baja, claves del bacatazo del PSOE', 22 November.

Girauta, J.C. (2010). *La Verdadera Historia del PSOE* (Madrid: Buenas Letras).

Juan, J. (2011). *Nada es gratis* (Barcelona: Destino).

Kennedy, P. (2007). 'Phoenix from the ashes: the PSOE government under Rodríguez Zapatero 2004–2007. A new model for social democracy?', *International Journal of Iberian Studies*, 20(3), 187–206.

OECD (2007). *Economic Survey of Spain 2007: Policy Brief* (Paris: OECD).

O'Kean, J. M. (2010). *España Competitiva* (Madrid: Ecobook).

Presidencia del Gobierno (2010). *Informe Económico del Presidente del Gobierno 2010* (Madrid: Oficina Económica del Presidente del Gobierno).

PSOE (2004). *Merecemos una España mejor, Programa Electoral, Elecciones Generales* (Madrid: PSOE).

PSOE (2008). *Motivos para Creer, Programa Electoral, Elecciones Generales* (Madrid: PSOE).

Salmon, K. (2010a). 'Boom to bust – reconstructing the Spanish economy. Part one: into recession', *International Journal of Iberian Studies*, 23(1), 39–52.

Salmon, K. (2010b). 'Boom to bust – reconstructing the Spanish economy. Part two: policy responses to the economic crisis', *International Journal of Iberian Studies*, 23(2), 83–91.

Zapatero, J. L. R. (2008). 'Discurso de investidura del 8 de abril de 2008', available at: www.lamoncloa.gob.es/Presidente/Presidentes/InvestiduraZapatero2008.

Zapatero, J. L. R. (2011). 'Intervención ante el Comité Federal', 26 November, available at: www.psoe.es/saladeprensa/docs/620147/page/intervencion-jose-luis-rodriguez-zapa tero-ante-comite-federal.html.

Zavala, J. M. (2010). *Las Mentiras de ZP* (Barcelona: Plaza y Janés).

11

Triumph and collapse: PASOK in the wake of the crisis in Greece, 2009–13

Dimitri A. Sotiropoulos

Introduction

When the Panhellenic Socialist Movement (PASOK) won the October 2009 general election, gaining 44 per cent of the vote, there was ample hope that Greece, governed by a stable socialist majority of 160 seats in a 300-seat Parliament and having an economy and a banking system little exposed to changes in the international economy, would be minimally affected by the global financial crisis raging since the autumn of 2008. In other words, it was widely thought that some of the chronic disadvantages of Greece, namely the absence of export-oriented production and the lack of foreign investments in Greek banks, would be an advantage in a period when export-oriented economies with a large share of foreign ownership in their banking sectors suffered rapid economic deterioration.

Moreover, PASOK triumphed in the 2009 election with an 11 per cent margin over its major competitor, the centre-right New Democracy (ND), and did not expect to face a strong opposition to fulfilling its electoral promise for economic development along Keynesian economic policy lines (Dinas, 2010; Gemenis, 2010; Pappas, 2010). PASOK had long government experience as it had won five general elections in 1981–2004, forming single majority governments on all five occasions (in 1981, 1985, 1993, 1996 and 2000). In 2009, the socialist Prime Minister, George Papandreou, the son of Andreas Papandreou who had founded the party in 1974, firmly controlled the governing party. He had been directly elected to the leadership of PASOK by all party members and party 'friends' twice, i.e. in 2004 and once more in 2007, when he was challenged by Evangelos Venizelos, a former PASOK minister and prominent party cadre, just after PASOK had lost the September 2007 general election to ND.

Fewer than three years after PASOK's 2009 electoral success, at the May 2012 general election, the socialist party lost over two million votes. It captured only

41 parliamentary seats, 119 fewer than in 2009. PASOK's share of the vote (13.2 per cent) was even under its lowest share ever (13.6 per cent, in 1974, i.e. in the first elections it had participated, just after Greece's transition to democracy).

In the same election of May 2012 ND also obtained its worst ever share of the vote (18.9 per cent). However, in the consecutive elections of June 2012, called because no government was formed out of the Parliament formed in May, ND sprang back to 29.7 per cent of the vote, whereas PASOK fell from 13.2 to 12.3 per cent. In other words, in fewer than three years PASOK moved from triumph to collapse. Even though Venizelos had replaced Papandreou, whom Greek voters largely associated with the economic crisis, at the head of the party in March 2012, PASOK suffered a heavy electoral blow. During the electoral campaign opposition parties reminded voters that PASOK was to blame, if not for causing the crisis, at least for mishandling it and that Venizelos had served as Minister of Finance during one of the peak periods of the crisis, between June 2011 and March 2012.

The crushing defeat suffered by PASOK in May and June 2012 is a case study of a governing party which became unelectable because of a combination of the international economic crisis, the Greek sovereign debt crisis and the party leadership's own policy mistakes.

This chapter attempts to answer the following questions: how is it possible to explain PASOK's passage from electoral triumph to collapse in a very short time period and is the economic crisis the exclusive reason for the party's defeat? How did the party fare after November 2011, when it switched from single party government to sharing power with other parties in coalition governments? How has the party tried to revamp its organisational structure and ideological profile after the defeat of 2012 and in the context of the ongoing economic crisis?

The chapter proceeds as follows. The first section considers how PASOK prepared itself for ascending to power while it was in opposition in 2004–09. The second section discusses PASOK's reaction to the economic crisis while in power in 2009–11. The third section covers the period PASOK participated in coalition governments, including how it lost the electoral battles of May and June 2012. The fourth section covers the period after PASOK's electoral defeat and its ninth party congress of February 2013. The concluding section attempts to appraise how PASOK responded to the economic crisis and what challenges lie ahead for this party.

PASOK in opposition, 2004–09

After it was founded in 1974, PASOK seldom remained in opposition. It was in power, enjoying more or less comfortable parliamentary majorities for nineteen out of thirty years (1974–2004) (Moschonas and Papanagnou, 2007). When Costas Simitis handed the party's leadership to Papandreou just before the election in 2004, PASOK seemed capable of regenerating itself even if it had been in power for the previous eleven years (1993–2004) (Sotiropoulos, 2013).

However, what followed was not regeneration but organisational decline. The new electoral procedure, introduced at the insistence of Papandreou, to elect the party's president through a direct vote of all card-carrying party members and registered 'party friends' was initially successful. In February 2004, when Papandreou ran unchallenged for the presidency of PASOK, more than one million voters cast their vote (1,020,146 votes cast according PASOK's official sources). Later on, however, the direct election did not attract such enthusiasm. In 2007, when Papandreou was challenged by Venizelos 769,156 votes were cast. In 2012, at the election of Venizelos to the party's presidency, only 236,151 voters appeared and in February 2013, at the election of representatives to the ninth congress of the party, participation was even lower, as only 112,016 party members cast their vote (Mavris, 2013: 13).

The dwindling participation in party life was not only the result of political alienation of socialist party members from the policies Papandreou followed after he rose to power in 2009. Declining enthusiasm about the party was also the result of two factors, i.e. the changing ideological profile of the party and the unpredictable fluidity of the party organisation in 2004–09, while PASOK was in opposition. Old party members were alienated by Papandreou's shifting focus on various postmodernist ideological themes, very different from the party's traditional profile, and also by his frequent experimenting with party structures and processes and the formation of an informal circle of close associates of the party leader, essentially a decision-making organ on the side of formal party organs.

PASOK's ideological and organisational shifts while in opposition
In detail, with the regard to the party's programme after 2004 Papandreou underemphasised traditional social democratic themes, such as development, economic inequality and labour relations. Instead he focused on participatory democracy, human rights and environmental protection (Moschonas and Pantazopoulos, 2010). This was a refreshing shift, but the party did not really elaborate these themes in a systematic fashion and its profile was characterised by ideological fluidity.

Papandreou's favourite theme of participatory democracy led to the establishment of virtual communities to engage in internet-based deliberations and of working groups, open also to non-members, in the seventh and the eighth party congresses (in 2006 and 2008). Papandreou underlined issues of collective identity with regard to women and minorities and in 2006 even invited a Greek Muslim woman to run as his party's candidate for governor of a region in northern Greece. As for economic development, he saw it as 'green development' and his constant reply to calls to specify the party's economic plans was that Greece should become a 'green economy' while job creation should take place in

environmental-friendly sectors. It was only in September 2009, a month before
the parliamentary elections, that Papandreou revisited traditional economic
policy issues, such as fiscal management and redistribution, on which he adopted
a traditional Keynesian line.

Although the party fought and actually won the parliamentary elections of 2009,
one should not forget that, while in opposition, it had become internally even
weaker than before. Since 1993 PASOK had become a hibernating party organisation owing to its very long tenure in government (Spourdalakis and Tassis, 2006),
but after 2004 the party was compartmentalised. For instance, before the seventh
party congress (2005) party members willing to discuss political issues were invited
to found or join relevant committees and 1,600 such committees were formed.
During party congresses, plenary sessions were few, as congress participants were
distributed to many different sessions running in parallel (Sotiropoulos, 2013).

Nevertheless, in the miserable performance of ND in government, which was
associated with economic stalemate and financial scandals that culminated in
2007–09, PASOK was given a chance to ascent once more to power, whatever
its own ideological and organisational weaknesses. Indeed, in October 2009,
PASOK achieved its largest electoral victory in the 2000s (Table 11.1).

PASOK confronting the economic crisis, 2009–11

As soon as PASOK ascended to power in 2009, it was confronted with Greece's
severe economic decline. Even though one should concede that between October

Table 11.1 Electoral results of PASOK in the 2000s

Year	Legislative elections (%)	Seats (number and %)	European elections (%)	Seats (number)
2000	43.8	158 52.7		
2004	40.6	116 38.7	34.0	8
2007	38.1	102 34.0		
2009	43.9	160 53.3	36.7	8
2012 (May)	13.2	41 13.7		
2012 (June)	12.3	33 11.0		

Note: The Greek Parliament has 300 seats. Greece had 24 seats in total in the EP in
2004, which fell to 22 in 2009.

2009 and November 2011, when PASOK's single majority government was in power, Greece did not exit the Euro-zone and did not default on its public debt, the truth is that the Greek economy deteriorated rapidly and that PASOK's performance in power was very disappointing.

PASOK's four mistakes in managing the economic crisis

PASOK has been accused of mishandling the crisis and causing the derailment of the economy. It is true, however, that Greece's fiscal problems preceded PASOK's rise to power and that the ND cabinets of 2004–09 bequeathed PASOK's governments with grave problems (Pagoulatos and Triantopoulos, 2009; Featherstone, 2011). Greece's fiscal problems did not rise under PASOK rule, as the public debt, which stood at 22 per cent of GDP in 1980, hovered around 100 per cent throughout the 1990s and was 102 per cent on the average in 2001–07 (Korliras, 2012: 62). In 2009, the year before the start of the crisis in Greece, the debt amounted to 129 per cent of GDP. Moreover, the country had been running budget deficits since 2003. In 2009 the budget deficit stood at −15.6 per cent of GDP, while the balance of payments was even more negative, i.e., −18 per cent of GDP (European Commission, 2011: 190).

This grave economic legacy of the past does not absolve PASOK, because after its ascent to power it committed four important mistakes: it wasted time before taking economic measures; later on it accepted the imposition of ineffective and unfair measures in exchange for Greece's bail-out; it was very reluctant in implementing structural reforms; and it did not attack tax evasion head-on.

To start with, just before the October 2009 elections Papandreou falsely claimed, that 'money is available, if one looks for money in the right place'. The country's already dire economic situation, sketched just above, should not have allowed for such a claim to be made. Papandreou promised to raise funds by imposing additional taxes on fuel consumption and on business profits. He thus raised false hopes for income improvement of the middle and popular strata, which were dashed only a few months later, when Greece resorted to the rescue mechanism.

PASOK's president also delayed to react when, upon coming to power, his Minister of Finance, George Papaconstantinou, and administrative officials informed him of the true condition of the Greek economy. Papandreou hesitated and in December 2009 even consented to a state budget informed by traditional Keynesian economic principles, whereas the government's limited revenue raising capacity was not at all commensurate to an expansionist policy. In fact, the Greek socialists were not alone in procrastinating over necessary measures. EU leaders, participating in EU's summit in February 2010, did not take action to protect the Euro-zone, although the signs of a possible Greek default were growing.

By May 2010, the PASOK government was left with no options and in fact, from then on, the hands of successive Greek government were tied (Zahariadis, 2013; Sotiropoulos, 2012). The Greek government resorted to the rescue mechanism put together by the European Commission (EC), the European Central Bank (ECB) and the International Monetary Fund (IMF). The three organisations formed a 'troika', represented by high-level technocrats who visited Greece regularly in 2010–12 and essentially shaped and dictated the country's new fiscal, income, pension and employment policies. The troika monitored the implementation of an austerity programme to which Greece committed in exchange for large international loans supplied in the form of rescue packages (the first package was drafted in May 2010 and the second in February 2012, while in the mean time, in June 2011, Greece's 'Medium Term Fiscal Strategy 2012–15' had been shaped along austerity lines).

The urgent need to avoid default led the PASOK government to make a second mistake with regard to the policy mix of the austerity package. This was mix of high interest rates, high taxation, deep cuts in public spending and no structural changes. The loans obtained by Greece came with high, almost 'punishing', interest rates, while the government raised taxes sharply and cut public sector salaries and pensions (Korliras, 2012).

The third mistake was that, although the rescue package contained relevant provisions, the socialist government hesitated to address structural problems of the economy. Such problems included the existence of a parasitic, sprawling public sector and of numerous heavily regulated and protected occupations (pharmacists, taxi and truck owners, notaries and many others). It is telling that not a single privatisation took place in 2010 and 2011.

On the one hand, PASOK did not want to tread in the turf of public sector unions, as public employees constituted one of its traditional social bases. For two years, 2010 and 2011, the government repeatedly cut the salaries of civil servants working in ministries and public organisations such as hospitals and universities as well as the welfare benefits offered by state-managed social security funds, but it did not affect the salaries and benefits of employees of state-owned enterprises until the winter of 2011. Preserving such discrepancies in the middle of economic crisis further eroded trust towards the socialist government.

On the other hand, the government passed legislation opening up access to occupations and professions, but was unable to overcome the extensive reaction of vested narrow organised interests stemming from among liberal professions and the self-employed. Three examples may show how vehement were such reactions. First, in the autumn of 2010, owners of trucks resisted the government's decision to issue new licences for trucks, by parking their vehicles in long lines along major thoroughfares and national highways and provoking further deterioration to the already grave traffic problems. Second, in July–August 2011, taxi owners fiercely resisted the government's earlier reversal of decision not to grant any new taxi licences, which was a promise made to them in 2010 but taken back in 2011. They used their taxis to occupy major streets and blocked access to ports and airports. Third, in 2010 and 2011, owners of pharmacies resisted the government's plan to grant licences for new pharmacies, by closing their shops a few days every single week for a period of several weeks and thus leading desperate customers to form long lines in front of their shops.

The fourth mistake of PASOK was the mishandling of tax evasion which is rampant among large businessmen, small shopkeepers and the liberal professions. The way in which two socialist ministers, Papaconstantinou and Venizelos, handled the so-called 'Lagarde List' offers a telling example. The list contained names of account owners and details of their bank accounts in the HSBC bank's branch in Geneva. It was confiscated by the French authorities in 2009, upon arresting Herve Falciani, a former bank employee of HSBC who had illegally downloaded personal data of HSBC's international customers. Many of the persons appearing on the data files were citizens of other EU countries, who had violated the tax legislation of their countries. Accused of tax evasion, they were obliged to pay taxes and fines. In 2010 Christine Lagarde, the then Minister of Finance of France, handed a list of Greek customers of HSBC to Papaconstantinou, the then Minister of Finance of Greece. However, neither in the period when Papaconstaninou was Finance Minister (October 2009–June 2011) nor in the period when Venizelos held this post (June 2011–April 2012) did the Greek government seek to tax any possibly unjustified wealth kept by Greek citizens in the said HSBC accounts in Switzerland.

The effects of PASOK's management of the economic crisis

After May 2010, more austerity measures followed which included spending cuts in the public sector, such as the elimination of the so-called 13th and 14th salary in 2010 and a further cut of 20 per cent on salaries in 2011 (European Commission, 2012). In March 2012, the government reduced the minimum wage in the private sector by 22 per cent, in order to increase the country's sinking competitiveness.

The said policy mix and government mistakes caused deep economic depression and a tremendous rise in unemployment. The economy, which had shrunk by −3.3 per cent in 2008 and 2009, shrunk by a further −10.5 per cent in 2010 and 2011. By the end of 2012 the Greek economy was in depression for a fifth year in a row, while in five years (2008–12) it had shrunk by 20 per cent (Eurostat, 2012a). At the end of 2011, Greek public debt had reached the level of 171 per cent of GDP. Chances are that without PASOK's rolling back of the state, the debt would have been even higher. It is to PASOK's credit that it managed to reduce the state deficit from −15.9 to −9.1 in a limited time period of two years (2010–11) (Eurostat, 2012b). However, this same policy had dramatic effects on the labour market.

The unemployment rate, which for two decades (1990–2010) fluctuated between 8 and 12 per cent, soared after the onset of the crisis: the rate was 21 per cent in 2011 and by mid-2012 had reached 25 per cent (European Commission, 2011: 34). Youth unemployment was always high in Greece: in 2006 unemployment in the 15–29 age group stood at 18 per cent. However, in 2011 it reached 33 per cent (Bank of Greece, 2012). Moreover, in December 2011, unemployment in the age group 18–25 reached 51.1 per cent, which along with the corresponding Spanish figure, was the highest in Europe.

Still, PASOK cannot be judged only on its unfortunate policy record in the economy. In 2009–11 the socialist government passed new, ground-breaking legislation in policy sectors other than the economy. In March 2010 it passed a law (L. 3838/2010) that allowed for the naturalisation of children of foreign migrants born after their parents had settled in the Greece. In July 2010 the socialist government passed a law (L. 3861/2010) which increased transparency in the public sector, as it required that all public documents related to hiring of personnel and public procurement are uploaded in official websites. If authorities do not obey, then government acts contained in the documents are invalid. And in August 2011 PASOK passed a law on university education (L. 4009/2011) which endowed Greek state universities with new organs, such as boards of trustees ('Councils') found in most university systems of Europe and North America. The law also promoted the managerial autonomy of each university and decreased the extensive politicisation of decision making within universities by limiting the crippling participation of political party-led factions of students in the selection of university authorities. (The latter law was amended in 2012 by the ND-led coalition government, but its basic principles remained intact.)

Explaining PASOK's adoption of neo-liberal economic policies

Left-wing critics of PASOK claim that the rescue package which the socialist government agreed with Greece's creditors was a typical neo-liberal policy package. Such critics add that it was this package rather than the long-term structural problems and earlier trends of the Greek economy in the 2000s, which caused the derailment of the Greek economy (Kouvelakis, 2011; Fouskas, 2012).

Nevertheless, in a period of extreme economic volatility, PASOK must be credited for repeatedly saving the country from default. At a time when the state coffers were empty, the PASOK government secured funds from bail-out packages, paying of course a high price in terms of austerity measures, i.e. measures of 'internal devaluation', on Greece's popular strata.

Indeed, Greece came to the verge of bankruptcy several times between May 2010 and December 2012. Successive governments (the socialist Papandreou government as well as the technocratic Papademos government and the tripartite Samaras government which succeeded it) had little room for manoeuvre. While in power, in 2010 and 2011, the PASOK government strived to close the gap between government expenditure and government revenue which in 2009 had reached €24 billion. In order to accomplish this task, it could either leave the Euro-zone and return to the drachma (a solution advocated by segments of the left, such as the Greek Communist Party and a few cadres of the radical left Syriza party) or to implement an austerity policy, while remaining in the Euro-zone.

PASOK's leadership correctly assessed that adopting again the drachma, the national currency of Greece before 2001 when it joined the Euro-zone, would be the worst option. Greece is a small, weak and open economy, with limited export capabilities and enduring patterns of high public spending. It has an economy which is far from self-sufficient and Greeks consume imported goods some of which are vital for sustaining decent living conditions (heating oil, gasoline, medicaments and even foodstuffs). A return to the drachma would have probably caused shortages of basic goods, high inflation, runs on the national currency (of the kind South-East Asian countries had encountered in the late 1990s) and soaring interest rates for any loans handed out from banks to businesses and individuals. In brief, exiting the Euro-zone would bring about economic collapse, if not a humanitarian catastrophe.

This was clearly an impossible option for Greek socialists who preferred to implement neo-liberal economic policies dictated to them from abroad. In 2010–12 the leaders of the strongest EU powers made it clear that Greece should fulfil the terms and conditions of the rescue packages. If not, Greece would be sanctioned with delays in receiving further financial aid or even suffer a cancellation of instalments of the rescue packages. Greece depended on such instalments and could only negotiate the pace at which the country would fulfil its obligations.

In view of the above, while the PASOK government may have not had enough room for manoeuvre, it probably did not put up a fight with the country's creditors. Anyway, as PASOK's record in opposition between 2004 and 2009 showed, it was probably unprepared to steer the economy in times of crisis. Eventually, as Gerasimos Moschonas has put it:

> PASOK failed to manage the sovereign debt crisis with fairness and effectiveness …
> The PASOK government did not negotiate adequately; 'adequately' means that it did not have either sufficient technocratic expertise or strong political will to negotiate on policy measures. Instead of a policy of chirurgical interventions to deal with the sovereign debt crisis and the state's incapacity, PASOK was led to adopt across-the-board spending cuts leading to a deadlock … Policy failures put PASOK into a worse negotiating position which in turn led to more ineffective measures. (2012)

Paradoxically, Greek socialists felt that their policy choice was vindicated by the fact that the ND party, which had rejected PASOK's policies in 2010, made an about-turn in November 2011. At that time, ND joined PASOK and the right-wing populist party LAOS in order to form a tripartite coalition government, headed by a technocrat (Professor Lukas Papademos). ND also followed the same policies when it came to power in June 2012, under Antonis Samaras who led another tripartite coalition government, this time relying on the MPs of PASOK and the pro-European Democratic Left party (DIMAR).

To sum up this section, PASOK was not alone in following neo-liberal policies and apparently had no other option but could have negotiated for better, fairer and more effective policy measures to deal with the economic crisis. Indeed, after Papandreou fell from power in November 2011, his successors also accepted the harsh austerity policies suggested by the troika. This was unavoidable, because the Greek state was unable to service its debts and at times was even close to stopping paying salaries and pensions to public employees. In order to implement the austerity programme, in 2010–2013 all three said governments (the Papandreou, Papademos and Samaras Cabinets) cut salaries and pensions, imposed a freeze on almost all social spending, delayed payments to private suppliers of goods and services to the state and pensioned off civil servants who were close to retirement age.

In 2012 the troika insisted that, given that even after two years into the economic crisis, there was no progress with structural reforms, the only way for Greece to regain ground with regard to competitiveness was to lower labour costs in the private sector, on top of previous decreases in public sector wages. The obvious result of all this was economic depression, accompanied by severe social effects. It was only natural that depression and adverse social effects would be reflected in shifts in electoral behavior, namely shifts which proved particularly damaging for PASOK.

Falling into the abyss: PASOK's abandonment of single party government and electoral collapse in 2012

While in power, Papandreou saw his party's parliamentary majority dwindle from 160 to 153 seats, as at various time points PASOK MPs voted against his policies and were thrown out of the party's parliamentary group. Eventually, in November 2011, Papandreou faced the spectrum of government fall, a development he himself actually provoked: he stunned the Greek and European publics by suddenly announcing that he would submit Greece's 'Medium Term Fiscal Strategy 2012–15', a policy package Greece had already agreed with the troika, to a national referendum. EU leaders saw this as an opportunity for Greece to voluntarily exit the Euro-zone, international markets reacted very negatively threatening the stability of the Euro and a revolt of PASOK MPs who were against Greece's disengagement from the Euro-zone followed. Papandreou handed power to Papademos and between November 2011 and May 2012 PASOK participated in his coalition government.

Soon, the symptoms of the economic crisis in Greece had worsened. In 2012, depression hit for a fifth year in a row, while unemployment reached 27 per cent in December 2012. Given that the last PASOK government was elected in October 2009, elections would have been normally held in 2013. However, the Papademos government lasted only for six months. It faced tremendous opposition from trade unions and from parties of the left which staged continuous demonstrations and occupations of government buildings.

Papademos also felt increasing pressure from the leader of ND, Samaras, who had hoped to win an easy victory. Thus, elections were called in May 2012. Samaras won the elections, but he obtained only 19 per cent of the vote and was unable to form a single majority government. PASOK obtained just over 13 per cent of the vote. In fact, no party was able to form such a government. ND and PASOK witnessed their electoral influence dwindle, as both parties together polled only 32 per cent of the vote. The radical left Syriza party came second, leaving PASOK in third place (Mavris, 2012).

Syriza surprised everyone by obtaining 17 per cent of the vote, while in October 2009 it had obtained 5 per cent and had come fifth. The results of the May 2012 elections amounted to an overhaul of the Greek party system, which until that month was one of the most polarised two-party systems in Europe. After the May 2012 elections, parties did not agree on a coalition government and elections were called again for June 2012. This time ND won by obtaining 30 per cent of the vote. Syriza came a close second with 27 per cent and PASOK came third with 12 per cent.

Given that PASOK had obtained 44 per cent in 2009, its electoral failure in 2012 was dramatic. Few people saw this electoral disaster coming. In an article published two months before the election day Gerasimos Moschonas predicted that 'PASOK will pay a heavy price because its policies do not correspond either to the needs of the country or to the interests of its traditional supporters' (2012).

Indeed, a diagnosis of PASOK's electoral catastrophe should be based on the fact that its social bases disintegrated almost completely in the elections of June 2012 (Table 11.2).

What is more, in the June 2012 elections PASOK polled very few votes from among the younger and middle-aged voters. It is telling that while PASOK's share of the total vote was 12 per cent, among those belonging to the 18–34 age group, only 6.7 per cent voted for PASOK; among those in the 35–54 age group, only 9.6 per cent did so. By contrast, among those over 65 years old, 20 per cent voted for PASOK.[1] In other words, PASOK may be appealing to an ageing segment of Greek society.

After its electoral collapse in the May and June 2012 elections, PASOK tried to reconcile the demands of its role as coalition partner of the ND party with the need to revamp its own political profile, in order to avoid falling into political irrelevance, if not extinction.

Table 11.2 PASOK's percentage share of the vote in each occupational category, 2004–12

	Election year (June)			
	2004	2007	2009	2012
Private sector employees	44	38	43	9
Public sector employees	43	40	42	10
Pensioners	33	36	46	23
Self-employed	42	37	43	10
Farmers	35	45	44	10
Students	46	41	41	1
Housewives	44	38	48	16
Unemployed	39	41	43	7
PASOK's national total vote	41	38	44	12

Note: 'Pensioners' refers to public sector pensioners, in 2004, 2007 and 2012, but to all pensioners in 2009. 'Self-employed' refers to small shopkeepers, artisans and craftspersons in 2004, 2007 and 2012, but to all those, plus professionals in 2009.
Sources: 2004 and 2007 elections, Public Issue, www.publicissue.gr/wp-content/gallery/tomos-2007-2/pinakas-6a.jpg; 2009 elections, joint exit poll of seven Greek public opinion companies, at http://tinyurl.com/exitpoll2009; June 2012 elections, Vernardakis (2012)

If PASOK had not supported the ND-led coalition government of Samaras, Greece would have experienced government instability. This would have been dangerous at a time in which government stability was most needed in order to overcome the economic crisis. However, this was unfortunate for PASOK's overcoming of its own crisis. As PASOK was a partner in the coalition government of Samaras, it did not have the time window or perhaps the courage to come to terms with the scale of its defeat. As a consequence, PASOK was in a state of limbo between participation in the incumbent government and regeneration in order to re-establish its lost credibility.

The day after: PASOK's reaction to electoral collapse and the first party congress in five years

For the first six months after the June 2012 election PASOK was in a state of shock. Fully understanding that it was unable to fill the political vacuum between ND and Syriza alone, PASOK made repeated gestures to the pro-European left party DIMAR, in the hope of a possible cooperation, but to no avail.

In the meantime, PASOK prepared for its ninth party congress that finally took place on 28 February–3 March 2013 in Athens. The first plans for this congress were laid down almost three years before, in September 2010 (Kovaios, 2010). The congress was scheduled to take place in the spring of 2011, but the further derailment of the Greek economy in 2011, in conjunction with Papandreou's chronic indecisiveness, led to delays. After Papandreou left the party leadership in March 2012, Venizelos, the new party leader, was also preoccupied with the crisis and PASOK's involvement in the coalition government formed in June 2012.

Since 2004, when upon the insistence of Papandreou the jurisdiction to elect the party's president was taken away from the congress and granted to direct elections by the party's base, PASOK's congresses lost their earlier political significance and symbolism. According to the party's statutes, congresses should take place every four years. Yet, for a period of five years (2008–13), no congress took place for the reasons explained above.

Venizelos, who had been elected President of PASOK in March 2012, convened the February 2013 congress in order to reshape the party's ideological profile and effect organisational changes as well as to consolidate his power base within the party through the election of a new Central Committee. The party leader's vision about the party was reproduced in a 'Declaration', i.e., a new ideological platform for PASOK, and also amendments to the party's statutes.[2] These documents signalled large-scale changes in PASOKs' physiognomy.

A long time has passed since PASOK's first 'Declaration' of September 1974. In that document, PASOK's profile was couched in three terms, namely 'national independence, popular sovereignty, social justice'. Almost forty years later, the 'Declaration' of March 2013 contained seven key terms. The seven key terms were the following: fatherland, democracy, freedom, justice, development, Europe and environmental sustainability. These terms reflected not only PASOK's change over time, but also an uncertainty about the party's ideology and an anxiety to offer an all-inclusive message to a deeply fragmented society subjected to the differential effects of the economic crisis.

The 'Declaration' plainly states that PASOK belongs to European social democracy. With regard to the party's stance towards the economic crisis, the 'Declaration' nods approvingly towards the PASOK government's commitment in 2009–11 to cooperate with Greece's creditors and international organisations in order to manage the sovereign debt crisis: 'a single word which signals a choice made by our party is Responsibility'.

Suggested amendments to the party's statutes included the reduction of the Central Committee size to 170 members who were responsible for electing a thirteen-member Political Council. The latter will convene on a weekly basis. There are provisions to prevent the emergence of a party oligarchy: party officials may serve up to three terms, while there is a requirement that in each election of the Central Committee or the Political Council or other party organs at least 30 per cent of the newly elected members should not have previously served in the same organ. Before each parliamentary election, the party's candidates will be elected in intra-party primaries.

However, such much needed reforms to make the previously overstaffed and slow party organisation lighter and more transparent coincided with a typical manoeuvre to control the party 'from above': in January 2013 Venizelos appointed an old party cadre, Yannis Souladakis, as president of the management committee of the party's ninth congress. The management committee, named Committee on the party's statutes and accreditation (EKAP), was in charge of carrying out the organisational and procedural motions to stage the congress and most importantly to monitor the dialogue among party members before the congress, the election of representatives to the congress and the accreditation of party members listed in the party's registry.[3]

This was a politically sensitive task as the total number and the names of PASOK party members had been disputed in previous occasions, during party congresses of the 1990s and the 2000s. For this reason, the elections of representatives to the party congress, scheduled for 24 February 2013, was a major political event for the party, as different factions of supporters and opponents of the party leadership would want to elect the largest number of representatives possible. The powerful EKAP committee, the nine members of which had been handpicked by the party leader himself, was different from the Central Organising Committee of the Congress (KOES), a large and rather decorative party organ entrusted to oversee the intra-party discussions on the way to the congress.

It is telling of the administrative incapacity and the uncertainty about the party's future course, that the said drafts of party documents, to be discussed in party cells before the congress and during the congress, were made available on 31 January 2013, only a few weeks before the start of the congress, and that the Secretariat of the KOES advised the party cells to meet twice, obviously in haste, within the same month in which the congress was scheduled to take place.[4]

It is not surprising then that in February 2013, on the way to the party congress Venizelos met with several challenges from his own party. First, a group of ten former socialist MPs and cadres, led by Michalis Karchimakis, the former Secretary General of the party (2010–12), claimed that there was lack of transparency in the preparations for the congress and that although the date of the congress was approaching rapidly, no debates were taking place in the party cells. Second, the self-proclaimed left wing of the party (the 'Left Initiative') publicly doubted if the party's leadership wanted to discuss the responsibilities of PASOK for the crisis and the rejection of austerity policies to which PASOK had consented in 2010–12 (Kechagia, 2013).Venizelos was also challenged by the former socialist Prime Minister, Simitis, who issued a short public announcement saying that he would not participate in the congress. He said that he did not want to participate in a 'photo opportunity', implying that he saw the whole process as a cosmetic exercise.

Finally, the party's leadership was challenged by the employees working in the party headquarters who have not been paid their salaries for twelve months. PASOK was unable to compensate its own employees, as in the middle of Greece's economic crisis the party itself was undergoing its own economic crisis: in mid-2012 PASOK had an outstanding debt of €112 million to various Greek banks. This was not unusual in the Greek party system as party financing has been based, among other things, on generous loans primarily issued to parties by state-owned banks. Notably, the ND party had a €120 million debt (Chassapopoulos, 2012).

PASOK's congress of 2013

The ninth party congress of the PASOK, which took place in March 2013 in Athens, may have been a new start, a sort of 'reboot', for a party that saw its electoral performance dwindle from 44 per cent of the total vote (in the parliamentary elections of 2009) to 13 per cent (in the elections of 2012). This was the first party congress after five years and it gave the party's leader, Evangelos Venizelos the opportunity to consolidate its position within the party. Congress participants contributed to the partial regeneration of the party by electing to PASOK's 170-member Central Committee a younger generation of party cadres. Among the cadres who received most of the votes and were elected to the first ten positions of the Central Committee, none had served as a minister in PASOK's successive cabinets in the 2000s, while almost all were in their thirties and forties. Moreover, the majority of the Committee members (65 per cent) were supporters of Venizelos rather than of the other factions which had dominated PASOK in the 2000s.[5]

The party cadres belonging to the faction once supporting Greece's former socialist Prime Minister, Papandreou, or those supporting the 'Left Initiative' did not do as well. They won a small share of votes and consisted of weak opposition groups in the new Central Committee. In brief, Venizelos dominated the congress and the newly elected party organs.

However, the congress was a missed opportunity to reunite the scattered political forces of former PASOK. Already before the elections of 2012, well-known cadres, such as former socialist ministers Louka Katseli and Haris Kastanidis, and MPs, such as Antonis Kotsakas and Alexis Mitropoulos, had rejected the austerity policies followed by Papandreou. Kotsakas and Mitropoulos, among others, expressed the left-wing populist views of the old PASOK of the 1980s, which were also espoused by PASOK voters who voted for the Coalition of the Radical Left (Syriza) in 2012. After PASOK participated in the coalition government of Antonis Samaras, formed in June 2012, the break with the left-wing populist wing became irreparable.

The ninth party congress could have been an opportunity for reunification not with the former PASOK faction which had been integrated into Syriza, but with the modernising faction which had more or less supported Venizelos since 2007, when the latter challenged George Papandreou for the party's leadership. It is telling that except for Simitis, the former PASOK president in 1996–2004, who refused to participate in the congress, formerly prominent socialist ministers and party cadres, such as Anna Diamantopoulou, and others associated with the era of Simitis, were also absent. After becoming party president in March 2012, Venizelos either felt strong enough not to make an effort to bridge the gap with the modernising faction or calculated that the inclusion of the socialist party elite which had served under Simitis would subtract more votes from PASOK than it would add.

Thus Venizelos managed to fully control the party, as shown by the fact that in the election of the thirteen-member Political Council (formerly known as the Executive Bureau) of PASOK, which took place at the first session of the Central Committee after the congress, Venizelos succeeded in having elected ten of his supporters as Council members.

There is no doubt then that, owing to the skill, experience and determination of its new leader, for the moment PASOK has avoided factionalism which may have ensued after the two consecutive disappointing performances of the party in the elections of May and June 2012. However, the fact that Venizelos has been unable to find allies among the former socialist elite reflects the correspondingly narrow electoral base of the party which, if anything, has continued dwindling even after the said elections.

Four different opinion polls, conducted in September 2012, i.e. only three months after the June elections, in November 2012 and in January and March 2013 showed that PASOK' s electoral appeal has shrunk even further: all four polls showed that if elections were held in any of these months, PASOK would obtain less than 10 per cent of the vote. What is worse, PASOK would probably trail behind the neo-Nazi party Golden Dawn which in the same opinion polls emerged as the third strongest party, behind ND and Syriza.[6]

Conclusion

The economic crisis which broke out in 2010 was not exclusively the result of the workings of neo-liberal capitalism, but the outcome of the combination of a model of growth based on accumulating public debt with the global financial crisis which had already started in late 2008. In Greece before 2010 state-owned and state-run companies dominated and in fact still dominate major sectors of the economy such as energy, land transportation, armaments and university education. Before the crisis, successive centre-right and socialist governments had not touched public sector salaries and pensions and had followed expansionist policies financed by government loans.

In the 2000s, all Greek governments and particularly the centre-right government of ND in 2004–09, which preceded PASOK in power, had sustained budget deficits. Such deficits resulted from excess government expenditure which was not matched by government revenue-raising capacity. Earlier governments had also allowed the public debt to get out of control; had neglected the deterioration of competitiveness and the current accounts balance; and had tolerated the existence of a narrow tax base, consisting of the salaried strata, while businesspersons, the self-employed and the liberal professions engaged in rampant tax evasion.

The austerity policies followed since 2010 reflect the neo-liberal consensus to which the Greek socialists have succumbed. In order to save Greece from default and remain in the Euro-zone, the PASOK government drastically cut salaries, pensions and welfare spending. Such policies were unavoidable given the legacies of policy choices of previous governments, but the mix of policies and the pace at which they were implemented reflected PASOK's own bias and political profile. The socialist government allowed unemployment to soar in the private sector, but it protected public sector jobs; it cut salaries across the board in the public sector, but did not privatise a single state-owned enterprise nor did it merge or reform any of the ministries and agencies of the central government.

In 2009–11 PASOK passed long-awaited reforms in policy sectors other than the economy (e.g. in migration, university education, transparency in the public sector). Nevertheless, in terms of a retrospective voting analysis, in 2012 voters judged PASOK for its economic policy and possibly on its disappointing record on fighting corruption. Even though in 2010 and 2011 PASOK had succeeded in reducing the state deficit and keeping Greece in the Euro-zone, it mismanaged the economic crisis. The Papandreou government proved unable to stabilise the public debt and limit the extent of economic depression and the ensuing unemployment. As a result, in the consecutive parliamentary elections of May and June 2012 PASOK took a heavy blow, as it received less than one-third of the votes it had obtained when it won the elections of 2009.

PASOK suffered defeat not only because voters punished it for adopting austerity policies or for tolerating corruption. Even though the mix of austerity policies was the primary reason behind the depletion of PASOK's ranks and the flight of voters towards parties to the left of PASOK, other reasons were present before it assumed power in 2009.

Such reasons included, first, the absence of a party structure other than the emaciated party organs which had survived the continuous experimentation with the party's organisation in 2004–13; and, second, the lack of a clearly recognisable ideological profile other than the blurred messages, broadcast by PASOK's leadership in the same time period, which created an unstable mix of ideas. The mix contained themes of PASOK's populist and nationalist rhetoric of the 1980s, major tenets of European social democracy and also post-materialist concerns (e.g. about environmental protection and the rights of women and minorities). The rhetoric of PASOK after Venizelos shifted somewhat, as the new leader emphasised his party's responsible stance throughout the crisis period, in order to contrast PASOK with Syriza which he accused of shallow populism and irresponsible policy promises.

In the future, it will be difficult for PASOK to regain its electoral strength, as since mid-2012 the Greek electorate has been divided between two poles, the conservative ND and the radical left Syriza. These two parties poll together about 60 per cent of the electorate, while populist right-wing and extreme right parties (Independent Greeks, Golden Dawn) attract another 20 per cent.

However, neither of the two large parties seems able to form single majority governments. The two right-wing parties are not potential coalition parties, as they place themselves too far off the centre of the political spectrum and have not even articulated a recognisable economic policy.

By contrast, PASOK still keeps a position in between ND and Syriza and may form a natural coalition partner of either party. Owing to the economic crisis and the unavoidable adoption of neo-liberal measures, the Greek socialists have lost political power and the confidence of their traditional electoral base. However, as long as PASOK does not completely disintegrate, which can happen because of internal factionalism or complete eradication in a parliamentary election of the current decade, it will keep an influential position in the centre of the party system. This position, coupled with its thirty-year-long experience in governing, may keep the socialist party afloat in Greek politics.

Notes

1 Personal interview with Professor Ilias Nikolakopoulos, electoral analyst, on 15 March 2013. His remarks were based on exit polls conducted in June 2012.
2 The new ideological platform of PASOK is available at: www.tovima.gr/files/1/2013/01/31/diakiripasok.pdf (accessed 19 February 2013).
3 The previous chairperson of the EKAP committee was replaced a few weeks before the congress. See http://archive.pasok.gr/portal/resource/contentObject/id/8b675c06–e2a2–4a04–be3f-a9ce264f8df1 (accessed 20 February 2013).
4 See the letter of P. Koukoulopoulos, coordinator of the Secretariat of KOE, addressed to party organisations on 31 January 2013, available at: http://archive.pasok.gr/portal/resource/contentObject/id/295ae121–7d97–4c64–8572–7d15365f1355 (accessed 21 February 2013).
5 See http://news.in.gr/greece/article/?aid=1231238139 (accessed 16 March 2013).
6 For the September 2012 opinion poll, conducted by polling company, Alco, see www.newsnow.gr/article/199367/dimoskopisi-alco-maxi-pasok-xrysis-avgis-gia-tin-4i-thesi.html. For the November 2012 poll, conducted by polling company, Pulse, see www.inews.gr/96/nea-dimoskopisi----katrakyla-gia-nd-kai-pasok--anodo-gia-syriza-kai-chrysi-avgi.htm. For the January 2013 poll, conducted by polling company, Metron Analysis, see www.star.gr/Pages/Politiki_Oikonomia.

aspx?art=164240&artTitle=nees_dimoskopiseis_skliro_mpra_nte_fer_nd_syriza_cha miles_ptiseis_pasok. For the March 2013 poll, conducted by polling company, Public Issue, see www.publicissue.gr/wp-content/uploads/2013/03/var-118–mar-2013.pdf (all sites accessed 15 March 2013).

References

Bank of Greece (2012). *The Greek Economy* (Athens: Bank of Greece Report, 6 April).

Chassapopoulos, N. (2012). 'No debt write-off for political parties', *To Vima*, 30 July, available at: www.tovima.gr/politics/article/?aid=468982 (accessed 21 February 2013).

Dinas, El. (2010). 'The Greek general election of 2009 – PASOK: the third generation', *West European Politics*, 33(2), 389–98.

European Commission (2011). *Statistical Annex to the European Economy*, autumn (Brussels: European Commission).

European Commission (2012). *The Economic Adjustment Programme for Greece: First Review*, Occasional Papers 123, December (Brussels: European Commission).

Eurostat (2012a). Eurostat data available at: http://epp.eurostat.ec.europa.eu/tgm/table.do?tab=table&init=1&plugin=1&language=en&pcode=tec00115 (accessed 3 November 2012).

Eurostat (2012b). Eurostat data available at: http://epp.eurostat.ec.europa.eu/cache/ITY_PUBLIC/2-22102012-AP/EN/2-22102012-AP-EN.PDF (accessed 3 November 2012).

Featherstone, K. (2011). 'The Greek sovereign debt crisis and the EMU: a failing state in a skewed regime', *Journal of Common Market Studies*, 49(2), 193–217.

Fouskas, V. (2012). 'Insight Greece: the origins of the present crisis', *Insight Turkey*, 14(2), 27–36.

Gemenis, K. (2010). 'Winning votes and weathering storms: the 2009 European and parliamentary elections in Greece', *Representation*, 46(3), 353–62.

Kechagia, V. (2013). 'PASOK suffering a nervous breakdown just before the party congress', *Ta Nea*, 19 February, available at: www.tanea.gr/news/politics/article/5002073/se-neyrikh-krish-ligo-prin-apo-to-synedrio (accessed 20 February 2013).

Korliras, P. (2012). 'The prospects of overcoming the crisis', *Economic Developments*, KEPE official journal, 18.

Kouvelakis, S. (2011). 'The Greek cauldron', *New Left Review*, 72, 17–32.

Kovaios, A. (2010). 'PASOK prepares its ninth congress', *To Vima*, 22 September, available at: www.tovima.gr/politics/article/?aid=355853 (accessed 21 February 2013).

Mavris, Y. (2012). 'Greece's austerity election', *New Left Review*, 76, 95–107.

Mavris, Y. (2013). 'The Post-election decline of PASOK', *Efimerida ton Syntakton*, 11 March.

Moschonas, G. (2012). 'PASOK's Suicide Mission', *Ethnos*, 17 March 2012, available at: www.ethnos.gr/entheta.asp?catid=25862&subid=2&pubid=63631569 (accessed 16 March 2013).

Moschonas, G. and Papanagnou, G. (2007). 'Posséder une longueur d'avance sur la droite: expliquer la durée gouvernementale du PSOE (1982–96) et du PASOK (1981–2004)', *Pôle Sud*, 27, 43–104.

Moschonas, G. and Pantazopoulos, A. (2010). 'Le PASOK et le rêve brisé de la Grèce', *La Revue Socialiste*, 39(3), 37–45.

Pagoulatos, G. and Triantopoulos, C. (2009). 'The return of the Greek patient: Greece and the 2008 global financial crisis', *South European Society and Politics*, 14(1), 35–54.

Pappas, T. S. (2010). 'Winning by default: the Greek election of 2009', *South European Society and Politics*, 15(2), 273–87.

Sotiropoulos, D. A. (2012). 'A democracy under stress: Greece since 2010', *Taiwan Journal of Democracy*, 8(1), 27–49.

Sotiropoulos, D. A. (2013). 'Greece', in J. M. de Waele, F. Escalona and M. Vieira (eds), *The Palgrave Handbook of Social Democracy in the European Union* (London and New York: Palgrave Macmillan), pp. 185–205.

Spourdalakis, M. and Tassis, C. (2006). 'Party change in Greece and the vanguard role of PASOK', *South European Society and Politics*, 11(3–4), 497–512.

Vernardakis, C. (2012). 'The elections of 17 June 2012 and the new cleavages in the party system', *He Avgi* (24 June).

Zahariadis, N. (2013). 'Leading reform amidst transboundary crises: lessons from Greece', *Public Administration*, 91(3), 648–62.

Part III

Towards a social democratic European Union?

12

Limits of consensus? The Party of European Socialists and the financial crisis[1]

Michael Holmes and Simon Lightfoot

Introduction

This chapter examines the response of the Party of European Socialists (PES) to the financial crisis. While the PES aims to play a role in coordinating the positions of social democratic parties throughout all EU institutions, the focus here is primarily on the role of the PES in the European Parliament (EP). This was the main forum in which the PES sought to develop a response to the financial crisis. We also treat the financial crisis not as a single phenomenon, but as a series of closely interrelated crises, ranging from the initial banking crisis to a recessionary crisis and finally to the crisis that enveloped the single currency. Therefore, it should also be pointed out that the crises were played out at multiple levels: at the level of individual national states, at the level of the European Union and at a global level.

The chapter has two objectives. The first relates to theories of the development of Euro-parties. There are two broad strands in this literature. The first of these argues that Euro-parties are of expanding importance. In their early study, Pridham and Pridham (1981) highlight, as have subsequent analyses such as those by Lightfoot (2005) and Hanley (2008), the emergence of transnational party structures in the EP and more broadly in the EU. These contributions argue that Euro-parties exhibit a growing and expanding influence over both their constituent national parties and over the EU's policies. The second strand in this literature, exemplified by Mair (2000), Schmitter (2000) and Sloam and Hertner (2012), acknowledges the growth in the number of Euro-parties, but argues that their influence – over either their constituent parties or the EU – is illusory. Therefore, part of our aim in this chapter is to assess whether the PES showed any meaningful influence during the financial crisis, or whether it was still only a marginal actor in the EU's processes. Our analysis will argue that generally the PES was not very influential in shaping policy at this time.

While the PES might not have been significant in these wider senses, it can still be used as a cipher which can decrypt the social democratic response to the financial crisis. It should be noted that each individual national social democratic party might not wholly endorse every nuance of PES policy statements. That being said, the PES stance can be taken as a broad indicator of a common social democratic position, which can therefore tell us about wider patterns of changes to European social democracy. Our second objective is to explore issues relating to social democracy through an analysis of the PES. The chapter will explore how the PES sought to build a common social democratic response to the financial crisis at the European level. We shall argue that despite significant attempts to construct a common position, in fact the PES's response to the crisis proved to be weak. We argue that the reasons for this weakness reveal wider problems of unity among social democratic parties in Europe.

In summary, we will argue that the PES's response to the financial crisis was reactive and incremental. In normal circumstances, these are good characteristics for fostering a common position among member parties. However, in the context of such a significant and serious challenge as the financial crisis, social democratic parties needed to attempt a more proactive and ambitious policy. We will also argue that the PES's response was strongly wedded to a pro-European perspective. Again, while in ordinary times this would make sense, the extraordinary circumstances of the crisis called for a more critical view of the direction that EU policy was taking. Although the PES eventually began to deal with the crisis in a more innovative and critical way, by that stage it had already lost leadership.

The PES is not solely to blame for its passivity. Indeed, we argue that one of the main challenges faced by the PES has been the very evident lack of unity among its constituent parties. In addition, another important feature which limited the ability of the PES and its parties to construct an effective response was their lack of capacity to shape things, due to their loss of power both in various national elections and in the 2009 EP elections. However, it does raise the question of why the PES and its members were unable to exploit the financial crisis and turn it to their electoral advantage at the height of the crisis.

Our analysis begins with a short summary of the background factors shaping the PES as a transnational party actor. The next section looks at the development of PES policy on the financial crisis. We argue that there were three distinct phases of the PES policy response. First, there was a period of limited reaction to the initial banking crisis, where the PES essentially reiterated existing policy proposals relating to financial regulation. Second, as the scale and scope of the crisis became more evident, the PES began to try to develop new ideas and policies, in particular by challenging the growing move towards austerity programmes and instead calling for ambitious investment programmes. Third, as the crisis moved on to become a very specific threat to the stability and security of the Euro-zone, the PES began to focus particularly on the future cohesion of the single currency and of the EU, trying to find a means of encouraging European unity. In the final section, we analyse the policy response. Our analysis is built primarily on an evaluation of party documents and press releases from both the PES itself and the Socialist Group (and latterly the Socialists & Democrats Group) in the European Parliament. Finally, we also draw on a selection of interviews with members of the PES, carried out in 2011.

Background: the capabilities of the PES

Social democracy has always laid claim to an internationalist commitment (Wilde, 1994; Sassoon, 1997). Although internationalism is by no means intrinsically synonymous with support for European integration, social democratic parties were among the first to try to build an organisational framework at the European level. A Socialist Group was created in the European Assembly in the 1950s, followed by the establishment of the Confederation of Socialist Parties in the European Community (CSPEC) in 1973, and then the foundation of the Party of European Socialists in 1992 (see Hanley, 2008). The main criterion for membership is that a party must be a member of the Socialist International, and must be from either an EU or a European Free Trade Area (EFTA) member state or a country on the verge of joining the EU. The membership in February 2013 stood at thirty-two full member parties, eleven associate and ten observer parties. It is possible for more than one party from each state to join the PES, so for a variety of historical and ideological reasons more than one member party exists in a number of countries.

The main decision-making organs of the PES are the congress, the leaders' conference and the presidency. According to party statutes, the congress is the supreme organ of the PES, responsible for laying down its political guidelines. Each member party can send delegates to the congress, with voting rights based roughly on 50 per cent of the weighting of votes in the Council of Ministers in conformity with the Treaty establishing the EU. Additionally, a number of delegates from each full member party, equal to one half of the number of its MEPs, can attend the congress. The leaders' conference meets twice a year, usually timed to coincide with European Council meetings. It can adopt resolutions and recommendations.

A number of events occurred in the early 2000s that mean that the PES today is a more independent party than ever before. In the early years it was very reliant upon its Group in the European Parliament for funding and staff. The EU Regulation 2004/2003 governing political parties at the European level and the rules regarding their funding clarified the roles played by each organisation and ensured that the PES was able to gain greater financial independence from its group (see van Hecke, 2010). The party was also able to employ its own staff, rather than rely on seconded officials from the EP Socialist Group (it currently (in 2013) has a staff of fourteen).

A further development was the establishment of a high-level presidency and a coordination team in 2001. The coordination team is in charge of administrative tasks, and the planning, preparation and financing of PES activities. The presidency is responsible for fixing the political direction of the PES. The presidency comprises a representative of each member party, from which the president and vice-presidents are elected. The roles of the president and vice-presidents are mainly administrative and symbolic, such as representing the PES, but the president in particular has proposal powers, which can be significant in shaping the agenda. In terms of decision-making capacity and authority within the PES, the party leaders' conference can adopt resolutions and recommendations. Within the party leaders' conference, Article 17.3 of the Statutes states that 'whenever possible, political decisions shall in principle be taken on the basis of consensus. If a consensus cannot be reached, decisions regarding policy areas subject to majority decision-making within the Council of the European Union shall be taken on the basis of a qualified majority' (PES, 2009a). Article 17.5 states that a 'qualified majority requires 75 per cent of the votes cast'. Votes shall only take place if at least two-thirds of the full member parties of the PES are present. Votes are cast per member party and organisation. The allocation of votes for a qualified majority per party and per organisation is equal to that party and organisation's number of delegates to the PES congress. However, Article 17.6 clearly identifies that if a 'full member party declares that it is unable to implement a specific decision taken by qualified majority, it can declare itself not to be bound by such a decision provided it indicates this intention before a vote is taken' (PES, 2009a). Interestingly, former PES Secretary General Ton Beumer downplayed the importance of qualified majority voting, arguing that the PES did not see outvoting national parties as progress towards their aim of influencing EU policy. Rather, he argued that the PES should continue its opinion-building role, a role that made the party 'more influential but less visible' (interview, Brussels, 2 March 2000).

There are two further difficulties in relation to being able to make the PES influential. First of all, there is a question mark over the extent to which social democratic actors in the EU have put forward a clear and distinctive message. Policies were developed in the late 1990s in the PES that had the potential to transform European society but the parties were too divided (see McGowan, 2001; Paterson and Sloam, 2007). When social democracy had its 'magical return' (Cuperus and Kandel, 1998) in the late 1990s, a time when thirteen out of the then-fifteen member-state governments were drawn from social democratic parties, the left failed to construct a distinctive vision. Indeed, perhaps even worse, 'it did not even try. It was clueless' (Sassoon, 2011: 138). Social democracy appeared content to collaborate in EU institutions with the EPP between 2004–09, which according to Marlière meant that in effect the PES parties had co-managed neo-liberal Europe (2011: 76). The second problem, perhaps allied to the first, is that social democracy has not been able to sustain a significant presence at the Council level in the EU during the 2000s. The 'magical return' proved to be fleeting and transient, so that an ongoing issue for the PES is actually having bodies on the ground in the Council.

The overall pattern of PES decision making reveals a very strong emphasis on consensus building across two main levels. First of all, it is evident internally within the PES, where the focus is on consensus and agreement among its member parties. Second, it is evident in terms of its relations with other Euro-parties at the EP level. This consensual approach has led in turn to the PES working in a very incremental manner. By their very nature, Euro-parties tend to provide guidance, not direction (interview, PES researcher, October 2011). Thus, the PES is inevitably more focused on facilitating and promoting a liaison between its member parties than on leadership. Despite the changes outlined above, to a large extent the PES can still be seen as a 'party of parties' (see Skrzypek, 2010) or a network of socialist parties (Moschonas, 2002). Indeed, it has to deal with an increasingly disparate collection of members. This is partly a consequence of the diversity resulting from enlargement. But it is also due to a certain lack of coherence in terms of identity.

For some time, the 'Social Europe' project acted as glue for social democratic parties, giving symbolic values and symbolic strengths. But the shared sense of identity has weakened. Once one goes past some rather non-contentious and bland assertions, member parties do not wholly agree about what constitutes the core social democratic values. A second general feature of PES decision-making is that it has a very strong pro-integration reflex, tending to automatically endorse the general direction of EU policy. The PES attempted to seize the 'window of opportunity' in the late 1990s to create a common economic policy, but the 'outcomes are meager' (Merkel *et al.*, 2008). On specific policies such as EU employment policies, the PES attempted to shape the agenda by aggregating policy inputs of social democratic parties and encouraging member parties to act cohesively with respect to the EU employment agenda. However, while the Employment chapter might 'bear the handwriting of social democrats', there was no real sustainable or significant solution to the problem (see Aust, 2004; Merkel *et al.*, 2008: 258). Given the problems with the employment chapter it is perhaps unsurprising that the PES failed to influence the Luxembourg process (Ladrech, 2000) or the EMU debate (Notermans, 2001). On tax harmonisation (see Külahci, 2010), it was clear that 'domestic self-economic interest (banking sector and industry structure and resulting interest group pressure) and institutional settlements (distribution and redistribution), and the corresponding electoral calculus, prove to be the key important factors for social democratic parties'. 'The relation within the PES was aggravated by substantial ideological differences between social democratic parties on, for instance, corporate and capital gains tax harmonization' (Merkel *et al.*, 2008: 258). Given the disagreements over economic policy, it is perhaps not surprising that the PES also finds it hard to construct a unified vision for the future shape of EU institutions (see Lightfoot, 2012).

The need for unity among social democratic parties in the EU has been highlighted as important, if the PES is to exert maximum influence over what Moschonas describes as a 'conservative system with little room for partisan logics' (2009: 11). Ladrech offers a more qualified analysis arguing that social democracy aims to use the 'EU as a complementary site for decisions and policy setting' (Ladrech, 2000: 55). Bailey (2009) argues that support for the EU enables social democratic parties to proclaim the possibility of social democracy at the supranational level, despite the absence of a substantive social democratic agenda. However, the financial crisis threw down a major challenge to the prevalent PES decision-making style. Suddenly, an incremental and consensual policy style and a pro-EU reflex seemed less appropriate. It has often been said of European integration that it is most likely to be pushed forward at times of crisis and when there is a clear challenge to be met. The same is true within the party federations, and the manner in which the PES has sought to respond to the financial crisis illustrates this well. The financial crisis presented a huge challenge to the PES, in terms of organisation, decision making and policy response. In the next section, we present a short summary of the events of the crisis, paying particular attention to the manner in which they involve a complex interplay of global, European, and national levels of activity. This will then be used as a basis for examining how the PES has responded in terms of decisions and policies.

The PES response to the financial crisis

At the start of the crisis, the initial response of the PES was built around one of their existing campaigns. As the financial crisis became apparent, the PES intensified its calls for the introduction of stronger regulation of hedge and private equity funds. This had already been on the PES agenda for a number of years. At a meeting of the Council of the PES in Sofia in November 2007, delegates unanimously endorsed a set of measures associated with strengthening arrangements for regulation of these kinds of funds (PES, 2007):

- there should be greater transparency of private equity and hedge funds;
- minimum reporting standards should be set for them;
- authorities should consider introducing limits on leverage to lower the risk of default;
- there should be effective taxation of fund managers;
- there should be greater consideration of workers' rights and protections in this field.

As can be seen, although they indicate the general approach of the party, these measures were of a rather broad and undefined nature. There is an absence of detail and, perhaps most evidently, authority and responsibility to actually do anything is predominantly left to other bodies.

This phase culminated in the publication of the Rasmussen Report, a report of the EP's Committee on Economic and Monetary Affairs, with PES President Poul Nyrup Rasmussen as rapporteur. This was passed in September 2008. The report dealt only with the narrow issues of greater regulation of hedge funds and private equity. Its key elements were (European Parliament, 2008):

- a harmonised EU approach to legislation in these areas;
- the introduction of mandatory capital requirements for all financial institutions;
- alignment of reward packages with longer-term outcomes, to reflect losses as well as profits;
- full transparency of remuneration packages for high-level executives and senior managers;
- greater disclosure, identification and transparency in the sector;
- allowing employees to be informed and consulted during leveraged buy-out takeovers;
- measures to counter 'unreasonable' asset stripping by companies in such buy-outs;
- action to avoid excessive debt caused by leveraged buy-outs;
- greater transparency in relation to the investment of employee pension funds.

As is the case with most EP reports, the final outcome was a somewhat watered-down compromise struck between the PES, the EPP and ALDE. Rasmussen himself noted that 'it could only be achieved with the agreement of all major political parties in the European Parliament. I am very satisfied that we have got everyone on-board with this compromise. It is a fair compromise and a first real step for better regulation' (PES, 2008a). The tone was more one of improved management than of any radical overhaul of systems. Nonetheless, the PES could claim to have taken 'the first big step to reduce the risk of further financial crises. But it is only a first step. The debate and the fight for better regulation will not stop here' (Rasmussen, in PES, 2008a).

By this stage, the PES was beginning to acknowledge that there was more to the crisis than simply inadequate regulation of certain areas of the financial services sector. The party's attention was shifting to include increasing reference to the need for concerted action to counter the growing threat of recession. The PES's approach to the worsening recession was based on three elements. First, as would be expected of social democratic parties, there was a strong commitment to investment to try to foster growth and to mitigate the worst recessionary impacts. In April 2008, the PES proposed setting up a European

Growth Initiative to be funded by special European Growth Bonds in order to try to achieve this (PES, 2008c). Second, there was a strong commitment to do so through European channels, arguing that 'Europe could create more jobs and kick-start its sluggish economy through making more investments together' (Rasmussen, in PES 2008a). But, third, there was a developing concern that there was a danger of austerity programmes being introduced.

In this second phase, the PES recognised that the crisis had moved beyond an issue of salvaging a number of financial institutions to become a significant threat to growth and prosperity. The party expanded its demands from simply a tightening of financial regulation procedures to a call for an EU-wide investment strategy to stave off recession. But the overall approach was one still based on an incremental and integrationist style. The only slight alteration was that a less consensual policy style was adopted in relation to conservative parties. Instead, the PES began to contrast their interventionist and reflationary social democratic strategy with the concentration on austerity advocated by parties of the right.

By 2009, the crisis had moved on even further, and the PES was acknowledging that 'we are now facing a crisis of an unprecedented nature', one which threatened to 'undermine European integration' (PES, 2009b). But the nature of the threat was still not clearly perceived. In the same document, the party was calling for better protection of non-Euro-zone currencies against speculative attacks. The sense of solidarity is admirable, the awareness of the impending Greek crisis less so. The PES was still focusing more on what it termed 'the excessive strength of the euro'. In April 2008, former SPD Finance Minister Hans Eichel was still content to declare that 'Economic and Monetary Union has been a stunning success and Europe can be proud of the way it has been managed' (PES, 2008c).

As the third phase of the crisis unfolded, the PES was forced to develop a new dimension to its policies. And this was among the hardest to construct, given the national differences that it inevitably entailed. The PES might have declared that 'Greece's economy will not fail ... partly because the EU is based on interdependence and solidarity' (PES, 2010a). However, that sense of solidarity was about to be very sorely tested.

The PES presidency issued a declaration stating that 'the principle of European solidarity is a financial and moral necessity. The Euro-zone member states must grant the required financial assistance to Greece immediately. Any further ambiguity is unacceptable' (PES, 2010b). The presidency identified three core measures that needed to be adopted. The first was an extension of their existing programme on financial regulation, calling for tighter regulation in the sphere of credit default swaps on sovereign debts. The other two were new features: first, calling for some form of 'European Mechanism of Financial Solidarity', and second, calling for the introduction of a financial transactions tax (also known as the 'Tobin tax').

However, the PES also accepted the need for the introduction of the Greek austerity programme. This is perhaps unsurprising, given that the government initially charged with implementing the plan – the PASOK administration of George Papandreou – was a fellow social democrat party. But despite some talk of 'put[ting] a gun on the table for all financial speculators to see' (Stavros Lambinidis, Pasok MEP, quoted in PES, 2010c), the focus was on working within existing approaches – reformist rather than radical.

By this stage, the PES began to shift a little from its traditional position of working within a pro-EU consensus. This was most evident in their growing challenge to the policies being advocated by the 'troika' of the European Commission, the European Central Bank (ECB) and the International Monetary Fund (IMF). From 2011 onwards, the official troika was imposing severe austerity programmes in Portugal, Ireland and Greece as the condition for bailing out their economies. In early 2012, the PES responded by sending an 'alternative troika' to Greece. This was intended to explore possibilities for a different approach, one that would attempt to balance debt alleviation with an economic stimulus programme.

The language now being deployed was very different from the previous one. Hannes Swoboda, the Austrian leader of the S&D group, talked in terms of locust and dictators. 'We have seen what locusts like hedge funds can do in the economic world. We cannot allow another swarm of locusts such as the Troika … to descend on the country and impose their ideas. This would amount to a dictatorship and not co-operation with a country which is part of the European Union' (PASD, 2012). The principle of pro-European solidarity was now being used as a reason to criticise EU policy. As one member of the 'alternative troika' put it, 'Greece is an old European country. We must show our solidarity and Greece has to remain not only European but inside the Euro-zone. This is not only vital for Greece but for all Europeans' (Elisa Ferreira, PASD, 2012).

This more critical position was apparent not just in relation to Greece. As discussions began to build around creating a new quasi-treaty to give the EU greater fiscal authority, the PES continued to argue that the EU was taking the wrong approach. Thus, PES President Sergei Stanishev argued that 'a fiscal compact on its own will not provide solutions' (PES, 2012a), while PES Secretary-General Philip Cordery dismissed an early draft of the compact as being 'so biased towards austerity only' (PES, 2012a). The evident concern of the PES was that the EU was becoming unequivocally identified with a right-wing agenda, and that this was alienating an increasing number of citizens across Europe. As Stanishev put it, 'the EU is at risk of being seen as part of the problem, imposing only pain through cuts and austerity. This is a breeding ground for populist anger' (PES, 2012b). It is no more than a mechanism to 'institutionalise austerity' (Stanishev, PES 2012c).

The PES demands were similar to what they had been arguing throughout the crisis – the use of the EU to promote growth to try to solve the financial crisis. This came alongside the long-standing PES calls for the introduction of financial reforms, involving tighter regulation of financial services and the introduction of the financial transactions tax. In addition, the PES now began to call for the creation of euro-bonds to help deal with the Euro-zone crisis, and also advocated the establishment of an independent European credit rating agency.

The PES response had clearly moved away from consensus to a more confrontational and political stance. Several key developments took place in 2012 that cemented this move. First of all, Martin Schulz was elected President of the Parliament in January 2012. He immediately emphasised a more confrontational style, beginning his term by declaring 'I will not be a convenient President' (Schulz 2012a), and stating 'I'm a fighter. I am trying to put the European Parliament in a confrontation with the heads of government' (*EU Observer*, 8 March 2012). He called for Parliament to be given greater rights to supervise budgetary powers of Euro-zone countries, a demand that has a particular resonance given the manner in which countries like Greece and Italy have seen their national parliamentary and electoral systems bypassed of late. Schulz has also talked in terms of giving the Parliament greater say in relation to the Commission presidency, a move that would give EP elections much greater competitive edge and profile.

A further important development came in the election of the Socialist Party's François Hollande as President of France in May 2012. Hollande came to power challenging the orthodoxy of the austerity programmes in place around Europe and calling for a re-examination of the terms of the Fiscal Treaty in order to try to find a means of promoting growth. Not surprisingly, Hollande's success was viewed with great enthusiasm. The PES's clear alternative political vision is evident in these statements. The result was a readiness to challenge the dominant policies in the EU in relation to the proposed fiscal treaty. PES President Stanishev set out the PES position: 'It is time to recognise that improved growth and jobs means clear public and private investment – full stop. This must become the new golden rule of EU policy. Without this, the treaty proposals remain 'unsatisfactory' (PES, 25 January 2012b). The PES position called for a significant and sustained investment programme focusing especially on green technology and development of sustainable infrastructure projects. The party's position was that the so-called 'fiscal compact' is an attempt to institutionalise austerity. It is far from being a comprehensive plan enabling the EU to get out of the crisis. The key concepts that are missing are growth and solidarity. Clearly, a debate has opened up about whether a continuing emphasis on neo-liberal financial orthodoxy and austerity was appropriate or not. In policy terms, a very clear left–right division has emerged, arguing at very least for some form of growth strategy to go alongside the Fiscal Treaty, if not even a more thorough reworking of the ideas contained in the treaty. However, there are clear divisions still within the PES, with the British Labour Party opting out of provisions for financial transaction tax.

Analysing the PES response

The PES would appear to have adopted a coherent approach to the financial crisis, one that reflects a gradual evolution from its existing policies to take account of the developing situation. Thus, the immediate response to the first phase of the banking crisis was to reassert the importance of stronger financial regulation. However, it is also one which at times seems to be following events rather than leading the way. This is a familiar issue with the PES, since 'current senior social democratic politicians are not renowned for taking risks. They have proved to be tentative about embracing new ideas, wary of changing direction, and lacking in inspiring leadership. They err on the side of caution' (Meyer and Rutherford, 2012: 6). In particular, the PES seems to have been reactive to the slide into recession and to the snowballing of the Euro-zone crisis.

This is not entirely its own fault. Social democratic parties suffered a series of electoral setbacks during this period, which significantly weakened their ability to engage with EU decision making at the highest level. Indeed, the PES itself was increasingly on the margins. PES representation in the EP suffered a serious setback in the 2009 election, when it lost thirty-four seats and saw its combined vote fall by almost 3 per cent. While the loss of seats was partly due to overall reductions in the size of the EP, and the losses were somewhat offset by the inclusion of MEPs from the Italian Democratic Party (though this necessitated renaming the Socialist Group in the EP as the Progressive Alliance of Socialists and Democrats), nonetheless the election was a clear blow to the PES.

The 2009 EP election result was damaging enough in its own right. However, in many EU states, social democratic parties suffered serious electoral reverses during roughly the same period. In 2007, social democratic parties were in power (either on their own or as senior or junior partners in coalitions) in fifteen out of the twenty-seven member states. But prior to the return to power of the Danish SD in the September 2011 election, the social democratic presence in EU governments had declined to just eight out of the twenty-seven. The German SPD, the Swedish SAP and the Spanish PSOE all suffered particularly severe electoral defeats. Even then, two of those five victories proved to be pyrrhic. The Portuguese PS under José Socrates had retained power in an election in 2009, but this proved to be short-lived, with the government remaining in office less than two years before being defeated. Similarly, the PASOK government in Greece, which had been elected to power in 2009, was superseded by a techno-cratic administration in 2011. In both cases, the exigencies of the financial crisis were at the heart of the problems of the social democrats. The PS government was defeated over its austerity plan while PASOK leader George Papandreou was forced to step down to make way for a national unity government to implement an austerity programme as a condition of the EU/ECB/IMF bail-out. Clearly, social democratic parties in government held a 'poisoned chalice' as a result of the financial crisis (Sassoon, 2011).

The fact that there were far fewer social democratic parties in government made it much more difficult for them to convey their ideas at Council level in the EU. This highlights the importance of governmental presence. For some social democratic members of the PES, participation in government made them far more reluctant to commit too much in a PES setting. Notably, the PASOK government in Greece was concerned with making sure that the PES did not make its life any more difficult than it already was. Similarly, the Austrian SPÖ, in a grand coalition government, was anxious to avoid excessively radical pronouncements from the PES, especially with regard to the European Council's handling of the crisis. These cannot by any means all be ascribed to the social democratic position on the crisis – there are far too many national issues cutting across. But it did pose a huge problem for the PES and its member parties.

In the past, there could be accusations of 'a lack of coherence within the PES' (Holmes and Lightfoot, 2007: 152). However, the financial crisis does not suggest such major ideological differences among PES parties. There is a broad consensus in support of many features, such as the introduction of financial stimulus packages and greater regulation of financial markets. Perhaps, wishfully, at one stage the PES viewed the crisis as 'the great defeat of neo-liberal capitalism' (PES, 2008b) and 'the end of unregulated market fundamentalism' (PES, 2008d). The PES boasted that 'we knew that the market could not do it alone, now everyone knows. We need more than ever a social democratic regulatory regime for financial markets' and declaimed 'Social Europe must triumph over greed and irresponsibility' (PES, 2008d). On the one hand, there is a clear ideological argument that under-regulation and unchecked market freedom have proved to be bad. But while declaring that 'free markets cannot ignore social morals', the PES goes on to conclude that what is needed is 'decent capitalism' (PES, 2008e), and to state that it 'wants markets to function better. For us, the market is our servant and not our master' (PES, 2008d).

Some differences emerged in relation to national positions, but these were muted at the PES level. There was at least still very strong commitment to the rhetoric of solidarity. Thus, the SPD did not go round PES meetings picking fights with its PASOK counterparts, nor vice versa. Indeed, there was a clear feeling that the SPD had adopted a principled European stance to the Greek crisis, refusing to make political capital out of the difficult position Chancellor Merkel found herself in. The SPD's actions appeared to epitomise the 'solidarity' message proposed by the PES, although there was a clear risk that this position could have come under pressure domestically with opinion polls highlighting German opposition to further transfers to Greece. There is also a sense that national positions trumped ideological positions. A potential cleavage existed between the so-called 'creditor' nations, such as the Netherlands, Finland, Germany and Austria, and 'debtor' nations, such as Greece, Spain and Portugal.

Interestingly, the social democratic parties of central and eastern Europe were relatively quiet on the subject. This might be due to the weak state of social democratic parties in the region, especially in Poland and Hungary. However, it also indicated that while parties in central and eastern European states were quite happy preaching austerity and fiscal rectitude in principle (see Holmes and Lightfoot, 2011: 47–50), in practice there was an awareness that their own countries' economies were not in a particularly strong condition. The lack of public squabbling is probably due to the fact that when such differences did occur, they did so in the form of the parties ignoring or sidelining the PES (we noted above that while the PES statutes allow for qualified majority voting, parties can opt out of decisions, and consensus is the norm). Much was made of the Spanish PSOE leader José Zapatero's failure to attend a PES Leaders' Meetings when he was prime minister, although the relatively low number of social democratic prime ministers made these meetings less useful than the meetings organised in the later 1990s.

The degree of consistency between policy statements at the national level and those at the European level would need to be tested in more detail to establish this, but there are some indications. In a letter to French President Nicolas Sarkozy, the PES suggested that the financial problems can be dealt with 'no budget transfers between Member States' (Rasmussen, 2008), an approach which smacks of trying to assuage some social democratic parties as much as conservative political leaders. The close working relations between the PS and the SPD appear to suggest that there was a high level of coordination in policy decisions between the two parties.

Conclusion

For social democrats, the financial crisis seemed to be partly a case of 'our day has come (again)', but also a case of 'the world won't listen'. On the one hand, policies and programmes that had seemingly been confined to the history books appeared to be making a sudden dramatic return to fashion. During the immediate aftermath of the crisis, it seemed at first as though the economic policy landscape had been drastically altered, with government parties of all political and ideological hues embracing various kinds of Keynesian-style demand management measures to deal with the crisis. The policy opportunities and possibilities for left-wing parties seemed to have opened up again after a long period of retrenchment and constraint. Thus, the financial crisis could have been a catalyst for a transformation in the fortunes of social democratic parties, a window of opportunity both to achieve power and to change policies (interview, PES researcher, October 2011).

However, this early impression quickly gave way to the adoption of more traditional neo-liberal governmental economic policy prescriptions. The threat of a sovereign debt crisis across the European Union, with some Euro-zone members displaying previously ignored unsustainable levels of diverging economic performance in regards to productivity and inflation rates, heralded a new focus on austerity, severe cutbacks in wages, employment in public sector provision and privatisation of state assets. Furthermore, not only were such policies being pursued at national level, they were also being championed within the EU.

The PES tried to argue that 'our social democratic way is the solution to the crisis – the well-regulated social market economy. In recent years, the conservative ideology of deregulation and neo-liberalism has been dominant. They argued that government was bad and the market was good. But markets without adequate rules are bound to fail. This crisis is the final proof' (PES, 2008b). The main problem with this was that the message did not get through to the electorate, if the EP and national election results are to be taken as evidence. The PES could point to some of its ideas being adopted at the European level, such as the financial transactions tax. However, the lack of visibility for the PES or social democratic parties means that the right-leaning parties who dominated the European Council could take the credit.

Social democratic parties were blamed for being 'part of the problem', perhaps not surprising given their support for neo-liberal policies during the 1990s, while conservative and liberal parties didn't appear to suffer to the same extent. Indeed, Manow *et al.* argue that in the late 1990s social democracy had 'more in common with its main competitors than with its own positions roughly three decades earlier' (Manow *et al.*, 2007: 32) and that 'the profound changes in the ideological orientation of left parties over the course of the 1980s and 1990s were more important for a liberal stance of the Council than the return of Social Democratic parties to national power in the second half of the 1990s' (Manow *et al.*, 2007: 22). Thus we can identify a clear paradox – social democratic policies and parties are most in favour of the European project, yet the European project damages their electoral chances the most. While it is too early to write off the social democratic left, the parties must seize this opportunity to redefine the European project to ensure the European electorate have a clear vision for the EU. Indeed, it is argued that the EU could be the vehicle for the left to rediscover an ideological zest. As Cramme argues, 'If social democracy is to rediscover its mission of marrying economic efficiency with social justice, it needs a new means and vehicles for change. In this process, the EU could be its best ally' (2012).

This was similar to the call of David Miliband, the former Labour Foreign Minister, that 'we must forge an opportunity to be internationalists of a hard headed and serious kind, or our policy solutions will have no traction at all' (2011: 137). Unless the PES parties can do this, thereby identifying policy solutions as social democratic ones in the minds of voters, PES member parties could find the political landscape of Europe redrawn to exclude them to the political margins.

Note

1 A much shorter version of this chapter will be published in A. Skrzypek (ed.), *Euro-parties and European Democracy* (Foundation for European Progressive Studies).

References

Aust, A. (2004). 'From "Eurokeynesianism" to the "Third Way": the Party of European Socialists (PES) and European employment policies', in G. Bonoli and M. Powell (eds), *Social Democratic Party Policies in Contemporary Europe* (London and New York: Routledge), pp. 180–96.

Bailey, D. (2009). *The Political Economy of European Social Democracy: A Critical Realist Approach* (London: Routledge).

Cramme, O. (2012). 'The power of European integration', in O. Cramme and P. Diamond (eds), *After the Third Way: The Future of Social Democracy in Europe* (London: I.B. Tauris).

Cuperus, R. and Kandel, J. (1998). 'The magical return of social democracy', in R. Cuperus and J. Kandel (eds), *European Social Democracy: Transformation in Progress* (Amsterdam: Friedrich Ebert Stiftung and Wiardi Beckman Stichting), pp. 11–28.

European Parliament (2008). 'Report with recommendations to the Commission on hedge funds and private equity', EP Committee on Economic and Monetary Affairs, rapporteur Poul Nyrup Rasmussen, doc. A6–0338/2008.

Hanley, D. (2008). *Beyond the Nation State* (Basingstoke: Palgrave Macmillan).

Hertner, I. (2011). 'Are European election campaigns Europeanized? The case of the Party of European Socialists in 2009', *Government and Opposition*, 46(3), 321–44.

Holmes, M. and Lightfoot, S. (2007). 'The Europeanisation of left political parties: limits to adaptation and consensus', *Capital & Class* 93, 141–58.

Holmes, M. and Lightfoot, S. (2011). 'Limited influence? The role of the PES in shaping social democracy in central and eastern Europe', *Government and Opposition* 46(1), 32–55.

Külahci, E. (2010). 'Europarties: agenda-setter or agenda-follower? Social democracy and the disincentives for tax harmonization', *Journal of Common Market Studies* 48(5), 1283–306.

Ladrech, R. (2000). *Social Democracy and the Challenge of European Union* (London: Lynne Rienner).

Lightfoot, S. (2005). *Europeanizing Social Democracy? The Rise of the PES* (London: Routledge).

Lightfoot, S. (2012). 'Left parties at an EU level from Laeken to Lisbon', in M. Holmes and K. Roder (eds), *The Left and the European Constitution: from Laeken to Lisbon* (Manchester: Manchester University Press).

McGowan, F. (2001). 'Social democracy and the EU: who's changing whom?', in L. Martell (ed.), *Social Democracy: Global and National Perspectives* (Basingstoke: Palgrave Macmillan), pp. 74–106.

Mair, P. (2000). 'The limited impact of Europe on national party systems', *West European Politics*, 23(4), 27–51.

Manow, P., Schäfer, A. and Zorn, H. (2007). 'Europe's party-political centre of gravity 1957–2003', *Journal of European Public Policy* 15(1), 20–39.

Marlière, P. (2011). 'The French Socialist party and European integration: faltering Europeanism', in D. Dimitrakopoulos (ed.), *Social Democracy and European Integration* (London: Routledge), pp. 51–82.

Merkel, W., Petring, A., Henkes, C. and Egle, C. (2008). *Social Democracy in Power: The Capacity to Reform* (London and New York: Routledge).

Meyer, H. and Rutherford, J. (2012). 'Building the good society', in H. Meyer and J. Rutherford (eds), *The Future of European Social Democracy: Building the Good Society* (Basingstoke: Palgrave Macmillan), pp. 3–9.

Miliband, D. (2011). 'Why is the European left losing elections?', *Political Quarterly*, 82(2), 131–7.

Moschonas, G. (2002). *In the Name of Social Democracy: The Great Transformation 1945 to the Present* (London and New York: Verso).

Moschonas, G. (2009). 'Reformism in a "conservative" system: the European Union and social democratic identity', in J. Callaghan, N. Fischman, B. Jackson, and M. McIvor (eds), *In Search of Social Democracy: Responses to Crisis and Modernisation* (Manchester: Manchester University Press), pp. 168–92.

Notermans, T. (2001). *Social Democracy and Monetary Union* (Oxford: Berghahn Books).

PASD (2012). 'Hannes Swoboda: we do not want another swarm of locusts destroying Greece', Brussels: PASD press release, 15 February, available at: www.socialist group.eu/gpes/public/detail.htm?category=NEWS&id=136688&request_locale=EN& section=NER (accessed 21 February 2012).

Paterson, W. and Sloam, J. (2007). 'Failing successfully: European social democracy in the 21st century', in K. Lawson and P. Merkl (eds), *When Parties Prosper: The Uses of Electoral Success* (Boulder, CO: Lynne Rienner), pp. 41–60.

PES (2007). 'European socialists vote for action on hedge and private equity funds', Brussels, PES press release, 22 November, available at: www.pes.org/en/news/ european-socialists-vote-action-hedge-and-private-equity-funds (accessed 27 August 2011).

PES (2008a). 'Strauss-Kahn right on fiscal policy change says Rasmussen', Brussels, PES, 28 January, available at: www.pes.org/en/news/strauss-kahn-right-fiscal-policy- change-says-rasmussen (accessed 27 August 2011).

PES (2008b). 'Taking Europe out of financial and economic crisis: an urgent European plan of action', PES leaders' declaration, 5 November, available at: www.pes.org/en/ news/socialists-demand-ambitious-recovery-plan (accessed 21 February 2012).

PES (2008c). 'Complacency over economic management would be fatal, warns Eichel', Brussels: PES press release, 30 April, available at: www.pes.org/en/news/complacency- over-economic-management-would-be-fatal-warns-eichel (accessed 27 August 2011).

PES (2008d). 'Goodbye to unregulated markets. Welcome to a new progressive roadmap for jobs and real value', PES presidency resolution, Brussels, 16 October, available at: www.pes.org/system/files/images/downloads/Presidency_Financial_Crisis-16–10–2008_EN.pdf (accessed 27 August 2011).

PES (2008e). 'Financial markets cannot govern us!', letter to Danilo Türk, President of the Republic of Slovenia, 19 May, available at: www.pes.org/system/files/images/downloads/Letter_President_Slovenia.pdf (accessed 27 August 2011).

PES (2009a). 'A new direction for progressive societies. PES statutes adopted by the 8th congress', PES, Brussels.

PES (2009b). 'A matter of urgency: a new progressive recovery plan for the European Union – the need for a new effort', PES, Brussels.

PES (2010a). 'Do they ever learn? The Greek crisis tells us to regulate hedge funds', Brussels, blog by P. N. Rasmussen, 23 February, available online at: www.pes.org/en/blogs/pouls-blog/do-they-ever-learn-greek-crisis-tells-us-regulate-hedge-funds (accessed 26 August 2011).

PES (2010b). 'Immediate European solidarity is a financial and moral necessity', Brussels, declaration on the Greek and Euro-zone crisis adopted by the PES presidency, 29 April, available at: www.pes.org/en/system/files/Adopted_PES_Presidency_Declaration_on_the_Greek_and_Euro-zone_crisis29042010_EN.pdf (accessed 4 October 2011).

PES (2010c). 'PES "Stabilization Plan" for Greece and Euro-zone "would put a gun on the table for all speculators to see"', Brussels, press release, 2 March, available at: www.pes.org/en/news/pes-stabilization-plan-greece-and-euro-zone-would-put-gun-on-table-for-all-speculators-to-see (accessed 4 October 2011).

PES (2012a). 'PES prime ministers meeting call on European Council to recognise need for investment', Brussels, PES press release, 30 January, available at: ww.pes.org/en/news/pes-prime-ministers-meeting-call-european-council-recognise-need-investment (accessed 21 February 2012).

PES (2012b). 'PES president calls for "concrete action" from Commission after meeting with Barroso', Brussels, PES press release, 26 January, available at: www.pes.org/en/news/pes-president-calls-concrete-action-commission-after-meeting-barroso (accessed 21 February 2012).

PES (2012c). 'PES verdict of European Council: an attempt to institutionalise austerity', Brussels, PES press release, 13 December, available at: www.pes.org/en/news/pes-verdict-european-council-attempt-institutionalise-austerity (accessed 21 February 2012).

Pridham, G. and Pridham, P. (1981). *Transnational Party Cooperation and European Integration* (London: HarperCollins).

Rasmussen, P.N. (2008). 'Letter to President Sarkozy', available at: www.pes.org/en/system/files/Lettre_PNR_a_Sarkozy_EN.pdf (accessed 27 August 2011).

Sassoon, D. (1997). *One Hundred Years of Socialism* (London: Fontana).

Sassoon, D. (2011). 'Response to David Miliband', *Political Quarterly*, 82(2), 138–9.

Schmitter, P. (2000). *How to Democratise the EU… and Why Bother?* (Maryland, MD: Rowman & Littlefield).

Schulz, M. (2012). 'Ich werde kein bequemer Präsident sein', 17 January, available at: www.martin-schulz.info/index.php?link=4&beriech=1&details=1&id=692 (accessed 21 February 2012).

Skrzypek, A. (2010). *Models of (S)electing a Pan-European Leading Candidate* (Brussels: Foundation for European Progressive Studies).

Sloam, J. and Hertner, I. (2012). 'The Europeanization of social democracy: politics without policy and policy without politics', in H. Meyer and J. Rutherford (eds), *The Future of European Social Democracy: Building the Good Society* (Basingstoke: Palgrave Macmillan), pp. 27–38.

Toole, F. O. (2012). 'Disarray of the left has spared the right its due', *Irish Times*, 21 February, available at: www.irishtimes.com/newspaper/opinion/2012/0221/1224312113141. html (accessed 21 February 2012).

Van Hecke, S. (2010). 'Do transnational party federations matter? (… why should we care?)', *Journal of Contemporary European Research*, 6(3), 395–411.

Wilde, L. (1994). *Modern European Socialism* (Aldershot: Dartmouth).

13

Palliating terminal social democratic decline at the EU level?

David J. Bailey

The debate over the role that the European Union might play in providing social democratic parties with an opportunity for 're-social democratisation', particularly in the light of ongoing ideological, organisational, electoral and programmatic decline, has a long heritage (Featherstone, 1988; Geyer, 1993; Ladrech, 1993; Aust, 2004; Strange, 2006; Bailey, 2005, 2009a). Indeed, both social democratic practitioners and academics have long debated the merits or otherwise of the European route to social democratic reinvigoration. As far back as 1973 the Socialist Parties of the European Community (the precursor to the present Party of European Socialists) adopted a policy statement, *Towards a Social Europe*, which included a commitment to European-level social policy, full employment, equality of opportunity, EC industrial policy, environmental regulation, worker participation and an EC incomes policy (Hix, 2002: 21). Similarly, writing in 1988, Featherstone (1988: 347) noted that:

> in the present conditions of world capitalism, there is a *need* for Socialists in Europe to seek supranationalist means to some of their traditional goals. The nation-state no longer has the capacity to fulfil the requirements of democratic socialism; the wider political and economic forces constitute the terrain on which Socialists need to base their actions. Whatever the past predilections of European Socialists, if they are to more effectively achieve some of their substantive policy objectives, they now have *no realistic alternative* but to seek solutions at the supranational level. [emphasis added]

Nevertheless, these ambitions have prompted a range of academic interpretations, with varying degrees of support for, and agreement with, the social democratic position adopted. This chapter explores each of these positions, arguing that, rather than side with either the optimists or pessimists within this debate, those critical perspectives which draw attention to the motives of social democratic party elites in heralding the supranational opportunities for re-social democratisation are better able to explain the current relationship between social democratic parties and the European Union.

In pursuit of supranational re-social democratisation

The question of whether, and to what extent, the European Union presents an opportunity for 're-social democratisation' forms part of a wider debate over the extent to which such a process of 're-social democratisation' is possible at *any* level, be it national or supranational (on which, see Bailey, 2012). Of course, in order to assess whether social democratic parties are adopting policy programmes that are more or less 'social democratic', we must first agree upon what the term 'social democracy' refers to. Yet such an attempt would suggest that there is an essential 'social democratic-ness' that can be defined without direct reference to the policies which social democratic parties adopt. In contrast to the view that (to paraphrase Herbert Morrison) 'social democracy is what social democratic parties do', the present chapter works with a conceptualisation of 'social democracy' as a political ideal, and assumes that we are therefore able to evaluate the degree to which a particular political programme is social democratic or otherwise.

Thus, the chapter adopts the view, outlined in more detail elsewhere (Bailey 2009a: ch. 2), that social democracy can be (and has been historically) defined as a commitment to three core goals: (a) the reform (rather than the replacement) of capitalist relations of production; (b) the attempt to realise these reforms through an electoral and parliamentary political strategy; and (c) that the reforms pursued will have a redistributive, levelling, egalitarian or decommodifying effect favouring social democratic parties' core electoral constituency (which comprises a broad subaltern group including (but extending beyond) organised labour), *subject to the constraints arising from the two prior commitments* (Bailey, 2012: 101). At least since the end of the First World War each of these ideals has been agreed to by all parties and party actors who have been considered to be, or considered themselves to be, 'social democratic' (Bailey, 2009a: 4). Further, the *extent* to which such parties can be considered 'social democratic' can be understood in terms of the level and scope of redistribution (in an egalitarian direction) or the decommodification[1] that has been sought and/or achieved (Esping-Andersen, 1990). As a result, the move since the early 1980s by social democratic parties across western Europe, to adopt a socio-economic programme that sought to encourage greater focus on the market as the mechanism underpinning resource allocation, has been viewed by many commentators as a process of 'de-social democratisation' as it has reduced the redistributive and decommodifying effects present within social democratic party programmes (Moschonas, 2002: 244).

These ideological and policy transitions within social democratic parties have been largely portrayed by party elites in terms of their resulting from the necessitating effect of changes to the structure of the global economy (Watson and Hay, 2003), as well as the effect such changes have had upon the scope for *viable* social democratic policies, due especially to problems of scale associated with unilateral action through individual nation states (for a classic statement along these lines, see Gray, 1996). As a result, much recent debate within social democratic parties has focused on potential opportunities through which to achieve a 're-social democratisation' of social democratic party programmes, and especially the opportunities (as afforded by an increase in scale) presented by the process of European integration (see, for instance, Strange, 2006). Such debate within the literature has tended to divide over the question of whether the European Union might present a supranational vehicle through which social democratic policies that have become unviable at the national level can be once more rendered viable. This debate, moreover, provides us with an insight into the question of how we might understand social democratic parties' supranational-level responses to the current Great Recession, and the kinds of outcomes that have occurred as a result.

The optimists: cosmopolitan social democrats

As noted, for those optimistic about the prospects of a supranational re-social democratisation of European social democratic parties, European integration offers an important opportunity to circumvent the obstacles that have impinged upon the social democratic project (i.e. those processes which are typically referred to as 'globalisation'). Thus, from this perspective, social democratic attempts to utilise the nation state as a means by which to promote redistributive and decommodifying public policies may have been hampered by problems associated with capital flight, increased international economic competition, and the conviction that state intervention results in less efficient decisions within the firm (and therefore ones which are unviable over the long term in a globally competitive environment). Nevertheless, such obstacles are largely viewed as a problem of both scale and intra-regional competition: the individual nation state is disempowered when capital is able to relocate to neighbouring nation states if the nation state seeks to implement decommodifying policies that are unpopular with capital holders. As such, the possibility of securing coordinated policies across supranational regions, most likely through economic policies adopted by the European Union, is believed to avoid intra-regional competition and increase the scale upon which such policies will be implemented, thereby re-enabling the adoption of social democratic policies *through supranational regional institutions* (see, for instance, Held, 2003). As such, in the light of the Great Recession, cosmopolitan social democrats might be expected to support calls for greater supranational governance, as a means by which to resolve the global economic crisis and to do so in such a way that ensures that more redistributive and/or decommodifying policies are implemented at the European level.

The pessimists: opposing neo-liberal Europe

More pessimistic social democratic commentators have tended to note a number of obstacles to the realisation of 're-social democratisation' at the supranational level. Thus, for supranational social democratic pessimists, the institutional and political obstacles internal to the European Union are such that the promise of re-social democratisation, purportedly to be achieved through coordinated supranational activity at the European level, is considered to be an unviable political project. Such sceptics point to the institutional barriers to social democratic outcomes being realised at the EU level, including the high decision-making threshold that results from the need for EU legislation to be approved by large majorities within the Council, European Parliament and Commission, the absence of a substantive supranational political community (outside of the bureaucratic Brussels community), and the path dependence created by the EU's historical focus on market liberalisation and economic (as opposed to social) integration (for more on these obstacles, see Bailey, 2008: 233–4).

Further, divisions within the social democratic party family itself tend to limit the adoption of a coherent and substantive social democratic agenda by social democratic party actors wishing to cooperate within the institutions of the European Union (Külahci, 2010). As a result of these obstacles, and in stark contrast to the claims of those more optimistic about the prospect for supranational re-social democratisation, critics have claimed that European integration has consisted disproportionately of the *removal and erosion* of opportunities for re-social democratisation, and in turn consolidated the process of de-social democratisation at the national level (Scharpf, 1999, 2010, has been one of the most consistent proponents of this view). Economic integration across the territory of the European Union precludes the adoption of national-level redistributive measures (as they would distort the free movement of goods, services, capital and labour), while the lack of opportunities for implementing redistributive or decommodifying measures at the supranational level ensures that the absence of a social democratic project is consolidated across the EU. For this reason, a number of social democrats have come to the conclusion that European integration is antithetical to social democratic ambitions and therefore seek a shift in sovereignty and decision-making capacity away from the supranational level and a(n) (re-)emboldening of national sovereignty, witnessing for instance the high level of Euro-scepticism among Swedish social democrats fearing that European integration will erode the social democratic achievements secured within the Swedish state (Aylott, 2008; Johansson and von Sydow, 2011).

In sum, for those fearing the erosive effect of European integration upon the European welfare model, we might also anticipate a degree of antipathy towards any attempts to further integration in response to the crisis. Similarly, if the claims of those pessimistic regarding the prospects for a supranational social democratic response to the crisis are correct, we might also expect that any anticipated or sought-after re-social democratisation (purportedly to be achieved through European coordination) will fail to materialise.

A critical perspective: palliating social democratic decline at the EU level?
Finally, scholars who are more critical of the social democratic strategy *per se* have tended to question the motives of social democratic party actors in seeking to promote a European-level social democratic agenda, especially given the apparently inimical institutional environment within which such an agenda is promoted. Rather than undertaking an evaluation of the prospects of the much hoped-for resurrection of social democracy at the European level, such critics argue, we should instead be considering the motives held by social democratic party elites in promoting such an expectation (given the apparently overwhelming obstacles to its realisation). As Moschonas (2009: 177) has noted, European social democrats have tended to 'take refuge in rhetoric' by advocating a Social Europe despite its weak prospects for realisation. Thus, as argued elsewhere, rather than understanding the pro-European discourse deployed by social democratic party elites as part of an attempt to achieve re-social democratisation at the European level, we might instead view it as an attempt to conceal the apparently irremediable failure of social democracy from social democratic constituents and voters, in an attempt to ameliorate the negative effects such failure has (or might have) upon the legitimation of social democratic parties and party elites themselves (Bailey, 2005, 2009a).

From this perspective, therefore, the expectation that social democratic values might be rendered realisable through European integration is more noteworthy for the role such an expectation plays in legitimating the contemporary social democratic party project than it is for the likelihood of its actualisation. If this is the case, we might seek to highlight and understand the role of social democratic party elites' statements on European integration, with regard to the Great Recession, in terms of any potential legitimating effects these statement have for party elites themselves.

There exist, therefore, three broad positions within the literature on the question of social democratic party actors and the expectations they might have for European integration as a means by which to respond to the global economic crisis. What follows is an attempt to compare each of these positions with regard to the actual responses witnessed by social democratic parties operating at the EU level, and in terms of the concrete achievements that have been realised in EU policy.

Social democrats and the Great Recession: a supranational opportunity?

In response to the Great Recession we have indeed witnessed a rearticulation, largely by social democratic party elites, of calls for a coordinated supranational response to the crisis, (ostensibly) seeking to instantiate a process of re-social democratisation, to be achieved through the institutions of the European Union. Thus, in March 2009 British Labour Party Prime Minister Gordon Brown gave a speech to the European Parliament in preparation for the forthcoming G20 Summit, in which he sought to set out a programme of financial regulation and stimulus that would be based on the model of supranational cooperation developed in the European Union:

> Instead of heading for the rocks of isolation, let us together chart the course of cooperation. That is in all our national interests. That is why I propose that Europe take the lead in a bold plan to ensure that every continent now makes the changes in its banking system that will open the path to shared prosperity, that every country participate and cooperate in setting global standards for financial regulation, and that every continent inject the resources needed to secure economic growth and jobs. (2009)

More substantively, a month later SPD vice-president Andrea Nahles co-wrote an article with Labour Party MP Jon Cruddas, in which they argued for a coordinated European programme, invoking traditional social democratic goals such as the prevention of unemployment, a more social Europe, public ownership/control of industry, a European minimum wage, and a return to collective bargaining and a stronger right to strike (Cruddas and Nahles, 2009). Such calls were echoed by Pierre Moscovici, National Secretary of the French Parti Socialiste. In this speech, Moscovici discussed the opportunities for left parties within the European Union, and argued that in a context of high unemployment, 'more than ever before, Europe appears as the only possible answer to assert power and identity in a globalized world' (Moscovici, 2011). Similarly, Olaf Cramme, director of the social democratic think-tank, Policy Network, has claimed that '[i]f social democracy is to rediscover its mission of marrying economic efficiency with social justice, it needs new means and vehicles for change. In this process, the EU could be its best ally' (2011: 12).

These views have perhaps been most fully fleshed out, however, in documents produced by the Party of European Socialists (PES), which typically takes responsibility for (seeking) the adoption of a coherent supranational social democratic policy agenda (Lightfoot, 2005; Hertner, 2011). For instance, in the wake of the Lehman Brothers' collapse the PES leaders adopted a 'plan of action', Taking Europe out of financial and economic crisis, which depicted the crisis as one of neo-liberalism – '[t]his crisis is the great defeat of neo-liberal capitalism' – and aspired to use the opportunity to promote a social democratic alternative through 'energetic and coordinated action from the EU and its Member States' (PES, 2008). A year later the 8th PES congress adopted a resolution, People First: A Progressive European Agenda, in which European social democrats again echoed their support for a *supranational* social democratic resolution to the Great Recession, claiming, '[i]n today's globalised world, no single nation can shape the future for its people. We believe that through cooperation and democratically shared sovereignty, the European Union can give our countries and our people the power we have lost to global forces.' This resolution went on to make a number of proposals, each of which would seek to promote a more redistributive and decommodifying agenda to be realised at the European level, including: a European recovery plan that would focus on job creation and social cohesion; financial market regulation that would end tax havens, prohibit excessive risk-taking, protect workers' interests and pursue a financial transaction tax; the promotion of a welfare state to ensure 'high social standards and protection in the long term' (in the form of 'needs-based social welfare benefits for all those who are retired, unemployed or unable to work', and the promotion of decent minimum wages, improved worker participation and more substantive employment legislation); and improved gender equality (PES, 2009). These proposals which, if realised, would amount to a substantive process of supranational re-social democratisation, were firmed up further still in 2010 with the PES's document 'A European Mechanism for Financial Stability', which called for the forthcoming EU bail-out fund to avoid an excessively disciplinary approach and to take into account the need for social cohesion among other factors, while (in contrast to the centre-right agenda) focusing explicitly on increasing tax revenues (of capital rather than labour) rather than reducing expenditure (PES, 2010). Similarly, in 2011 the PES presidency sought to oppose 'a culture of sanctions and punishment' which it claimed was being promoted by the centre-right, instead advocating a focus on jobs, growth, democratic accountability and the role of social partners (PES 2011a, 2011b). Finally, the PES Ministers for Social Affairs and Employment agreed in October 2012 that they would call for a 'Social Union' that would focus on jobs and social cohesion, in order 'to strengthen the support for the European integration project among workers and those citizens which have been hit hard by the crisis' (PES, 2012). The PES has, therefore, consistently set out an agenda for supranational 're-social democratisation', in the light of the Great Recession, to be achieved through coordinated activity that utilises the expanded scale and therefore opportunities afforded at that level (in contrast to the constraints experienced at the national level).

In sum, social democratic party actors have throughout the Great Recession sought to advocate a coordinated supranational response that would consist of a reflationary programme focused on jobs, growth, protecting the vulnerable, achieving financial market and remuneration regulation, a tax on financial transactions and a form of economic governance that would ensure social cohesion and jobs were not forfeited by any attempt to limit public debt and deficits. Finally, any move to balance public finances should, social democrats focused on the EU level have argued, include an increase in tax revenues (secured from capital rather than labour), rather than reducing expenditure. Many of these proposed policies, therefore, would potentially have a redistributive and/or decommodifying effect (and therefore represent a form of supranational 're-social democratisation'), in that they would seek to curtail the wealth-accumulating opportunities of financial capital while securing the improved economic circumstances of the poor, vulnerable and workers. This focus on social cohesion and jobs, if achieved, would have the potential to remove elements of economic coercion upon those on lower incomes.

In short, we witness social democratic party actors continue to adopt an optimistic, cosmopolitan social democratic position as outlined above, viewing the Great Recession as a crisis-*cum*-opportunity through which to realise such an agenda. These initiatives have subsequently been promoted within the institutions of the European Union, witnessing for instance the PES leaders' tabling of its 'declaration on strengthening the Euro-zone and preparing the EU2020 Strategy' at the European Council meeting of March 2010 (PES, 2010).

EU-level developments: prospects for re-social democratisation?

In contrast to the proclaimed social democratic (and especially PES) ambitions outlined above, the outcomes witnessed at the EU level have been less promising for those seeking a supranational re-social democratisation, and in that sense tend to confirm the views of both the pessimists and more critical scholars sceptical about the possibilities available for reconstructing a social democratic alternative at the supranational level. Thus, a brief overview of the key social and economic policies that have emerged at the European level since the onset of the Great Recession highlights the absence of substantive redistributive and/ or decommodifying policies achieved through supranational-level coordination, with the obstacles discussed by those pessimistic about the prospects for EU-level re-social democratisation continuing to play a role in hampering a more substantive social agenda from coming to fruition.

Financial regulation

The financial crisis of 2008 was viewed by many to have resulted from an over-liberalisation of the global financial industry (Seabrooke and Tsingou, 2010). As a result, and as we have seen above, many actors (including social democratic party actors) looked to supranational and global regulation of the financial industry as a necessary development in order to avoid a repeat of the financial crisis. The European Union moved towards the adoption of such measures in agreeing to a system of EU-wide financial regulation at the June 2009 European Council. These measures included: a European Systemic Risk Board (ESRB) and a European System of Financial Supervisors (ESFS) to regulate and oversee the financial system; the Alternative Investment Fund Managers Directive (AIFMD) to regulate hedge fund managers, private equity firms and real-estate funds; and the Capital Requirements Directive (which came to be known as CRD3) that required the capitalisation of banks and included a ban on multi-year guaranteed bonuses and would defer large bonuses over three years with the possibility of claw-back if profits declined. Each of these initiatives, however, experienced significant opposition from member states within the Council (largely centred around the UK) and centre-right parties within the European Parliament who were opposed to tight regulation. As a result, the ESRB and ESFS were both limited to the coordination of *national* supervisors and systems of regulation, rather than the creation of substantively new supranational regulations, thereby enabling the initiative to be agreed to by those member states such as the UK that favoured 'light-touch' regulation (Buckley and Howarth, 2010: 120, 125–7; 2011: 125). Further, in order to appease member states' concerns over the potential relinquishing of national sovereignty associated with this new system of financial regulation, it was decided that the ESRB would have thirty-seven voting members. This has significantly impeded its ability to undertake a firm and coherent supervisory role, reflecting a commonplace tendency for 'soft' governance at the EU level (Hodson, 2011). Opposition from (particularly) the UK government therefore ensured that the new 'European Supervisory Authorities' would not impinge too greatly upon domestic regulations.[2]

In the case of the AIFMD, divisions within both the Council and the European Parliament, between those favouring greater regulation (Germany, France, and the Socialists and Democrats in the European Parliament) and those seeking a lighter touch (especially the UK), resulted in the legislation being watered down so that initial attempts to prohibit excessive speculation were essentially avoided. As Buckley and Howarth (2011: 139–40) put it

> AIFMD can be seen very much as a British government victory in the Council and a lobbying victory for industry. The most controversial proposals, including plans to impose fixed caps on leverage and capital requirements, were either removed or watered down significantly … Even in the post-financial crisis world of politicized financial regulation, the industry lobby and its allies were able to shift EU policy on AIFM significantly.

With regard to CRD3, the European Parliament sought (unsuccessfully) to introduce a cap on bonuses at 100 per cent of salaries (Buckley and Howarth, 2010: 134), although a watered-down version of this proposal was later successfully reintroduced under CRD4. More recently, we have witnessed a proposal to regulate over-the-counter derivatives (European Market Infrastructure Regulation (EMIR)), which has witnessed member states block attempts by the European Parliament to embolden the regulatory capacity of the European Securities Markets Authority (ESMA) that would be created by the EMIR (Buckley *et al.* 2012: 104). Similarly, in setting a maximum liquidity coverage ratio, the Commission sought to appease German and French concerns over

excessively restrictive banking regulations under the new CRD4 (Buckley *et al.*
2012: 110–11). Thus, while agreement between eleven member states to draft
an EU financial transaction tax has recently been reached (January 2013), the
failure to include all member states (with the UK, Sweden and the Netherlands
being most opposed) suggests that any tax agreed will need to consider the
impact it will have upon the financial markets, and therefore will likely be
limited in impact by both the opt-out of the 'non-FTT' 16 and the competitive
pressures that this will create within the single European market.[3]

In sum, therefore, while a number of financial regulation measures have been
introduced at the European level, opposition (especially, although by no means
exclusively, from the UK (Buckley *et al.*, 2012)) has been sufficient to ensure that
any regulations adopted are sufficiently 'light-touch' to avoid the imposition of
measures that would have a significantly detrimental or redistributive effect, and
in many cases will not exceed already-existing measures existent at the national
level.

Economic governance

In response to the collapse of Lehman Brothers in September 2008 the EU
member states agreed the following month (albeit following a period of damaging unilateral policy announcements by member states) to a €2 trillion pledge to,
in the words of Hodson and Quaglia, 'recapitalize and, if necessary, take shares
in European banks'. While acting to stabilise the EU economy in the short term,
this rescue package did so in such a way that focused support on savers. This
stimulus measure was agreed in late 2008 and arguably presented opportunities
to introduce measures targeted specifically at lower-income groups. However,
the actual stimulus agreed contained little opportunity for inter-member state
redistribution (Hodson and Quaglia, 2009: 942–3), and was anyway predominantly an aggregate of already-existing spending pledges by member states
(Barber, 2008). Indeed, redistributive policy mechanisms already in place at the
European level, particularly the structural funds and the globalisation adjustment fund, have been largely viewed as ineffective on the grounds that they are
both too small to have an impact upon the effects of the post-2007 crisis,[4] and
that applicant member states and regions face excessively difficult technical barriers to accessing the funds.[5]

Further, the immediate moves at the beginning of the global crisis to shore
up the Euro-zone have now clearly led to sovereign debt crises in a number of
the Euro-zone's peripheral countries. These were initially responded to in the
form of the European Financial Stability Fund (€440 billion), which sought to
secure member governments against potential sovereign debt crises, and which it
was agreed would be replaced by the permanent European Stability Mechanism
(€500 billion) from 2014. In May 2010 an initial bail-out for the Greek debt
crisis was agreed on that would provide €110 billion (funded by both the EU

and the IMF). This was combined with the introduction in May 2010 of the ECB's Securities Markets Programme (purchase of private and public debt) (*c.*€77 billion by May 2011), although this led to strained relations within the ECB, with Axel Weber (Bundesbank President) opposing the policy and also largely being held to explain the exit of Juergen Stark as the ECB's chief economist in September 2011 (Hodson, 2011: 237). The experience of adopting supranational-level bail-outs, therefore, has witnessed member state reluctance inhibiting the potential for anything beyond the bare minimum required for the particular national economy receiving the bail-out to not become bankrupt (and arguably not even enough to avoid that). This, we might conclude, potentially rules out more redistributive measures between member states being agreed upon. Indeed, the difficulty experienced in gaining approval for the minimal scheme agreed on for Greece in summer 2011 – including a tense vote in the German Bundestag, the need for a German Constitutional Court ruling, and opposition from Slovakia, Austria and Finland – seems to confirm this view. As a result, and in contrast to social democratic ambitions, therefore, the implementation of bail-outs for Greece and the attempt to resolve the Euro-zone debt crisis have been accompanied by austerity measures which sought to reduce government expenditure and public service provision. For instance, the Article 126(9) recommendations to Greece in February and May 2010 under the terms of the Stability and Growth Pact were increasingly prescriptive on the need for austerity measures (Hodson, 2011: 240–1). This focus on austerity measures and fiscal surveillance appeared to be further echoed by both the introduction of the 'European semester' system and the subsequent 'euro-plus pact' that was agreed by Sarkozy and Merkel (albeit eventually sidelined by inaction).[6] Similarly, the second major Greek debt bail-out, agreed to by the European Council in June 2011, included an agreement by the Greek government to cut public sector employment by 20 per cent.[7] Further, the measures introduced to ensure greater economic coordination, or a preliminary form of economic government – for instance, with the so-called 'six pack' of secondary legislation adopted in December 2011 – was largely oriented towards ensuring reduced government spending and fiscal constraints. As a result, Udo Bullmann MEP, speaking on behalf of the Socialist group, criticised the legislation, claiming that, 'there exists another path out of the crisis. The reform is an austerity pact.'[8] It would appear, therefore, that any newly adopted EU-level fiscal or monetary policies are highly unlikely to result in the formation of a redistributive supranational economic governance regime.

Social policy

EU social policy developments during the Great Recession fall into three key areas: labour market regulations, pro-employment policies and anti-poverty initiatives. Each of these, however, have witnessed similar trends to those outlined above, with weak EU-level governance undermining the capacity for more substantive measures that might otherwise have a redistributive or decommodifying effect.

In the area of labour market regulations, divisions between member states have continued to limit the extent to which supranational labour market regulations could be used to increase protection for employees. For instance, in April 2009 the Council and European Parliament failed again to agree on a resolution to the long-running dispute over attempts to revise the Working Time Directive and remove the national opt-out that have significantly hampered the impact of the directive,[9] with commentators continuing to believe that the prospects of a resolution were low two years later.[10] Similarly, in June 2011 the Pregnant Workers Directive was blocked after two years of negotiations due to opposition from the UK and Germany in the Council.[11] The so-called 'fourth' anti-discrimination directive has also been blocked since its proposal in 2008 as a result of opposition from a number of member states, led by Germany.[12] Opposition within the Council, therefore, continued to hamper the scope for more substantive labour market regulation to be introduced throughout the period of the Great Recession.

With regards to pro-employment and anti-poverty policies, the most headline-grabbing developments were the two flagship initiatives included within the EU's 10-year strategy, Europe 2020, which was adopted in June 2010 – 'An agenda for new skills and jobs and the European platform against poverty and social exclusion'. While much of Europe 2020 was given a wary reception by those seeking a more substantive 'social Europe', on the grounds that for many it consolidated a model focused solely on a market-based model of growth, the inclusion of the two social initiatives did at least represent a formal reincorporation of headline social targets following their removal from EU economic strategy in the 2005 review of the Lisbon Process (Vanhercke, 2011: 155–7). That said, neither of these initiatives appear particularly focused on securing a 're-social democratisation' agenda. Thus, the 'Agenda for new skills and jobs' is focused on increasing the proportion of the working-age population in work to 75 per cent, largely through greater flexibility and incentivisation within the labour market, and improving information available to people with regard to the skills needed for employment.[13] As such they represent the continued focus on labour market participation as the means by which social policy is to be achieved at the European level; hardly, therefore, a process of labour decommodification.

With regard to anti-poverty policies, the European platform against poverty and social exclusion, which aims to lift at least 20 million people out of the risk of poverty and exclusion, has been criticised on the grounds that it resulted from a downscaling of ambitions at the EU level following the inability of member states to agree on ways in which to measure poverty, with the end result being a compromise whereby member states can choose for themselves between one of three ways in which poverty is measured.[14] Further still, it remains unclear how the Commission will be able to enforce these commitments (Vanhercke, 2011: 150).

In sum, the record of EU-level policy making in response to the Great Recession does not suggest that divisions within the Council and between the Council and European Parliament have abated to any visible extent, resulting in the ongoing inability to agree policies at the European level that go beyond a minimal commitment to market building. As such, and as a number of scholars have noted for a considerable time, European integration appears destined for the foreseeable future to continue to promote market liberalisation without being able to adopt some form of more substantive redistributive or decommodifying measures to complement market liberalisation at the supranational level, as pursued by social democratic parties.

Conceptualising social democratic responses: faith retention and blame displacement

As the critical perspective on supranational re-social democratisation outlined above suggested, the continued absence of a substantive 'Social Europe' raises the question of why social democratic party actors continue to focus on the prospects for re-social democratisation at the European level. It is the claim of this chapter that in order to understand the EU-level response of social democratic party actors to the Great Recession, we need to situate social democratic parties historically. In particular, we should view social democratic parties in terms of the inherent tension that we might consider to be constitutive of them. Thus, on the one hand, and as already discussed, social democratic parties have been historically constructed around the pursuit of policies that will have a decommodifying effect upon their electoral constituency. On the other hand, however, in moving to a position marked by accommodation with capitalism, especially since 1945, social democratic party actors also need to adopt policies that are able to secure continued capital accumulation in order to reproduce the society over which they govern. This in turn tends to require intensified exploitation, or what might be termed 're-commodification', in order to create new opportunities for growth (Harvey 2006, 183–203; Bailey, 2009a: 35). Social democratic party actors must, therefore, simultaneously achieve visible gains in terms of decommodification for their constituents *and* oversee the recommodification of many workers who form the same group of people within their core constituency (Bailey, 2009a: 36). If we consider the Great Recession to represent the growth to limits of the most recent model of capital accumulation (Kotz, 2008; Crouch, 2011; Harvey, 2011), therefore, those seeking to reproduce capitalist relations must identify new opportunities for intensified exploitation. Thus, as Carlin (2011) puts it, '[t]he focus of supply-side reforms must be on the twin objectives of measures that raise productivity growth and that allow the growth of nominal wages to be controlled'. Indeed, such measures have already begun (Clark *et al.*, 2011: 12). In such a context, social democratic parties arguably face a process of terminal decline, as they are unable to realistically identify opportunities for substantively decommodifying public policies or be associated with attempts to mobilise popular demands for such policies, due to their necessarily overriding concern with identifying opportunities for recommodification.[15] Social democratic party elites therefore face further disillusion and disaffection within their core constituency, in part explaining the defeat of the PES in the 2009 European Parliament elections.

In this context, this chapter argues, we can understand claims by social democratic party elites to be seeking a supranational re-social democratisation, in terms of the opportunities that such claims have to conceal or obfuscate this purported process of terminal social democratic decline. First, the call for supranational re-social democratisation enables a process of blame displacement, whereby social democratic party actors are able to conceal the notion that the Great Recession in part poses the failure of social democracy, and instead allows those actors to point towards the demands made by, and/or policy omissions existent at, the EU level in seeking to explain problems experienced by social democratic parties. For instance, in adopting austerity measures in line with EU and IMF demands, the Greek PASOK government repeatedly focused on the necessity of adopting such measures in order to remain within the Euro-zone, witnessing Papandreou implore the Greek Parliament (including his own PASOK party members) to put aside their objections to the austerity measures and vote in favour, in order 'to avoid bankruptcy and keep Greece in the euro core'.[16] Acting to remind the electorate of these demands, moreover, the government was quick to highlight (and oppose) EU–IMF demands for privatisation, with government spokesman George Petalotis reported as saying '[t]he behaviour of the European Union, International Monetary Fund and European Central Bank representatives ... was unacceptable ... We asked them to help and are fully meeting our obligations. But we did not ask anybody to meddle in the internal matters of the country.'[17] Similarly, as Donadio and Kitsantonis (2011) pointed out with regard to the impact of the crisis on Greece, Greek Prime Minister George Papandreou 'said the European Union was also to blame for failing to call the previous government on its dubious statistics'.

Second, and more importantly, the voicing of ambitions for re-social democratisation at the supranational level presents the possibility of social democratic faith retention, whereby social democratic party actors seek to retain the conviction of remaining social democratic constituents that it is possible that, despite the apparent failure of social democracy *in the short-term*, and provided social democrats are able to coordinate their activity *at the supranational level*, the social democratic project will continue to be both pertinent and feasible.

The virtue of the European Union in terms of faith retention, moreover, is that any failure to realise such initiatives can be portrayed as a problem relating to the institutional difficulties and obstacles already noted – and not related to the more fundamental problems associated with the need for recommodification and the failure this represents for social democracy more generally. Witness, for instance, the response of German Socialist MEP Mechtild Rothe (who chaired the Parliament's delegation in the relevant talks), to the failure to reach a deal on the Working Time Directive in April 2009 – thus, while noting that the Parliament had come forward with proposals, she claimed, 'it was not possible to agree with the Council. There was nothing forthcoming from the Council, we were bitterly disappointed by that.'[18]

Conclusion

This chapter argues that social democratic parties' European response to the global economic crisis is in keeping with a course of events that we have witnessed social democratic parties following since at least the mid-1970s and the breakdown of the Keynesian consensus and Bretton Wood system. Social democratic parties have struggled to adapt to the economic, political and ideological terrain that they have been faced with since the mid-1970s. This was (partly) resolved for many West European social democratic parties through the move to 'new' social democracy in the 1990s, involving a process of ideological moderation and abandonment of much of the traditional commitment to decommodification, compensated in part by reference to the (unrealisable) promise of more substantial traditional social democratic policy outputs at the European level (Bailey, 2009a). The restructuring of global capitalism associated with the collapse of the 'privatised Keynesianism' model (Crouch, 2011: ch. 5) in 2007–08, however, places greater pressure upon social democratic party elites to abandon their commitment to decommodification. As such, we see a continuation of preceding social democratic party strategy vis-à-vis European integration.

In exploring this strategy, the chapter suggests that support for European integration, in a context of heightened pressure to accede to the economic necessity of welfare retrenchment, offers social democratic parties the opportunity to both: (a) displace blame away from the limits to social democracy and project it instead onto the (less fundamental) limits of the European Union; and (b) seek to retain the faith of those who remain social democratic members, supporters or voters, *with the promise of supranational-level social democratic achievements to come at some point in the future*, despite the increasingly apparent inability of social democratic parties to realise such goals (at either the national or supranational level) or to reconcile the contradictory goals that constitute social democracy. A key question we might wish to explore in coming years, therefore, is the extent to which social democratic party elites will be able to continue with such a strategy.

Put differently, will there come a point at which the promise of supranational social democracy is so untenable that even its utility for faith retention and blame displacement will be negated? And, if so, what then for social democratic parties?

Notes

1 The term 'decommodification' is used here to describe the extent to which individuals are removed from the compulsion to sell their labour power on the labour market.
2 http://euobserver.com/19/30749 (date of access for this and subsequent URLs in this chapter: 15 August 2013).
3 http://euobserver.com/news/118810
4 http://euobserver.com/886/29806
5 www.ft.com/cms/s/0/8cd8016c-b9d3–11df-8804–00144feabdc0.html
6 www.ft.com/cms/s/0/453e91a4–cbf7–11e0–9176–00144feabdc0.html#axzz1XrPxLqgB
7 www.ft.com/cms/s/0/1a1df098–d942–11e0–884e-00144feabdc0.html#axzz1XONWpoi6
8 http://euobserver.com/economic/113761
9 http://ec.europa.eu/social/main.jsp?catId=157&langId=en&newsId=498&furtherNews=yes
10 www.euractiv.com/socialeurope/gloomy-prospects-working-time-directive-talks-news-504242
11 www.euractiv.com/socialeurope/ministers-shelve-maternity-leave-directive-news-505646
12 http://euobserver.com/social/114856
13 http://eur-lex.europa.eu/LexUriServ/LexUriServ.do?uri=CELEX:52010DC0682:EN:NOT
14 www.euractiv.com/priorities/eu-set-lower-poverty-reduction-ambitions-news-494871
15 Of course, while it is in principle possible that social democratic party actors faced with a dilemmatic choice between economic growth and redistributive/decomodifying public policies could choose the latter, the structure of incentives for the party elite, and patterns of behaviour inculcated among the broader party membership, are such that its prospects are remote (Bailey, 2009b).
16 http://news.smh.com.au/breaking-news-world/greek-pm-survives-confidence-vote-20110622-1gdw7.html
17 www.brecorder.com/business-a-finance/banking-a-finance/2732-greece-blasts-eu-imf-asset-sale-demand.html
18 http://euobserver.com/851/27898

References

Aust, A. (2004). 'From "Eurokeynesianism" to the "Third Way": the Party of European Socialists (PES) and European employment policies', in G. Bonoli and M. Powell (eds), *Social Democratic Party Policies in Contemporary Europe* (London: Routledge), pp. 180–96.

Aylott, N. (2008). 'Softer but strong: Euroscepticism and party politics in Sweden', in A. Szczerbiak and P. Taggart (eds), *Opposing Europe?: The Comparative Party Politics of Euroscepticism, Volume 1: Case Studies and Country Surveys* (Oxford: Oxford University Press), pp. 181–200.

Bailey, D. J. (2005). 'Obfuscation through integration: legitimating "new" social democracy in the European Union', *Journal of Common Market Studies*, 43(1), 13–35.

Bailey, D. J. (2008). 'Explaining the underdevelopment of "Social Europe": a critical realization', *Journal of European Social Policy*, 18(3), 232–45.

Bailey, D. J. (2009a). *The Political Economy of European Social Democracy: A Critical Realist Approach* (London: Routledge).

Bailey, D. J. (2009b). 'The transition to "new" social democracy: the role of capitalism, representation, and (hampered) contestation', *British Journal of Politics and International Relations*, 11(4), 593–612.

Bailey, D. J. (2012). 'The impossibility of social democracy: from unfailing optimism to enlightened pessimism in the "re-social democratisation" debate', in G. Strange and O. Worth (eds), *European Regionalism and the Left* (Manchester: Manchester University Press), pp. 101–18.

Barber, T. (2008). 'Europe's shrinking stimulus packages', *Financial Times*, 16 December.

Brown, G. (2009). Speech to the European Parliament, 24 March.

Buckley, J. and Howarth, D. (2010). 'Internal market: gesture politics? Explaining the EU's response to the financial crisis', *Journal of Common Market Studies*, 48(1), special issue, 119–41.

Buckley, J. and Howarth, D. (2011). 'Internal market: regulating the so-called "vultures of capitalism"', *Journal of Common Market Studies* 49(1), 123–43.

Buckley, J., Howarth, D. and Quaglia, L. (2012). 'Internal market: the ongoing struggle to "protect" Europe from its money men', *Journal of Common Market Studies*, 50(1), 99–115.

Carlin, W. (2011). '10 questions about the Eurozone crisis and whether it can be solved' (UCL European Institute), available at: www.ucl.ac.uk/european-institute/comment_analysis/eurozone/2011_09_WCarlin_Eurozone_layout.pdf.

Clark, I., Heyes, J. and Lewis, P. (2011). 'Verities of capitalism: neo-liberalism and the economic crisis of 2008–?', Paper presented at the 6th ECPR General Conference, University of Iceland, 25–27 August.

Cramme, O. (2011). 'The power of European integration: social democracy in search of a purpose', policy network paper, available at: www.policy-network.net/publications_download.aspx?ID=7555.

Crouch, C. (2011). *The Strange Non-Death of Neoliberalism* (Cambridge: Polity).

Cruddas, J. and Nahles, A. (2009). 'A new path for Europe: society led by markets and profits has failed. We are offering an alternative for the democratic left', *Guardian*, 8

April.

Donadio, R. and Kitsantonis, N. (2011). 'Greek leaders win bitter budget vote; as police fight protesters with tear gas, Socialists unite to tighten spending', *International Herald Tribune*, 30 June.

Esping-Andersen, G. (1990). *The Three Worlds of Welfare Capitalism* (Cambridge: Polity).

Featherstone, K. (1988). *Socialist Parties and European Integration: A Comparative History* (Manchester: Manchester University Press).

Geyer, R. (1993). 'Socialism and the EC after Maastricht: from classic to new-model European social democracy', in A.W. Cafruny and G. G. Rosenthal (eds), *The State of the European Community, Vol. 2, The Maastricht Debates and Beyond* (London: Lynne Rienner), pp. 91–106.

Gray, J. (1996). *After Social Democracy: Politics, Capitalism and the Common Life* (London: Demos).

Harvey, D. (2006). *The Limits to Capital* (London: Verso).

Harvey, D. (2011). 'The enigma of capital and the crisis this time', in C. Calhoun and G. Derluguian (eds), *Business as Usual: The Roots of the Global Financial Meltdown* (New York: New York University Press).

Held, D. (2003). 'Global social democracy', in A. Giddens (ed.), *The Progressive Manifesto: New Ideas for the Centre-Left* (Cambridge, Polity), pp. 137–72.

Hertner, I. (2011). 'Are European election campaigns Europeanized? The case of the Party of European Socialists in 2009', *Government and Opposition*, 46(3), 321–44.

Hix, S. (2002). '1957–1994', in S. Hix and U. Lesse, *Shaping a Vision: A History of the Party of European Socialists, 1957–2002* (Belgium: Party of European Socialists, European Parliament).

Hodson, D. (2011). 'The EU economy: the Eurozone in 2010', *Journal of Common Market Studies* 49(1), 231–49.

Hodson, D. and Quaglia, L. (2009). 'European perspectives on the global financial crisis: Introduction', *Journal of Common Market Studies*, 47(5), 939–53.

Johansson, K.M. and von Sydow, G. (2011). 'Swedish social democracy and European integration: enduring divisions', in D. G. Dimitrakopoulos (ed.), *Social Democracy and European Integration* (London: Routledge), pp. 117–56.

Kotz, D. (2008). 'Contradictions of economic growth in the neoliberal era: accumulation and crisis in the contemporary US economy', *Review of Radical Political Economics*, 40(2), 174–88.

Külahci, E. (2010). 'Europarties: agenda-setter or agenda-follower? Social democracy and the disincentives for tax harmonisation', *Journal of Common Market Studies* 48(1), 1283–1306.

Ladrech, R. (1993). 'Social democratic parties and EC integration: transnational party responses to Europe 1992', *European Journal of Political Research*, 24, 195–210.

Lightfoot, S. (2005). *Europeanizing social democracy?: The Rise of the Party of European Socialists* (London: Routledge).

Moschonas, G. (2002). *In the Name of Social Democracy: The Great Transformation: 1945 to the Present* (London: Verso).

Moschonas, G. (2009). 'Reformism in a "conservative" system: the European Union and social democratic identity', in J. Callaghan, N. Fishman, B. Jackson and M. McIvor (eds), *In Search of Social Democracy: Responses to Crisis and Modernisation* (Manchester: Manchester University Press), pp. 168–92.

Moscovici, P. (2011). 'The left in Europe: what does the future hold?', *Social Europe Journal*, 21 January.

PES (2008). 'Taking Europe out of financial and economic crisis: an urgent European plan of action', PES leaders' declaration adopted 5 November.

PES (2009). 'Resolution no. 1: People first: a progressive European agenda', adopted by 8th PES congress, Prague, 7–8 December.

PES (2010). 'A "European mechanism for financial stability": a progressive response to the Euro-zone sovereign debt crisis', adopted by the prime ministers' and leaders' conference, 25 March.

PES (2011a). 'PES statement on European economic governance', adopted by the PES presidency, 24 February.

PES (2011b). '"From economic chaos to economic governance": A call to the European Council for an alternative strategy based on investment and modernisation', adopted by the PES leaders' conference, Brussels, 23 June.

PES (2012). 'Towards a social union: declaration of the PES ministers for social affairs and employment', adopted 4 October.

Scharpf, F. (1999). *Governing in Europe: Effective and Democratic?* (Oxford: Oxford University Press).

Scharpf, F. (2010). 'The asymmetry of European integration, or why the EU cannot be a "social market economy"', *Socio-Economic Review*, 8(2), 211–50.

Seabrooke, L. and Tsingou, E. (2010). 'Responding to the global credit crisis: the politics of financial reform', *British Journal of Politics and International Relations* 12, 313–23.

Strange, G. (2006). 'The left against Europe? A critical engagement with new constitutionalism and structural dependence theory', *Government and Opposition*, 41(2), 197–229.

Vanhercke, B. (2011). 'Is the "Social dimension of Europe 2020" an oxymoron?', in C. Degryse and D. Natali (eds), *Social Developments in the European Union 2010* (Brussels, ETUI), pp. 141–74.

Watson, M. and Hay, C. (2003). 'The discourse of globalisation and the logic of no alternative: rendering the contingent necessary in the political economy of New Labour', *Policy and Politics*, 31(3), 289–305.

14

Reforming Europe, renewing social democracy? The PES, the debt crisis and the Euro-parties

Gerassimos Moschonas

How to effect a transition from the type of organization characteristic of the pre-paratory stage of the socialist movement – usually featured by disconnected local groups and clubs, with propaganda as a principal activity – to the unity of a large, national body, suitable for concerted political action over the entire vast territory ruled by the Russian state? ... It is clear that the Russian Social Democracy should not organize itself as a federative conglomerate of many national groups. It must rather become a single party for the entire empire. (Rosa Luxemburg, 1904)

The era of problematic reformism[1]

Analyses that see only Europe's 'liberalism' underestimate the fact that the Community's model of political economy is fundamentally twofold: it is pro-duced both by liberalisation and by a certain (uneven, fragmented and minimal) kind of federalism. Europe is notable for a remarkable concentration of powers in certain sectors – monetary policy and structural policies are two examples of quasi-state policies (Jabko, 2009: 264–5). Thus, European integration is the still-incomplete product of two almost simultaneous processes that reinforce one another: the building of Europe *through the market* and the building of a *political* Europe. Paradoxically, despite social democratic aspirations (political Europe as a counterweight to the market), the politicisation of integration through a dense, rigid, institutional apparatus has consolidated and solidified the liberalisation of Europe. It was the building of a political Europe that gave liberal economic solu-tions such a long-term advantage (Moschonas, 2009). Such was the irony – and unanticipated ruse – of the politicisation of the process.

The setting has changed dramatically. One aspect of this change is critical. The European dynamic has progressively and significantly reduced the space allowed to the forces of the nation and to national governments. Ironically, the great transfer of authority unleashed by the Community renaissance has generated a framework of weak dual power: a *simultaneous* power deficit both at the national level and at the level of Europe proper (for a more detailed analysis, see Moschonas, 2012b: 235–6). In a sense, as Cramme aptly notes, 'half-way federalisation has brought the worst of both worlds to the fore' (2011: 11). This double deficit differentiates the EU fundamentally from the United States, as the structure of the European system does not embody a centralising logic comparable to the dynamic of American federalism (Magnette, 2001). While globalisation has everywhere weakened the core component of what might be called 'governance', the dual deficit in question is *specifically* European. It is in a way the direct product of the rebirth of Europe and it undoubtedly deprives all parties in government of some of their influence. But this applies even more in the case of the social democratic parties, which have traditionally made public (national) power the principal lever of their political action.

Compared with the political systems produced by the nation state, the European system has complicated the strategies of 'strong reformism' (Dunphy, 2004) in unprecedented fashion, at national and European levels alike. The national level is no longer relevant for the adoption of a credible social democratic strategy, while the European level is neither sufficiently structured and unified, nor sufficiently flexible, to facilitate the implementation of a European social democratic strategy. There is nothing surprising, then, about the fact that the leap forward in the political and economic capacities of Europe has coincided with a leap backward in the reforming capacities of the parties of the left. Europe poses a major problem for the left – and not only because it is liberal. It poses a major problem because the European regime is complex, cumbersome and institutionally inimical to change (Tsoukalis, 2005). The EU is 'a tricky place for center-lefts to work' (Ross, 2011: 332). The renaissance of Europe – the extraordinary strengthening of the EU since the mid-1980s – has ushered the left into a new era, one of *problematic reformism* (Moschonas, 2009; for a more qualified view, see Ross, 2011: 327–9, 338).

The crisis as political opportunity

The European dilemma facing socialism over the last two decades can be encapsulated as follows: either destabilise the European Union or further destabilise social democratic identity. With the financial and economic crisis triggered in 2007–08 (and which soon became a crisis of the European project) the terms of this dilemma were for the first time posed more favourably for the left. If Europe was an accelerating factor in the social democratic crisis, the same Europe, thanks to its own deep crisis, was now providing a major window of opportunity for a left that had been having a rough ride. Breaking the negative cycle (Moschonas, 2009: 180), which had prompted a crisis of the social democratic imaginary, has been tabled as an issue by the European crisis. The financial crisis on the one hand, and the sovereign debt crisis on the other, have restored the possibility of European reform.

Unquestionably, this period of turbulence found social democracy in a depleted state. Most of the socialist parties were in opposition, particularly in the key countries of Germany and France. In addition, three socialist governments – in Spain, Portugal and especially Greece – were in a weakened position because their countries were seen as part of the problem, rather than as part of the solution. The reduction in the size of the socialist group in the European Parliament, following the result of the 2009 European elections, had further weakened the influence of the centre-left. Given its minority status, social democracy was not in a position to impose any conception it had of an 'alternative Europe'.

However, despite its drawbacks, being in opposition has a liberating aspect: it makes risk-taking and researching new programmatic horizons easier. In times of uncertainty, upheaval and even chaos, a political force can recover lost ground. Moreover, for the *first* time in its history, the Party of European Socialists (PES) was naturally well placed to become the organic framework for coordinating socialist action. The minority participation of socialists in European institutions favoured such a role, which would have consisted of steering the socialists' political and programmatic activity through the PES and the leaders' conference. It must also be stressed that the intellectual environment was highly favourable. The crisis gave rise to an outpouring of ideas, policy proposals and scientific documents. This intellectual and political activity represented a veritable turning point in the literature on European integration that was addressed to the 'general public'. In particular, the innovative proposals formulated in the left-wing public sphere (and which derived from the social democratic current as well as from radical left-wing tendencies) were of high quality. The scale of the crisis, the strong resurgence of interest in Europe and, above all, the theatre of operations (the socialists' oppositional status) had created a context conducive to strengthening the PES's organisation and visibility. Social democracy was able to influence decisions (via 'external pressure')[2] and establish itself as a sort of European 'opposition', a vector of a different conception of Europe, albeit a minority one. Faced with the crisis of the European project, socialists had a great and unique opportunity to revitalise their European strategy.

The programmatic leap forward of the PES

The initial phase of the crisis began with the Greek collapse and ended in the beginning of May 2010 with the signing of the first Greek rescue plan on 2 May 2010. During this period, socialists were conspicuous by their virtual absence. It would, however, be unjust not to point out that during this phase a number of specific proposals were formulated – proposals that left behind the kind of soothing generalities of which the Euro-parties are past masters. Three of them are particularly significant: the insistence on a 'firm policy for regulating financial markets'; a European tax on financial transactions;[3] and, particularly since March 2010, a proposal to establish a 'European mechanism for financial stability' (PES, 2010c) (the PES has been a pioneering force in promoting this mechanism). Moreover, the PES adopted a more partisan and confrontational style in contrast to its traditional discourse, which tended to be formulated in an equivocal, imprecise and irresolute manner.

Nevertheless, despite the progress made in launching a rather straightforward attack on particular problems, social democracy's marginalisation in the initial phase of the crisis has no precedent in the history of European integration over the last forty years. Social democracy as a whole has not succeeded in promoting its agenda. The failure, however, lay less with the PES than with the national parties (or, at least, the most influential of them), which failed to cooperate effectively and to promote a distinctive social democratic vision for the resolution of the debt crisis and the reform of the EU. Without a coordinated and powerful message focused on the issue of the moment (the Greek problem), the programmatic 'offer' of the social democratic family lacked political distinctiveness and intellectual force.

The second phase opened with the agreement to the Greek rescue package and extends to the time of writing (February 2013). It must be said that, having lost the first battle, socialists then rallied, albeit only partially and gradually. During this period, European socialism advanced in a less disorderly fashion in the direction of an effective political response. There is now a significant body of socialist programmatic thought concerning European reform. Even if it is sometimes fleeting and vague about the measures proposed, it is both more concrete (when compared with the traditional idle chatter of the Euro-parties) and more left-wing than past programmes. In addition, the thematic range is much broader, and a tough tone and alarmist accents dominate. The PES has demonstrated that it is not an 'empty shell'.

The new political–programmatic formula has been developed around four major themes:

1 The first, regarded as a 'matter of urgency' and a central priority, is focused on financial regulation – the strengthening of European supervisory authorities; a stricter control over derivatives and speculative funds; the regulation of private ratings agencies; and the creation of an independent European ratings agency. This initial series of proposals is highly prominent in the PES's new rhetoric, and constitutes a central element in the distinctive new brand of European socialism.

2 The second theme, which is concerned with solving the debt problem, revolves around the establishment of a 'European mechanism for financial stability'. It should be noted that the proposal for Euro-bonds (initially intended to finance

long-term investments) (PES, 2010d) has been progressively integrated into the strategy of establishing a European Stability Agency that would issue Euro-bonds for the purposes of common management of a specified portion of cross-border public debt and investment.[4]

3 The third theme is articulated around the 'European pact for jobs and social progress with a view to equitable growth'. This involves a European pact for a minimum wage above the poverty threshold; more aggressive use of European structural funds; active employment policies; inclusion of a social clause in every piece of European legislation to better protect the rights of workers faced with a jurisdiction that prioritises economic liberties; an active European industrial policy for sustainable and qualitative growth; and a strengthening of the financial resources of the European Investment Bank (see, among others, PES 2010e, 2010f, 2011a). This section of the PES's formulations is distinguished neither by its detail nor by concrete measures. It frequently confines itself to stating and juxtaposing policy-oriented ideas without the requisite 'costed' articulation. It is a road map containing a vision and many good ideas, but not a real programme.

4 The forth theme concerns repairing public finances and it advocates the use of new financial instruments, both fiscal and non-fiscal. Obviously the tax on financial transactions is the *flagship measure*, serving as an emblem of the new brand image of post-financial-crisis socialism.[5] Alongside this pet theme, a green tax and resolving the issue of tax evasion and fraud through European cooperation, among other measures, round off this set of objectives.

In general, it might be noted that the programmatic strategy we have just briefly summarised marks a *political break*, despite being at times cursory when it comes to the measures proposed. The PES now counts among its assets a more elaborate, solid and rich discourse, a more systematic agenda, and a significant number of policy proposals. The PES has gradually brought *renewal* to the European strategy of the left, with the emphasis placed on the articulation of an 'alternative policy'.

The 'paradoxical' failure of social democracy

Nevertheless, the PES (and the social democratic family) has neither been able to take centre stage nor to 'remedy' the deficit in the European imaginary of socialism by restoring the credibility of the narrative of reform. Given the general frenzy of the period, this mediocre result is cause for surprise, especially considering the important programmatic progress that has been made. Extenuating circumstances are certainly not wanting. Out of necessity, the pace of the crisis has given governments and, as a result, parties of the centre-right, a decisive role. Yet the balance of forces does not explain everything.

The mediocre result stems from three main causes:

1 Socialist strategy contained *certain key ideas,* as well as certain concrete measures, for reforming Europe, however these ideas remain mainly on paper. In practice, the PES, bereft of a centralised structure and an institutionally powerful elite, has not transformed its ideas into an offensive and powerful message.[6]

2 National social democratic parties have not really taken things up. For want of solid relays in national societies (and the European Council), the PES has found itself without structured political and institutional support.[7] A link between the policies proposed, on the one hand, and European citizens and institutions, on the other, has never been established. National parties, acting as gatekeepers and selecting which messages and policies would be brought to the attention of national electorates or of European institutions, did not play the game. Only at a later stage – mainly after June 2011, given the failure of European policies concerning the debt crisis – have national social democratic parties adopted more convergent policies. The 'haircut' of part of the Greek debt and, more significantly, the emphasis on growth strategies and the severe criticism of austerity policies, have unified social democratic parties and have reduced the divergence between the programmatic statements of PES and the policies of its member parties. All in all, social democracy has not been able to propose a social democratic project for Europe.

3 With the unprecedented austerity measures they have adopted, the socialist governments of southern Europe (and, in the first instance, the Greek government) have significantly contributed to a further loss of bearings within the socialist family. The discrepancy between the economic strategy of socialist governments and that of the PES (geared to growth) – two strategies *highly unequal* in their visibility – has shattered the discursive unity of European socialism's strategy. As a result of circumstance, the PES has not been able to establish itself as a powerful actor, just as during the 2009 European elections it proved itself incapable of proposing an alternative candidate to José Manuel Barroso (Hertner, 2011: 342–3). Once again the moderate left has become lost in the middle of its own contradictions.

In sum, the PES 'failed' even as it assumed its role: such is the 'paradox' brought on by the crisis management. This paradox is apparent: if socialism does not succeed in more successfully imposing or promoting its agendas and options, fault should not be laid at the door of the PES. In fact, the crisis has dramatically illustrated something that was already known: the multilevel, polycentric structure of the European regime is reproduced, albeit not in identical fashion, within European party families. The multiplicity of levels and centres of power and influence *within* the socialist family (both inside and outside the PES) has created an enormous problem of effectiveness – and practical coherence.[8] It has posed a significant problem of *collective coordination* and *strategic centre and leadership*. In sum, what was lacking were not ideas as much as the *mechanisms* of the realisation and *effective* implementation of a left-wing reformist project. But this lack should not surprise us, as it is inherent in the very matrix of the system's functioning. The 'paradox' of the PES's success and the family's semi-failure (positive programmatic balance sheet, weak political performance) illustrates this basic fact. Ironically, what began as a real success story (the programmatic leap forward of the PES) ended up as a very poor 'goal achievement'.

Programmatic consolidation: the crisis as a critical juncture

The basic thematics of the new programmatic discourse, however interpreted, are the pillars of a new agenda. We will call it a *post-third-way* agenda because its key components (focused on the strategy of market regulation) go beyond the programmatic elaborations and governmental actions of social democracy in the decades of the 1990s and 2000s.[9] How has the PES arrived at this point?

The evolution of the PES into a more 'programmatic party' is something that occurred gradually. The great turn towards the new orientation took place in 2008 and 2009 and was expressed through the programme for the European elections of the same year. For the first time, the party presented a programmatic document covering a wide thematic spectrum and with a very evident emphasis on left-wing mottos and proposals. For all its weaknesses (there is much that is too general, and the 'Manifesto' does not describe the tools for attaining the objectives it posits), the pre-electoral programme politicises European issues on the basis of the right–left axis, takes a more aggressive-than-usual stance against the Europe of the markets, and for the first time describes, albeit somewhat vaguely, the features of a 'progressive Europe'. The programme published in the run-up to the 2009 European elections already reflected a qualitative change in the programmatic building of the PES. The tendency was reinforced through the first half of 2010 in the light of the special conditions generated by the debt crisis, a crisis moreover focused on the socialist governments of southern Europe.

In actual fact, the debt crisis has energised the PES, accelerating, enriching and refining a process of programmatic construction that had already been initiated in the past. Although, in one guise or another, they had been formulated in the previous months, the basic features of the new programmatic profile were presented in full at the PES Council in Warsaw on 2 December 2010. Since then the PES has been producing quite detailed analyses, well focused overall and making strong political points. The new programmatic profile represents a break not only in terms of the programmatic history of the PES but also by comparison with the programmatic profile of the other Euro-parties.

The influence of many actors and factors contributed to the ultimately favourable outcome. The Rasmussen leadership and the elite surrounding the secretary general of the party, Philip Cordery, made a decisive contribution to formulating the new orientation. The president of the PES pursued policies of activation and empowerment of the party, buttressed moreover by a dynamic and ebullient personal style of action. Rasmussen's long-term (2004–11) presence at the head of the PES (he was the longest-serving party president) contributed to the emergence of stable operational rules, to elite cohesion, and to a reinforcement of supranational (as opposed to inter-partisan) functioning of the party. Furthermore, and perhaps paradoxically, the unsatisfactory degree of participation by national leaders at the Conference of Leaders *de facto* reinforced the role of Rasmussen and the Brussels mechanisms and so, indirectly, the supra-national operational logic of the PES.

However, the programmatic progress in question would never have been possible had it not received the green light from two centrally important parties: the French Socialist Party (PS) and the German Social Democratic Party (SPD). Notwithstanding the reservations of German public opinion, the German Social Democrats have been adamant in their implementation of the line that solution of the debt problem presupposes 'more Europe'. With the passage of time, the German social democratic stance has acquired greater weight and coherence, and the failure of the austerity policies imposed on Greece has played a role in this. The voluntaristic stance of the French PS, according central importance to activation of the EU in the direction of market regulation, has had a positive effect and has greatly contributed to the programmatic leap that can be seen in the party. The French PS has to a significant extent undertaken the role of *entrepreneur*, to employ David Hanley's term (2008: 204–5).[10] Furthermore, the action of George Papandreou within the PES, but also of the PASOK delegation within the Socialists and Democrats group, without being central, should not be underestimated. During the first period of the crisis, PASOK had a vital interest in activating both the Socialists and Democrats group and the PES in the direction of a social democratic response to the debt crisis.

In addition, the crisis has introduced, for the first time in such a conspicuous manner, a division of roles: the PES has assumed the role of 'thinking strategically', with the parliamentary group attending to day-to-day tasks of parliamentary work. In the final analysis, the very sound programmatic work was the collective result both of the action of specific national parties and of an 'endogenous' elite that has slowly established itself and gradually come to coordinate and lead the programmatic upgrading of the party. The fact that the great majority of socialist parties have been in opposition has not only made it easier for the party to be mobilised but has also imparted a greater freedom of movement to the PES leadership. Without the constraints of governmental management, without the commitments entailed by greater socialist participation in the European Council, it has been easier for left-oriented ideas to be adopted.

If every institution is an 'incomplete contract', with a long road of improvement ahead of it, the economic crisis has functioned as the 'critical juncture' – to borrow the terminology of historic institutionalism – for acceleration of programmatic change within the PES. The direction of change confirmed the hypothesis of Liesbet Hooghe and Gary Marks that the centre-left has an inclination to identify ideologically with regulated capitalism and that the more the discussion inside the EU tends to focus on the issue of market regulation (at the expense of market making), the more the left, or at least the moderate left, tends to be 'pro-European', meaning that it seeks solutions at the European level and reinforces a strategy of 'more Europe' (Steenbergen and Marks, 2004: 9; Hooghe and Marks, 1999).

Towards a policy-seeking party?
The end of 'programmatically unstructured politics'

As Simon Lightfoot argues, 'the evidence in the literature that Europarties can be seen as policy-seeking parties is based upon two premises: the ability to create common policies for the EU and the ability to influence the outcome of EU policy making' (2005: 9). To these we will add a third premise – namely, the ability to affect the policy orientation of member parties and to influence policy making at the national level.[11] Now, the PES has evolved from a party able to define *policy-oriented ideas* (designated by Lightfoot as 'policy orientation') into a party able to define 'specific policy proposals' (Lightfoot, 2005: 15, 19). This evolution undoubtedly represents a step forward towards a *policy-seeking* model of partisan construction. Nevertheless, the discrepancy between the programmatic statements of the PES and the policies of its member parties in government clearly shows that the real degree of influence of the PES, both at the European and at the national level, is still limited.

Consequently, however loosely and broadly one defines the term 'policy-seeking party', the PES, like the other Euro-parties, still falls short of being a real policy-seeking party. Without full collaboration from the national parties that constitute it, it is not in a position to promote its policies and 'to move from the statute of agenda-follower to the one of agenda-setter' (Külahci, 2010). In essence, the stance of the member parties, particularly while in government, has been the real measure of the power and the programmatic integration of the PES. Our analysis of the debt crisis therefore serves to confirm both old and less old (but not for that reason invalid) arguments, such as the one formulated by Lightfoot in 2005 that 'domestic policy imperatives and ideological differences between the member parties hindered the development of a true policy-seeking party' (144). If the PES has, from 2004 on, taken important steps towards strengthening its organisational capacities and internal cohesion and if, moreover, from 2009 onwards, it has made significant moves toward programmatic integration, it nevertheless remains a 'second-order' party (Heidar, 2003: 3). The Europeanisation of programmatic content in the sense of real 'programmatic convergence' among the PES member parties remains very limited (Hertner, 2011: 344). For a number of national party leaderships, 'the price of supporting stronger Euro-parties does not seem justified by the benefit' (Ladrech, 2006: 76).

So, did nothing at all important occur in the course of this eventful period? Any such interpretation would be mistaken. The debt crisis has contributed to the inauguration of a new phase in the development of Euro-parties. With its programmatic leap forward, the PES crossed a threshold: the period of 'programmatically unstructured politics' seems now definitely over.[12] But inaugurating a new phase does not mean that a new era – and a new game – has begun. It rather means that programmatic strengthening is now to be carried to a higher level. The PES has opened the door to new possibilities, and our hypothesis is that now other Euro-parties might have to walk through it.[13]

More generally, throughout the period of the crisis and the institutional redistribution of roles (2008–12), exactly as in the previous period (that of the 'normal' functioning of Europe), a significant role for Euro-parties was not found. No theory about the nature and dynamic of the Euro-parties can underestimate or neglect this basic fact; nor can any theory underestimate the real success story of programmatic consolidation of the PES. Reality is both composite and stubborn. And it furnishes strong arguments against the simplistic views of optimists and pessimists alike towards the dynamics of Euro-parties.

Discussion: the PES, the Euro-parties and the future of social democracy

The social democratic adoption of the neo-liberal globalisation rationale was based on the premise that the liberation of markets would increase overall social wealth and so could easily be combined with the social guarantees of the European model. This overly optimistic analysis entailed what Wolfgang Merkel (referring to British New Labour) aptly called 'criminal neglect' of the supranational control of globalisation (2001: 53). The socialists promoted hundreds of small ideas for alleviating the costs of liberalisation for the underprivileged classes, but they did not promote even one comprehensive idea, or even one large-scale initiative, for controlling the new global economic game (Moschonas, 2002: 261–7). The collapse of market self-regulation, which has twice proved to be catastrophic (in the 1930s and in the second half of the 2000s), swept away the social democratic ideological and programmatic stance that was formulated in the second half of the 1990s around the ideas of the Third Way. 'When crisis hit,' wrote Henning Meyer, 'social democrats were at best perceived as politically clueless and at worst as collaborators in a failing project' (2012: 153).

The exogenous shock of the economic crisis acted as catalyst both for the ideological defeat of the Third Way strategy and for promotion of a large-scale programmatic revision within the PES. The leadership of Poul Nyrup Rasmussen, whose capacity for promoting programmatic reform was strengthened by the financial and fiscal crisis and by the crucial fact that the majority of socialist parties were in opposition, was favoured by the circumstances: programmatic creation and renewal would be enacted chiefly via the PES, as was our hypothesis. The period of programmatic innovation commencing in 2008, in the run-up to the European elections of the following year, was accelerated, and took on the character of intensive change, from March 2010 to the end of the same year, to be followed by a phase of stability, that is to say, small changes in the framework of the new programmatic equilibrium that had been forged.

As far as the socialist parties of the member states were concerned, many of them pursued a programmatic course that was similarly oriented. But the programmatic and policy innovation of the parties in question, which is still in progress, was incomplete. It was much slower and more contradictory than that of the PES and its ideological imprint was not, and is not, striking and clear-cut. Moreover, the socialist parties of the countries most affected by the crisis of indebtedness (notably those of the European south) did not adopt the same blueprint for change or, to the extent that they did adopt it – in words, rhetorically – this did not have any effect on their governmental practice, which remained focused on policies of austerity and fiscal discipline.[14] The Socialists and Democrats group in the European Parliament adopted an intermediate programmatic course that, although clearly more moderate, was closer to that of the PES than to the policies followed by the governing socialist parties.[15]

Given this constellation of different positions inside the European socialist family, the course of the PES, and to some extent the Socialists and Democrats group, was perhaps a little insular. Undoubtedly the socialist elites of Brussels and Strasbourg were communicating the new *état d'esprit*, the general change in the ideological climate that had developed within the socialist family, in the first instance after the collapse of Lehman Brothers and then after the choice of austerity policies as a means of dealing with the debt crisis. However, they articulated more comprehensively and more effectively than the social democratic elites of the member states, more comprehensively and more effectively than any national socialist party, the post-third-way atmosphere that predominated in the ranks of the socialists. And indeed the policy proposals of the PES went much further than any 'average' social democratic party (assuming that there could, hypothetically, be such a thing, which we know there cannot) would be inclined to accept and/or to implement. They shifted the ideological and programmatic centre of gravity of the socialist family so far to the left as to render it – in effect – no longer a centre of gravity, in the sense that it no longer represented the mainstream view of the socialists.

The Union of Socialist Parties of the European Community (USPEC), wrote Guillaume Devin in 1989, remains fundamentally 'the tool of national socialist policies, less for transcending them than for legitimising them by a common formulation' (282). The PES of today, heir to the Union, is no longer the 'tool of national policies'. On the contrary, it confirmed its autonomous role by shaping to a great extent its own reformist agenda. It was this agenda that the socialist group in the EP was influenced by and to a certain extent that the national parties, or at least some of them, were inspired or influenced by even though only rhetorically. From such a point of view the PES did not function as a party of the least common denominator, namely as a 'party of parties' according to the theory of the Euro-parties. However, this entailed losses. Without functioning as a party of parties and without simultaneously being – or being in the position to become – a real party, it 'lost contact' with some national parties. Some important member parties, precisely because they considered themselves not bound by the new orientation of the PES, or in any case judged that the PES 'does not count', adopted a kind of 'laissez-faire' attitude. Rather than coming into conflict with the PES leadership and the national parties supporting the new programmatic orientation, they preferred a policy of 'discreet' distancing or silence (it was mainly the British Labour Party and to a less significant degree the Spanish PSOE that opted for the latter).

The programmatic leap forward of the PES contributed to the renewal, even if that was limited, of the politics of the European social democracy. Nevertheless, it concurrently contributed to the 'emergence' of the major weaknesses of the PES. As the latter tended to assume a role that exceeded its real power, not only did it face difficulty in promoting its politics efficiently (an issue that this chapter emphasised), but it was also at a loss to fulfil its unification function within the social democratic family. The PES of the Rasmussen–Cordery period was a Europarty that tested its potentialities to the (extreme) limits. What was the result of such a game? On the one hand, the PES widened the horizon of the Euro-parties' actions. On the other hand, it revealed how limited such horizon is in the current phase of European integration. Everyone who attempts to cross borders shall meet the border guards sooner or later. Not by mere coincidence have they been named 'gatekeepers' in the theory of the Euro-parties. The well-entrenched balance between 'pleasing the principals' and developing a truly transnational agency will take a long time to change (see Gagatec and Van Hecke, 2011: 13).

Compared to other Euro-parties, the PES is a programmatic pioneer. It has transcended the old practice of 'programmes without a programme' – this having been a hallmark of the historic building of the Euro-parties. The PES paved the way for 'parties at the European level' to become programmatic parties, but also to become less consensual and more confrontational. It would nevertheless not be wise to overestimate the value of this 'programmatic renewal'. The crisis, the remarkable response of the PES, and, notwithstanding that response, the (relative) ineffectiveness of its action, have shown that there is a major – and structural – disparity between transnational party actors, national parties, and the structure of European decision making. The major lesson of the crisis is that the PES, despite the innovative activism of its leadership team, has not acquired the requisite influence and has not proved capable of going beyond the congenital weaknesses of the 'Euro-party' form. The underdevelopment of Euro-parties, exactly as David Bailey has shown for the underdevelopment of Social Europe, needs to be understood as the outcome of a 'series of obstacles existing at multiple strata', of 'interconnected and deep-rooted constraints' (Bailey, 2008: 237–8).

If it returns to power, today's social democracy is better prepared and more coherent than that of the 1990s. The important step forward taken by the PES creates a favourable programmatic context. But confronted with the constraining logic of institutions and the complexity of the European machinery, the fine programmes and *chic soirées* of the social democratic European elites are insufficient. Furthermore, the emphasis often placed on transnationalism underestimates the Union's evolution towards intergovernmental solutions and ignores the extreme pressure of events and the reality of intra-socialist divisions. The power of the nation is unique. It is still this magnificent (and intellectually puzzling) identity–event that largely determines European developments. While contemporary socialism represents the most *Europeanised* political current on the continent (Caramani, 2010), and the PES constitutes a more coherent transnational pole than the forces represented by the European People's Party, the 'nationalization of socialist consciousness' (Berger, 2012: 13) that has taken place since the end of the nineteenth century still remains predominant and damages any social democratic offer or strategy that does not use national vocabularies and does not aim at national electorates. If the future of Europe is in the 'transnational', then that future seems remote. Will socialists resort to 'cooperative strategies' in Europe and accomplish their 'third refoundation' (Weber, 2011)? The recent history of social democrats, along with their internal disagreements,[16] warrants pessimism. All the factors impeding the advance of reformism in Europe remain operative. The institutional logic of the EU, needless to say, tends to favour status quo ideas.

The new Europe, as described in the new Pact for budget discipline of the twenty-five, is more conservative, more recessionary, more German, less coherent, and above all, *less* capable of meeting the requirements of the European social model. Undoubtedly, the successive waves of emergency measures for saving the Euro-zone are reshaping the European Union. The process of twofold construction of Europe, on the one hand through the markets, liberalisation and insistence on fiscal discipline and, on the other, through 'extra-market' actions and institutions, such as the European Stability Mechanism (ESM), continues unabated. Because of the violent pressures being exerted by the debt crisis, this process is contradictory, opportunistic and chaotic. 'The eurozone's aircraft is being redesigned while crashing' (Wolf, 2012). Nevertheless, the redesigning is happening. What is missing from it is the prospect of a social democratic Europe.

If social democracy is to offer a better solution to the problems of the EU, this 'better solution' will be largely inter-partisan or intergovernmental rather than the product of a transnational type evolution. This is the reality of the current balance of forces, this is the lesson learned from the crisis of European governance and the weak political performance of the social democratic family. Parties at the European level will long remain – despite their clear reinforcement – weak structures unlikely to function as a true political force. If social democrats wish to avoid Samuel Beckett's 'fail again, fail better', it is in their interests to sketch with power and clarity the outlines of an alternative policy and the strategic centre of its conception and implementation.

Notes

1 The chapter is based on the examination of the official documents and resolutions of the PES and on a large number of interviews with cadres of the PES and members of the Group of the Progressive Alliance of Socialists & Democrats in the European Parliament. These interviews began during 2011 and continued up to the time of the writing of this chapter (February 2013). The chapter presents the first conclusions from a work still in progress, and is a heavily reworked version of an earlier short non-academic article (Moschonas, 2012a).

2 Historically, exercising influence through 'external pressure' (when the socialists were in opposition) has been part of the power of the social-democratic movement. German social democracy illustrates this 'external pressure' in an extreme fashion (Berger, 2000: 223–4).

3 See PES (2010a); also, the 'establishment of a European Union Financial Transaction Tax (FTT) and stronger financial regulation, in particular on Credit Default Swaps on sovereign debts and the banning of naked short-selling' are central in the strategy of the PES (2010b).

4 According to the PES (2010e) 'the issuance of debt securities tied to investment projects at the European level – Eurobonds – can raise additional funds for growth related investments and provide a real European added value...In the longer run Eurobonds could also provide Member States with breathing space in pooling part of their national debts together and convert it in a common bond that would lower interest payments, enhance financial stability in the monetary Union, create a liquid and unified European bond market and strengthen budgetary surveillance'; see also the important – and politically more confrontational – joint press statement by Poul Nyrup Rasmussen, President of the PES and Martin Schulz, President of the Socialists and Democrats Group (S&D) in the European Parliament, 13 December 2010, available at www.pes.org/en/news/eurobonds-and-european-stability-agency-are-gps-eurozone-ship-desperately-needs).

5 For a detailed description of the PES's stance on this matter, see PES (2011b); also see the two reports promoted by PES MEPs, Pervenche Berès (PS, France) and Anni Podimata (PASOK, Greece).

6 The policy of the PES, as it emerges from official texts, indicates that the positions

adopted by the PES's leaders' conference are invariably more timid and qualified than those of its president or council.

7 George Papandreou's participation in the Conference of Leaders was systematic, in contrast to the option taken by other leaders of 'opportunistic' participation (or no participation at all), particularly in the case of the Spanish and Portuguese prime ministers.

8 The 'arm's-length policy' adopted by Spanish and Portuguese socialists towards their Greek counterparts, particularly during the first months of the crisis (when Greece was not reputable company), is an excellent example both of the problem of effectiveness and of that of collective coordination in the socialist family.

9 Enhancing the dynamism of the market rather than of curbing it was a central component of the Third Way ideology, see Callaghan (2006: 191–2); on this 'tension-ridden project', see the crucial work, nuanced and innovative, of Jenny Andersson (2010: 149).

10 What is certain is that the centre of gravity of the PES and, even more so, of the socialist group's leadership was not structured around the Franco-German axis.

11 Take for example the strong, and ultimately successful, pressure exerted by the leaders of the EPP on the Greek centre-right New Democracy party, obliging it to participate in a grand coalition government with PASOK.

12 We borrow the term 'programmatically unstructured politics' from Kitschelt *et al.* (2010: 306). The writers have used the term in the context of their study of the party systems of Latin America.

13 During the same period, under the pressure of the crisis, other European parties also improved their programmatic analyses (indicatively: the Party of the European Left and the European Green Party). This has not however occurred, or has occurred to a much lesser extent, with the European People's Party. On the Party of the European Left, see Moschonas (2011).

14 PASOK, which governed alone between 2009 and 2011 and since then has been junior partner in all governing coalitions, has identified more than any other socialist party with neo-liberal austerity policies. This is so despite its radical past that situated the PASOK on the left of the other members of the European socialist family.

15 The interviews we had with members of the socialist group revealed a divergence between the politics of the PES and the options of the Group of the Progressive Alliance of Socialists & Democrats in the European Parliament. The strong, flexible and effective leadership of Martin Schulz (2004–12) provided firm guidance to the socialist group, reinforcing its cohesion. Nevertheless, even though Schulz's policies introduced left-leaning touches and colouration to the group's overall image and placed great emphasis on the priority of a growth strategy, they always had one eye fixed on the possibility of a grand coalition and on agreements with the European People's Party. The discreetly minoritarian role of the French PS inside the Socialists and Democrats group, in distinct contrast to its active role in the PES, reflects this divergence. Michael Holmes and Simon Lightfoot's observation that 'the PES had clearly shifted from working within a pro-EU consensus' accurately conveys the general tendency towards 'a more confrontational and political stance' (2012: 5–6). It does, however, overestimate its scope. The PES has become

distanced from the consensual logic, though this is less true of the parliamentary group.

16 For an interesting study of the points of agreement and disagreement, see Dimitrakopoulos (2011). This volume covers the socialist parties of five countries, namely Germany, France, the UK, Greece and Sweden.

References

Andersson, J. (2010). *The Library and the Workshop: Social Democracy and Capitalism in the Knowledge Age* (Stanford, CA: Stanford University Press).

Bailey, D. (2008). 'Explaining the underdevelopment of "social Europe": a critical realization', *Journal of European Social Policy*, 18(3), 232–45.

Berger, S. (2000). *Social Democracy and the Working Class in Nineteenth and Twentieth Century Germany* (London: Longman).

Berger, S. (2012). 'Social democratic trajectories in modern Europe: one or many families?', in H. Meyer and J. Rutherford (eds), *The Future of European Social Democracy, Building the Good Society* (Basingstoke: Palgrave Macmillan), pp. 13–26.

Callaghan, J. (2006). 'Old social democracy, new social movements and social democratic programmatic renewal, 1968–2000', in J. Callaghan and I. Favretto (eds), *Transitions in Social Democracy* (Manchester and New York: Manchester University Press), pp. 177–93.

Caramani, D. (2010). *The Europeanisation of Electoral Politics: An Analysis of Converging Voting Distributions in 30 European Party Systems, 1970–2008*, National Centre of Competence in Research (NCCR), Working Paper No. 42.

Cramme, O. (2011). 'The power of European integration: social democracy in search of a purpose', policy network paper, September.

Crespy, A. (2009). 'La fabrique du socialisme européen. Derniers développements au PSE', Brussels, International conference, Le Parlement européen, un parlement comme les autres?, Université libre de Bruxelles, 29 April.

Devin, G. (1989). 'L'Union des partis socialistes de la Communauté européenne. Le socialisme européen en quête d'identité', in *Socialismo Storia* (Milan: Franco Angeli).

Dimitrakopoulos, D. (ed.) (2011). *Social Democracy and European Integration: The Politics of Preference Formation* (London and New York: Routledge).

Dunphy, R. (2004). *Contesting Capitalism? Left Parties and European Integration* (Manchester: Manchester University Press).

Gagatec, W. and Van Hecke, S. (2011). 'Towards policy-seeking Europarties? The development of European political foundations', EUI working papers, European University Institute, Robert Schuman Centre for Advanced Studies, Florence, RSCAS.

Hanley, D. (2008). *Beyond the Nation State: Parties in the Era of European Integration* (Basingstoke: Palgrave Macmillan).

Heidar, K. (2003). 'Parties and cleavages in the European political space', Arena Working Papers, July.

Hertner, I. (2011). 'Are European election campaigns Europeanized? The case of the Party of European Socialists in 2009', *Government and Opposition*, 46(3), 321–44.

Holmes, M. and Lightfoot, S. (2012). 'The PES and the financial crisis: the revitalisation of social democratic politics', paper for the FEPS Next Left Programme, Berlin, 8–9 November.

Hooghe, L. and Marks, G. (1999). 'The making of a polity: the struggle over European integration', in H. Kitschelt, P. Lange, G. Marks and J. Stephens (eds), *Continuity and Change in Contemporary Capitalism* (Cambridge: Cambridge University Press).

Jabko, N. (2009). *L'Europe par le marché: Histoire d'une stratégie improbable* (Paris: Presses de Sciences Po).

Kitschelt, H., Hawkins, K. A., Rosas, G. and Zechmeister, E. J. (2010). *Latin American Party Systems* (Cambridge, New York: Cambridge University Press).

Külahci, E. (2010). 'Europarties: agenda-setter or agenda-follower? Social democracy and the disincentives for tax harmonization', *Journal of Common Market Studies* 48(5), 1283–306.

Ladrech, R. (2006). 'The promise and reality of Euro-parties', *European View*, 3, 73–80.

Lightfoot, S. (2005). *Europeanizing Social Democracy? The Rise of the Party of European Socialists* (London, New York: Routledge).

Magnette, P. (2001). 'Les contraintes institutionnelles au développement des partis politiques européens', in P. Delwit, E. Külahci and C. V. de Walle (eds), *Les Fédérations européennes de partis. Organisation et influence* (Bruxelles: Editions de l'Université de Bruxelles), pp. 57–66.

Merkel, W. (2001). 'The Third Ways of social democracy', in R. Cuperus, K. Duffek, J. Kandel (eds), *Multiple Third Ways* (Amsterdam/Berlin/Vienna: Friedrich-Ebert-Stiftung), pp. 27–62.

Meyer, H. (2012). 'The challenge of European Social democracy: communitarianism and cosmopolitanism united', in H. Meyer and J. Rutherford (eds), *The Future of European Social Democracy, Building the Good Society* (London: Palgrave Macmillan), pp. 152–65.

Moschonas, G. (2002). *In the Name of Social Democracy. The Great Transformation* (London, New York: Verso).

Moschonas, G. (2009). 'Reformism in a "conservative" system: the European Union and social democratic Identity', in J. Callaghan, N. Fishman, B. Jackson and M. McIvor (eds), *In Search of Social Democracy: Responses to Crisis and Modernisation* (Manchester: Manchester University Press), pp. 168–92.

Moschonas, G. (2011). 'The European Union and the dilemmas of the radical left: some preliminary thoughts', *Transform!*, 9, 8–23.

Moschonas, G. (2012a). 'Trapped in Europe? Problematic reformism, the PES and the future', *Queries*, 2(8), 80–88.

Moschonas, G. (2012b). 'La panne des voies réformistes en Europe. La social-démocratie à l'épreuve de la gouvernance européenne', in D. Cohen and A. Bergounioux (eds), *Le socialisme à l'épreuve du capitalisme* (Paris: Fondation Jean-Jaurès/Fayard), pp. 233–54.

PES (2010a). 'Economic coordination and financial reform for a stronger and fair recovery', agreed by PES prime ministers and deputy prime ministers, 10 February.

PES (2010b). 'Presidency declaration on the Greek and euro-zone crisis', Brussels, 29 April.

PES (2010c). 'A "European mechanism for financial stability", a progressive response to the Euro-zone sovereign debt crisis', adopted by the prime ministers' and leaders' conference, 25 March.

PES (2010d). 'Sortie de crise: notre réponse progressiste', joint declaration of PES and S&D group in European Parliament, adopted by PES presidency, 10 June.

PES (2010e). 'A European employment and social progress pact for fair growth', PES policy paper adopted by PES council, Warsaw, 2 December.

PES (2010f). 'A progressive way out of the crisis, recovery vs. austerity: PES strategy to resolve the dilemma', PES policy paper, annexed to political statement adopted by PES prime ministers' and leaders' conference, 16 June.

PES (2011a). 'Europe is in the wrong hands', declaration adopted by PES leaders' conference, Athens, 4 March.

PES (2011b). 'A European FTT, for a fair contribution from the financial markets', declaration adopted by PES presidency, 14 April.

Ross, G. (2011). 'European center-lefts and the mazes of European integration', in J. Cronin, G. Ross and J. Shoch (eds), *What's Left of the Left* (Durham, NC: Duke University Press), pp. 319–41.

Steenbergen, M. and Marks, G. (2004). 'Introduction: models of political conflict in the European Union', in G. Marks and M. Steenbergen (eds), *European Integration and Political Conflict* (Cambridge: Cambridge University Press), pp. 1–10.

Tsoukalis, L. (2005). *What Kind of Europe?* (Oxford: Oxford University Press).

Weber, H. (2011). *La nouvelle frontière, pour une social-démocratie du XXIe siècle* (Paris: Seuil).

Wolf, M. (2012). 'Why the eurozone may yet survive', *Financial Times*, 17 April.

Postface

Death by a thousand cuts?

Ashley Lavelle

The extraordinary economic events of the past five years have put mercurial capitalism and its propensity for mass destruction on full display. Over the course of its convulsive history, capitalism has given rise to many crippling episodes of regression, with all the attendant waste of human potential: this most recent calamity began as simply one – albeit highly damaging – instance of speculative mania in a long line of such upheavals going back at least as far as the tulip bubble of 1636–37 (Kindleberger, 1996: 4). But as Marlière notes in this collection (Chapter 6), the more perceptive observers have understood the current downturn as a 'crisis of capitalism', and not merely a 'financial' collapse. Whatever its immediate causes this time round, the crisis at one level merely reflects bipolar capitalism's manic swings between boom and slump. Reflecting on an earlier 'world economic crisis' in 1921, Leon Trotsky observed that, by turns, 'capitalism does live by crises and booms, just as a human being lives by inhaling and exhaling'. Yet, the irrational and chaotic savagery of the market renders virtually impossible any forewarning of when or where a crisis will strike, or how much havoc it will wreak. Thus government leaders, agency officials and mainstream commentators were all caught napping by the sudden turn of events. Callaghan in his focus on the British case notes the foolhardy glee and wishful thinking that characterised much orthodox opinion in the run-up to the crash. This recalls previous incantations on the healthiness of the market just prior to an unanticipated debacle, perhaps the most dramatic case in point being the praise President Calvin Coolidge heaped on the US economy in 1928 for its 'tranquillity and contentment ... and the highest record of years of prosperity' (cited in Galbraith, 1961: 30).

In spite – or perhaps because – of the sheer power of the wrecking-ball effect of the slump, there has been little attempt to tame capitalism's wild ways, for Callaghan argues that a hallmark of debate on the financial sector in Britain post-2007 has been its 'timidity'. He cites some of the important theoretical works on finance capitalism and its relationship to imperialism that were developed in the early part of the twentieth century by Vladimir Lenin, Nikolai Bukharin and Rudolf Hilferding, and which influenced early British Labour's enmity towards the stockjobbers, though Callaghan wryly adds that these were not necessarily well received by politicians with their heads down trying to keep the capitalist system in working order.[1] Such studies have never been more relevant in terms of achieving the understanding of monopoly capitalism that has proved so elusive to establishment economists. But now, as then, social democrats hardly have time for such discomforting analyses when they have set themselves the immediate task of preventing the capitalist economy from caving in on itself!

Thus the amenability of capitalism to state intervention is as much a theme of discussion as capitalist crisis itself. Importantly, Callaghan challenges some of the received wisdom about social democratic responses in the 1930s: those who were fortunate to assume power when economies were reviving in France, Sweden and New Zealand were able to enact some reforms, but the British and Australian Labo(u)r governments in office at the time of the Great Depression had a very different experience – one that included succumbing to the dominant economic and business articles of faith. Indeed, the Scullin Labor government in Australia responded to the crash with major cuts to wages and pensions, splitting the party in the process (Denning, 1982). Further afield, Callaghan suggests that in the US the Democrat Roosevelt's New Deal was hardly Keynesian, and nor was it creditable for the later economic upswing (in reality achieved only when the war machine was set in motion in the US and the world at large; see Kolko, 1976: 155). All in all, there was a comparatively small presence by the state in the economy of the 1930s. Debunking other myths, Callaghan makes the point that an overstatement of social democratic strength during the post-war boom serves to render a false novelty to the apparent impotence of social democracy in negotiating politics and economics in the age of so-called 'globalisation'. What is commonly referred to as the golden era of social democracy was not in fact a simple one of progressive social democratic administration, for the emergence of the welfare state and mixed economies did not always have social democrats to thank. Keynesian demand management was supposed to be the linchpin of shrewd social democratic policy making, but the truth is that this same Keynesian demand management was in tatters after the return of international recession and the emergence of stagflation in the 1970s. At the time Keynesian measures initiated in response to the contraction either had no impact, or made matters worse (Harris, 1983: 73–99). Callaghan goes on to say that the actual part played by conscious government policy in generating full employment during the post-war boom is questionable – indeed, some have argued that a 'permanent war economy' consisting of inflated arms spending and the nuclear race were more important in sustaining consistent high economic growth (Kidron, 1974: 19– 20). It is thus mistaken for some well-meaning economists to contend that, by changing their tack from slash and burn to stimulus, governments could put a speedy end to the crisis (for example Krugman, 2012). While correct to point to the contractionary effects of austerity, such advocates ignore Keynesianism's imperilled state in the 1970s, as well as capitalism's chronic problems of profitability to which government spending can make little long-term difference (Callinicos, 2012).

Capitalism's immunity to attempts at smoothing its operation goes some way towards explaining the lack of willingness on the part of social democratic leaders to act against it. As Callaghan notes, many government leaders in the post-war era were persuaded for a time by the efficacy of Keynesianism, whatever its real acumen in staving off slumps. More recently, however, social democrats have largely abandoned any belief in the need, or capacity, of government to restrain capitalism in the interests of the majority. For instance, vis-à-vis the retreat hastily beaten by France's François Mitterrand in response to hostile economic conditions in the early 1980s, New Labour's Tony Blair made sure to disabuse all supporters of any notion that he planned to interfere with the market, which was now accepted as both wondrously beneficial and inevitable. According to Ryner in his chapter, Blair had gone as far as celebrating Mitterrand's backsliding (see Chapter 4). Former National Executive Committee (NEC) member of the British Labour Party, Liz Davies, observed at first-hand that for the Blairites global capitalism was 'liberating and progressive' (2001: 186). Blair himself argued that fiscal rectitude, low taxes, labour market flexibility, reduced regulation for business and free trade, were all once written off as the preserve of the right but were now 'the agenda of a modern progressive centre-left' (2004). It was clear that economic realities would not thwart a Blair Labour government's plans for social democratic reform along traditional lines of reducing inequality and boosting social spending, because there were no such plans to begin with. Callaghan concludes his chapter with the indictable fact that after thirteen years at the helm of the economy, New Labour left British society one of the most unequal in the industrialised world (see Chapter 5).

The pricking of the New Labour bubble is one of the more delicious comeuppances to flow from the crisis, for long were we forced to listen to Messrs Blair and Brown pontificate about the righteousness of their economic policy path, their overcoming of the cycle of 'boom and bust', and the merits of the market, to which, in any case, there was no alternative. The latter is the subject of Marlière's contribution, who reminds us of the policy convergence that characterised the politics of Britain under New Labour governments at one with the Tories on economic matters (see Chapter 6). Marlière also observes how Labour's spending plans, even before Britain drifted into the epicentre of the crisis, were based on what economic growth levels – or, in other words, the health of the capitalist economy – would permit. This is an important point, for others, including Callaghan and Ryner in their respective contributions, have suggested that economic growth levels largely determined what social democrats could do (see Chapters 4 and 5). Marlière also mentions the watershed nationalisation of banks such as Northern Rock: indeed, the panicky government takeovers of some of the citadels of finance have constituted 'the greatest nationalizations in world history', though governments were loath to refer to them as such (Callinicos, 2010: 8). Marlière is rightly sceptical about whether the New Labour leopard has changed its spots; a leadership shuffle and some bank-bashing rhetoric aside, there has been little concrete sign of policy renewal, and more pointedly its imprimatur has been given to virtually every cut made by the Cameron government, the consequences of which have been dire.[2] This mirrors trends elsewhere such as in Germany, where as Schmidt (Chapter 8) observes the SPD has expressed few regrets about its policies under Schröder (see below). Like its continental European counterparts, the British government has implemented policies whose severity would not have been contemplated only a few years ago: as the old adage has it, every crisis presents an opportunity, and this one has afforded elites in Britain the chance to drive through policies they might never have imagined in their wildest dreams of neo-liberal utopias. But, had it not been unceremoniously dumped by the British people, Labour under Brown would have done little different.

As egregious a case as New Labour may be, it has been indicative of the rapprochement concluded with capitalism and the market by social democrats and others on the broader left, especially in the wake of the Cold War (Lavelle, 2005). Unlike elements of the far left and far right (see below), social democracy is not well placed to exploit the ideological and political opportunities arising from the crisis since, as Andersson and Ryner note in their contributions (Chapters 4 and 7), it was culpable for many of the neo-liberal policy changes that unleashed the crisis in the first place, including for example the Swedish social democrats' (SAP) deregulation of credit markets in 1985. Andersson also cites the work of Esping-Andersen and his stress on 'decommodification', something with real bite in a world in which anything not nailed down is turned into a commodity. But tackling commodification would require overcoming social democracy's quarantining of politics from economics – orienting toward parliamentary activity (politics) while allowing the levers of industry (economics) to remain in the hands of the CEOs – as well as doing something about alienated labour. Andersson argues that a defining question for social democrats historically has been 'what to do about capitalism'. Today, at best, this is a question in social democracy's too hard basket. At worst, as we saw above, capitalism is viewed by social democrats as a force for good.

Could this change? Andersson estimates that a Herculean effort would be required by social democracy in order to revise the pro-capitalist changes it has engineered in its policies. Indeed, she suggests that, such has been the wholesale junking of old principles over the last two decades or more by social democrats, especially in Britain and Sweden, executing an about-turn would be not only be 'politically costly, but also ontologically difficult', and the turnaround would be comparable to the Third Way reprogramming of the 1980s and 1990s. Yet, it can be argued that while the latter went completely with the grain of capitalism and elite opinion – in Ryner's eyes, the Third Way and neo-liberalism were largely synonymous – a shift in the opposite direction would cut the other way, in the process attracting manifold greater resistance in elite quarters, and making it much less likely to occur in light of social democracy's general preference for class conciliation over conflict. Sections of capital, such as the banks, may come in for an occasional tongue-lashing, but capitalism, industry and finance in general are on safe ground.

For some commentators, social democracy's pacific disposition towards neo-liberalism is related to the pressures of globalisation and Europeanisation, both of which are regarded as among the leading constraints on policy making. These themes are taken up in Chapter 14 by Moschonas, for whom social democracy was more at ease in the simpler 'national era'. While some of the less sophisticated contributions to the literature have declared the end of reformism at the behest of globalisation (see, for instance, Gray, 1996), the more insightful analyses have acknowledged that neo-liberal policies – including freer trade, market deregulation and foreign investment liberalisation – have played more than a bit part in bringing about globalisation, in and of itself a contentious term involving numerous dubious assumptions (Weeks, 2001). European federalism, on the other hand, is a very different beast to its counterpart in America, in competition with which the EU in part came into being (Martell, 2001: 223). Supranational European institutions notwithstanding, Moschonas homes in on the absence of a centralised body empowered to impose an international solution – presuming one could be found – to an international problem in an anarchic world system of independent states. On the other hand, the existence of an international structure that could override national governments would not represent progress per se: witness ECB President Mario Draghi's support in late October 2012 for the idea of a 'super-commissioner', a post in which power would be vested with the capacity to veto national budgets (BBC, 2012).

The themes of the role in the crisis of the EU, and social democrats' responses, are pursued further in Chapter 13 by Bailey, who argues that, for social democrats bent on shirking responsibility for their failure to adopt more redistributive and progressive measures, the mirage of re-social democratisation via Brussels provides a welcome distraction. As Moschonas notes, there is a telling contradiction between the more reflationary strategy of the Party of European Socialists (PES) and the austerity fixations of social democrats on their home turf. This of course brings to mind the debate, to which Bailey refers, as to how the EU can best be understood, and how it interacts with social democracy. Some social democrats had initially held out hopes that the EU might offer a way around the problems of globalisation, in particular multinational companies' state hop-ping in a quest to find optimal conditions for capital accumulation. Indeed, as Bouillaud suggests in Chapter 9, the French Socialists still appear to be clinging to the prospect of Europe offering some kind of shelter from neo-liberal capital-ism. But Bailey points to the inbuilt institutional brakes on the realisation of a redistributive agenda in Europe, including: the necessity for EU legislation to be approved by large majorities within the Council, the European Parliament and the Commission; the lack of a genuinely supranational political community transcending bureaucratic circles in Brussels; and the path dependency created by the EU's historical focus on 'market liberalisation and economic (as opposed to social) integration'. Of course, it hardly needs mentioning that the EU is partly what its member states make it; and its member states have been embrac-ing neo-liberalism independently of anything taking place at the regional level.

The reasons for this are not specific to Europe. For instance, the world capi-talist system has been beset by steadily falling economic growth rates since the 1960s: whereas global growth in that tumultuous decade averaged around 3.5 per cent and in the 1970s 2.4 per cent, in the 1980s and 1990s the figure shrank to 1.4 and 1.1 per cent respectively, while the early years of the twenty-first century had barely seen them reach 1 per cent (Harvey, 2006: 42). This in turn exerts pressure on governments to remedy the sclerosis through policies that facilitate capital accumulation and generate investment and growth, resulting in the so-called Washington Consensus prescriptions that Harvey regards as the modern equivalent of the enclosures as spurs to profit making (2003: 158). This helps account for the obstinacy of social democratic support for neo-liberalism: following the discrediting of Keynesianism, and in light of the perceived need to do something to resuscitate a lifeless global economy, stimulation of investment through dramatically pro-capital neo-liberal policies seems like the only option for managing capitalism effectively. European elites remain wedded to the neo-liberal project irrespective of whether or not it can revive what Harman (2010) appropriately called 'zombie capitalism'. In this context, Bailey gets to the heart of the matter when he dismisses talk of 're-social democratisation' in Europe as mere play-acting in a desire to deflect attention from the palpable failure of social democracy to challenge neo-liberalism locally.

Here it is helpful to examine the behaviour of the PES, which is also the subject of Chapter 12 by Holmes and Lightfoot, who raise the spectre of irrel-evancy for the regional organisation. This is, in part, because of the low level of participation in the forum by governing social democratic leaders (for example José Luis Rodríguez Zapatero's no-shows at PES gatherings while he was Spanish Prime Minister) and the absence of clear unity among members, but also, perhaps more importantly, because of the realist tendencies exacerbated by the crisis and the lack of binding powers at the Party's disposal. And yet, the PES has also dealt itself out of the equation by, for example, accepting the necessity of austerity in Greece, with all too tragic results: more than a third of those living in democracy's cradle have been driven below the poverty line, while over a quarter have been thrown on the unemployment scrapheap (Smith, 2012). In 2011 the suicide rate rose by 25 per cent, as one crestfallen pensioner undertook the ultimate protest action when he shot himself in the head in front of the Greek Parliament: on his person was found a suicide note in which he lamented being robbed of his benefit by the government, leaving with him no choice other than taking his own life if he were to avoid the indignity of upending trash cans in a quest for food scraps (Lowen, 2012). Needless to say, these hapless citizens form part of the core of the traditional social democratic base.

In these circumstances, it is scarcely surprising that one of the standout political manifestations of the crisis has been the thrashings meted out at the polls to officiating social democrats. Perhaps the most striking electoral collapse has been that of the Greek social democrats (PASOK). Sotiropoulos in Chapter 11 surveys the wreckage left by the economic crash, PASOK's handling of it, and its broader political and ideological torpor in the preceding years: from a comfortable parliamentary majority of 160 out of 300 seats and 44 per cent of the popular vote in October 2009, the party occupied just 41 seats and only 13.2 per cent of the vote in May 2012. As unemployment reached 25 per cent around the time it was ejected from office, PASOK bears a heavy responsibility for the social misery that has brought soup kitchens to Athens and which has seen some parents give up their children for adoption because they can't afford to feed and clothe them (Smith, 2011; Price, 2012). In some senses, as Sotiropoulos notes, PASOK surfed to power in 2009 on a wave of economic woe and financial scandals that rocked the New Democracy Government. While its electoral meltdown is not totally reducible to the economic catastrophe, the age-old syndrome of social democracy playing doctor to an ailing capitalist patient is all too evident here.

A further case in point, discussed by Kennedy in his contribution (Chapter 10), is the Spanish Socialist Workers' Party's (PSOE) humiliation in 2011 – when it received less than a third of the vote – after its resounding victory just three years earlier; along the way some four million Spaniards deserted the PSOE. The blowback from the neo-liberal misadventure has indeed been inglorious, something symptomatic of the electoral volatility to which social democrats have always been subject due to the gulf between their supporters' aspirations and the sobering reality of social democracy in power. But, in the case of Spain, Kennedy quite rightly disputes the idea that the crisis was the sole cause of the PSOE's unravelling, which in fact reflected its paltry record prior to the slump. Ryner makes a similar point, noting the derisory performance of social democrats at the 2009 European elections, including the humbling of the German SPD – so often a barometer of the health of social democracy because of its size and strategic importance in Europe's most populous country and biggest economy – which scored its worst result since the Second World War. On the other hand, as Schmidt details in Chapter 8 on Germany, the cycle of austerity followed by electoral crisis preceded the global recession in the case of the SPD, whose former chancellor turned Gazprom consultant Gerhard Schröder engineered the most serious cuts to the welfare state since the Second World War following the 2002 federal election. Indeed, Schmidt traces the party's problems to the fallout from the different economic context wrought by the end of the post-war boom in the 1970s. Nevertheless, the global slump did hit the SPD squarely in its electoral heartlands, as its share of the vote was cut to less than a quarter at the 2009 election.

On the surface, the French Socialists' fortunes have been somewhat brighter. But as Bouillaud explains in his contribution (Chapter 9), the securing of the prime ministership and presidency in 2012 reflected a 'simple pendulum's movement' in French politics as citizens tired of the conservatives' policies. Its electoral revival is unlikely to last for long, as the party's policies parallel those of other social democrats in the abandonment of any remnants of class politics: the infamous 75 per cent tax on individual salaries exceeding €1 million – struck down by the French Constitutional Court in December 2012, forcing the government to revise the policy – was symbolic amid its general inaction and designed to convey an impression that the president did have some progressive economic reforms after all.

Relevant here is Ross's important comment that, however hollow their organisation and membership structures and however tarnished their record, social democratic parties can still pull off the odd electoral victory, in part because the mainstream right, too, is in disarray in many places, but also because the electoral volatility of the times means that sharp swings of mood are commonplace in a context in which voters are given very limited options by the mainstream parties: who can forget the heady days of the late 1990s when social democrats commanded the treasuries of thirteen of the then-fifteen EU member states? (see Chapter 2) Much was made at the time of this achievement, which seemingly heralded the dawning of a new red tide. Yet, as Braunthal (2003: 25) argued, the ephemeral nature of this success – within a few years most of them had been swept from office – was a product of social democrats' betrayal of these voters' hopes for more redistributive policies. The list of fallen social democratic idols, including Schröder, Jospin, Persson and Blair/Brown, is a long one. Regardless of any electoral victories in the future, the long-term sores of social democracy are only likely to calcify, as triumph predictably gives way to treachery and defeat.

The events of Europe today, Moschonas argues, mirror those of the 1930s, which had also put paid to the myth of 'market self-regulation'. This time around, the crisis hammered the final nail in the coffin of the so-called 'Third Way', though Moschonas is charitable enough towards the latter to consider it as part of a laudable effort to prepare social democracy for the 'new era'. He contends that the way is opened now, as it was in the 1930s, for the imagining of 'a post-liberal Europe'. Importantly he also points to the action on the streets and interventions by radical intellectuals. He is no doubt referring to vibrant movements including the Spanish *indignados*, one of the most significant formations to arise from the revolt on the continent. The *indignados* occupied the political space vacated by the absence of opposition on both the left and right to neo-liberalism, unemployment and cutbacks. The movement's occupation, however, was more than metaphorical, as semi-permanent activist encampments took root on public land in Barcelona, Madrid, Valencia, and beyond (Castañeda, 2012). Discussions and debates within these forums did not amount to parochial responses limited to the plight of ordinary Spaniards, but instead canvassed all issues great and small, including the building of alternative economies to capitalism in the twenty-first century. The *indignados* movement quickly caught on, fanning out beyond Spain to reach cities as far abroad as Rome and Athens (Marquand, 2011). More broadly, protests, riots and general strikes have been nigh on daily occurrences across Europe in recent years. In mid-November 2012, coordinated strikes and demonstrations were staged across twenty-three different countries – the largest anti-austerity protests ever to grace the continent. As these words were written, the EU was preparing to launch a raid on the savings accounts of Cypriot citizens to fund a bank bail-out, provoking once again uproar and mass protests in the streets.

It is social democracy's bipartisan support for neo-liberalism in the wake of the crash that has opened up opportunities for other political combatants: Ryner points to successes for Trotskyites in France and for the Left Party in Germany, but also to gains for the far right. Ross in his chapter also points to the spawning of revolts on the left and reaction on the right to the austerity measures that were enacted in response to the economic meltdown and in which social democrats have so often had a hand. He notes that the social democrats' 'big tent' approach has run its course, as its large membership base has slowly withered away and its mass support in the electorate has almost evaporated. Moreover, social democracy has been blindsided by social movement activists, first beginning in significance in the 1960s and 1970s, re-emerging with vigour in the late-1990s with the 'anti-globalisation movement', and exploding with the present anti-austerity mobilisations. The radical '1960s and 1970s rebellions' emerged almost completely independently of social democrats – in point of fact, as Schmidt argues in the case of the German SPD, the movements had arisen partly in opposition to some social democratic policies, such as on nuclear energy – who often viewed the movements with disinterest, if not disdain. Ross also identifies the way in which social democrats have been unable to quell the rise of the far right, whose anxious supporters are often victims of the same 'reforms' in whose implementation social democrats have often been complicit.

This conveys a sense of the danger with which the historical moment is pregnant, as the reactionary far right jostles with the progressive movements to steer Europe in a different direction. What is happening here is indicative of the polarisation occurring across Europe, as both far right and far left are vying for overlapping constituencies (Callinicos, 2012). Andersson, in her chapter, draws our attention to the 'major' development in the form of the election to the Swedish Parliament of the far right for the first time since 1991. In 2010, the cynically named Sweden Democrats secured representation in the country's national Parliament, scoring 5.7 per cent of the vote and securing twenty seats from which to spout their poisonous views. At the same time, as Ryner notes in his chapter, there was a continued decline in confidence in Swedish social democracy in the lead-up to its 2010 defeat. In polls taken in late 2012, the Sweden Democrats, whose leading members often share histories with neo-Nazi or racist organisations, ranked third most popular among voters and was tipped by some to hold the balance of power in the Parliament post-2014 elections (*Daily Times*, 2012). The current economic gloom is only likely to exacerbate these trends. With the fascists gaining a foothold in the Riksdag, the potential for a racial backlash is all too real in the heart of Scandinavia.

So it is in Europe. Needless to say, the growth of the far right on the continent did not commence with the events of the last few years. Even so, the crash has given a major fillip to the racists and xenophobes. In Greece, where the human toll of austerity and recession has perhaps been greatest, the Golden Dawn – which as Sotiropoulos notes has risen to the position of Greece's third most popular party – has had significant success:

> Imagine a scene from a dystopian movie that depicts our society in the near future. Uniformed guards patrol half-empty downtown streets at night, on the prowl for immigrants, criminals and vagrants. Those they find are brutalised. What seems like a fanciful Hollywood image is a reality in today's Greece. At night, black-shirted vigilantes from the Holocaust-denying neo-fascist Golden Dawn movement – which won 7 per cent of the vote in the last round of elections, and had the support, it's said, of 50 per cent of the Athenian police – have been patrolling the street and beating up all the immigrants they can find: Afghans, Pakistanis, Algerians. So this is how Europe is defended in the spring of 2012. (Žižek, 2012)

According to Žižek, Greece's racists and fascists, venomous as they are, do not constitute the most pressing danger: it is the proponents of austerity, those scything through social programmes with reckless abandon, who pose the most urgent threat. The latter's actions are not only occasioning much greater misery, they also help bring the racists out from the woodwork, providing a platform and an audience for views that in different circumstances would most likely fall on deaf ears. For these reasons, Žižek (2012) has thrown his support behind Syriza, the counterpoint to the far right Golden Dawn, which like its opponent on the far left is capitalising on the discontent with mainstream parties' handling of the crisis and the broader failure of established politics to serve up anything other than more economic pain.

Undoubtedly the most shocking instance of the racist cloud hovering over Europe since the onset of the global financial crisis has been the massacre in Norway perpetrated by Anders Behring Breivik, who murdered seventy-seven people in July 2011 in coordinated bombing and shooting attacks. This was not simply the product of the psychopathology of a lone assailant with racist, Islamophobic, anti-feminist and anti-Marxist views. It was also indicative of the state of Europe itself and the racial anomies unearthed in the wake of the recession. The actions of Breivik can be seen as part of a tidal wave of Islamophobia washing over the region (Hockenos, 2012), where right-wing anti-Muslim political forces such as Norway's Progress Party, of which Breivik was formerly a member, have triumphed to become, at the time of writing, the third largest party in the Norwegian Parliament and probably a member of the coalition government.

Social democratic parties must shoulder a large share of the blame for its role in cementing the neo-consensus in elite politics, for the retrenchment policies that have increased the bitterness in society, and, as a result, for creating the fertile ground on which the likes of the Progress Party can pose as an alternative. It is not necessarily the left who will make the most from the crisis of capitalism, and having a progressive policy on paper is not sufficient to progress, for as Andersson argues in Sweden old elements such as the (formerly Stalinist) Left Party have become 'increasingly weak' and tired. Agency thus remains as critical as ever.

Conclusion

It is not just in their responses to the economic downturn that social democrats have been found wanting of late. There is a growing sense that social democrats have had little to say – or do – about some of the central problems of modern citizens, including the congestion, pollution and creaking infrastructure that plague the world's cities; the scourge of psychological depression – tipped by the World Health Organization to be the ailment afflicting more people in the world than any other by 2030 (BBC, 2009) – and other mental health problems such as eating disorders and obsession with body image, whose best indicator is the booming trade in cosmetic surgery; the so-called obesity epidemic; growing problems with abuse of drugs – including ever more dangerous and exotic varieties – and alcohol; and the extreme alienation and hyper-commodification of life that has produced such consumer ingenuities as gift vouchers for divorce (Kenber, 2009).

The global economic downturn may have pushed these into the background, but there is no doubt that social democracy has reached an impasse on many levels. If it doesn't seize the opportunity presented by this crisis to move leftward and reorient away from neo-liberalism and global capitalism, it most likely never will. The available evidence suggests that it won't, providing some rays of sunshine in which those on the far left and, disturbingly, on the far right can make hay. As Schmidt pointedly concludes, there is a clash between the need for traditional social democratic policies and their unrealisability within the constraints of contemporary capitalist political diseconomy – a conflict that almost inevitably will provoke the quest for 'socialist alternatives'. Far from it being likely that this search will be spearheaded by old social democratic organisations, we should rather expect to see the initiative taken by 'new left parties, such as The Left in Germany, extra-parliamentary movements, and labour activists willing to overcome the corporatist traditions that still dominate union practices today'. Whatever happens, a rocky road lies ahead for Europe and, *ipso facto*, the world.

Notes

1 On the other hand, Hilferding occupied several political posts in Germany prior to the Nazis' rise to power.
2 The UK's *Guardian* newspaper has devoted a series on its website to sorry tales of the most vulnerable people at the sharp edge of the government's fiscal rectitude, including single mothers forced to cope with £50 a week less; disabled people whose payments have been limited to one year; victims of domestic violence – which kills two women every week in the UK – affected by closures and cuts to refuge services; and students with learning difficulties stripped of their subsidised travel to and from college (available at: www.guardian.co.uk/commentisfree/series/the-cuts-get-personal, accessed 1 December 2012).

References

BBC (2009). 'Depression looms as global crisis', *BBC News*, 2 September, available at: http://news.bbc.co.uk/2/hi/8230549.stm.

BBC (2012). 'Draghi backs eurozone super-commissioner plan', *BBC News Business*, 28 October, available at: www.bbc.co.uk/news/business-20116668.

Blair, T. (2004). Prime minister's speech to Goldman Sachs on the economy, 22 March, available at: www.number-10.gov.uk/output/Page5555.asp (accessed 1 October 2007).

Braunthal, G. (2003). 'The SPD, the welfare state, and Agenda 2010', *German Politics and Society*, 21(4), 1–29.

Callinicos, A. (2012). 'The second coming of the radical left', *International Socialism*, 135, available at: www.isj.org.uk/index.php4?id=819&issue=135.

Castañeda, E. (2012). 'The *indignados* of Spain: a precedent to occupy Wall Street', *Social Movement Studies*, 11(3–4), 309–19.

Daily Times (2012). 'Swedish anti-immigration party climbs to third place in polls', 13 November, available at: www.dailytimes.com.pk/default.asp?page=2012\11\13\story_13–11–2012_pg4_6.

Davies, L. (2001). *Through the Looking Glass: A Dissenter Inside New Labour* (London: Verso).

Denning, W. (1982). *Caucus Crisis: the Rise and Fall of the Scullin Government* (Sydney: Hale and Iremonger).

Galbraith, J. K. (1961). *The Great Crash: 1929* (London: Penguin).

Gray, J. (1996). *After Social Democracy: Politics, Capitalism and the Common Life* (London: Demos).

Harman, C. (2010). *Zombie Capitalism: Global Crisis and the Relevance of Marx* (Chicago: Haymarket).

Harris, N. (1983). *Of Bread and Guns: The World Economy in Crisis* (Harmondsworth: Penguin).

Harvey, D. (2003). *The New Imperialism* (Clarendon: Oxford University Press).

Harvey, D. (2006). *Spaces of Global Capitalism* (London and New York: Verso).

Hockenos, P. (2012). 'He's not alone', *Foreign Policy*, 19 April.

Kenber, B. (2009). 'Law firm offers divorce gift vouchers', *Telegraph*, 22 February, available at: www.telegraph.co.uk/news/newstopics/howaboutthat/6833434/Law-firm-offers-divorce-gift-vouchers.html.

Kidron, M. (1974). *Capitalism and Theory* (London: Pluto).

Kindleberger, C. (1996). *Manias, Panics and Crashes: A History of Financial Crises* (3rd edn, New York: Wiley).

Kolko, G. (1976). *Main Currents in Modern American History* (New York: Harper & Row).

Krugman, P. (2012). 'How to end this depression', *New York Review of Books*, 24 May, available at: www.nybooks.com/articles/archives/2012/may/24/how-end-depression/?pagination=false.

Lavelle, A. (2005). 'After the "end of history": the "vanishing of opposition"', Roundtable on the Politics of Opposition, Research School of Social Sciences Political Science Program Seminar Series, Australian National University, 7 October, available at: www.parliamentarystudies.anu.edu.au/pdf/events/2005/lavelle.pdf.

Lowen, M. (2012). 'Greek unrest after pensioner suicide beside Parliament', *BBC News Europe*, 5 April, available at: www.bbc.co.uk/news/world-europe-17620421.

Marquand, R. (2011). 'Occupy Europe: how a generation went from indifferent to indignant', *Christian Science Monitor*, 29 October, available at: www.csmonitor.com/World/Global-Issues/2011/1029/Occupy-Europe-How-a-generation-went-from-indifferent-to-indignant.

Martell, L. (2001). 'Capitalism, globalization and democracy: does social democracy have a role?', in L. Martell (ed.), *Social Democracy: Global and National Perspectives* (Basingstoke and New York: Palgrave Macmillan), pp. 205–34.

Price, M. (2012). 'Greece's poor queue for food aid in Athens', *BBC News Europe*, 9 March, available at: www.bbc.co.uk/news/world-europe-17299660.

Smith, H. (2011). 'Greek economic crisis turns tragic for children abandoned by their families', *Guardian*, 28 December, available at: www.guardian.co.uk/world/2011/dec/28/greek-economic-crisis-children-victims.

Smith, H. (2012). 'I fear for a social explosion: Greeks can't take any more punishment', *Guardian*, 12 February, available at: www.guardian.co.uk/world/2012/feb/12/greece-cant-take-any-more.

Trotsky, L. (1921). *The First Five Years of the Communist International, vol. 1*, Report on the world economic crisis and the new task of the Communist International, Second Session, June, Part II, available at: www.marxists.org/archive/trotsky/1924/ffyci-1/ch19b.htm.

Weeks, J. (2001). 'Globalize, globa-lize, global lies: myths of the world economy in the 1990s', in R. Albritton, M. Itoh, R. Westra and A. Zuege (eds), *Phases of Capitalist Development: Booms, Crises and Globalizations* (Basingstoke: Palgrave Macmillan), pp. 263–82.

Žižek, S. (2012). 'Save us from the saviours', *London Review of Books*, 25 May, available at: www.lrb.co.uk/v34/n11/slavoj-zizek/save-us-from-the-saviours.

Index